THE MURDER OF ALEXANDER LITVINENKO
TO KILL A MOCKINGBIRD

For Valentina

THE MURDER OF ALEXANDER LITVINENKO
TO KILL A MOCKINGBIRD

BORIS VOLODARSKY

WHITE OWL
AN IMPRINT OF PEN & SWORD BOOKS LTD
YORKSHIRE – PHILADELPHIA

First published in Great Britain in 2023 by
PEN AND SWORD WHITE OWL
An imprint of
Pen & Sword Books Ltd
Yorkshire - Philadelphia

Copyright © Boris Volodarsky, 2023

ISBN 978 1 39906 017 2

The right of Boris Volodarsky to be identified as Author of
this work has been asserted by him in accordance with the Copyright,
Designs and Patents Act 1988.

A CIP catalogue record for this book is available from the British Library.

All rights reserved. No part of this book may be reproduced or transmitted in
any form or by any means, electronic or mechanical including photocopying,
recording or by any information storage and retrieval system, without permission
from the Publisher in writing.

Typeset in Times New Roman 10/12 by
SJmagic DESIGN SERVICES, India.
Printed and bound in the UK by CPI Group (UK) Ltd.

Pen & Sword Books Ltd incorporates the Imprints of Pen & Sword Books
Archaeology, Atlas, Aviation, Battleground, Discovery, Family History, History,
Maritime, Military, Naval, Politics, Railways, Select, Transport, True Crime,
Fiction, Frontline Books, Leo Cooper, Praetorian Press, Seaforth Publishing,
Wharncliffe and White Owl.

For a complete list of Pen & Sword titles please contact
PEN & SWORD BOOKS LIMITED
George House, Units 12 & 13, Beevor Street, Off Pontefract Road,
Barnsley, South Yorkshire, S71 1HN, England
E-mail: enquiries@pen-and-sword.co.uk
Website: www.pen-and-sword.co.uk

or

PEN AND SWORD BOOKS
1950 Lawrence Rd, Havertown, PA 19083, USA
E-mail: uspen-and-sword@casematepublishers.com
Website: www.penandswordbooks.com

Books by the same author

Nikolai Khokhlov, WHISTLER: Self Esteem with a Halo (2005)
The KGB's Poison Factory: From Lenin to Litvinenko (2009)
Stalin's Agent: The Life and Death of Alexander Orlov (2014)
Assassins: The KGB's Poison Factory 10 Years On (2019)
The KGB: A New History, Vol. I (2023)

'Why do I so dislike Putin? This is precisely why. I dislike him for matter-of-factness worth than felony, for his cynicism, for his racism, for his lies, for the gas he used in the Nord-Ost siege, for the massacre of the innocents, which went on throughout his term as President … His outlook is the narrow, provincial one his rank would suggest; he has the unprepossessing personality of a lieutenant colonel who never made it to colonel, the manner of a Soviet secret policeman who habitually snoops on his own colleagues. And he is vindictive.'

Anna Politkovskaya,
Putin's Russia (2004)

Miss Maudie explains to Scout: 'Mockingbirds don't do one thing but … sing their hearts out for us. That's why it's a sin to kill a mockingbird.'

Harper Lee,
To Kill a Mockingbird (1960)

Contents

The Murder of Alexander Litvinenko:
  A Short Bibliographical Essay Instead of Acknowledgements viii

Definitions of Key Terms xx

About This Book: A Tribute to Forsyth xxviii

Prologue: A Machine Starts to Grind, then Stops xlv

Chapter 1   The Family and the KGB Coup d'État 1

Chapter 2   Berezovsky: The Rise and Fall of a Wise Man 20

Chapter 3   The Escape 34

Chapter 4   A Coterie of Friends and Foes 47

Chapter 5   The Frenzied World of Private Spying 68

Chapter 6   Italy 85

Chapter 7   Storm Clouds are Gathering 100

Chapter 8   To Kill a Mockingbird – Part I 114

Chapter 9   To Kill a Mockingbird – Part II 136

Chapter 10   The Third Man 161

Chapter 11   The Litvinenko Inquiry 174

Epilogue 196

Appendix: The KGB Successors: December 1991–December 2022 200

Notes 205

Index 228

The Murder of Alexander Litvinenko

A Short Bibliographical Essay Instead of Acknowledgements

The extraordinary death in London of a low-level Russian defector in November 2006 caused an unprecedented reaction among the world's mainstream media. The polonium poisoning of Alexander 'Sasha' Litvinenko has given rise to an astonishing wealth of polemical, scholarly, scientific, propaganda, and counter-propaganda material. In the years since then, articles in newspapers and magazines, books, television documentaries and even theatre productions have never stopped coming out. A new impetus was given by the British government decision to finally hold public inquiry of the case, which was concluded in January 2016. Reviewing Lucy Prebble's take on the Litvinenko story – *A Very Expensive Poison* at the Old Vic – Susannah Clapp writes in *The Observer* (Sept 2019): 'A spotlit Vladimir Putin leans out from a theatre box, implacable, scornful. A giant golden phallus rears up on stage. Handprints made luminous by radiation glow along the side of the proscenium arch. And a woman walks towards the audience to talk of her husband's murder in a London hotel – and the dreadful delay of the British government in bringing the facts to light.'

The woman is Marina Litvinenko, played by MyAnna Buring, a Swedish-born British actress. In an interview Marina said she had felt nervous going to the theatre, partly because she didn't know what to expect. She obviously liked what she saw because half a year later all three of them – Marina, Lucy, and MyAnna – together attended the Critics' Circle Theatre Award 2020 ceremony at the Prince of Wales Theatre in London's West End. In October 2021, Lucy Prebble's play premiered at the Švandovo Theatre in Prague.

In the meantime, an opera, *The Life and Death of Alexander Litvinenko*, which took almost a decade in the making, finally had its world premiere at Grange Park Opera in Surrey in July 2021. In *The Times*, Richard Morrison's review was headed 'A worthy tale of murder and mayhem – shame about the music [by Anthony Bolton, a former banker]', calling the score 'drearily atonal' and complaining that Kit Hesketh-Harvey's libretto was 'stodgy'. Ivan Hewett entitled his review in the *Daily Telegraph* 'a thrilling story, bold staging, but not there yet' writing that the opera was 'exciting but flawed ... hobbled by a hectic score'.

The Murder of Alexander Litvinenko

The opera is in two acts with a prologue. In a prologue set in a London hospital, a chorus tells of a radioactive poison polonium and Litvinenko, on his deathbed, gives his final speech. Act I shows Litvinenko and his wife Marina reminiscing on their six years in London and his former work as an FSB officer. There are also scenes about the Moscow theatre hostage crisis – the seizure of the crowded theatre by Chechen terrorists in October 2002 and the reporting of the event by Anna Politkovskaya, a brave Moscow journalist; Litvinenko's experiences in Chechnya during the war between Russia and the Chechen Republic of Ichkeria; his refusal to assassinate the oligarch Boris Berezovsky; and an Interfax press conference for the Russian media in November 1998 where Litvinenko and his fellow officers publicly denounce the FSB.

In Act II Berezovsky assists the escape of Litvinenko and his family to the UK; at a birthday party hosted by Berezovsky Litvinenko meets his former colleague, Andrey Lugovoy; Politkovskaya visits London where Litvinenko warns her that in Moscow her life is in danger – she nevertheless returns to Russia and is murdered in her apartment block on Putin's birthday. Lugovoy comes to the UK and poisons Litvinenko by putting polonium in his tea during a meeting at a London hotel; the final scene returns to Litvinenko's final speech against Putin and his death. Heartbroken Marina (Rebecca Bottone, soprano) sings a lament.

As usual, among many works dealing with the case, and first of all one should mention books and articles published in the West, there are some of political and historical importance, but there is also a certain amount of rubbish. For obvious reasons, the most extensive bibliography is to be found in English and, to a much lesser extent, in Russian.

Panorama, an investigative documentary series on BBC One, revealing what they believe is 'the truth about the stories that matter', was the first to commission a private company named Blakeway/3BM to produce a documentary, *How to Poison a Spy*, with John Sweeney. The work started as soon as it became known that Litvinenko was poisoned and he gave an exclusive interview to the BBC Russian Service. My article, 'Russian Venom', was published in *The Wall Street Journal* on 22 November 2006, in which I suggested that the mysterious substance that was killing Sasha, whom I had met in London about a year before, must be a radioactive poison.

Sasha Litvinenko died at University College Hospital at 21.21 on Thursday, 23 November. On the same day, in the morning, when Litvinenko was still alive, John O'Mahony, the film director, called me and a couple of days later he and Fiona Stourton, executive producer, were waiting at the cigar bar of the Connaught Hotel in Mayfair to discuss the plot. At that meeting, I agreed to act as the chief consultant and shortly after the funeral arranged interviews with all major participants of the drama including Sasha's Italian friend, Mario Scaramella, who came especially from Naples to talk to us. In January, John Sweeney left for Moscow to discuss the case with Dmitry Peskov, Putin's press secretary, against which I, fully aware of the BBC's ridiculous political correctness, categorically protested.

As expected, Peskov stubbornly insisted that 'Russia has not done that and it is absurd even to think about that'. But Marina, Litvinenko's widow, said it was the work of Russian agents, John retorted, sitting opposite him and looking straight into Peskov's eyes. 'If she said that Russia has killed Sasha,' repeated Peskov without a hint of embarrassment, 'she is a liar in these words.' The film ends with Marina's statement or warning, proved to be prophetic: What happened with my husband, she says, can happen again. The list of people whom the Kremlin wants to kill is not finished yet. Okay, what will they use now to kill other persons? An atomic bomb?

'Will Putin go nuclear?' the world was asking less than two decades later.

'Much depends on how Putin perceives the threat to the Russian state and his rule,' was the unpromising answer. I looked at the calendar. The date was 4 October 2022. Was Sasha Litvinenko perceived as a threat to the Russian state and Putin's rule?

Precisely because Russia had been under Putin for over two decades, any objective study of the regime's crimes was strictly forbidden and not a single book or article could be published on the Litvinenko case if they were not approved by Putin's propaganda machine reflecting the Kremlin's view on the events. Even in the West, some newspaper articles were quite openly pro-Kremlin and in my first book, *The KGB's Poison Factory: From Lenin to Litvinenko* (Frontline Books, 2009), I devoted a lot of space discussing the work of Ketchum, a global public relations firm with headquarters in New York that became the principal PR partner of the Russian president's press office.

Peskov contracted Ketchum in or about May 2006 to advise the Kremlin. James Robinson, writing for *The Observer*, found out that a posse of PR professionals was involved, including the BBC's former Moscow correspondent Angus Roxburgh, the author of *The Strongman: Vladimir Putin and the Struggle for Russia* (I.B. Tauris, 2011) and Tim Allan, who used to work for Tony Blair before he set up his own PR firm. The campaign was being handled by Ketchum's Brussels-based sister company, GPlus, which was co-founded by Peter Guildford, a former civil servant at the European Commission. Guildford began his career as a journalist, becoming Brussels correspondent for *The Times* during the late 1980s. He then became official EU Spokesman, working under Romano Prodi, President of the EU Commission.

Guildford, in turn, subcontracted the British part of the business to Portland Communications established by the already mentioned Tim Allan, a public relations consultant serving as Tony Blair's adviser and then deputy director of communications at 10 Downing Street.[1] Allan became head of corporate communications at BSkyB after he left politics with impeccable contacts in the press. And if initially it was about repackaging 'an autocratic East European leader [Putin] with a new image that would make him palatable to a Western audience', their capacities were used in full after the Litvinenko poisoning became a world affair.

'As the Politkovskaya murder was followed by the Litvinenko murder, and then by the Russian invasion of Georgia, I began to wonder whether the very reason the Kremlin had decided to take on a Western PR agency was because they knew in advance that their image was about to nosedive,' Roxburgh later wrote.[2] It must be added that for over a decade a good number of well-known British and American journalists had been falling over themselves to ensure that Moscow's position expressed by Peskov in our film became widely known to the Western public.

At least one such publication is analysed in detail by Yuri Felshtinsky, a Russian-American historian and friend, as well as a co-author with Litvinenko of *Blowing Up Russia: The Secret Plot to Bring Back KGB Terror* (Encounter Books, 2007). Felshtinsky was a Fellow at the Hoover Institute, University of Stanford, and the first US citizen to receive a doctorate from the Russian Academy of Sciences. In his latest work with Vladimir Popov, *From the Red Terror to the Mafia State* (Nash Format, 2021), Felshtinsky refers to the article by Dimitri Simes, 'The Litvinenko Matter: Kremlin Conspiracy or Blofeld Set-Up?' published in *The National Interest* on 6 December 2006, a day before Litvinenko's sealed casket was buried in an isolated section of the historic Highgate Cemetery.[3] 'This article,' the historian writes, 'had little to do with politology but had a lot to do with Kremlin's campaign to minimize the political damage inflicted by the Russian Secret Service operation in London, with the cover-up operation called damage control. Kremlin involved Simes in this operation immediately.'

During my research for this book, I called Yuri many times on various occasions asking for his comments, opinions, or just to share his memories of this or that episode related to Berezovsky or Litvinenko and his work with both. Yuri's detailed answers followed immediately, for which I am very grateful.

Martin Sixsmith, another former BBC Moscow correspondent, is the author of the very first book published in London on the Litvinenko case with an appropriate title, *The Litvinenko File: The True Story of a Death Foretold* (Macmillan, 2007). Martin honestly collected and systemised all information that could be gathered in such a short period of time – from late November 2006 to early April 2007 – before the book came out. As a researcher, Sixsmith didn't have much to rely on because his book was on sale well before the director of public prosecutions, Sir Ken Macdonald, made his official statement announcing that the Crown Prosecution Service had decided to charge Lugovoy with the murder of Litvinenko based on the material of the Metropolitan Police investigation. What Martin Sixsmith managed to do was to meticulously study all available police reports and other nuggets of information that became available and interview all people who had anything to do with this case to make his own conclusions. Researched, written, and published in record time, it is a very decent investigative work which has not lost its relevance even today, when a lot more has become known, and almost all documents including witness statements, police records, and experts' assessments are in the public domain in addition to the long and detailed Litvinenko Inquiry Report. Forgetting several minor errors that are not worth mentioning, perhaps the only serious flaw is in the last chapter, which the author called 'A Final Reckoning'. After briefly visiting Moscow while researching the book and talking to the people he knew, Martin wrote: 'My Kremlin contacts responded to my questions and left me with the firm belief that Putin did not order the killing [of Litvinenko].'

The Murder of Alexander Litvinenko: To Kill a Mockingbird

From 1980 to 1997, Martin Sixsmith worked for the BBC as a foreign correspondent in Moscow, Washington, Brussels, and Warsaw. He was reporting from Moscow when the Soviet system crumbled first under Mikhail Gorbachev and then Boris Yeltsin. He also reported from Poland at the time of the Solidarity (*Solidarność*) uprising and was the BBC's Washington correspondent during Bill Clinton's first term as US president. A very experienced journalist, Sixsmith also spent five years as a civil servant working as director of communications for various government departments. Still, back in 2007 he failed to understand what Christopher Booth, another former BBC Moscow bureau chief, grasped very quickly, comparing Putin to Michel Foucault with novichok and tanks (which today may be viewed as flattery).

'Among the many compliments paid to Vladimir Putin's version of tyranny is a supposed special and novel gift for devious information warfare,' Booth writes. 'The truth is that he is merely an inheritor of the ingrained governing DNA. Pathological lying to foreigners and one's own citizens is [his] standard operating procedure.'[4]

Another important book that came out soon after the events was a joint work by Alex Goldfarb and Marina Litvinenko entitled *Death of a Dissident: The Poisoning of Alexander Litvinenko and the Return of the KGB* (Free Press, 2007). The most important element here is that this is a story written by participants, first-hand witnesses of all events described in the narration. Dr Goldfarb is a Russian-American microbiologist and human rights activist who received his PhD from the Weizmann Institute in Israel, did his post-doctoral research at the Max Planck Institute for biochemistry in Germany, and worked as assistant professor at Columbia University in New York. For many years Alex had been an adviser, friend, and assistant to Boris Berezovsky, as well as Sasha's mentor and teacher, who arranged the Litvinenkos' immigration to the United Kingdom – an offence under British law. Goldfarb also served as Sasha's unofficial spokesman during the last two weeks of his life.

I read the book many times as soon as it was published and later, when a new fully updated version came out. Initially, it struck me as a rather biased interpretation of events, and indeed it is written from a clear perspective of a member of the Berezovsky team. But later, especially after Putin unleashed the biggest war in Europe since the Second World War, with his army bombing and invading Ukraine, committing crimes unseen since Stalin and Hitler, the authors' position seemed fully justified. 'You may succeed in silencing one man. But a howl of protest from around the world will reverberate, Mr Putin, in your ears for the rest of your life' – Alex Goldfarb was one of the authors of these prophetic words and the one who read them when Sasha's final statement was released to reporters outside University College Hospital.

'I have written the personal story,' Alex explains, 'with the benefit of first-hand knowledge. I have written the history with confidence that it conveys Sasha Litvinenko's beliefs and conclusions, and my own. I do not propose that I am a neutral observer. I do maintain that I am an honest one and one who, with Marina's assistance, can best speak for Sasha.'

Definitions of Key Terms

Spy – the main purpose of adding the word 'spy' to the list of key terms in this book is (a) because very few people really know what a spy is, and (b) because in hundreds or maybe thousands of media reports, books and articles about Litvinenko, he was erroneously referred to as a spy: Russian, British, or both. Ben Emmerson QC, representing Sasha's widow Marina, even claimed that 'Mr Litvinenko had been for a number of years a regular and paid agent and employee of MI6'.[9] It is amazing that even a renowned British barrister specialising in, among other subjects, international criminal law, sometimes acting for and against the Government of the United Kingdom, does not understand (or pretends not to understand) the difference between a 'paid agent' and 'employee', especially when it concerns the Secret Intelligence Service of his own country. As a matter of fact, Sasha Litvinenko could have never been 'an employee' of MI6 because to be able to apply, one needs 'to be a British citizen and to have lived in the UK for the majority of the ten years before applying'. Judging by all available information, Litvinenko was a paid agent of the Service, also sometimes acting as a consultant. There is also a difference between intelligence officers (IO) and spies.

Based on a classic definition, a spy can be described as a person employed by a government to secretly obtain classified information which another government does not want to disclose. According to MI5, 'Espionage is the process of obtaining information that is not normally publicly available, using human sources (agents) or technical means (like hacking into computer systems). It may also involve seeking to influence decision-makers and opinion-formers to benefit the interests of a foreign power.' Wikipedia combines espionage, spying, and intelligence gathering, describing them as 'the act of obtaining secret or confidential information (intelligence) from non-disclosed sources or divulging of the same without the permission of the holder of the information for a tangible benefit. A person who commits espionage is called an *espionage agent* or *spy*'. With the advent of private investigative business and firms that offer investigative support, business intelligence, risk assessment, dispute resolution, forensic and litigation consulting, and due diligence checks (add other catchphrases), the profession of a private spy or private investigator and analyst has become popular and profitable. During the last year of his life, Litvinenko also acted as a freelance contractor (sometimes referred to as subcontractors or simply subs) to several British private investigative firms.

Volna ('Wave') – the KGB/SVR name for the secret channel of delivery of hazardous materials to and from Russian territory. Usually, Aeroflot international flights are used for the purpose. A sealed container with material is placed in the pilots' cabin, where one of the pilots is an intelligence officer, agent, or a co-optee. According to Alexander Kouzminov who served in the 12th Department of KGB's Directorate S (Illegals) regular dealing with VOLNA shipments, the use of this method of clandestine transportation increased after the collapse of the Soviet Union in 1991.

About This Book

A Tribute to Forsyth

> Two and two equal four. The trouble is, in that world of shadows and distorting mirrors what may or may not appear to be two, when multiplied by a factor that may or may not be two, could possibly come out as four but probably will not.
>
> Frederick Forsyth, *The Fist of God* (1995)

Most people become celebrities because of their extraordinary lives. Sasha Litvinenko became a celebrity because of his extraordinary death. Not that his life was entirely uninteresting. Born in the city of Voronezh in southwestern Russia, on the crossroads between Moscow, Georgia, Ukraine, and the Urals, he arrived in this world in December 1962, one month before term, weighing less than 2.5 kilograms. Looking back, either with the benefit of hindsight or really remembering some little things associated with the birth of her only son, his mother Nina said in an interview with an American journalist that a woman in another bed in her maternity ward told her that all eight-months babies became famous. Whether all of them become famous is hard to establish, but among the famous people born prematurely one can name Sir Isaac Newton, Sir Winston Churchill, Albert Einstein, Mark Twain, and Anna Pavlova, one of the world's most famous ballerinas.

Exactly like in the spring of 2022, when a dangerous confrontation between the civilised world and Putin's Russia was threatening the existence of our planet, the Cuban Missile Crisis of October 1962, when Litvinenko was born, had been a result of a dangerous confrontation between the United States and the Soviet Union. Having managed to build a number of nuclear warheads, the USSR imagined itself to be one of the nuclear superpowers and this largely unfounded idea quickly led to the moment when the two states came closest to the nuclear conflict. Then, the Soviet leader seems to have been better informed and much more sober-minded than the Russian president six decades later because, after only a few weeks, the crisis was peacefully resolved.

The situation was very similar. Nikita Khrushchev, the First Secretary of the CPSU, and John F. Kennedy, the US president, met in Austria to discuss important political issues at the Vienna Summit in June 1961. And in June 2021, US president Joe Biden and the Russian President Vladimir Putin met at the historic Villa la Grange in Geneva, Switzerland, for their first face-to-face meeting since Biden took office in January, trying to resolve a number of existing conflicts. Unfortunately, instead of conflict resolution, the confrontation between Russia on the one hand and the USA and NATO on the other led to Russia's invasion of and war in Ukraine.

Litvinenko was not destined to live to these days, but like other children of history he was born and lived in the Soviet Union, witnessed its collapse, its difficult transition into the new millennium, and the formation of new, democratic Russia that no one could have imagined might ever happen. At the crossroads of centuries, he had served in the KGB, FSK, and FSB, where he had reached the rank of a senior investigative officer, fighting against organised crime and corruption. One day, Litvinenko rebelled against the state and his secret service, served his term in the FSB prison and managed to leave the country illegally. Having settled in London with his wife, whom he truly loved, and their small son, he joined the team of a Russian business tycoon, a former academic declared by the Kremlin their Enemy Number One.

Sasha was not born into a happy family, rather it was a short-lived college marriage. Alex Goldfarb, Litvinenko's friend and mentor, and his mother Nina recall that at the age of three Sasha was sent to live with his paternal grandfather in Nalchik, a small town in the northern Caucasus, while both his parents formed new families and produced new children. His father Walter, a medical student, after graduation from university abandoned the family to build a second life in the faraway place – Russia's Sakhalin penal colony, one of the largest penal colonies in history, where he served as a medical doctor. When Sasha was 9, living with his grandfather and going to school, his mother and stepfather produced a daughter of their own, Svetlana. When he turned 17, his father, discharged from the army, returned to Nalchik with his new wife and their three children – Tatiana, Vladimir, and Maxim.

I met Walter and Maxim, Sasha's half-brother, in London in December 2006. Maxim, who lived in Italy, seemed a bit reserved but otherwise all right, but Walter I did not like. He made flowery speeches accusing Putin and the Kremlin of every imaginable crime, and would hold forth at length. I remember somebody saying (was it Jeaniene Frost, an American fantasy author and the *New York Times* correspondent?), 'I despise flowery speech, since those who use it are usually guilty of the worst betrayals later.' This turned out to be true and sometime later Walter Litvinenko betrayed his son, his friends, Sasha's family and all those who were helping him for several woeful weeks when his elder son was dying in a London hospital.

When Walter, with his wife and three children, moved in, the grandfather's house became too small for all and Sasha, feeling sidelined, decided there was no other way for him but to join the army. He was a good sportsman, just out of high school, following in his father's and grandfather's footsteps, so a career in the army seemed right for him. By then, his mother, stepfather, and their daughter were living in Fryazino, a small town 25 km away from Moscow, which was later granted the status of Naukograd, a 'science city'. The whole R&D in Fryazino concentrates on radio electronics and communication systems and first of all serves the defence industry.

Like his father, Litvinenko was drafted into the Internal Troops, a paramilitary police-like force of the Ministry for Internal Affairs and, after a year in the army, he secured a place at the Internal and Border Troops military academy in Ordzhonikidze (now Vladikavkaz), in North Ossetia. In 1985, after graduating from the academy, he was commissioned in the Dzerzhinsky division,[1] military unit no. 3419 in Balashikha. Today it is known as the 4th Operational Duties Regiment. The task of his battalion was to escort valuable cargo of the Gokhran: precious metals and germs, and the company where Sasha served was rather special because part of the job was cargo security escort to destinations abroad. As it happens, soon a KGB major from military counterintelligence approached him with an offer you cannot refuse, namely, to become a KGB collaborator.[2] Sasha said he did not hesitate to sign an agreement and was enlisted as an agent. In 1988, he left Balashikha and set out for the Officer Military Counterintelligence School No. 311 in Novosibirsk, Siberia. That was the beginning of Litvinenko's KGB career as an operational officer that lasted until his arrest.

In his book *The Lubyanka Criminal Gang*, first published by the International Foundation of Civil Liberties (a non-profit organisation established in New York and financed by Berezovsky) in 2002, Litvinenko summed up his eleven years in the KGB. 'In my biography,' he says, 'there are episodes about which I do not want to speak. Even the Constitution protects a person from being compelled to incriminate oneself. Suffice it to say that I have never killed anyone, never kidnapped anybody, was never involved in protection "krysha" racket and did not seek to be cut in on criminal profits. And there ain't no blood on my hands. I'm not ashamed of anything and therefore sleep peacefully in my bed.'

Remarkably, Litvinenko could say this after having served in such different KGB-FSK-FSB units as Military Counterintelligence, Division of Economic Security, Anti-Terrorist Centre's Directorate of Operations (DO), and even the URPO, the FSB directorate focusing on major international, national, and regional organised crime groups that control large segments of the illegal activities. Sasha, Goldfarb explains, 'Kept secret files on mobsters, studying their personal affairs, their networks, their contacts with businessmen and politicians. What Sasha knew – and how he knew it – was rarely revealed in court. Yet to official investigators, his stuff was priceless. He solved crimes before charges were made. He worked behind the scenes. He eavesdropped. He recruited and ran agents.'

In August 1997, quite unexpectedly, the then director of the FSB Nikolai D. Kovalev, Putin's predecessor in this post, transferred Litvinenko to the URPO, a newly created semi-official supersecret department within the Russian Security Service, whose offices were located inside an old four-storey unmarked residential building at 34/1 Novokuznetskaya Street, far away from the FSB head office. 'You will report to Colonel Gusak,' Kovalev said. Alexander Gusak was Sasha's former colleague at the DO and that was perfectly all right, but this new directorate was headed by General Yevgeny Khokholkov and there was nothing Litvinenko could do about it – or so he thought.

The problem was, Sasha's former boss at the Anti-Terrorist Centre's Directorate of Operations General Vyacheslav Volokh suspected that the URPO and Khokholkov, one of his former subordinates, could one day become an unwelcome competition to his directorate. According to Goldfarb, Volokh asked Sasha to dig up dirt on his potential rival. However, the ATC only existed until July 1998 when Kovalev was fired and Vladimir Putin became new director of the FSB. The Anti-Terrorist Centre was reorganised into the Department for the Protection of the Constitution. In September, General Gennady P. Zotov was appointed its head and Volokh was given a comfortable job overseas, working undercover as a counsellor at the Russian embassy in Stockholm. In its turn, the URPO was disbanded and Khokholkov temporary transferred to the State Tax Service. The dismissal of both Kovalev and Khokholkov was a result of a joint effort of Berezovsky and Litvinenko.

A year later, in a December 1999 interview to a Russian newspaper, Eyer Winkler, a former high-ranking staffer with the National Security Agency (NSA), stated that 'corruption in the Russian Government, their foreign intelligence service, and in the GRU (military intelligence) allows Russian organised criminal groups to use these departments in their own interests'. His idea was that criminal groups from the former Soviet Union were getting more and more active not only inside the country but also internationally and that intelligence services or at least some of their officers got involved in those illegal activities.

Whether Volokh's assignment in Sweden was related to investigating this claim is unknown. In February 2001, Sweden arrested a worker of the Swiss-Swedish engineering giant, ABB ASEA Brown Boveri, on suspicion of spying for Russia. Two days later, the case was dropped, the man released, but Volokh had to leave the country. In November 2002, Sweden expelled two Russian diplomats for spying on radar and missile guidance technologies developed by Ericsson, a Swedish multinational telecommunications company headquartered in Stockholm, for the Saab JAS 39 Gripen fighter jet. Five current and former employees of Saab had been investigated. In the meantime, Volokh suddenly left the Security Service (FSB) and got a job as deputy chairman at the State Fisheries Committee, which looks very much like stern chastisement for a lieutenant general and former commander of the ATC.

At a press conference on 17 November 1998, Litvinenko and four officers from his department accused the leadership of the URPO of planning (and actually ordering) the assassination of Berezovsky, who until recently had served as Deputy Secretary of the Security Council. Four days earlier, Berezovsky published an open letter to Putin, drawing attention of the FSB director to the fact that Litvinenko and his friends, after revealing their information to him, had been accused of 'preventing patriots from killing a Jew who had robbed half of Russia'. All FSB officers who took part in the press conference were suspended, and in March 1999 Litvinenko was arrested. Berezovsky could not help him because since early November 1997 his tenure on the Security Council had come to an end. Although well before the press conference in spring 1998, he was appointed executive secretary of the Commonwealth of Independent States (CIS), it was not the same.

In September, the hardliner Yevgeny Primakov, who had served as the foreign intelligence chief (SVR director) and then foreign minister, became the Prime Minister of Russia, succeeding Berezovsky's ally Viktor Chernomyrdin. Thus, another avenue of influence was blocked. In addition, in early December 1998, President Yeltsin dismissed Berezovsky's only reliable contact in the Kremlin, Valentin Yumashev, the influential chief of Yeltsin's staff, better known as Presidential Administration (officially, Presidential Executive Office). Berezovsky's link to the president was through Yumashev and Tatiana Dyachenko, Yeltsin's daughter, who was Yumashev's friend and companion and would later become his wife.

The press conference sealed Litvinenko's reputation as a turncoat who, against all odds, had rebelled against the system. In December, Elena Tregubova, the Kremlin correspondent for *Kommersant*, one of the leading Russian papers which would soon be bought by Berezovsky, managed to arrange an interview with Putin, expecting to learn a bit more than he usually revealed about his plans for the future. At the time, the FSB director was a public figure.

Having learned that he did not expect to keep his post after Yeltsin's retirement, Tregubova asked about the press conference where Litvinenko and his colleagues accused the Service of planning extrajudicial executions. 'Personally, I cannot exclude that these people really frightened Boris Abramovich [Berezovsky],' Putin said. 'He had been a target for assassinations before. It would only be natural for him to believe that yet another attempt on his life was in the making. But personally, I believe that with the help of this scandal [those] officers simply tried to secure a future job market for themselves. After all, some of them even moonlighted as security guards for him.' After a moment's thought, he added: 'This conference demonstrates that our *Sistema* has baleful trends. Therefore, I disbanded their entire unit…'

On 25 March 1999, Litvinenko was arrested and hauled off to the notorious Lefortovo prison, a drab yellow four-storey building not too long ago used for mass executions and tortures. In November, a judge at the Moscow military court found him not guilty but right in the courtroom he was arrested again and transferred to Butyrka. It is the oldest and largest Moscow prison, serving as a pre-trial facility. Compared to Butyrka, hell is a health resort. He was released on bail shortly before Christmas.

Among many people who surrounded Berezovsky, there were two whom he trusted and whose opinion valued. Both are naturalised American citizens from Moscow who left Russia long ago. One is Yuri Felshtinsky, an academic historian who lost his parents at the age of 17 and later emigrated to Boston via Vienna, a transit point on the emigration route of Soviet Jews. Felshtinsky arrived in the United States in April 1974. Here he was educated at Brandeis University, a private

About This Book

research university in Massachusetts sponsored by the Jewish community, and earned his PhD in history from Rutgers University in New Jersey. Felshtinsky first met Sasha, by that time an FSB lieutenant colonel, on the day he was getting ready for that press conference.

Another was Alex Goldfarb. Alexander Goldfarb is almost the same age as Berezovsky. He emigrated from the USSR in 1975. In the Soviet Union, Goldfarb studied biochemistry at Moscow State University (MGU), received a PhD from the Weizmann Institute in Israel in 1980, continued his post-doctoral research at the famous Max Plank Institute for Biochemistry (MPIB) in Germany, and then worked as assistant professor at Columbia University in New York. He also directed the Tuberculosis in Siberian Prisons project funded by George Soros. According to Soros's biographer, Goldfarb was among the first group of Russian exiles in New York whom Soros invited to brainstorm his potential Foundation in Russia and, in 1991, managed to persuade the philanthropist to donate 100 million dollars to help former Soviet scientists survive during what became known as the 'wild ninetieth'. From 1992 to 1995, he had served as Director of Operations at Soros's International Science Foundation, also managing several of Soros's projects in Russia. In 2000, together with Dr Paul E. Farmer, he was still involved in one of such projects to contain an epidemic of tuberculosis in Russian prisons.

> In the spring of 1995, in Russia, Goldfarb was introduced to Boris Berezovsky. Alex later recalled: 'He had summoned me because I worked for George Soros, hoping to lure that legendary billionaire into becoming his backer in major privatisation deals that were on the horizon. I had more or less guessed why I had been invited to Berezovsky's tea table. What I did not realise was that I was about to enter a new planet of the solar system – Boris World – which I would be navigating for the next decade.'[3]

The meeting took place at Berezovsky's dacha in Rublyovka, an enclave of the Kremlin and near-Kremlin superrich inhabitants in the western suburbs of Moscow. At the time, during the first months of the First Chechen War, Alex was overseeing a Soros-funded relief operation of providing assistance to the besieged population of the Chechen capital Grozny, transformed by Russian troops into a slaughterhouse.

A new life for him began with the new millennium when he headed the New York-based Berezovsky Foundation (which would later become known as the International Foundation for Civil Liberties, or IFCL). Some time after Litvinenko was released from prison, Goldfarb asked Boris to introduce him to Sasha because, parallel to other engagements, he had still been running a public health project sponsored by Soros aimed at TB prevention and control care in prisons. 'I wanted to quiz Sasha about the medical services in Lefortovo,' Alex explains.

Quite by chance, Berezovsky established his famous LogoVAZ Reception House to accommodate visiting dignitaries on the same street as the offices of the URPO, at No. 40 Novokuznetskaya, and it was equipped and guarded incomparably better than its FSB neighbour. Goldfarb recalled that on any given day The Club, as he called it, was full of visitors among whom were popular TV personalities, ministers, Duma deputies, journalists, and Western businessmen, as well as people no one knew. Among such strangers was an unremarkable young man in a jeans suit who often sat in a corner. Although they saw each other several times, only later did Alex learn that the young man was Litvinenko.

Felshtinsky also met Sasha there, in the LogoVAZ Club. Many years had passed since that earlier meeting, but in the first days of Putin's war in Ukraine Yuri remembered Sasha saying: should Putin come to power, he would start purges. People would be killed or arrested. 'I can feel this,' Sasha insisted. 'He will kill all of us as well. Trust me. I know what I am saying.'[4] The year was early 2000 and Putin had not yet been formally elected as the President of Russia. In those days, Felshtinsky was investigating the apartment blocks bombings of September 1999 that occurred in several cities across Russia, claiming the lives of more than 300 people. Before Bucha and Mariupol, that was the largest terrorist act ever committed on the territory of the former Soviet Union.

Back then, Felshtinsky somehow came to the conclusion that those explosions were organised by the former KGB, which had been dissolved eight years earlier and split into several independent agencies. He thought the idea was to blame the Chechens, creating a *casus belli* to start the Second Chechen War.

Wise people do not start wars that they believe will be long and costly. And, quoting Clausewitz, 'no one starts a war or rather, no one in his sense ought to do so without first being clear in his mind what he intends to achieve by the war and how he intends to conduct it'. Events in Ukraine have demonstrated that Russian leaders launch wars because they fool themselves into thinking the war will be quick, cheap, and successful.[5] As usual, the military campaign unleashed in Chechnya in September 1999 was portrayed by the Russian leadership as a limited and carefully targeted counter-terrorist operation aimed at eliminating the threat to Russia.[6] The same reason was used to justify the war in Georgia in August 2008, the annexation of Crimea in February-March 2014, the direct military involvement in the Syrian civil war in September 2015, and the invasion of Ukraine in February 2022.

Strategically, the Chechen war was intended to be a breakthrough in the revival of the Russian Army. But preparing for the second war in Chechnya, Russian leaders in their habitual manner were trying to kill two birds with one stone.

One objective was to win the war and impose the Kremlin's political will. In the Red Banner Yuri Andropov Institute and the Defence Ministry's Military Academy they were taught that to get the iron dice of war rolling, one must first convince the public that it is necessary and wise. However, unbiased military observers quickly noticed that no amount of PR spin could hide the fact that the victory had not taken place, and, as one of them commented, 'the presidential denial of the Army's continuing degradation was not made any more convincing by the supporting roar from the top brass'.[7]

About This Book

Also, for the first time since the Bolshevik revolution, the war was used to promote Putin's popularity before his election as the country's leader. After Lenin, there was no election. On the eve of the new millennium, it was a bit more complex because besides the acting president, eleven more candidates were nominated. Unfortunately, the Union of Right Forces (SPS), which emerged from the December 1999 parliamentary vote with real momentum, ranking fourth, failed to endorse a presidential candidate. One of its founding members, Konstantin Titov, was on the ballot as an independent candidate, while Sergey Kiriyenko and Anatoly Chubais backed Putin. Other prominent liberal figures wavered. Boris Nemtsov, former deputy prime minister and Security Council member, one of the co-founders of the SPS, said in an interview, 'If, in 1996, the choice was between primitive Communism and primitive capitalism, the choice in the year 2000 will be between an oligarchic regime of mongrels and a popular, democratic regime.' From the end of August 1999 to the end of March 2000, when the election took place, hidden puppeteers sought to make their colourless candidate visible, well aware that a successful local war would secure this candidate's easy march to the Kremlin. Putin won the elections in the first round.

Felshtinsky, an academic historian, was aware of all that but there were still many things he did not know or understand. He needed somebody from the secret services' ranks to give him some tips or to explain. So, he flew to Moscow to see Litvinenko and ask for his help. 'The same night in Moscow,' Felshtinsky writes, 'we also discussed Alexander's escape. He had been released from prison but was under 24-hour surveillance by the FSB.' When he came to talk to Sasha, Yuri noticed that two cars with surveillance teams were following Litvinenko during the day and at night a car was always on duty in front of his house. Felshtinsky realised that as a renegade and whistle-blower, this former FSB lieutenant colonel and experienced criminal investigator had no future in Russia and his arrest was just a matter of time.

In May 2000, Felshtinsky flew to Moscow to join Alex Goldfarb and Pavel Arseniev, the Berezovsky Fund's representative in Russia, who were helping Boris to write a lengthy memorandum concerning Putin's recent decree dividing Russia into seven federal districts and his proposal of a number of federal laws. This memorandum, which was published in *Kommersant* at the end of the month in the form of a letter to the president, called for a wide and open public discussion of these draft laws. In Berezovsky's opinion, such measures were anti-democratic, did not correspond to the declared goals and objectives, and could cause more harm than good. The work consumed a lot of time and resources, but one day Felshtinsky took a break to meet with none other than Sasha's former boss General Khokholkov. He decided to make a pitch on behalf of his friend by exploring Boris's reputation while it was still worth something. It was his first and last attempt to negotiate with the FSB, trying to obtain some kind of immunity for Sasha Litvinenko.

'Isn't there any way to leave Litvinenko in peace?' Felshtinsky asked.

It was a good try, but it failed. Back in Sasha's apartment, Yuri was very open about the situation.

'It's bad. You and Marina have to get out of here. You won't survive until the end of the year. In the best case, they'll put you in prison. In the worst, you understand...'

The plan was simple. With his internal passport not valid for foreign travel, Litvinenko was to cross the Russian border to a nearby former Soviet republic, all fifteen of which have become new independent states after the dissolution of the Soviet Union. In the meantime, Marina, who had a passport allowing her to travel abroad, would buy a tour and fly with their son to some remote place like Cyprus, Egypt, or Spain. As soon as Felshtinsky knew that Sasha had crossed the border and Marina with Tolik had successfully left Russia, he, as an American citizen, would contact a US embassy, quickly arrange an asylum for the family, and the mission could be considered accomplished. In real life, however, the venture was so new for them all that many of the pitfalls could hardly have been foreseen.

In the middle of the road, Felshtinsky got sick and tired of problems and returned to Boston, and Goldfarb took over. On the morning of 1 November, safely inside London Heathrow Terminal 2, four of them followed the exit signs, briefly stopping for Goldfarb to make a telephone call. Alex was calling George Menzies, a solicitor hired to represent Sasha's interests. Alex and George had first communicated to discuss all particulars when they were leaving Turkey from the freshly inaugurated international terminal of the Istanbul Atatürk airport. George was now waiting in Arrivals on Level 1 with all necessary papers to secure a smooth passage for his new clients. After having been convinced that the way was clear, Goldfarb let Sasha approach a border control official. 'I am KGB officer,' Litvinenko said in broken English, 'and I ask political asylum.'

On 14 May 2001, George Menzies called Sasha. 'The Home Office has just granted you political asylum,' he said. 'Could you come to my office to sign some papers? Fine, and please congratulate Marina and Tolik.' It was some two years before a discreet appointment was arranged for Litvinenko to meet a MI6 officer. They would later call him 'Martin' in the official documents, just for the record.

* * *

In the period of six years that Litvinenko resided in London, he did so many things to irritate and anger the vindictive Master of the Kremlin that one can only wonder how he managed to last so long.

One of the things that sealed his fate was the fact that he did not only manage to flee from the country with the help of Berezovsky and his people without any assistance from the secret services of Britain or the USA (or, for that matter, any other country), but he also settled in London where he was living a rather prosperous, pleasant, and carefree life doing what he most enjoyed doing. There, as in Russia, Litvinenko became one of the trusted lieutenants of the Kremlin's Enemy No. 1, Berezovsky, who was paying him a generous allowance much higher than most of his former FSB colleagues were getting. This could easily motivate others to defect and join the Berezovsky camp.

About This Book

Almost immediately Sasha got involved in the so-called Cassette Scandal, also known as Kuchmagate. It began in November 2000 and its consequences reverberated throughout Ukrainian society for two decades, doing irreparable damage to the career of Leonid Kuchma, the second president of independent Ukraine. It is also said to have given rise to the non-Communist opposition, which led to the protests that sparked the Orange Revolution.

Working with two prominent academics, Felshtinsky and Goldfarb, Litvinenko co-authored two books in 2002. One, originally entitled *The FSB Blows Up Russia* (later published in English in both Britain and the USA as *Blowing Up Russia*) was a result of the Felshtinsky investigation enhanced by Litvinenko's professional knowledge and experience. Some chapters from the book were first published in Moscow by *Novaya Gazeta* in August 2001, with the full text coming out in Russian in the USA several months later (New York: Liberty, 2002). Another book, *The Lubyanka Criminal Gang* (New York: Grani, 2002) was written in the form of interviews given by Litvinenko to a journalist from *Novaya Gazeta*, Akram Murtazayev, with Goldfarb writing a foreword. There, Litvinenko talks about the FSB, his 1998 press conference, Russian politicians and public figures, and his escape from Russia. The book contains some keen observations, for example, 'Everything that Putin says needs to be constantly double-checked because he is always lying.' Or 'Patrushev can kill for his fatherland, but he will never die for it.' Or '[Putin's rise to power] marked a major watershed in Russian politics: people with money versus people with secret service IDs.' The publication of both books was financed by Berezovsky's foundation.

Apart from financing research, writing, and promoting *Blowing Up Russia* in the media, Berezovsky also funded a documentary produced by a professional French team based on the book. The subject was the apartment bombings in several Russian cities that took place in September 1999. As in the book, the theory proposed by the film makers was that the bombings had not been a terrorist act by Chechen separatists, as the government claimed, but a covert operation organised by the FSB to provide a justification for another war in order to establish full control over Chechnya. Another, even more far-reaching aim, according to the authors, was to boost Putin's political prospects because, in August, Boris Yeltsin named him the acting prime minister and his chosen successor for president. The film screening and panel discussions were arranged at the Royal United Services Institute (RUSI) in London and the Woodrow Wilson International Centre for Scholars in Washington, DC, in March and April 2002.

To pursue this course further, Berezovsky, a former Kremlin insider, encouraged and supported the establishment of a Commission to conduct a public investigation of the allegations. The Commission consisted of fifteen prominent members, among them several MPs, human rights activists and politicians. As Goldfarb testified during the inquest hearings, it was planned that Sasha, as a former FSB officer, 'would be essentially the face of the campaign to inform the public opinion and the powers that be that the FSB might have been involved in the apartment bombings'.

The Murder of Alexander Litvinenko: To Kill a Mockingbird

At least two of the Commission members, Sergey Yushenkov, an MP, and Yuri Shchekhochikhin, a journalist from *Novaya Gazeta*, lost their lives. Yushenkov was one of the founders of the political party Liberal Russia together with Berezovsky and Vladimir Golovliov. Golovliov was assassinated in August 2002. Yushenkov was shot dead near his house in Moscow in April 2003. Shchekhochikhin was poisoned and died in Moscow in July 2003, a few days before his scheduled departure to the USA, where he agreed to speak to the FBI, who wanted to interview him.

In 2003, Litvinenko was one of those who helped his friend and patron to received political asylum in Britain, which Berezovsky considered a very big personal success having reasonable grounds to believe that now it would be much more difficult for the Kremlin to get hold of him. He was right.

It was quite obvious from the evidence presented to the Litvinenko Inquiry that the profile that Sasha established during the time that he had lived in London was considerably greater than simply a member of the Berezovsky entourage. During those six years, he had managed to create a reputation of his own as a journalist, campaigner and commentator, and an outspoken one at that. The coroner quoted an expert's characterisation of Litvinenko as one of the most 'prominent and ebullient' of Putin's critics, whose 'denunciations were fierce'. In July 2006, Litvinenko published an article on one of the opposition websites accusing the Russian president of paedophilia, an insult that Putin could not ignore.

As already mentioned, Litvinenko was also involved in the Cassette Scandal, sometimes referred to as Kuchma tapes. A member of President Kuchma's security detail, Mykola Melnichenko, secretly recorded conversations between Kuchma and a number of officials, about fifty-five individuals, and then smuggled those tapes with him abroad. Berezovsky became involved as one of the funders of a project to transcribe the tapes and make them public. For a time in 2002, and then again in 2005, this transcription work had been carried out in London. A website (5element.net) was set up and a Berezovsky team of Goldfarb, Felshtinsky, and Yuri Shvets were directly involved in transcribing, translating, and verifying the texts. Shvets is a former KGB major who had worked undercover in Washington, posing as a TASS correspondent, before he decided to move to the United States forever with his family. They settled in Sterling, Virginia, from where Shvets was summoned to London to work with the tapes in mid-May 2002. Here, he was introduced to Litvinenko and Berezovsky. Litvinenko's part was to accompany Melnichenko, whom he quickly befriended, and check whether the transcripts contained any links between President Putin and Russian organised crime.

As the coroner put it in his Litvinenko Inquiry statement, another strand of Sasha's activism that deserves mention was his involvement with the Chechen cause. Akhmed Zakayev, deputy prime minister of the Chechen Republic of Ichkeria in exile (later prime minister), gave evidence that at his request Litvinenko, who became his close friend, served on a War Crimes Commission that was established under Zakayev's chairmanship to collect evidence of the Russian war crimes in Chechnya. This work included identifying names of the Russian troops and special forces commanders and soldiers suspected of having committed war crimes, crimes

That is surely true and I can vouch for it.

Alex was of great help when I was writing my first book on the Russian secret services' operation against Litvinenko, and I relied on his excellent memory and first-hand knowledge of events related to Sasha and Boris again while researching this book. Answering my question of whether Boris Berezovsky read the manuscript before it was sent to Ed Victor, an American literary agent based in London, the son of Russian-Jewish immigrant parents who became a legend in the industry, Alex said: 'No, he didn't. I had to run after him to answer my questions. The fact is that the book was written in English, and he did not have an attention span for this. Boris only read a Russian version when it came out.'

Among Ed's friends was Michael Mann, a famous American screenwriter, director, and producer. By the end of October 2007, sufficiently inspired by what he had read, Mann appreciated the merits of Goldfarb's work with Marina by signing on to direct a feature film based on their book while Columbia Pictures had snapped up rights to *Death of a Dissident*. Very soon Mann, who earned his Master of Arts at the London Film School, arrived in the British capital. During the next few months we were spending a lot of time together discussing the details of the future blockbuster at Claridge's, where he stayed, because Michael, who is best known for his distinctive crime dramas starring Oscar-winning actors and Hollywood legends, decided I should be the film's chief consultant. At the end of June 2009, after the London premier of his movie *Public Enemies* (with Johnny Depp and Marion Cotillard), to which Michael invited all three of us – Marina, Alex, and myself – we still talked about the future film, the production of which was about to start.

Alan S. Cowell, a British journalist and a former foreign correspondent for the *New York Times*, who was their London bureau chief when the Litvinenko story became a major media event, was based in Paris, working for NYTimes.com at the time his book *The Terminal Spy: A True Story of Espionage, Betrayal, and Murder* (Doubleday, 2008) was published. But long before it happened, Warner Bros purchased film rights to Cowell's forthcoming work for Johnny Depp's production company. Depp would produce the film and could star in it, *Variety* announced. However, nothing happened until February 2010, when the British filmmaker Mike Newell (*Harry Potter and the Goblet of Fire*) revealed he was trying to bring the Litvinenko story to the big screen based on Cowell's book.

While, to my great regret, Michael Mann's project stalled and was as good as dead and buried, none of the mentioned films had been completed. I secretly rejoiced because I did not too much like what Cowell had written. The author claims to have included 'interviews and conversations with contacts and the key players' in Austria and Israel, among other places, but I did not find any, for the obvious reason that there were no 'key players' from these two countries involved in the Litvinenko case. Generally, the book is a typical example of news-style reporting without analysis, a considerably detailed but superficial piece missing the big picture.

In the book, there are also some ridiculous statements, as when, for example, the author quotes a former KGB colonel, Stanislav Lekarev, who allegedly said that 'he had worked in the 1950s at a secret KGB laboratory producing polonium' and that 'polonium was used once in the case of Khokhlov', a Soviet defector. Both these facts – a secret KGB laboratory producing polonium and Khokhlov's alleged polonium poisoning – are pure inventions.[5] But the most amazing passage deals with Deputy Assistant Commissioner Peter Clarke, head of Counter Terrorism Command (CTC) of the Metropolitan Police in 2006–2008. According to Cowell:

> Clarke asked MI5 to check on the whereabouts of all the thirty-plus known operatives of the Russian SVR foreign intelligence service based in London in the weeks leading up to Litvinenko's poisoning. More used to bugging and tailing suspected Islamic terrorists, MI5 scrambled, calling on its own counterintelligence resources – including a clandestine double agent within the SVR establishment [?!] – to track the movements of the Russian spies in late October, assembling information from agents, intercepts, and surveillance teams. Within days, a British security officials said, MI5 compiled a dossier that seemed to show no direct involvement in the poisoning by the known SVR spies in Britain.
>
> In one sense, that conclusion came as a relief. An assassination by the known SVR operatives would have been an unequivocal act of hostility – not just toward the Russian émigré community but also toward British sovereignty. The exoneration of the SVR, by contrast, left open a slender possibility that Litvinenko's death was simply an act of extreme criminality rather than a display of supreme arrogance by the Kremlin.[6]

Cowell's book is based not on primary sources but on interviews, newspaper articles, hearsays, and catchy headlines without offering any clue to why Sasha was murdered, who did it, how, and, most importantly, *cui prodest* – who benefited. Extreme criminality? 'If he had lived his latter years as a crusader seeking regime change in Russia,' Cowell writes, 'Alexander Litvinenko died in vain, and his death offered a cruel warning to others who might emulate him.' By the time the Litvinenko Inquiry was completed and its report published, *The Terminal Spy* became obsolete, with the following events showing that when Cowell was facing the most important questions to which he was expected to give clear answers, he got it all wrong.

Sasha Litvinenko did not die in vain and while I was writing these words, the responsible world leaders and the media became united in their conclusion: he's gotta go! 'Putin has left the world no other option but regime change' – an article with this title was published in the *Daily Beast* in October 2022. In his article, David Rothkopf puts it bluntly: 'Vladimir Putin must go. His demented Kremlin speech [30 September], during a ceremony in which he feebly asserted Russia was annexing portions of Ukraine, made the strongest case for the necessity of regime change in Moscow that any world leader has yet to make. But it has been clear the Russian dictator must be removed from office for a long time now.'

Luke Harding's book *A Very Expensive Poison: The Definitive Story of the Murder of Litvinenko and Russia's War with the West* (Guardian Faber, 2016) is, unlike Cowell's, based on the Litvinenko Inquiry material, personal meetings with many participants, and the author's many newspaper reports. A British journalist and author of several bestselling books, Harding wrote extensively on the Litvinenko case both from London and Moscow, where he had resided as the *Guardian* correspondent since 2007. Some four years later, in February 2011, on the way back to Moscow Harding was stopped by the border officials, refused re-entry to Russia, and deported the same day. In September, his book *Mafia State: How One Reporter Became an Enemy of the Brutal New Russia*, was published. In it, the Litvinenko story occupies a considerable part, but a full exposé is in *Very Expensive Poison*, brought out after the Litvinenko Inquiry Report was made public.

Harding's is a serious effort to write a definitive story but, alas, no 'definitive story' is ever possible when dealing with a complex intelligence operation like the murder of Litvinenko in London. Nevertheless, and disregarding several errors (one of the least important ones is an incredible assertion that Putin's grandmother was Lenin's cook), this is a substantial piece of work which attracted the attention of Lucy Prebble, whose theatre play is based on it.

I especially liked one episode because it had to do with Sasha's father, Walter Litvinenko, whom I brought to film the BBC interview together with Litvinenko's half-brother Maxim, at the location chosen by John O'Mahony. It was a typical red-brick London building at 2 Audley Square, a place described in several spy books. Facing the camera, Walter was very eloquent accusing Putin and his secret services of poisoning his son. Like in Stalin's time, Walter said, only Putin could have authorised this murder in London. 'I know it was Putin who killed Sasha,' he repeated, his eyes welling with tears. Four years later, in 2010, Luke Harding flew from Moscow to Italy, where he arranged to visit Litvinenko senior and his family, who by that time resided in the seaside town of Senigallia on the Adriatic coast.

The family were in poor shape. 'Walter blamed their misfortunes in exile on Silvio Berlusconi, Italy's prime minister, whose close friendship with Putin was well known,' Harding writes. Tatiana, Litvinenko's half-sister, blamed Berezovsky. 'He is clearly not interested in us,' she complained. Tatiana and her husband had both worked for the FSB in Nalchik, Litvinenko's hometown, but after his defection, their careers were ruined. Berezovsky had initially supported the Litvinenkos in exile, as he supported Marina and Tolik, Sasha's young son, but by the time Harding visited Walter, Maxim, and Tatiana in Senigallia, his money had run out.

In February 2012 I saw Walter Litvinenko again, this time in a news programme prepared by Channel One on Russian television. In an interview from Montemarciano in the Italian Province of Ancona, Litvinenko senior said he had come to understand that his late son was a traitor, 'a British spy'. Walter asked his *rodina* (motherland) to forgive him for Christ's sake and allow him to go back to

Russia. 'In an affidavit, sworn in September 2012 before Russian officials,' Harding writes in his book, 'he said he now believed Lugovoi [*sic*] was innocent, and that polonium had been "skilfully placed" to incriminate him. The real murderer, he suggested, was Alex Goldfarb', a CIA agent. This was said on the set of *Let Them Talk*, a popular Russian television programme broadcast in March 2018, where Walter hugged Lugovoy and shook his hand. After this show, the family's business was said to have suddenly improved. Goldfarb likened the encounter between a father and an alleged murderer of his son to a scene from the *Iliad* and filed a complaint for malicious defamation with the US District Court in New York's Southern District against two Russian television stations: RT America and Channel One.

My own book, *Assassins: The KGB's Poison Factory 10 Years On* (Frontline Books, 2019), unlike the first volume, contains only one chapter where the Litvinenko case is summarised in brief. I must confess that although my research was based on the Litvinenko Inquiry Report of January 2016, I ignored or overlooked many primary sources that were used in full in the current work, based almost exclusively on primary sources. I am very grateful to the experts of the National Archives (TNA) in Kew as well as to the TNA's Freedom of Information Centre for declassifying several documents at my request that were pertinent to this research. I must also thank FCDO Historians – experts in diplomacy, intelligence, political documents, and archives who were happy to share their knowledge but whose names unfortunately may not be published.

My principal error in the previous two volumes dealing with the Litvinenko case concerned the time and place when Sasha was poisoned. I was confused by two witness statements, fully documented by the Metropolitan Police and reconfirmed to me in person by those two witnesses. The first was David Kudykov, Sasha's good friend with whom I got acquainted at the funeral on 7 December, which I attended in the company of Oleg Gordievsky.

David lives in London. Originally from Riga, Latvia, he was a partner in a shipping company. When Litvinenko called him, David said, he was abroad taking care of one of their cargo vessels in the Netherlands, but Sasha's telephone call reached him in Berlin on the way back to London. The time was about 1.45 pm and, according to David, Sasha was calling from a hotel. Later, David repeated the same on camera to the BBC team in my presence while John O'Mahony was filming. This footage never appeared anywhere. David said that he listened to what Sasha had to say very attentively and himself asked questions. According to David, he got an impression that Sasha was in the company of two people, at least one of whom he knew well, and they discussed the possibility of transporting liquefied natural gas (LNG) and copper to Latin America. Sasha's companions, David said, and the way they were answering or, rather, were unable to answer his simple questions, left an impression that they had little to do with any business. They did not know elementary terms of the trade, were confused about prices, and could not tell CIF from FOB. Kudykov told his friend that the deal looked unrealistic and advised against it. According to David, he had been questioned for four hours by the police regarding this telephone call and signed a witness statement, also providing his phone number. I was surprised when later I did not find David's name and his statement among the investigation documents. But Goldfarb's statement about an early meeting at the Millennium was on file.

'At some time in November, probably the 19th or 20th, an interview by Oleg Gordievsky appeared in *The Times* claiming that Litvinenko in addition to meeting Scaramella also met a Russian contact on November 1, 2006,' Alex testified. 'I contacted Berezovsky by phone and he said that he knew about that meeting from Litvinenko. I then asked Litvinenko and he confirmed that the meeting took place in the Millennium Hotel. There were two Russians: Andre [*sic*] Lugovoy and another man unknown to Litvinenko who he called Vladimir. To my recollection he said *the meeting was before the meeting with the Italian Scaramella* [italics added] but I am not certain of this.'[7]

My second witness was Mario Scaramella, Sasha's Italian friend, whom he met later on the same day, 1 November, at Piccadilly Circus at about 3.00 pm. As they walked down Piccadilly, they were talking. 'Alexander explained to me,' Mario later testified, 'that he wanted to start a business in the trade of natural resources. He explained to me that in Russia the state companies that deal with natural resources are afraid of the secret services and do as they tell them. He told me that he had a friend in the secret services who knew the president of one of these companies and therefore he could supply any product at a very low price. He told me that he was closing or had [just] closed a deal with a load of copper. He concluded his explanation by saying: "Millions, Mario, millions!" Because his English was not very good, I did not understand what he meant the first time and I asked him to repeat what he had said, which he did.'[8] A CCTV camera captured them both at 3.10 pm walking along Piccadilly.

All this and the fact that the table at Itsu, an Asian eatery where they dropped in for a chat and for Sasha to grab a quick bite before his planned meeting with Lugovoy at the Pine Bar of the Millennium Hotel, was later found to be contaminated with polonium, made me think that Litvinenko was quite definitely poisoned before the Pine Bar meeting. And there was no mistake because the evidence collected during the police Operation AVOCET clearly identify the table at Itsu and the place where Litvinenko was sitting on that day with Mario as contaminated with polonium, although only slightly.[9] The seat where Scaramella was sitting was also contaminated, but much less so.

I admit that this version of mine might have misled several people, including Sixsmith, Guzzanti, and Gordievsky, who mentioned it in their writings and interviews. After studying all police documents related to that day, it seems that the only time and place where Litvinenko could have been poisoned was the Pine Bar on the late Wednesday afternoon of 1 November 2006.[10] The only remaining question is who did it.

I am very grateful to members of the SO15 Counter Terrorism Command investigation team, Lisa Harman and Michael Hoban, with whom I had a chance to interact during the Litvinenko investigation. It was my first encounter with

Metropolitan Police officers and I was hugely impressed by their professionalism, style of work, and communication skills that makes the British police in general and especially London's Metropolitan Police far superior to any other police service anywhere in the world. SO15 or Specialist Operations branch within the MPS was established as a result of the merging of the Anti-Terrorist Branch and Special Branch, bringing together intelligence, operations, and investigative functions to form a single command. It all happened in October 2006, virtually days before they were entrusted to investigate the Litvinenko poisoning, something new to most of the officers especially because it was not an ordinary crime but a sophisticated operation of Russian Intelligence Services (RIS) on British soil.[11] Usually, it would have been a job of the Security Service (MI5) and Special Branch.

It is impossible to understand the Putin regime – call it a dictatorship or an autocracy, scholars use them synonymously – and its crimes committed during more than two decades in power of 'a lunatic with small man syndrome', as British Defence Secretary Ben Wallace said, without a few important monographs. Most of them are in English or were translated into English. These are books by Anna Politkovskaya, *Putin's Russia* (London: The Harvill Press, 2004) and *A Russian Diary* (London: Harvill Secker, 2007); Nataliya Gevorkyan, Natalya Timakova, and Andrei Kolesnikov, *First Person* (New York: Public Affairs, 2000), translated by Catherine A. Fitzpatrick, whose work leaves much to be desired; Steve LeVine, *Putin's Labyrinth: Spies, Murder, and the Dark Heart of the New Russia* (New York: Random House, 2008); Mikhail Zygar, *All the Kremlin's Men: Inside the Court of Vladimir Putin* (New York: Public Affairs, 2016); two articles by Masha Gessen, 'Dead Soul' (*Vanity Fair*, October 2008) and 'The Wrath of Putin' (*Vanity Fair*, April 2012), as well as her book *The Man Without a Face* (New York: Riverhead Books, 2012); Catherine Belton's *Putin's People* (London: William Collins, 2020), although one must take many things that the author says with a pinch of salt; and the latest book by Yuri Felshtinsky and Michael Stanchev, *Blowing Up Ukraine: The Return of Russian Terror and the Threat of World War III* (London: Gibson Square, 2022). For Russian speakers, the book by Yuri Shulipa, *How Putin Kills Abroad* (Kiev-Berlin: Institute of National Politics, 2021) may be a useful guide.

While working on my third book on the murder of Alexander Litvinenko, I had to apply to the 'council of wise advisors', concilium in Latin, for help and expert assessment. I am indebted to several scientists with whom I discussed various aspects related to complex poisons and poisonings, and especially to Nicholas 'Nick' Priest, at the time Professor of Environmental Toxicology at Middlesex University; Professor John Harrison, Oxford Brookes University, Faculty of Health and Life Sciences; Professor Bogdan Skwarzec, a specialist in polonium, its chemistry, occurrence in nature, bio-accumulation, determination and radiotoxicity for humans at the Faculty of Chemistry, University of Gdańsk; and Dr Peter Steier, Assistant Professor at the Institute for Isotope Research and Nuclear Physics at the University of Vienna.

As always, two of my teachers and friends, Professor Sir Paul Preston in London (*A People Betrayed: A History of Corruption, Political Incompetence and*

Social Division in Modern Spain, 1874–2018, London: William Collins, 2021) and Professor Ángel Viñas in Madrid provided invaluable support and guidance throughout my work on this book, especially those parts that concerned Spain. In turn, former Italian senator Paolo Guzzanti, another good old friend and author of *Il mio agente Sasha* (Rome: Aliberti, 2009) was instrumental in explaining Litvinenko's work in Italy for the Mitrokhin Commission of the Italian parliament that Paolo had headed.

    Last but not least, I want to express my profound gratitude to all those who have helped to make this book possible. Almost twenty years after Russian agents murdered Sasha Litvinenko in London, Jonathan Wright, the publisher for the White Owl imprint of Pen & Sword Books, decided to commission this work, expecting a fresh look at a seemingly well-known case. Lisa Hooson has, for many years, been unfailingly helpful regarding requests and queries related to research and various publishing issues. Charlotte Mitchell, editor and production assistant, was very encouraging and enthusiastic, especially when working on the book cover. In the meantime, I was very pleased to find out that in addition to all her skills, Charlotte is a Spain and Spanish-language specialist. And I am immensely grateful to Cecily Blench, herself a prize-winning author, for her close and sympathetic reading of all the chapters.

    Finally, I want to thank my wife Valentina, to whom this book is dedicated, as were all my previous works. Throughout many years of our marriage, she has unfailingly supported everything I have done, also helping to research archives, generate ideas, and navigate through the murky world of Russian espionage and deception. And, of course, she has always been my first reader and critic.

    Grateful to all these successful, intelligent, well-educated, and kind people, I remain solely responsible for any errors herein.

Boris B. Volodarsky,
London and Vienna, February 2023

Definitions of Key Terms

Agent – someone who works for the government or its security or intelligence services. This is a basic definition and there may be different 'agents' including foreign agents, secret agents, double agents, agents-in-place, agents-of-influence, access agents, support agents, source agents and human assets. Regarding Soviet and Russian Intelligence Services (RIS), not all but many agents sign the letter of allegiance with the Service and may receive remuneration or benefits in various forms, depending on the position of an agent. For example, journalists recruited as agents may get access to information which is otherwise not usually shared with the media based on which they may produce sensational news stories. Thus, an 'independent Russian journalist' who for whatever reason resides, say, in London may suddenly announce that a high-ranking official in Moscow is going to be dismissed or arrested, explaining that this information was received from some unnamed secret sources in the FSB. Or a British or American journalist suddenly publishes 'strictly confidential' information which was 'shared' with him or her during a recent visit to Moscow. In the KGB, this is known as 'active measures', which is part of media manipulation, in itself an element of complex influence and propaganda operations.

A typical example of a double agent and at the same time agent-in-place is Sergey Skripal, who as an officer of Soviet and then Russian military intelligence (GRU) was recruited to work for Britain, providing information first from his undercover intelligence post in Madrid and later from the GRU headquarters in Moscow, where he had been based after his recall from Spain.

In his book *Organised Crime Group 'The Lubyanka Syndicate'* (also translated as *Lubyanka Criminal Group* or *The Gang from Lubyanka*, 2002), Litvinenko explained the difference between agents and **confidants**. 'An agent,' he said, 'has a personal file in the Service's registry and receives regular assignments, while a confidant is there to occasionally run errands for his handler.'

Case Officer – a secret service officer charged with building and managing relationships with agents and informants. Case officers run their human assets by maintaining good, friendly relations with them in order to collect raw intelligence.

Centre – in Russian intelligence jargon, the 'Centre' or Moscow Centre was the headquarters of the First Chief Directorate (FCD, foreign intelligence) of the KGB

Definitions of Key Terms

and its predecessors especially during the first Cold War (1947–91). All Soviet agents abroad reported to and received their instructions from the Centre, which was first located at the KGB building on Lubyanka Square in Moscow and later at the FCD compound in Yasenevo near Moscow, currently the headquarters of the SVR.

Clandestine – usually understood as something which is done in secret. Clandestine operations, however, have their specifics and are different from **covert** operations, which is confusing to most people. In the tradecraft, a clandestine operation is carried out in such a manner that it remains in secrecy. That is, the operation itself and the agency responsible for it remain unknown so that complete deniability on behalf of the government is possible. A typical example of a clandestine operation is the murder of Boris Berezovsky in the UK.

Clean phone – usually a prepaid mobile phone used for secure communication between an agent and his intelligence service handler. As long as this phone number is unknown to the opposite side, it cannot be located, monitored, or tapped.

Confidant or confidential source – a person who can be trusted with secret matters and on whose services an intelligence officer can usually rely. The worldwide success of the tiny Israeli secret service known as the Mossad, Hebrew for Institute, is partially because it can rely on the international network of what they call helpers and voluntary assistants, in Hebrew, sayanim.[1] This system has operated inside Russia for years but since the borders of the country opened and a certain part of the educated population settled in the West, the KGB and its successors picked up the idea of the 'Russian World' (Russkiy Mir), a concept put forward in the 1990s. It was officially adopted by the Russian administration and Putin decreed the establishment of the state-sponsored Russkiy Mir Foundation as a global project in 2007. The Foundation even managed to set up the Laboratório de Estudos Russos (LERUSS) at the largest Brazilian public university. The Russian World is headed by Vyacheslav Nikonov, the grandson of Molotov, one of the most ruthless of Stalin's henchmen placed in charge of Soviet foreign affairs. Among non-specialists, Molotov would be remembered for the Molotov-Ribbentrop Soviet-Nazi Pact signed in August 1939, and the Molotov cocktail. The term was coined by the Finns during the Winter War between Soviet Union and Finland as a pejorative reference to the then Soviet foreign minister. Quite out of the blue, Nikonov was awarded the honorary degree of doctor honoris causa by the University of Edinburgh in July 2012.[2]

Although all major intelligence operations abroad are planned and executed by the SVR officers and agents those involving the Russian World network are partially controlled by the FSB through its resident agent, officially accredited as a diplomat at the Russian embassy, and by a so-called group leader also resident in the country.

Like the sayanim of Mossad, Russian confidants are never or at least rarely brought into operations, just asked for favours. And they are assured that the help they are asked to provide is not against the country of their current residence and always for the benefit of their motherland, which may or may not be true.

When Litvinenko was a young lieutenant in the Dzerzhinky Division, he later explained, 'out of the 1,000 officers and men in the regiment there could be 170 sources and confidential sources'.[3] According to him, FSB officers use confidants for errands rather than assignments.

Covert – something which is not openly acknowledged (or displayed). Exactly like **clandestine**, a covert operation is planned and executed in secrecy, but while its consequences cannot (or are not intended to) be concealed, the identity of the initiator and the agency (or organisation) are protected and must remain secret at all costs. Typical examples of covert operations are the assassinations of Anna Politkovskaya and Boris Nemtsov in Moscow. In the poisonings of Alexander Litvinenko in Britain, the operation was clearly planned as clandestine, but as a result turned out to be covert, with Russian propaganda still vehemently denying that the Kremlin was behind it. On the contrary, the attempted poisoning of Alexey Navalny has been an operation initially planned as covert, but without any doubt authorised by the Kremlin and proved to have been executed by the FSB.

Dangle – usually refers to an intelligence officer or agent who is instructed to pretend that he or she is interested in defecting to or being 'turned' by the adversary's intelligence service. In most cases, dangles act as walk-ins or offer their services to a foreign intelligence service of another country, giving various plausible reasons. Dangles may also serve as agent provocateurs or double agents, collecting intelligence for their original agency and feeding disinformation to their 'new masters'. In recent intelligence history, one of the best examples of an intelligence officer acting as a dangle is Alexander Zhomov.[4]

FSK – the Federal Counterintelligence Service was the successor of the Ministry of Security and predecessor of the FSB. It existed between December 1993 and April 1995, with the head office at No. 2 Lubyanka Square in Moscow, the old KGB building. It had a staff of 75,000 people and was commanded first by Nikolai Golushko, former chairman of the Ukrainian KGB, and then by Sergey Stepashin, who would also serve as the first director of the FSB from April 1995.

FSB – Federal Security Agency of the Russian Federation, one of the indirect successors of the Soviet KGB and the principal security agency of Russia. Following the collapse of the USSR and the attempted coup d'état of August 1991, the KGB was dismantled and a new structure – Federal Security Agency (AFB, 29 November–19 December 1991) was formed. The Agency quickly grew into the Ministry of Security of the Russian Federation (24 January 1992–21 December 1993) which was transformed into the Federal Counterintelligence Service (FSK, 21 December 1993 – 3 April 1995) of RF.

Definitions of Key Terms

The FSB is a successor to the FSK and takes care of internal counterintelligence, counterterrorism, organised crime, surveillance, and border protection. In addition, it is responsible for all sorts of intelligence operations on the territory of the former Soviet Union. Contrary to popular wisdom, the FSB is neither the KGB of post-Soviet Russia nor the equivalent of the British Security Service (MI5) or the American FBI. The FSB of today is roughly comparable to the United States Department of Homeland Security (DHS) minus customs, minus immigration, minus disaster prevention. As if to amplify the difference, they added the so-called Special Purpose Centre to the FSB structure.[5] From the first day of its formation in October 1998, the Centre has been commanded by Colonel General Alexander Tikhonov, who reports to First DD. Two special units within the FSB Special Purpose Centre – Directorate 'A' (Alpha Group) and Directorate 'V' (Special Group Vympel)[6] are authorised to act under the direct control and orders of the Russian president. Officers of Alpha and Vympel are trained to carry out covert as well as clandestine operations, both domestically and internationally. Both units also have a role in anti-terrorist operations in Russia and abroad (Syria).

Informant – someone who secretly gives information to the police, security service, or someone in authority. In the law enforcement world, informants or informers (aka stool pigeons) are officially known as confidential human sources, whose motivations may be very different. They are usually divided into self-interest (financial reward, revenge, and so on), self-preservation (fear of reprisals or arrest), conscience (guilt or genuine desire to help law enforcement agencies), and even mischief. In the KGB, informants were known as *seksots*, which is a Russian portmanteau meaning 'secret collaborator'. In KGB reports, informants were designated as 'sources', 'reliable sources', or sometimes 'sources of operational information'. They usually signed a confidential collaboration agreement and received regular remuneration.

Instantsiya – in KGB and GRU parlance: the highest authority, which, after the death of Stalin and until the collapse of the Soviet Union in 1991, was the Communist Party Central Committee at 4 Staraya Square in Moscow. Both Soviet foreign intelligence services were primarily collection agencies responding to specific or general requests for information from the ruling Communist Party leadership and the armed forces. With this, the chairman of the KGB and his deputies reported to the head of the Administration Department of the Central Committee and sometimes directly to the general secretary of the CPSU, while the director of the GRU reported to the chief of the army general staff. After the approval of the responsible authorities, scientific and technical intelligence was directed to the consumers. Political intelligence, which, apart from the KGB, was also collected by the Foreign Ministry mostly through embassies and consulates, as well as by the Soviet news agencies TASS and APN and Soviet journalists accredited as foreign correspondents abroad, was analysed, edited, abridged, and, when necessary, sent to the top party officials. The Instantsiya also issued directives to conduct special operations which may be active measures (after the war – disinformation, propaganda, and deception as part of the political warfare), provocations and deep penetration with a view to sabotage, assassination (also known as terminations), and general mayhem. The term 'wet affair' (or 'wet job' and sometimes 'wetwork'), loved by many spy writers, is obsolete and has not been used since the 1920s. The term 'liquidation' is also out of use.

After Putin came to power in March 2000, the presidential administration located at the very same address on Staraya Square had been executing complete oversight of almost all Russian secret services (with the exception of the Presidential Security Service and Rosgvardiya), to a certain extent, like the Cabinet Office in the UK, bringing an overall coherence to the tasking of the Services, to assessing their product and to determining their resource needs and performance.[7] But as always happens in Russia, there are a lot of flaws in this arrangement.

Investigator – in one of his books, Litvinenko described his FSB role as *razrabotchik*, explaining that his job included collection and analysis of information on suspects who might be involved in terrorist activities, espionage, serious organised crime, and (he forgot to name) proliferation of weapons. An FSB investigator (razrabotchik), according to Litvinenko, is an operational officer's highest professional qualification, which requires the combination of professional competence, education, and skills. While working at the FSB headquarters in Moscow, Litvinenko was very proud to have been trusted with the investigator's job, giving assignments to agents and confidants as well as to surveillance teams to covertly monitor targets' movements, conversations, and other activities. His group, he said, was involved in the operational support of the investigation which usually resulted in arrests and criminal charges.

Kontóra – a Russian slang word meaning, among other things, the KGB. The word was borrowed from the German *Kontor* and is colloquially used to refer to an office or bureau. As a reference to the KGB (and later its successors), it also formed a pun exploiting the same acronym, KGB (*Kontora Glubokogo Bureniya*, verbally 'deep drilling office'), which sounds alike but has a different meaning.

Krysha – in Russian, 'krysha' literally means 'roof' but, as Amy Mackinnon explains in her article in *Foreign Policy* (14 June 2020), the word took another meaning in the late 1980s and is now associated with protection. Protection from criminals and organised crime groups (OCG) that flourished as the Soviet state collapsed. 'Its trajectory,' she writes, 'charts the evolution of power in Russia as the gangsterism of the 1990s was brought to heel, making way for the political violence of President Vladimir Putin's rule in the 21st century.' After private business was allowed in Russia, small businesses and even large companies became rather easy pickings for predatory protection rackets and criminals took as much as a 30 per cent cut of profits.

In the absence of a functioning police or court system, the protection offered by gangs was welcomed by many business owners, Ms Mackinnon claims, quoting an assistant professor of political science at the John Jay College of Criminal Justice, who confirmed: 'It was something people trusted, more than the state.' In the lawlessness of the 1990s, it was almost impossible for a business to survive without hired muscle.

The *Foreign Policy* article takes a new twist, suggesting that:

> Under Putin, Russia entered a period of long-craved stability and prosperity, and the lawlessness of the 1990s faded … When Putin assumed the presidency in a very staged handoff from the ailing Yeltsin in 1999, it became clear he would brook no challenge to the state's authority. Many gang members were killed or imprisoned. Other residents of the Russian underworld managed to use their connections to manoeuvre their businesses into semi-legitimacy.

This, however, represents only one face of the coin.

The problem is that under Putin, the state has merged with organised crime and the officers of the Russian secret services and the police have assumed the role of krysha, while some diplomats and intelligence officers operate as criminals being actively involved in extortion, money laundering and drug trafficking. As seen by many experts, the regime has given way to a marriage between kleptocracy and organised crime. An article with the self-explanatory title 'Gangs and Gulags: How Vladimir Putin Utilizes Organized Crime to Power his Mafia State' by Dylan McIlvenna-Davis in *Berkeley Political Review* (16 December 2019) mentions Solntsevskaya OCG as the largest organised crime group in the world, ranking above both the Japanese Yakuza and the Mexican Sinaloa cartel in terms of overall revenue. It is no secret in Russia that the FSB serves as this gang's krysha.

Officer (in the KGB-FSB-SVR parlance: *sotrudnik*) – a staff member of a secret service. In the KGB and its successor organisations, all officers had military ranks from lieutenant upwards.

Oligarch – the term is widely used in the media to describe very rich or sometimes simply rich Russians, which is wrong. The *Cambridge Business English Dictionary* defines 'oligarch' as 'one of a small group of powerful people who control a country or an industry'. In its turn, the *Oxford Advanced Learner's Dictionary* adds that Russian oligarchs became rich after the collapse of the former Soviet Union, specifically pointing to 'the power of the oligarchs to influence the government'. That is, a Russian oligarch is a fabulously wealthy person who, very importantly, has the power to influence the decision making on the state level.

In one of the analytical articles published on the eve of the 2000 Russian presidential election on the Radio Free Europe/Radio Liberty site, Floriana Fossato recalls a situation when Boris Nemtsov and Anatoly Chubais, both of whom served as deputy prime ministers, launched an attack on Berezovsky, describing him as the main advocate of oligarchic capitalism. An independent Russian news agency Interfax reported Berezovsky's reaction. Because an oligarchy is a merger of power and capital, he said, the choice is straightforward: either Nemtsov is not a deputy prime minister, or those whom he attacks are not oligarchs.

Podstava – used in modern Russia both in intel-speak and in everyday life. In informal English, it means a set-up, a ploy, or a hoax, 'a situation in which someone cheats or tricks you, especially by making you appear guilty when you are not' (*Macmillan English Dictionary*). In other words, 'a cunning plan or action designed to turn a situation to one's own advantage' (*Oxford Languages*). In Russian intelligence lingo, it may denote a sting operation which is set up to catch a person who has committed or is attempting to commit a crime. It may be launched many years after the crime has actually been committed. For example, in 1997, the FBI used a sting operation to catch up a former colonel of the US Army Reserve who had been spying for the Russians in the 1970s and 1980s. The operation was a typical *podstava* which went on for three years until the suspect was finally arrested in June 2000. He was convicted of spying and died in a high-security US federal prison fourteen years later.

Rules (by the rules) – the code of conduct which is used to govern the lives of the members of criminal groups. In Russian, it is translated as *zhit'* (live) or *déistvovat'* (act) *po ponyátiyam* (according to the unwritten rules). As one report has put it, 'organised criminals, like prisoners, live outside the law, and in response to this outlaw status they, like prisoners, develop a set of norms and procedures for controlling conduct within their organisation'. The general directives making up the prisoners' code are, in fact, characteristic of the code of good thieves everywhere. In order to maintain their status as leaders of illegal criminal groups or organisations, crime bosses must promulgate and enforce similar codes of conduct.[8] Many officers of Russian law enforcement agencies often act not according to the law but according to the unwritten rules that every member should know, which may or may not be the same as the criminal code of conduct.

Sistéma – in this case, *sistema* (system) means organisation. Generally, it refers to the inner structure of the Soviet and Russian state, backed, supported, and infiltrated by corrupt Russian secret services and police. Although it had always existed in Russia before and after the Bolshevik revolution, during the Putin years *sistema* became known as 'the vertical of power' which is probably one of the best general summaries of Russia's political system and its ambiguities. As someone noted, to go or to rebel against the system – *idti protiv sistemy* – is a heinous crime. It means to betray it, to act against the existing harmonious order of things both in the country and within its secret services because, as it was demonstrated in 1989–91, the main weakness of this regime is that it can be integrally endangered or even destroyed by any change of form.

About This Book

against humanity, or genocide in Chechnya for presentation to the International Criminal Court in The Hague.

During the inquest hearings it was also established that in or about 2003 Litvinenko started collaborating with the British Secret Intelligence Service (SIS), also known as MI6. From 2004, he had been entered in the Service Registry as a paid agent for various intelligence assignments abroad. He was also consulting SIS's Russian Desk on Russian organised crime in Europe, travelling to various countries to assist their law enforcement agencies on SIS's request.

Litvinenko also provided information on the Russian secret services to the Mitrokhin Commission of the Italian parliament. Vasili Mitrokhin was a senior KGB archivist who defected to Britain, bringing with him a huge handwritten personal archive that contained copies of almost all the KGB documents of enormous historical value that he had ever dealt with during his years of service. Together with an eminent British intelligence historian, Professor Christopher Andrew, he worked on a book which came out in two volumes as *The Mitrokhin Archive* (1999 and 2005). A certain part of the Mitrokhin documents remained classified and some of them, dealing with specific countries, MI6 sent to the secret services of those countries for study and analysis. Among others, Italy also received such files.

In 2002, the Italian parliament established a commission, which became known as the Mitrokhin Commission, to investigate matters related to the Mitrokhin documents. The Commission was headed by Senator Paolo Guzzanti. One of his assistants arranged contact with Litvinenko through another former Soviet intelligence officer living in the UK in order to get an insider's perspective on how Soviet and Russian secret services operate. In January 2004, Litvinenko travelled to Italy, where his half-brother Maxim lived, to help the Commission. He stayed in touch until 1 November 2006, when he was poisoned and went into hospital. Mario Scaramella, an amateur investigator and Litvinenko's contact involved in collecting information for the Commission, was one of the few persons who met Sasha in London on that fateful day.

Among other information that Litvinenko shared with the Mitrokhin Commission was his claim that Romano Prodi, an Italian politician and senior civil servant, who had twice served as prime minister of Italy and, in between, as President of the European Commission, had been a KGB agent.

In 2005, British authorities arranged Litvinenko's contact with the Spanish Centro Nacional de Inteligencia (CNI), which was acting as both its foreign and domestic intelligence agency, involved in investigating Russian organised crime in Spain. At about the same time, the British National Crime Agency (NCA) together with the Spanish authorities were involved in a multi-agency operation codenamed CAPTURA to detain criminals wanted by the UK who were hiding in Spain. In their turn, MI6 took a keen interest in Kremlin-connected oligarchs. It had been established that several Russian top officials close to Putin had maintained regular informal contacts with Russian organised crime lords based in Spain and operating in Europe, which gave reasonable grounds to suspect some of the Kremlin's inhabitants of political corruption.

The Murder of Alexander Litvinenko: To Kill a Mockingbird

Litvinenko met with José Grinda Gonzalez, a Spanish anti-corruption prosecutor, in July 2006 and was supposed to testify in Spain on 10 November. A 500-page report filed by the Spanish prosecutors two years after Litvinenko's death provided details of several criminal networks uncovered in Spain, whose bosses were ostensibly linked to the highest rungs of the Russian government. The National Court of Spain, based on 'very serious evidence against them', issued arrest warrants for several Russian top officials close to Putin's circle. Litvinenko's main contribution to the Spanish authorities' fight against corruption and organised crime was his 'thesis', which he was able to justify based on his personal knowledge and experience, that Russian secret services and law enforcement agencies controlled organised crime groups and sometimes even directed their activities both in Russia and abroad.

As if all that was not enough, in 2005 and 2006, Litvinenko was involved in what the coroner called 'private security work'. From the text of Sir Robert Owen's final report for the Litvinenko Inquiry in January 2016, it is obvious that the coroner is not quite aware of what this work entails. What are known as corporate investigative firms are actually private spies who are usually former professional spies now retired and for hire. Like, for example, Christopher Steele, a former SIS intelligence branch officer who was in charge of the Russian Desk at the Secret Intelligence Service (MI6) head office at Vauxhall Cross in 2004–2009. His private company Orbis Business Intelligence, which he founded together with another former intelligence officer as soon as he left MI6, would provide 'strategic advice, mount intelligence-gathering operations and conduct complex, often cross-border investigations', according to their site.

There is little question that private investigators take on legitimate assignments – still, everyone in the industry knows its secret, as one recent assessment of this tricky business reveals. This secret lies in the simple fact that the big money is made not by exposing the truth but by concealing it. 'Spies-for-hire,' Barry Meier writes, 'are part of a wider web of enablers – lawyers, public relations executives, "crisis management" consultants – who serve the powerful and wealthy. But what makes private operatives unique is that they are the unseen part of that web, taking on the kinds of jobs that other people don't know how to do or don't want to get caught doing.'

In the case of Litvinenko, he did not know how to do this job and was not afraid of getting caught, but was simply anxious to try his hand at private spying. He started working with three private investigators that, like Orbis, offer enhanced due diligence, anti-money laundering, business intelligence, fraud investigation, as well as complex litigation and business resolution advice and support, plus a lot of other discreet services. And failed.

Sasha Litvinenko was poisoned during a meeting set up by a man whom he considered his good friend, business partner, and hope for the future. This man's name was Andrey Lugovoy. At the time of writing, he is alive and still basking in the glory of his success in the Litvinenko affair, promoted to the State Duma (Russian parliament) and awarded the Order of Merit by President Putin. In response to

About This Book

British demands, Moscow refused to extradite him. The poisoning was a result of a complex, well-planned and well-executed covert operation that had lasted for over a year and had been carried out by a large group of people both in Moscow and London. At the final stage, Lugovoy was accompanied in London by his two friends and former classmates, Vyacheslav Sokolenko and Dmitry Kovtun.

Kovtun was brought into this operation shortly before, on 16 October, and according to the plan should have been acting as a distraction. Distraction means to divert the mind or attention of a target away from something, a known spycraft trick. In magic, it is called misdirection and is used to direct audience's attention towards one thing so it does not notice another. On that day, however, Kovtun also managed to contaminate himself while handling the container with radioactive poison without any protective clothing and safety glasses, leaving traces of radiation everywhere he went. Professionally speaking, having no idea of what substance he was dealing with, Kovtun accidentally suffered external radiation exposure, probably due to a leak in a vial containing the substance or incorrect handling, or simply carelessness. Although usually such exposure is not a hazard to the outside of the body, in this case it could have been extremely high and as a result Kovtun received radiation-induced injuries and some two weeks after the exposure had to undergo a lengthy treatment in a specialised facility in Russia. After six months, they told him he was all right and, for some time, he enjoyed life like Lugovoy, taking part in press conferences, making political statements, and giving interviews. In or about 2015, Kovtun disappeared from the public radar. On 4 June 2022, he died. To the best of my knowledge, he left no will and did not make a final statement.

Contrary to him, Sasha Litvinenko left a political testament that during all those years of Putin and his regime in power in Russia has become more and more relevant. Sasha's statement was released to reporters by Alex Goldfarb on the day after Sasha's death:

> You may succeed in silencing me, but that silence comes at a price. You have shown yourself to be as barbaric and ruthless as your most hostile critics have claimed. You have shown yourself to have no respect for life, liberty or any civilised value. You have shown yourself to be unworthy of your office, to be unworthy of the trust of civilised men and women.
>
> You may succeed in silencing one man. But a howl of protest from around the world will reverberate, Mr Putin, in your ears for the rest of your life.

* * *

All wars must teach lessons. If they do not do so they were fought in vain and those who died in them did so for naught.[8] The poisoning of Alexander Litvinenko started the Second Cold War, which after less than two decades escalated into Russia's war of aggression against Ukraine, making many people think we are on the brink of World War III.

The previous wars taught at least three lessons, if the powers have the wit to learn them. The first is that it is madness for the forty advanced economies of the world, with decent standards of living, a substantial accumulation of industrial capital, modern technologies, and institutions that are firmly embedded within the global economy to offer the leader of an aggressor state a face-saving compromise that will only enable future aggression. 'No country in Europe or beyond,' the Chief of SIS warns, 'should be seduced into thinking that unbalanced concessions to Russia bring better behaviour.' Having come to power as a wartime president and having at his disposal instruments like nuclear, biological, and chemical (NBC) weapons to support his aggressive stance, such a leader will always rely on a war as the best way to secure his leading position. For two decades, Putin's regime was allowed to arm itself to a frightening level by a combination of political foolishness, bureaucratic blindness, and corporate greed. Military loss and the eventual destruction of that war machine combined with an economic recession and financial crisis generated by sanctions could create a real opening for a major change in the authoritarian aggressor state. Such a regime cannot and must not remain in power.

The second lesson concerns information. At the end of the First Cold War and following the collapse of the Soviet Union, foreign delegations rushed to Moscow in large numbers. Among them were groups of former CIA officers who naively believed that since the Berlin Wall had fallen, the main adversary became a cooperation partner. Many hoped that the great confrontation between Russia and the West could safely be curbed. The reality showed the opposite and Russia, China, and Iran remained the 'big four priorities' within the intelligence community for the next decades, the fourth being international terrorism (Richard Moore, 'C' of SIS).

At the end of the twentieth century, technical advantages in the gathering of intelligence were so impressive and the threat to the *free world* seemed so insignificant that Western governments were led to believe that human relationships and networks could now be downgraded. The proliferation of weapons including conventional armaments and WMDs became a source of great concern and counting terrorism – the highest priority of the international community. In areas related to intelligence collection, especially in what concerned Russia and its satellites, the budgets and human resources were dramatically reduced. In the meantime, Western societies as well as former Soviet republics and Warsaw Pact members became thoroughly penetrated by agents of influence, confidential contacts, collaborators, traitors, and ideological moles. Even most advanced tech gadgets and modern supercomputers could not see them.

While all countries were pouring money into mastering artificial intelligence (AI), quantum computing and synthetic biology, Russia was developing New Generation Warfare to address the West, always considered by the Kremlin as Russia's main adversary. 'As practiced in Ukraine, Russia's new generation warfare

About This Book

is manifested in five component elements: political subversion, proxy sanctuary, intervention, coercive deterrence and negotiated manipulation,' according to the expert.[9] Russia's annexation of Crimea and the war in Ukraine that followed eight years later took many by surprise, although American and British intelligence did not only predict the invasion of Ukraine but were also instructed to make their knowledge public, weeks in advance. Still, when the war started, Western agents and analysts were seeking to get inside the Russian president's head, trying to figure out what might be the next move.

Artificial intelligence and quantum computing could not help here. What becomes plain is that for certain tasks in certain places there is still no substitute for the oldest information-gathering device on Earth with the talent to turn complex data into human insight. Forsyth calls it the Human Eyeball, Mark One.

The third lesson deals with deception and self-deception. All warfare is based on deception, while appeasement is a result of self-deception. Edward Wood, also known as Lord Irwin, Viscount Halifax and Earl of Halifax, then the Leader of the House of Lords and later British Foreign Secretary, after a meeting with Hitler, wrote to the Prime Minister Neville Chamberlain: 'Hitler was sincere when he said he did not want war.' It was November 1937 and, as an appeaser, he wanted to believe it. This pre-war deception of Eden, Halifax, Chamberlain, and their fellow travellers was a self-induced kind. As correctly noted by Andrew Rawnsley, 'appeasement, the fatal delusion that Nazi Germany could be contained by buying it off with concessions, was the most momentous British mistake of the 20th century'.

Another mistake, this time in the twenty-first century, was made by Tony Blair twice. First, when he visited Russia at the KGB's request in March 2000 before Putin was even confirmed in his post as Russian president. After the visit, Blair told the BBC: 'He [Putin] was highly intelligent and with a focused view of what he wants to achieve in Russia.' Twenty years later we knew exactly what he wanted to achieve. Second, when the Labour government under Blair's leadership failed to properly respond to the act of radiological terrorism in November 2006. The poisoning of Alexander Litvinenko in London by a polonium compound was a typical case of a radiological weapon attack with all characteristic features of such an attack.[10] Although there was a formal reaction, the UK's response to the Litvinenko murder was described as 'late, lame and lamentable'. The government expelled four Russian diplomats and official contact with the FSB was suspended. The Blair government tried to discuss the UK's concerns with its European partners, but according to the Chatham House report, 'the EU's somewhat tepid response fell short of its hopes'. Although the war in Europe was delayed by the Labour government's appeasement toward Russia, it was not too long in coming.

Speaking ahead of a visit to Britain, the first state visit by a Russian leader in nearly 130 years, Putin said: 'Tony Blair and I have a very good and trusting contact.' Like Tony Blair, the US president George W. Bush also looked the man in the eyes. 'I was able to get a sense of his soul,' Bush said. 'I found him to be very straightforward and trustworthy.'

Litvinenko was a simple man but he also had his chance to look Putin in the eyes. He quickly realised the man had no soul. 'I feel very upset that this criminal Putin sits at the G8 as its Chairman, at the same table as the British prime minister Tony Blair,' Sasha said in his last police interview, three days before his heart stopped beating. 'Having sat this murderer next to themselves at the same table Western leaders have actually untied his hands to kill anyone, anywhere.'

Litvinenko was not Lazarus... and not Nostradamus. But his predictions turned out to be correct.

Two Labour governments under Tony Blair and Gordon Brown stubbornly resisted any confrontation with Russia. In July 2013, Theresa May, the home secretary representing the Conservative government of David Cameron, sent a letter to the coroner, Sir Robert Owen, explaining the reason for the decision not to hold a public inquiry into Litvinenko's poisoning.

'May I begin by assuring you,' Ms May wrote, 'that the government shares your concern to make certain that the tragic death of Mr Litvinenko is properly investigated.' However, the government decided against holding a public inquiry. Why? 'It is true,' Ms May explained, 'that international relations have been a factor in the government's decision making.'

Giving due credit to the Counter Terrorism Command (SO15), a Specialist Operations branch within London's Metropolitan Police Service, this book seeks to make certain that Sasha's poisoning is properly investigated with the benefit of hindsight. And that conclusions made by the Litvinenko Inquiry in January 2016, like all other historical cases, could and must be reassessed in order to establish the truth, regardless of how various political actors influence our world.

In November 2006, the first question producers of BBC *Panorama*'s programme about the murder of Alexander Litvinenko asked me when I arrived in London was 'who and why'. Today, I feel like I can answer. To begin with: it was not polonium-210...

Prologue

A Machine Starts to Grind, then Stops

The government has cut the budget of the anti-corruption unit tasked with investigating dirty Russian money in 'Londongrad', one of the leading British newspapers revealed in March 2022. The article, focusing on how British corruption investigators and law enforcement agencies are being 'massively outgunned' by the so-called 'oligarchs' from the former Soviet Union, put the blame on the prime minister's decision to reduce the aid budget. According to media reports, following this decision ministers have slashed spending on the International Corruption Unit (ICU) by 13.5 per cent...

Spring in Vienna was unusually cold and unfriendly that year, and the city's main railway station, the newly constructed Hauptbahnhof (Hbf) was full of refugees from Ukraine. Here they were getting free meals, mineral water and tea, anti-Covid masks, and tickets to different destinations in Austria that had agreed to accept Ukrainians who had to leave their country, running away from the Russian bombs, mines, and missiles. Ukrainian women and children were also running away from the Russian soldiers who did not spare anyone's lives when Ukrainian troops were forcing them out of occupied Ukrainian territory. The Bucha massacre, revealed to the world on 2 April, with the corpses of the dead lying randomly on the streets, would be remembered forever. As if that was not enough, Russian forces left some bodies booby-trapped with explosive devices to cause more deaths and casualties – a tactic they learned from ISIS, which stands for the Islamic State of Iraq and Syria, a terrorist organisation.

There are two special express trains in the Austrian capital that take passengers from the centre of Vienna to its only international airport. Remarkably, the one leaving the Hbf every hour is even faster, better, and considerably cheaper than the widely advertised CAT, City Airport Train, a non-stop commuter service connecting Schwechat and the City Air Terminal.

Iberia, the flag carrier airline of Spain that promises to take you from Vienna to Adolfo Suárez Madrid-Barajas in three hours non-stop, is not my favourite, but there's hardly any better choice. As a compensation, the seriously renovated and expanded Vienna International Airport with a wide selection of excellent frequent traveller lounges is extremely comfortable and cosy, providing a lot of opportunities for a proper rest before the flight.

Waiting for the boarding call and browsing international newspapers provided here free of charge, I found out there were several British agencies responsible for investigating international bribery, corruption, and money laundering offences. Two organisations – the National Crime Agency's International Corruption Unit (ICU) and the Serious Fraud Office (SFO) – share prime responsibility for investigating allegations of corruption while the police, NCA, and HM Revenue and Customs (HMRC) are the principal authorities to deal with domestic and international money laundering. In their turn, the Crown Prosecution Service (CPS) prosecutes cases investigated by the enforcement agencies.

The man who was waiting for me in Madrid knew it all and perhaps even much more. In one of the interviews, he said that the unique position to go after Russian organised crime with few restraints became possible to a large extent thanks to his country's empowered anti-corruption unit, la Fiscalía Anticorrupción. 'If there weren't a centralised organisation with all its powers, things would be very slow,' meaning that coordination between different agencies is not always good enough and usually slows things down.

A kind of a celebrity in the small world of international anti-corruption experts, Senor José Grinda Gonzalez, a Spanish prosecutor hailed as a frontliner in the fight against the Russian mafia in Spain, is well known in both Britain and the USA. Some years ago, he was much quoted by the British media when he publicly stated that Britain's contribution to fighting Russian organised crime was zilch. 'It is less than negative,' he said, 'it just doesn't exist.' Quoted by *The Independent* after speaking at the Hudson Institute, a conservative American thinktank based in Washington, DC, Mr Grinda said Britain was suffering 'economic contamination'. According to him, UK politicians 'had been linked to oligarchs' and the country was riddled with 'oligarchs that have taken dirty money'.

This requires an explanation.

The British government has committed to passing the Economic Crime Bill to make it harder for oligarchs to hide laundered wealth. Remarkably, the word 'oligarch' is being used quite incorrectly by both the Russian-language and English-language speakers, including journalists and politicians, not to mention simple people on the street. According to the *Oxford Advanced Learner's Dictionary*, an oligarch is 'an extremely rich and powerful person, especially a Russian who became rich in business after the end of the former Soviet Union'. This widely accepted definition neglects the most important trait of the oligarchs – the power to influence the government of their country. Therefore, everybody is confused and, in most cases, people use the word 'oligarch' to describe any person who has managed to amass considerable wealth, which may include government mandarins, military, intelligence and police officers of various ranks, business people, and mafia chieftains. When MPs are speaking about their agencies being 'massively outgunned by rich defendants' lawyers', they grandstand, making a political argument just to boost their status because they know this is how the modern world is organised. Those who have more money have better houses, schools, cars, hospitals, wines, and defence attorneys – this is just the way it is. In what concerns law enforcement agencies, resources are important but there should also be something else.

Prologue

Mr Grinda, the Spanish anti-corruption prosecutor whom I was going to meet in his modest office at the Fiscalía Especial Contra La Corrupción y la Criminalidad Organizada on Calle de Manuel Silvela in Madrid, realised he needed to find the root of the problem. Grinda was assigned to work on Russian organised crime cases in March 2006. In July, he went to London to meet Alexander Litvinenko, a young former lieutenant colonel of the Russian FSB.

As it turned out, many people in the West are deeply mistaken about the place and role of the FSB in Russia. They think it is the modern name of the old Soviet KGB, which is wrong. Anyway, Mr Grinda was aware that Litvinenko was a former senior officer of the URPO, an FSB department, similar to his own, established to investigate and prevent Russian organised crime cases. Nobody in the West knew the Russian organised crime scene better than Sasha Litvinenko, Sasha being a shortened version of Alexander. What José Grinda learned during those meetings in July 2006 completely changed his view on Russia and on his own job.

Litvinenko explained to him that since Vladimir Putin, a former KGB officer first appointed director of the FSB, then prime minister and then acting president, was elected the President of Russia in March 2000, the framework for fusion between Russian intelligence services and Russian organised crime under the direction of the Kremlin had been established. The so-called Family of Boris Yeltsin, the ailing incumbent president who retreated to his dacha on New Year's Eve giving over his office and the country to the man he hardly knew, appointed Putin expecting that he would preserve the status quo and leave the untouchables untouched. Instead, by the end of Putin's first term – and that would go on for over two decades – the country had been completely changed. What is more, while the Russian economy was being transformed, the social life of the people and the way many Russians assessed the state of their own country and its place in the world underwent equally drastic changes. Irrespective of their age, they were now a new generation, Generation Z. Western researchers were amazed to find out that in February 2023, a year after the Russian invasion of Ukraine, a large percentage of the country's population still supported Vladimir Putin, had increasingly negative views of the 'collective West', especially Britain, the USA, and NATO, and were nostalgic for the Soviet era. Leaving the departure gate and boarding the aircraft, I was wondering whether, sixteen years before the war in Ukraine, José Grinda and Sasha Litvinenko were able to advance as far as predicting this tragic turn of events.

It seems they were. During their meeting in London in 2006, Litvinenko laid out before his guest a strong argument proving that Vladimir Putin is not only fully implicated in Russian organised crime but that he and his close circle control all important mafia activities. Sasha directly accused the Kremlin of having organised crime groups do whatever the official Russian authorities cannot or for various reasons do not want to do. 'It is rare that criminals in a country make up its government,' Yuri Felshtinsky, Litvinenko's co-author, wrote in the foreword to their book. And about Putin as a mass murderer, Litvinenko reminded his Spanish colleague how the FSB killed more than 300 innocent people in September 1999 to create a pretext for the Kremlin to go to war with Chechnya in order to get Putin elected. Known as the Russian apartment bombings, these were a series of explosions that hit four apartment blocks in several cities across Russia. The bombings triggered the Second Chechen War. Litvinenko also pointed out that as part of this war, the battle of Grozny, which ended with the Russian seizure of the Chechen capital in February 2000, devastated the city like no other since World War II. Three years later, the United Nations declared Grozny the most destroyed city on Earth because the Russian troops literally razed the city to the ground.

In 2005, there were two very successful anti-money laundering and organised crime operations conducted by the Spanish police in collaboration with Interpol and Europol. One, codenamed WHITE WHALE, was in March near the Costa del Sol, and another, codenamed AVISPA, in June. During the first operation, over 250 million euros had been recovered and among the seized items were forty-two luxury cars, a yacht, two private planes, paintings, and other valuables. According to the reports, Spanish, French, Finnish, Russian, and Ukrainian nationals were among the forty-one apprehended criminals. The results of Operation AVISPA were no less impressive, in spite of the fact that two out of three main targets about whom Litvinenko provided valuable information managed to escape. Nevertheless, with Litvinenko's help, investigators were able to identify important clues to the nature of the relationships between criminal networks and corrupt Russian officials.

AVISPA, 'wasp' in English, consisted of three parts. In June 2005, during Phase I, in a sweeping operation conducted by the Grupo Operativo de Seguridad (GOS) de la Guardia Civil (Spanish Civil Guard Operative Security Group) that involved 400 officers from the Costa del Sol and elsewhere in Spain, twenty-eight suspected 'Russian Mafia' members, mainly Georgian and Ukrainian nationals, were arrested. In the course of Phase II in 2006, nine additional suspects were apprehended and, a few months later, in 2007, Phase III resulted in three more arrests. According to the secret report of the US embassy in Madrid, which leaked to the media, that included the Spanish national government's number two official in the Catalan region for allegedly helping members of the Russian organised crime network secure work visas to allow them to enter the country legally. A year later, the Spanish flagship daily *El Pais* published a detailed article claiming that Litvinenko provided important information on the former Soviet organised crime leaders, resident in Spain since the 1990s but active in Russia and Europe, to GOS officials during a meeting 'in a European city'.[1]

Since Russian organised crime has become interwoven with the Russian state, it is not just a problem for Russian people only, Litvinenko reasoned. Grinda agreed. Moreover, the Spanish prosecutor developed this idea observing that as Russian organised crime went global, attempts to stop it lagged. At that time, they both thought that Russian criminals, seizing all kinds of assets in the West and establishing themselves in Europe and America, would one day become dangerous. But they could have never imagined that less than two decades later the whole of Russia would become dangerous to the civilised world.

Prologue

The publication of *Blowing Up Russia* did not get any attention until Litvinenko's death in November 2006. Even then, Western leaders did not change their attitude to Putin. They did nothing when Russia invaded Georgia in 2008, and when it invaded and subsequently annexed Crimea in 2014 in violation of all international agreements. In early February 2022, leaders of two great European powers, France and Germany, were still visiting Moscow allowing Putin to humiliate them further by placing first the French president and then the German chancellor at the far end of a five-metre-long table to listen what he had to say. Political observers immediately recalled September 1938, when Neville Chamberlain and Édouard Daladier rushed to meet Hitler, reminding the world once again of the futility of appeasing totalitarian states.

This time, Britain was above reproach and made everyone respect her leaders, who pledged the UK's unwavering support to Ukraine.

At 4.00 am on 24 February, the world woke up in another reality. Soon Moscow started to talk about the Third World War quite seriously. Flying to Madrid, I wanted to ask Mr Grinda what he was going to do now.

CHAPTER 1

The Family and the KGB Coup d'État

> Three main forces took part in the struggle for power [in 1996]: the communists, the oligarchs, and the secret services. Russian businessmen were so absorbed in the fight against the communists that they failed to notice how people in uniform stabbed them in the back.
>
> Alexander Litvinenko, *LPG* (2002)

In late November 2002, BBC News reported that the oil tanker *Prestige*, which had been leaking oil off the north-west coast of Spain, had sunk after breaking apart, taking thousands of tonnes of fuel with it. After being kept out at sea for six days, it split up and went down spilling 50,000 tonnes of oil into the Atlantic and polluting miles of coastline of Galicia and over a thousand beaches in Spain, France, and Portugal. Fishermen and local authorities affected by the spill were demanding 2.2 billion euros (£1.8 bn) in damages while the court documents put the total damage at nearly four billion euros.

The *Prestige* had set sail from St Petersburg, Russia. The ship flew under the Bahamas flag, but was insured in the UK as part of a Swiss fleet with a Greek captain and Filipino first mate. The oil, which the Spanish workers had been scraping off the beaches for weeks, belonged to the Russian Alfa Group. The unfortunate tanker was owned by a Liberian-based company called Mare Shipping and chartered by the Swiss-based Crown Resources registered in Zug. Investigators quickly found the company's direct links to CTF Holding in Gibraltar and CTF Holding SA in Luxembourg which, in turn, acted as a parent to many of Alfa Group's legal entities in Russia and around the world.

One of the leading personalities of the Alfa Group Consortium was a Russian businessman, economist and politician Petr Aven, who until March 2022 headed Alfa-Bank, the largest private bank in Russia. In addition to his many talents and achievements, Aven wrote a book about his former boss that he called *Berezovsky's Time* (2018), which is based on interviews with people who had been close to the tycoon and who agreed to share their thoughts about Berezovsky, Litvinenko and Putin. They also discussed how it could be that an average bureaucrat from St Petersburg who was a former lieutenant colonel of the provincial KGB virtually unknown to anybody suddenly became the autocratic ruler of the country which, at least at the time of writing, covered about one-eighth of the world's land surface.

Aven was born in Moscow in 1955 and educated at Moscow State University (MGU) where he also received his PhD in economics in 1980. After about a decade, working at the Institute for Applied Systems Analysis of the USSR Academy of Sciences, he joined the International Institute for Applied Systems Analysis (IIASA) in Laxenburg, Austria.[1] When Boris Yeltsin became the President of Russia, he asked the young economist 'to assist in the transition to a market economy, specifically assigning him to make the rouble convertible and find a solution to Russia's foreign debt'.[2] In 1991 Aven was appointed Minister for Foreign Economic Relations in the new Yeltsin government. There, one of Aven's initiatives was to hire Kroll Inc., an American corporate investigations firm, to hunt down the Communist Party's hidden treasures: gold, precious stones, hard currency deposits and works of art. 'They didn't find anything,' he later said in an interview.

After leaving the government in December 1992, he became an economic adviser to Berezovsky, remaining his associate for many years, although he soon left Berezovky's LogoVAZ to start a career in politics and big business. 'In the early 90s,' *Forbes* later quoted him, 'it was crucial to be able to be friends, to build relationships. The role of informal relationships is very important in Russia in general, it definitely means much more here than in the West.' When Berezovsky had to leave the country, becoming the leader of an anti-Putin opposition abroad, they stopped communicating because Boris accused Aven of collaborating with 'the bloody regime'.[3] This was probably correct because four days after the Russian invasion of Ukraine, on 28 February 2022, the UK sanctioned Aven and the *Financial Times* reported that the European Union blacklisted him and had all his asserts frozen together with those 'of Russia's leading oligarchs and allies of Putin', also imposing travel bans. Nevertheless, the book seems like a genuine attempt to understand Boris's motives, ambitions, and his role in Russian politics. And his complex relations with people who had been close to him all those years.

Strange as it may seem, perhaps the most unusual and controversial figure among them all is Valentin Yumashev. During Yeltsin's tenure as president (1991–99), Yumashev served as a Kremlin adviser and the chief of the presidential administration (PA) and was one of the key figures who brought Putin to power in 1999. A man without a university degree, Yumashev made an astonishing career from a caretaker in the Soviet writers' dacha colony of Peredelkino to the editor-in-chief of a popular political magazine *Ogoniok* to a member of Yeltsin's family – first as a leader of the tight group of Yeltsin's personal advisers and one of the president's speechwriters, and then as a husband of one of Yeltsin's daughters – a kingmaker who only stepped down as Putin's 'unpaid adviser' in April 2022. In an interview with Aven, Yumashev mentioned that he had personally hired some top Putin aides, 'like Serge Prikhodko and Liosha Gromov', to work at the presidential administration.[4] At the time of the interview (October 2014), they were still in the Kremlin.

Many people, including the historian Yuri Felshtinsky and his co-author Vladimir Popov, a former lieutenant colonel of the Fifth Directorate of the Soviet KGB, believe Yumashev had been a KGB agent or a co-optee since his young years. They are not alone and there are plenty of arguments in favour of this version except that Yumashev strongly denies it while any documentary proof is missing. Even if he signed a collaboration agreement with the security service in the 1970s, that was definitely over after the collapse of the Soviet Union some twenty years later.

It was Aven who introduced Yumashev, then deputy editor, to Berezovsky in 1994. After a while, Yumashev realised that Boris was a very gifted person with outstanding levels of aptitude, incredible charm, and an unconventional mind. When, in March 1997, Yeltsin appointed Yumashev head of his presidential administration, he invited Berezovsky to be his informal or unofficial adviser. 'Boris visited me at the Kremlin quite often,' Yumashev said, 'but contrary to conventional wisdom, Berezovsky and President Yeltsin had a face-to-face meeting only twice. Besides those two meetings, they never met either in the Kremlin or at home. A belief that Berezovsky could barge into the president's office whenever he wanted is just a myth.'[5]

No one ever argued that Berezovsky played the first fiddle in the Russian presidential election of 1996. In January, a group of Russian oligarchs headed by Berezovsky attended the World Economic Forum (WEF) in Davos. There, in the Swiss Alps, Berezovsky proposed a scheme that saved Boris Yeltsin – and Russia – from certain defeat in the upcoming election. Other leading oligarchs supported him. Masha Levinson, the WEF director at the time, recalled:

> The members of the Russian delegation, and particularly the business leaders, became deeply concerned about the popularity of [Gennady] Zyuganov and the likelihood of a victory of the Communist party. Many were infuriated that Zyuganov was saying one thing in Russia and another thing in Davos, appearing in the guise of a modern moderate rather than a hard-line Communist. They decided to take action and to throw their financial weight behind Yeltsin's campaign. The unwritten collective pledge became known as the Davos Pact.

Goldfarb argues that Boris's first meeting with the president took place shortly after Davos, in late February 1996 when Yeltsin met with the Davos group in the Kremlin. Those present were Boris Berezovsky, Vladimir Gusinsky, Mikhail Khodorkovsky, Vladimir Potanin, and Mikhail Friedman. They explained to the ailing president that he was being deceived, his popularity rating was less than 10 per cent, and his most trusted bodyguard, head of the Presidential Security Service General Alexander Korzhakov was going behind his back, secretly trying to push forward his own candidate to be appointed the prime minister, which would make him the official successor. 'What's going on around you is a disaster,' Yeltsin was told. 'People see it, so many in the business community are trying to cut a deal with the Communists and the rest are packing their bags to flee abroad. And our motivation is pure: if you lose, the Communists will hang us from the lampposts.'[6] They proposed to create an analytical group, change the campaign staff placing

Anatoly Chubais in charge, and start an effective Western-style election campaign based on new strategies with the full backing of the media, all these activities funded by the oligarchs. According to Goldfarb, after the meeting Berezovsky stayed behind for fifteen minutes to discuss the details because he worried that the president was not completely sold on the plan.

* * *

While the Russian delegation was still in Davos (the WEF meeting that began on 20 January went on until 6 February), one of Litvinenko's agents reported that transcripts of conversations in the prime minister's office were circulating in Moscow. That could only mean that the office was bugged. A secret investigation revealed that bugging devices were almost certainly placed by Korzhakov's people as part of an operation to dismiss the current prime minister and install Korzhakov's protégé.

Naturally, Sasha's Operations Directorate could not compete with the almighty Presidential Security Service (SBP), a direct successor of the so-called *lichniki* – personal close protection unit of the Ninth Chief Directorate of the KGB. The SBP was headed by Korzhakov, who personally created it in 1991. Formally it was subordinate to the GUO, Chief Directorate for Protection,[7] but in reality SPB had always been a top-secret elite service above all other secret services of Russia. As expected, as soon as Litvinenko submitted a report to his boss General Volokh, Korzhakov came, seized all investigation materials, and said he would inquire into the case himself. Nobody could do anything because the recently appointed FSB director Mikhail Barsukov previously headed the GUO and was Korzhakov's pal.

Noticeably, at that period, three young officers joined the protection service which, after the KGB was disbanded, changed its name several times. The first was Vladimir Valuyev followed by Vyacheslav Sokolenko, and the last Andrey Lugovoy, who had previously served in the Kremlin Regiment. All of them served in the GUO and not, as erroneously stated in many sources, in the FSO or SBP.[8] In fact, the trio left the service before the FSO was established to start some private security business. They will become direct participants (and should be considered prime suspects) in the Litvinenko operation in London.

Shortly after the affair, Litvinenko was summoned to the Lubyanka's executive floor where he was informed that his new important assignment would be to report on Berezovsky. In mid-February, Berezovsky himself called him and proposed that they meet.

'Here's what you need to know,' Berezovsky said as soon as a neatly dressed male secretary invited Litvinenko to his office at The Club and closed the door. 'Until quite recently I was on very good terms with your bosses, Korzhakov and Barsukov. But now we've split. And I want to warn you that you may have problems if you remain connected to me.'[9] Everybody knew that Litvinenko was in the FSB team who had investigated an assassination attempt on Berezovsky in June 1994. They met, Sasha formally interviewed Boris and told him who he thought could have solicited the businessman's murder and why, after which they exchanged telephone numbers and agreed to stay in touch. Although the investigation had stalled, they saw each other a few times on different occasions during the next few months.

When, in March 1996, an important television personality, a popular journalist and TV anchor who had recently become a new director general of the ORT Public Russian Television (now Channel One), was gunned down at the door of his Moscow home, Berezovsky called Litvinenko again. This time, he urgently needed Sasha's help because a squad of Moscow police officers were at The Club, ready to arrest Boris on murder charges. Sasha promptly arrived and after fierce negotiations and a flow of telephone calls, Boris was saved. As expected, the killers were never found but after that day, Goldfarb writes, 'Boris and Sasha developed a bond shared only by people who have faced mortal danger together – not friendship or attachment, but a special kind of loyalty that no other can surpass.'[10]

At the end of April, only two months before the Russian presidential election, Dzhokhar Dudayev, the Chechen separatist leader who was the first president of the Chechen Republic of Ichkeria, was assassinated by a Russian missile strike (some say there were two explosions) while using his US-made satellite phone. Litvinenko later claimed that the technology needed to intercept a satellite phone call was provided to the Russians by an agent within the FBI.

The Russian government never released details of this operation. Dudayev was succeeded by an interim president, his former vice president Zelimkhan Yandarbiyev, who was assassinated in the Qatar capital Doha by three Russian GRU (military intelligence) agents in February 2004. One of them claimed diplomatic immunity and was released and two others were returned to Moscow in December in what appeared to be a goodwill gesture by the Qatar authorities. After the 1997 popular elections, Dudayev's former chief of staff Aslan Maskhadov was elected president. According to the official version, he was killed in an operation conducted by the FSB special forces in March 2005 and buried in an unmarked grave. Akhmed Zakayev, one of his closest allies, who acted as his spokesman and foreign minister, was elected prime minister of the Chechen Republic of Ichkeria in exile in November 2007.

Since January 2002, Akhmed and his family had been residing in the UK where they became close neighbours to the Litvinenkos in Muswell Hill in the North London Borough of Haringey. Zakayev is a very nice, intelligent, and cultured man, a former leading actor of the Grozny Drama Theatre. Marina Litvinenko says that in London Akhmed and Sasha became best friends. But Alex Goldfarb asserts they knew about each other long before, in fact since the First Chechen War. 'We were aware of an intelligence officer who often came from Moscow operating against us from the FSB office in Nalchik,' Zakayev once told him. Nalchik was the capital of Kabardino-Balkaria in the foothills of the Caucasus Mountain range between Europe and Asia, Litvinenko's hometown. 'We ran an agent of our own at Nalchik FSB,' Zakayev explained. 'He reported that the officer's name was Alexander Volkov, and that he was a local. It was no trouble for us to establish that his real name was Litvinenko, since many people knew his father's family.'[11] On his part, Litvinenko knew about Zakayev, who in February 1996 was appointed commander of the entire Western Group of Chechen forces and in early August led his men in the decisive raid on Grozny, which became known in the West as Operation Zero Option, when Chechen fighters regained and kept control of the capital. Zakayev's war record later paved his way to high politics.

In July 1996, Boris Yeltsin was re-elected by a wide margin and three months later, on 29 October, Berezovsky was appointed Deputy Secretary of the Security Council. For the first time in his life, Boris became a civil servant and this was a rather important government post serving under Ivan Rybkin, whom Yeltsin made his National Security Adviser, and Mikhail Mityukhov, professor at the leading Moscow Law School, who was appointed First Deputy Secretary. In his memoirs, Yeltsin recalled that it was the idea of Chubais, then the Kremlin Chief of Staff (head of the Presidential Executive Office), who told the president how important it was to invite intelligent people, even if they were difficult and out of the ordinary, to work in the government.

A year later, on Tuesday, November 4, Boris Nemtsov, first deputy prime minister, accompanied by Chubais, by now also first deputy prime minister, visited Yeltin at his official residence, known as Gorki-9, insisting that Berezovsky should be removed from the post. They explained that he was one of the central players in the conflict between the government and Russia's big private business and if he were removed from the Security Council, he would immediately lose his clout. 'No one will be interested in his opinion,' they said, 'and the conflict will end.'[12] Had Boris become less intelligent or more ordinary during that year?

Yeltsin summoned Yumashev, who until March 1997 had worked in the administration as political adviser on mass media relations and later, succeeding Chubais, as the Kremlin Chief of Staff, asking for his advice. Yumashev, who had ghostwritten Yeltsin's memoirs, writes that he personally was against dismissing Boris, but the president easily succumbed to persuasion because he did not like Berezovsky. In his book, Yeltsin explains:

> Why did I fire Berezovsky in November? My motivations are probably more difficult to explain than it might seem at first glance. I never liked Boris Berezovsky, and I still don't like him. I don't like him because of his arrogant tone, his scandalous reputation, and because people believe that he has special influence on the Kremlin. He doesn't. I never liked him, but I always tried to keep him on my team. A paradox? Perhaps. But those who are professionally engaged in politics or governance will understand.

Remarkably, in spite of all that, Berezovsky managed to become a leading member of what would later be known as the Family, President Yeltsin's small inner circle that included his daughter Tatiana, her associate and later husband Valentina Yumashev, his successor as the Kremlin Chief of Staff Alexander Voloshin, Boris

Berezovsky, and the Family's financier Roman Abramovich. This was a Russian version of what is known in America as 'Kitchen Cabinet' (referring to the group of unofficial advisers to US president Andrew Jackson, in office 1829–37). Now, the question is: who brought in Putin?

There's a striking discrepancy in versions typical to Putin's biography, which is part of the Seven Seals of the Kremlin. As the Freedom House 2022 report on Russia stressed, 'There is little transparency and accountability in the day-to-day workings of the government. Decisions are adopted behind closed doors by a small group of individuals whose identities are often unclear to the public, and are announced to the population after the fact.'

In his answers to the authors of the first ever book about himself, Putin explained that it was Pavel Borodin, head of the Administrative Directorate of the President (UDP) who made him an offer to move to Moscow and become a member of Kremlin staff. After his boss, the mayor of St Petersburg Anatoly Sobchak, lost his re-election bid to his deputy in early June 1996, Putin said, he had been without a job for a few months. Why Borodin, whom he barely knew, made him such an offer, he didn't know. According to Putin, after Borodin recommended him, Nikolai Yegorov, the Kremlin Chief of Staff before Chubais, invited him to Moscow, offering the position of deputy chief, which Putin accepted. All necessary papers were ready for President Yeltsin to sign but then Yegorov was suddenly dismissed from his post and Chubais simply eliminated the deputy chief position, so nothing happened.

Some time passed, and one Alexey Bolshakov, a fellow Petersburger, now serving in Moscow as first deputy prime minister, met Borodin at a reception and reproached him for not keeping his word.[13] Then goes a very long and rather unbelievable story until, Putin said, in August 1996 he ended up in the government building on Moscow's Staraya Square as Pavel Borodin's deputy in charge of the legal division. And because Borodin also headed what is now Chief Directorate for Federal Property, Putin was also made responsible for the Russian Property Abroad Department, where he remained until March 1997.

At the same time, another Sobchak deputy, Alexey Kudrin, who had worked in St Petersburg between 1990 and 1996, was appointed deputy Kremlin Chief of Staff under Chubais in August 1996. It was not a random choice. Back in Leningrad (later St Petersburg), Chubais headed the Committee for Economic Reform of the Executive Committee of the City Council, where Kudrin was his deputy. In 1991, Kudrin became deputy chairman of the Mayor's Office Committee in charge of the special economic zone (SEZ). There he was introduced to Putin, who headed External Relations and, as a poet said, they met by chance and became friends by choice. By the end of the year the KGB was dissolved, which for Putin was another catastrophe after the loss of the Soviet Empire. Until the end he would strive to restore both of them but in his own particular way.

According to Borodin, he and Putin got acquainted when Putin helped to arrange some medical treatment for Borodin's daughter, who studied in St Petersburg, in 1995. In June 1996, when Sobchak lost the elections, he invited Putin to Moscow, but Chubais was categorically against it. Unable to place his protégé in the Kremlin staff over the head of its chief, Borodin hired Putin as his own deputy at the UDP where, he claimed, Putin remained for nine months until March 1997. Then Chubais moved to the government as first deputy PM and no one could stop Putin from taking office at the PA.[14] In mid-March, Putin was transferred to the Presidential Administration, now headed by Yumashev, and put in charge of its Control Directorate, a place that served Borodin's plans well.

* * *

At that time, only a handful of people in Moscow knew the name of Beghjet Pacolli, an ethnic Albanian from Kosovo. Pacolli had worked in Austria and Switzerland and in the early 1990s met Borodin, then the mayor of Yakutsk in east Siberia, which ranks as the coldest city in the world. Pacolli, Borodin said, first acted as an interpreter, working for a Swiss firm, Interplastica, but then founded his own company that he called Mabetex, which was ever since involved in many construction projects in the Republic of Sakha of which Yakutsk is the capital city. When Borodin was transferred to Moscow in November 1993, Pacolli followed in his footsteps. There is no doubt that besides Borodin, who subsequently became Pacolli's business associate on the eastern side of the crumbling iron curtain, both Putin and the Family should have known the Albanian (or at least about his existence) rather well because a wide stream of extremely lucrative contracts soon started to flow from Moscow in the direction of Lugano, a beautiful small city in the Swiss canton of Ticino, where Mabetex was registered.

Interviewed by Aven, Yumashev recalled that it was Chubais whom he asked to help find the right staff for the PA and Chubais personally recommended Putin. This seems to be true because both Chubais and Yumashev remained Kremlin high-flyers close to Putin until spring 2022 when both resigned following the Russian attack on Ukraine. At the end of March, Bloomberg reported that Chubais had left Russia.

Very soon, the former KGB lieutenant colonel impressed the new Kremlin Chief of Staff as a very good worker. In May 1998, Yumashev appointed Putin his first deputy, that is, first deputy chief of the presidential administration.

Quite by chance, Putin's appointment coincided with what would become internationally known as Kremlingate or the Mabetex affair. Earlier that year, one Philipp (later Felipe) Turover visited the Office of the Attorney General of Switzerland, then headed by Carla del Ponte, and presented evidence of the corruption at the heart of the Kremlin. Turover accused Pavel Borodin of laundering Russian budget funds and of massive kickbacks paid by Mercata, the sister company of Mabetex. The main protagonist of the scandal and at the same time the key player in the affair was Pavel Borodin and a few people close to him like Viktor Stolpovskih, the founder and owner of a small construction firm in Yakutsk, then headed by Borodin as the mayor. In 1995, Stolpovskih, together with Andrey Siletsky, Borodin's son-in-law, bought the dormant Swiss company

Mercata Trading & Engineering SA. Transfers of large sums of money began when Stolpovskih acquired an offshore company, Lightstar Low Voltage Systems Ltd., registered at the Isle of Man. At the end of May 1996, Mercata and Lightstar concluded a brokerage agreement wherein Lightstar acted as a sales agent and Mercata as a principal.[15] The details of the case are rather well known.

In August 1996, Borodin's office awarded two contracts worth $492 million for refurbishing the Kremlin Palace and Moscow's Chamber of Audits to Mercata. The work was done by Mabetex, while Marcata paid a $62,5 million 'commission' to Lightstar as a broker at their Midland Bank account on the Isle of Man. Whatever was left for Lightstar owners, the rest was distributed to the fourteen suspects named by the Swiss investigation including Borodin, his daughter and her husband, who between them received over $25,6 million in four payments to accounts in Geneva, Nassau and Guernsey in 1997–98. According to the media reports, Yeltsin's wife and his two daughters, Yelena Okulova and Tatyana Dyachenko, were also implicated in the case because their massive credit card expenses were covered from the same money. In his interviews with Aven, Yumashev never mentioned the Mabetex scandal.

Interlude: Felipe Turover, con artist from Boadilla

Philipp was born in Russia in 1964 to the family of a well-known and well-respected Moscow linguist, Genrikh (Enrique in Spanish) Yakovlevich Turover, who headed the department of Romance languages at what is now the Moscow State Linguistic University. Turover senior is the author of the best Russian-Spanish dictionary, who was often asked to serve as interpreter for top-level government delegations.

In 1982, Philipp finished what was known in the UK as a night school for the working classes (in Russia, it used to be called an evening school for young workers), and worked as an accountant at the Moscow society for the protection of nature. At the age of 19, he married Dolores, the daughter of a Spanish woman named Rosa Seijó from the generation of los niños de la guerra civil española (children of the Spanish Civil War) who had been evacuated to the Soviet Union during the war in Spain. Philipp and Dolores were allowed to emigrate to Spain, where their son was born.

After a while, Philipp, now a Spanish citizen known as Felipe, divorced her, but Dolores continued to live in Boadilla in the vicinity of Madrid together with her father-in-law and his wife Natasha. Felipe continued his studies in Spain and France and also travelled to Mexico, coming back to Spain before the dissolution of the Soviet Union. His trip to Mexico, which would otherwise cause questions, was fully justified because his father was teaching Russian to the Mexican ambassador in Moscow and his sister-in-law got married to an embassy official. As he was a Sephardic Jew by origin, Felipe also obtained an Israeli passport and a Swiss residence permit while preserving his Soviet document in the name of 'Philipp

Turover-Chudinov'. This allowed him to travel to Russia without any visa and he returned to Moscow in 1988, well equipped to do perestroika business.

It was perfect time for people like Turover. In August 1990, a secret memorandum from Gorbachev's newly elected Deputy General Secretary issued instructions to hide Communist Party assets using joint ventures between Russian and Western firms. The party and the KGB were to transfer CPSU funds to the West through all available channels.[16] In November 1990, an offshore company named Fimaco was registered in Jersey on the instruction of Viktor Gerashchenko, the last chairman of the State Bank of the USSR. Russian officials claimed that Fimaco was 100 per cent owned by the Russian Banque Commerciale pour l'Europe du Nord (BCEN) – Eurobank in Paris. Billions of dollars were reportedly transferred to the West using its bank accounts.[17] Yuri Skuratov, Prosecutor General of Russia since October 1995, opened a criminal investigation, asking Gennady Seleznyov, the Communist chairman of the State Duma, to provide explanations. Seleznyov assigned his personal assistant, Yevgeny Limarev, to investigate the matter and report. His answer is not on file but years later, during the Litvinenko Inquiry hearings, Limarev testified: 'I was supporting Mr. Seleznyov. I was working on some projects that would – that could help him financially abroad, first of all [in] Switzerland.'[18]

According to media reports of the time, Turover's financial dealings were of a much lower class. In Moscow, he established good friendly relations with Igor Voronov from the General Prosecutor's Office and through him with Skuratov. An article in *El Pais* provides a lot of examples of Turover's 'business deals', and Russian sources add a story when Dmitry Rumyantsev, head of Human Resources Department at the PA in June 1993, became one of Turover's victims by entrusting him a five-digit sum of his hard-earned US dollars to deposit on a numbered account in the Banca del Gottardo that Turover had promised to open.[19] As in several previous cases, something didn't work as planned – the money disappeared and Turover had to urgently flee to Switzerland.

Seeking to solve his problems by obtaining a protected witness status, he travelled to Bern and knocked at the office of Carla del Ponte, promising to provide testimonial evidence and disclose all that he had learned about secret financial deals of the Kremlin officials. Soon the scandal received worldwide attention and almost overshadowed the accomplishments and democratic achievements of Boris Yeltsin and his administration.

The last time the Russian and Spanish media mentioned Turover was in 2022 in a long article published by *El País*, the leading Spanish newspaper. It tells the story of how one day in January 2021, a new guest showed up at the door of an elderly couple's home in Villaviciosa de Odón, outside the Spanish capital. Like so many others before him, Felipe Turover had booked a room through the online platform Airbnb. 'Turover, 56, had a shaved head, an athletic body and spoke perfect Spanish except for his "r" sounds, which suggested a Russian background,' the article stated. He came across 'as friendly, educated and composed – an ideal guest who was going to stay for just 10 days'. It turned out the man decided to stay as long as possible without paying any rent.

The landlords finally learned some details about their now unwanted guest from Catherine Belton's book *Putin's People* (2020). Belton spoke with him for three days in Boadilla del Monte, 'a sleepy market town in the hills near Madrid'. 'He was from the elite of the Soviet foreign intelligence service,' she writes. 'It was May 2013, more than twenty years since the scheme was set up, and Felipe Turover, a former senior officer for the foreign intelligence directorate of the KGB, was telling for the first time the story of how he helped Putin set up the St Petersburg oil-for-food scheme.'[20] But the Spanish newspaper's article tells another story, more important for this chapter, of how Turover ended up in Bern.

> Primakov tasked Turover with handing over sensitive information about Yeltsin and other Russian politicians to Swiss prosecutors. In the summer of 1999, the Italian daily *Corriere della Sera* revealed that part of that information involved Yeltsin and his daughters, and the scandal grew. Turover realized that his own life was in danger. He said that Putin met with him at a Moscow hotel one night in mid-September and coldly informed him over a cup of tea: 'You have two weeks to leave the country. If you don't go, we either lock you away or we liquidate you.' A week later, Turover showed up in Switzerland.

The *Corriere della Sera* article mentioned here was written by two Italian investigative journalists, Carlo Bonini and Giuseppe D'Avanzo, who would also figure prominently in the Litvinenko case, especially in relation to his work in Italy.

Unlike Catherine Belton, the *El País* correspondent knew that as early as the 1990s, international media articles were already labelling Turover as a charlatan. 'It is possible,' the article stressed, 'that part of his tale, such as the alleged meeting with Putin, is an exaggeration or even a complete fabrication.'[21] This is obviously correct because Turover spoke to the Swiss attorney general more than a year before the *Corriere della Sera* article described the Kremlingate affair.

Three months later, in March 2022, the newspaper noted that Turover was still living in the same room without paying a cent.

***

In his book, Goldfarb describes how one day in the middle of June 1998, that is, four weeks after Putin became first deputy chief of the presidential administration, Yumashev invited Berezovsky to the Kremlin, asking his opinion about his new deputy.

'Why?' Boris inquired.

'Because we are considering him for the FSB directorship,' Valentin said.

'I support him 100 percent,' Goldfarb quoted Boris who, in his words, endorsed Putin's candidacy.[22]

Yumashev disagreed with this version of events. Recalling the situation during his interview with Aven, he said that it was the young Russian prime minister

Sergey Kiriyenko who advised Yeltsin to appoint Putin as the new FSB director. Yumashev didn't explain why but said that Yeltsin immediately agreed with this proposal. In his memoirs, Yeltsin never mentioned the episode and never explained why he appointed Putin. It is, however, very doubtful that Kiriyenko's opinion could have any weight in this matter.

Born as Sergey Israitel to the family of a Jewish father and Ukrainian mother, he was educated in Gorky (later Nizhny Novgorod) at the shipbuilding faculty of the Water Transport Institute where his father was teaching, and adopted his mother's name. Kiriyenko's Jewish grandfather is said to have been a devoted Communist and member of the Cheka, but it was a liability rather than an asset in the early 1990s. Kiriyenko continued working in Gorky under Boris Nemtsov, the governor of the region from November 1991 to March 1997, when he agreed to join the federal government. In November 1997, Kiriyenko succeeded Nemtsov as Minister of Fuel and Energy before Yeltsin suddenly appointed him prime minister of Russia in March 1998. Kiriyenko remained in this post for less than half a year and resigned in August in the middle of the financial crisis because Russia was not able to pay its debts.

Rather, Yamashev seemed to prevaricate when Aven asked him about Putin's appointment to the FSB and Goldfarb was probably right that Yumashev consulted with Berezovsky shortly after Putin became the security chief. Yeltsin probably didn't mind and did not care too much because he fully trusted Yumashev and his own daughter Tatyana, whose influence on his decision making was hard to overestimate. As the newspapers wrote about another similar case (when the President sacked his entire government in March 1998), 'the decision had been carefully planned with the involvement of Tatyana Dyachenko, the President's daughter and confidante, Valentin Yumashev, head of the Kremlin administration and ghost writer of Mr Yeltsin's two books, and Boris Berezovsky, a business tycoon and veteran Kremlin intriguer.' At the time, all three were quite interested in stopping the activities of Swiss prosecutors. Concerning Russia, they were sure they had everything in hand, but suddenly things didn't quite go as planned.

With Putin in place as a new FSB director, Viktor Ilyukhin, the Chair of the Security Committee of the State Duma (Parliament) with statutory responsibility for oversight of the Russian secret services, claimed that he had received evidence that part of the $4.8 billion bailout loan granted to Russia by the International Monetary Fund (IMF) had been stolen, which was one of the key factors leading to the financial crisis of August 1998. Ilyukhin stated that payments were made to bank accounts linked to the Family and that some $235 million were transferred to a company in which Leonid Dyachenko, Tatyana's husband, was a principal shareholder.[23]

In the meantime, the Mabetex scandal was mushrooming. At the end of January 1999, Swiss prosecutors searched Mabetex offices in Lugano. It is not illegal for Swiss companies to pay 'commissions' to foreign officials, but in that case Swiss authorities were assisting their Russian colleagues to investigate alleged bribery of the Kremlin staff. On 18 March, Skuratov sent a team of prosecutors to Borodin's office, who began confiscating documents. On 23 March, when Carla del Ponte was due to arrive in Moscow, they continued seizing documents and also searching the Moscow offices of Mabetex. While Jacque Ducry, the Tessin prosecutor from Lugano whose people raided Mabetex headquarters, was part of the Carla del Ponte delegation visiting Moscow, Swiss magistrates from the canton of Vaud started investigating two companies in Lausanne, both belonging to Berezovsky, that had been used for the hard currency transactions on behalf of Aeroflot.

Back in March 1996, Berezovsky had invited Litvinenko to accompany him on a business trip to Switzerland. It was Sasha's first travel out of the country and he was very excited because besides the luxury of going abroad, which most former Soviet citizens could only dream about, Berezovsky arranged for him a diplomatic passport, a cover document, as Sasha proudly explained later. It was issued in the name of 'Alexander Volkov', allegedly the Second Secretary of the Russian embassy in Bern. Boarding Berezovsky's private jet at a Moscow airport, Litvinenko met Lena Gorbunova, the gorgeous girlfriend of Boris, Arkady 'Badri' Patarkatsishvili, Berezovsky's Georgian friend and business partner, Olga Safonova, whom Badri would secretly marry, their young son David, and Olga's son Roman. On the way to Switzerland, they made a short stop in Salzburg, where Badri and his family disembarked, and upon landing in Zurich rented a Mercedes, travelling by car to Lausanne via Bern.

Before leaving Moscow, Badri called Konstantin Bushlanov, head of the Aeroflot office in Vienna, and asked him to arrange a meeting at Salzburg Airport, named after Mozart, and a nice hotel somewhere close to the city. At the time, my wife and I lived in Vienna publishing a luxury magazine called *Business Lunch* for high-net-worth travellers from the former Soviet Union. Its print editions were also distributed on board Aeroflot international first- and business-class flights, so Konstantin called our office and we booked a beautiful hotel at the Gaisberg, a mountain to the east of Salzburg. Hotel Schloss Mönchstein was an oasis of tranquillity and relaxation, with very personal service and a breath-taking view over Salzburg and the area. We soon became quite friendly and visited Olga and her children often, especially because from time to time Badri had to fly to Lausanne to discuss business with Boris.[24] It later turned out that Boris, Badri and their financial wizard Nikolai Glushkov were redirecting the whole hard currency cashflow of Aeroflot to be accumulated in one Swiss bank account which could further be used for bank guarantees, leasing, spare parts purchase, service, and so on. This complex business model would subsequently develop into the notorious 'Aeroflot case' investigated by both Russian and Swiss prosecutors that would haunt Berezovsky for many years to come.

In March 1999, Director of the FSB Putin became Secretary of the Security Council succeeding Nikolai Bordyuzha, who had also served as the Kremlin Chief of Staff since previous December when the President fired Yumashev. Bordyuzha, a KGB general who was viewed by some analysts as a possible successor to President Yeltsin, was sent to Copenhagen having been appointed the Russian ambassador to Denmark.

On Friday, 6 August 1999, at a meeting attended by Yumashev, Tatyana, Chubais and Voloshin, it was decided that Putin must be urgently made the new prime minister of Russia.[25] On Monday, 9 August, Putin's appointment as acting prime minister was made public. Aven asked Yumashev whether Berezovsky or Abramovich were also present at that Friday meeting. No, Yumashev said, the fact that Berezovsky took part in this decision making was just another myth among many deliberately spread by Berezovsky to show his role as a kingmaker. Nevertheless, he added, about four or five days earlier, Boris rushed to Putin, who was away on holiday in Biarritz, and told him: Volodya, it is all settled, you shall be the next president.[26] Habitually addressing Putin by a short form of his first name, Berezovsky was unaware that the meaning of the name Volodya is 'universal ruler'.

On that Monday morning, Putin was initially appointed first deputy prime minister and, several hours later, prime minister which, according to the Russian constitution, is the first candidate to succeed an incumbent president in case of sudden illness, death, or resignation. It is possible and even certain that in his interview with Aven many years later Yumashev, himself a master of an underhand intrigue, was not telling the whole truth because on the same day President Yeltsin in his televised message to the nation named Putin as his successor. For the Family no other option existed because they were quite convinced that Putin was the only person who, when elected, could protect them. At the end of the day, they were right. Berezovsky and his people, including Litvinenko, were another story.

The incumbent prime minister Sergey Stepashin, a KGB general who had previously headed the Federal Counterintelligence Service (FSK) and was the first FSB director, resigned on the same day. Like General Bordyuzha before him, Stepashin was considered by the Family as a possible successor to the president. In his book *Operation Successor* (with Vladimir Pribylovsky, 2004) historian Yuri Felshtinsky stresses that it was not by chance that all four presidential candidates in 1999 – Bordyuzha, Stepashin, Putin, and Yevgeny Primakov – were top KGB figures. Primakov was effectively blocked by Berezovsky because, as he honestly told Yeltsin, if such staunch Communists came to power, many, including the Family, would soon be hanging from lampposts. There were personal reasons too because, in the words of Alex Goldfarb, 'for Primakov, no one personified capitalist evil more than Boris Berezovsky'.

The acting president Vladimir Putin fired Borodin in January 2000, transferring him to an unimportant Kremlin post of state secretary of the Russia-Belarus Union. Though an obvious demotion, the new post came with perks like a formal rank equal to that of a prime minister plus status allowing to travel abroad with a diplomatic passport. A year later, in January 2001, Borodin was arrested in New York's JFK International Airport on a Swiss arrest warrant while on his way to the inauguration of the US president George W. Bush. He remained in a Brooklyn jail until April, when he was extradited to Switzerland. After the Russian government agreed to pay 5 million Swiss francs (CHF) in bail, Borodin was released, having promised to return to Geneva for questioning. In March 2002, Bernard Bertossa, Geneva Prosecutor General, found Borodin guilty of laundering CHF 38 million

(US$22.4 million) and ordered to pay a fine of CHF 300,000 (US$175,000).[27] The charges against Borodin stemmed from the Mabetex case.

***

It was probably a coincidence that as soon as Litvinenko started to collaborate with the Mitrokhin Commission of the Italian parliament and the Italian magistrates, prosecutors in the Italian town of Trento issued arrest warrants against the former head of the Russian state agency for import and export of defence-related and dual use products, technologies and services (RosVooruzhenie, later RosOboronExport), his mistress, and their financial consultant. Former KGB General Yevgeny Ananyev, his mistress Olga Beltsova, and financial consultant Giulio Rizzo were accused of money laundering millions of dollars through several Italian banks, the chief of the Financial Police in Trento stated in an interview. Litvinenko was not involved in this case, which was only one part of a larger investigation carried out by Swiss, Peruvian, and Italian authorities since 2000. The operation was codenamed MATRIOSHKA.

In 1998, Ananyev oversaw the sale of three MIG29 fighter jets to Peru via Belarus. His Peruvian partner was Vladimiro Montesinos Torres, then chief of the National Intelligence Service of his country and presidential adviser. From the deal, worth $117 million, they decided to divert slightly more than 10 per cent, that is $18.4 million, of which Montesinos collected his 'commission' of $10.9 million and Ananyev pocketed the rest, $7.5 million. While the assets of Montesino were frozen in Switzerland, Ananyev transferred $5 million to his bank account in Lugano, from which he started sending smaller sums to the account of his mistress at the local branch of the Austrian Raiffeisen Bank, Cassa Raiffeisen Nova Levante in Vigo Di Fassa.

The arrest warrants were issued in June 2004. Ananyev managed to escape to Russia, Beltsova was detained and placed under house arrest and Rizzo escorted to jail. As the *Moscow Times* reported, a Peruvian court convicted Montesinos Torres of corruption and drug trafficking and sentenced him to nine years in prison. But that was not the end of the story.

In November 2005, the Trentino prosecutor Stefano Dragone signed European arrest warrants (EAW) for a group of Russian citizens suspected of kickbacks and money laundering. This time, they were accused of laundering $62.52 million in kickbacks from Mercata for contracts to refurbish the Kremlin awarded almost a decade earlier. 'Two weeks after awarding Mercata its contracts,' the *Wall Street Journal* wrote after the case had been successfully closed and forgotten in Moscow, 'Mr. Borodin had his rendezvous with Swiss bankers on the Boulevard des Philosophes.' He was accompanied by his daughter Yekaterina Siletskaya and her then husband and Borodin's son-in-law Andrey Siletsky who, according to the company filing in Lugano, was Mercata's vice president. Together they signed forms to open bank accounts in the name of two offshore companies, Somos Investment in Cyprus and Amadeus & Carmina Foundations in Panama. Borodin, according to documents submitted to the bank, was the beneficial owner of both entities.[28]

The Murder of Alexander Litvinenko: To Kill a Mockingbird

Millions of dollars paid by Moscow to Mercata were partly redirected to various offshore accounts, including those of Borodin and his relatives, through Lightstar, controlled by Stolpovskih, while instructions on the distribution of the fees in Midland Bank were provided by a Geneva attorney, Gregory John Connor, Lightstar's second director. Most of those offshore companies, their accounts, and banks were named in the investigation paper published by the European Institute for Crime Prevention and Control in Helsinki in 2004. Amazingly, both Ananyev and Beltsova were also involved and their names were again included in the EAW alongside those of the daughter and former so-in-law of Pavel Borodin, as well as of Borodin himself; Margarita and Andrey Nerodenkov, daughter and son-in-law of the former chairman of the Russian State Customs Committee Anatoly Kruglov, himself a multi-millionaire.[29] Other people accused by prosecutor Dragone of money laundering were less well known. Although the full money laundering scheme was not disclosed by the prosecutors, it was suggested that one of the elements was investments in the Italian real estate.

All available documents show that although Litvinenko actively collaborated with the Italian authorities between 2004 and 2006, he was not involved in any of the above investigations. However, the Kremlin might have thought differently.

One of the most amazing dialogues in the already mentioned book by Aven, related to Litvinenko, is with Lena Gorbunova. Elena, aka Helena Gorbunova, whom many, including Goldfarb, call Lena Berezovskaya, the third wife of Boris, was Berezovsky's long-term partner. Together they had two children but after many years she broke up with Boris in 2012 and was then pursuing him in a British court for a share of his assets. Nevertheless, Lena was ever-present at Berezovsky's side as he was fighting 'an epic legal battle', as the world media have labelled it, against Roman Abramovich, who turned from a business partner into a bitter enemy.

'I should probably start from the very beginning,' she said, answering Aven's question about what was subsequently called the world's biggest litigation battle. 'And, specifically, why Boris filed this lawsuit in the first place.' According to her version, one day in spring 2006 Litvinenko brought some documents that revealed that a contract had been placed on his life. Not on Sasha's life; Roma (Roman Abramovich) and two other persons were allegedly planning Berezovsky's assassination. The order for murder was placed directly with the FSB, Litvinenko claimed.

It was in 1997, she explained, that Berezovsky was planning to team up with Mikhail Khodorkovsky and his Yukos Oil company which was badly affected by the economic recession. Boris wanted to kick Abramovich off and make Khodorkovsky the president of their joint enterprise.[30] That would be the end of Roma.

'But why?' Aven asked. 'If something like that really happened it was long ago. And you say Litvinenko brought those documents in 2006?'

> Yes, because those documents only surfaced in 2006. In our papers I have found letters from Boris's lawyers asking what they should do with Litvinenko. Boris told Litvinenko not to proceed any further with the case because it might look stupid and would make no sense

anyway. But after Litvinenko's poisoning, sometime in early 2007, Boris thought that perhaps Litvinenko had been murdered because he had found those documents. And maybe Litvinenko's death was a sign shown to him to see that he would be the next victim. So, Boris decided to defend himself and the best way to do it, he thought, would be to show his insidious enemies to everybody. So far as the legal proceedings were going on, he believed he would be safe. But when the case was decided [on 31 August 2012] and he lost, Boris realised that he had also lost his physical protection.

She said Berezovsky managed to prolong his life, but only until March next year. Then, it was all over.

***

The year 2006 started off very well. On 23 January, Berezovsky was the toast of London, holding his black-tie 60th birthday party at Blenheim Palace, the seat of the Dukes of Marlborough, birthplace and home of Sir Winston Churchill. 'A string quartet was playing as 200 guests sipped pink champagne by a magnificent fire,' writes Heidi Blake who was not there but saw a lot of documentary footage working on the TV series *Once Upon a Time in Londongrad* (2022). 'In the centre of the room,' Edward Jay Epstein adds, 'was an ice sculpture representing St. Basil's Cathedral on Red Square, coated with mounds of beluga caviar.' Ed was not there either but went to Russia instead. There, he saw Red Square and the Lubyanka with his own eyes. In Moscow, he also saw a spectre.[31] What came out as a result only the lazy did not criticise.

In the picture of them at Blenheim Palace kindly shared with this writer, four happy men – Litvinenko, Berezovsky, Zakayev and Felshtinsky – are posing for a photograph on that very day in that very palace which served as the wartime headquarters of the British Security Service (MI5).

Those who were not there cannot know that before the great party in Woodstock, there was a small private reception in Berezovsky's office in London's Mayfair. Only very good old friends were present and Petr Aven managed to meet one of them, the Russian-American mathematician Vitaly Greenberg.

'Among other things,' Dr Greenberg told Aven, 'we discussed Berezovsky's new status as a sworn enemy of Russia and how he was literally hunted down by them [the Kremlin]. Sasha Litvinenko was there and with him we talked a lot about this problem. Now, here comes Boris and tells me that he is going to a restaurant to pick up some sashimi for me. And I ask Litvinenko, "Very well, and who is going to oversee it?" That is, well aware of the threat to their lives they lived absolutely carelessly without thinking that one moment someone could poison them.'[32]

A spectre is haunting Europe – the spectre of Communism, Marx and Engels wrote as a manifesto for the revolutionaries who gathered in London in November 1847. Mr Epstein saw the wrong spectre in Moscow. What he missed was a spectre of Putin's assassins, haunting Europe.

'Amazingly, there was another case where an assassin was operating here in the UK. We've never named him,' writes Andy Hayman, former Assistant Commissioner for Specialist Operations of the Metropolitan Police. The period in question was between 2006 and 2007 and he had just completed the investigation of Litvinenko's poisoning, of which he was in charge.

Two years after the Counter Terrorism Command under his leadership sent a file of evidence on the Litvinenko case to the Crown Prosecution Service (CPS), Mr Hayman tried to avoid giving too many details of this second plot. Today, it is no secret any more but in the light of what Lena Gorbunova has said, Litvinenko's worries for the safety and indeed life of his patron seem perfectly justified.

In 2006, MI6 received intelligence that some unidentified individuals in Moscow were plotting to assassinate Boris Berezovsky. The CX report probably landed on the desk of Charles Farr (later Sir). It was then directed further to Special Branch and its investigative wing. Because they knew each other, it is possible that Litvinenko was also briefed with advice to talk to Berezovsky and warn him without disclosing any details. Neither Lena nor Boris's lawyers whom she mentioned ever saw 'the Litvinenko documents' that she referred to in an interview with Aven.

When Andy Hayman was informed about a possible attack, the job of the police was to thwart it. The information was that a potential assassin was not a UK national, possibly specifying that he began his criminal career in the 1970s with burglaries in Moscow, was involved in the violence of the gangsters' wars in the 1980s, and in the 1990s helped Boris Berezovsky build up his business empire. Later the man collaborated with the FSB, then was tasked with detaining and annihilating some key figures in the Chechen militant groups. It was the FSB, it was reported, that now planned to dispatch him to London.

'We devised a scheme, putting our best "assets" on standby to follow the assassin covertly,' Hayman writes. 'The target could potentially have been high profile.' Obviously, the police had to inform their political masters and, as expected, in the corridors of Whitehall it caused uproar.

> They favoured a different solution. They were concerned that if the country from which this individual came discovered one of their citizens was being followed it could damage the UK's relations with that country. A series of meetings was held, there was much to-ing and fro-ing between departments and, to our annoyance and disbelief, the police plan was rejected ... I understood that the foreign secretary Margaret Beckett was not happy. She had supported us in previous cases but now she favoured a different solution to the one we were planning. I believe she had a conversation with the home secretary [John Reid], who decided to call another meeting.

Finally, the case went as high as the prime minister's office at Downing Street. Tony Blair discussed it with his adviser on foreign affairs, Sir Nigel Sheinwald, and the covert operation initially planned by Special Branch (which, after merging with Anti-Terrorist Branch SO13 in October 2006, became Counter Terrorism Command) was back on.

By the end of June, the potential assassin, whom Andy Hayman describes as a professional hitman, became increasingly frustrated because he could not accomplish his mission. Finally, he and a person who accompanied him were detained and taken to Paddington Green police station, where for two days detectives questioned them. Both were then handed to Immigration, who seized their visas and deported them. 'We had amassed new intelligence and I believe we saved the target's life, and in so doing sent a strong message to any would-be assassin that we'd be on to them,' Mr Hayman said.

When British media reported the story (about a month after the events), Charles Farr, who had previously served as MI6's director of security and public affairs, was appointed Director of the Office for Security and Counter-Terrorism, so Andy's boss. At the end of his book's chapter which he called 'On Superpowers and Spies: The Litvinenko Murder and a Second Assassination Attempt', Hayman writes: 'I believe as a result of this incident any would-be assassin will think twice before trying to operate in the UK again. It worries me though that this assassin is still at large.'[33]

In fact, the assassin did not last too long – soon after his return from London, the man was kidnapped in the centre of Moscow, taken to Chechnya, and killed.

Andy Hayman OBE resigned from the service in December 2007.

NB: In November 2002, when the oil tanker *Prestige* sank in front of the northwest coast of Spain and caused one of the largest oil spills in the world of seafaring on European shores, parts of the Alfa Group's network attracted public attention. As already mentioned, the tanker had been chartered by the Swiss-based company Crown Resources, owned by CTF Holding. Through offshore-leaks affair documents, it became known that numerous offshore companies were involved, from the Caribbean to Russia. Suddenly, the East German Ministerium für Staatssicherheit (MfS), better known as the Stasi, came to light, and specifically its Chief Directorate 'A' (Hauptverwaltung Aufklärung, HVA) under Markus 'Misha' Wolf.

It was one of the most effective spy agencies of the Cold War. Putin's KGB career in foreign intelligence began there, in the Stasi's directorate in Dresden, where Markus Wolf kept his secret guesthouse (later purchased by an Austrian agent of the HVA) for important visitors from the Lubyanka and the local KGB staff like Lazar Matveyev, Stanislav Androsov, Sergey Chemezov, Nikolai Tokarev, Vladimir Agartanov and Captain Putin. 'In wicked acts he outdid them all,' to quote a famous historian.

For the first and only time in connection with this Alfa Group scandal, the name of Franz Thomas Alexander Wolf, a German businessman born in Berlin in May 1953, came to light. According to the leaked documents, Mr Wolf had been serving as the plenipotentiary representative of the Crown Finance Foundation in Liechtenstein, which is part of the CTF Holding company in Gibraltar, and as director in numerous other companies of Friedman's Alfa empire. It is not hard to guess that Franz Wolf is the son of Markus Wolf, one of the best-known spymasters, who had been the Stasi's number two for over thirty years.

CHAPTER 2

Berezovsky: The Rise and Fall of a Wise Man

Without Berezovsky, there would be no Sasha Litvinenko. Boris Berezovsky is an extraordinary figure, hugely underestimated by the West. 'I am a businessman who turned to politics, an entrepreneur, and a communications executive,' he writes in his book *The Art of Impossible* (2006), published both in Russia and in the USA. 'But in Russia and in the West, I have been called an oligarch, someone who wielded unknown power in the Yeltsin years and who does not believe in democracy. This was an unfair portrayal, but I never felt seriously compelled to refute it until recently.'

The book, which covers three volumes and was co-authored and edited by Felshtinsky is, unfortunately, little known. Boris further explains:

> The current situation in Russia has made it necessary for me to tell the world of concerns I have for the future of democracy there...
>
> I had hoped that Mr. Putin would preserve the fundamental accomplishment of the Yeltsin era – the national commitment to democracy – while correcting some of the mistakes from that time. But his performance in the year he has been in power – he was elected in March but has been running the country since August 1999, when Boris Yeltsin named him as his successor – has been a disheartening disappointment. Not only did Mr. Putin not start solving these pressing problems, but he initiated the dismantling of some revolutionary achievements of the Yeltsin era.
>
> He has formally (so far only formally) destroyed the basis of the democratic federation by replacing elected representatives in the upper chamber of the Russian parliament with appointees. Moreover, he abrogated for himself the power to dismiss regional governors elected by the people. In doing so, the new president concentrated all the country's political power in his hands.
>
> Most recently, he has taken steps to subordinate the mass media and has begun using law enforcement agencies to put pressure on both independent businesses and political opponents...
>
> Mr. Putin continues to insist on a military solution to the ethnic conflict in Chechnya, a path leading nowhere. The fear of the

authorities' unchecked power has begun to find its way back into the everyday lives of ordinary Russians.

By and large, Mr. Putin is gradually heading toward authoritarian rule. For ages the supreme leader of Russia – be it a Tsar, general secretary or president – wielded practically unlimited power...

It would be wrong to say that we were friends with Berezovsky – he had many associates but only one or two true friends like Yuly Dubov[1] – but we knew each other. Like Litvinenko, I had his private phone number and he had mine, but unlike Sasha we phoned and met only a few times. There was a period when I needed his financial support, working on my first book about Russian poisonings, and Boris immediately agreed to provide a grant through his IFCL. For reasons independent of him, it never materialised and now I am quite happy that it did not happen. At least I can in all conscience say that I never received money from Berezovsky. But many, very many people did receive it: British lords, Russian, European, American, and other politicians and MPs, ministers and PR specialists, bureaucrats of all ranks, army, intelligence, and police officers, journalists, actors and actresses, husbands, wives, children, and young women. Even heads of states and terrorists. If you want names, ask Alex Goldfarb, the IFCL director.

There are many books written about Berezovsky. From *The Godfather of the Kremlin* (2000) by Paul Klebnikov – not only an unfortunate but also an erroneous title – and *A Self-Portrait or The Hanged Man's Notes* (2013) by Yuri Felshtinsky, to *The Time of Berezovsky* (2018) by Petr Aven, personally presented by the author in Waterstones Piccadilly where Litvinenko used to meet some of his contacts. But I believe the most authoritative among them remains *Death of a Dissident* (2007), written by Goldfarb when Boris was still very much alive and kicking. Advertised as a story about Litvinenko penned with Marina's help, it is certainly a treatise about Berezovsky and the title fits perfectly with the content. The title says it all. Whatever the authors planned or wanted, it is Berezovsky who was a dissident, another 'prophet unarmed' and then 'prophet outcast' like Trotsky, not Sasha Litvinenko. About six years before a coroner recorded an open verdict on the death of probably the most interesting, controversial, and mysterious figure of the post-Communist Russia, when Goldfarb's book was published nobody could know that Berezovsky, who directly or indirectly financed it and was one of its very first readers, was already as good as dead.

In the tight circle of Berezovsky's associates, Litvinenko was by far not the first victim. A new political party, Liberal Russia, formed in March 2002, was not registered in Moscow until they agreed to expel one of its leaders, founders, and sponsors. The name? Boris Berezovsky. All formalities were completed in October of the same year. The party was then duly registered by the Ministry of Justice but in May 2003 its Central Council met again and re-elected Berezovsky as the party's co-chairman together with Sergey Yushenkov, MP, Vladimir Golovlev, MP, and Boris Zolotukhin, former member of the first democratic Russian parliament (1993–95).

Golovlev was killed in broad daylight near his house in Moscow by multiple gunshots to the head in August 2002. Yushenkov was murdered in the same manner in April 2003. Following those high-profile assassinations, Zolotukhin resigned as co-chairman of the party in March 2004 and the party was abolished. Another co-chairman, Mikhail Kodanev, was charged with organising the contract killing of Yushenkov and sentenced to twenty years. Eight years later, he suddenly announced that he had received instructions from Berezovsky and Patarkatsishvili to hire a hitman, which he did against his will. Kodanev was released from prison in May 2018 – as if by design, ten years after Badri died, aged only 53, and five years after Berezovsky's dead body was found in a mansion belonging to his former wife.

Boris was a mathematician and as such would be one of the few individuals who could truly appreciate this mathematical coincidence (with integers simultaneously satisfying multiple seemingly unrelated criteria). One may say that it was easily predictable that the former oligarch would die a violent death. Some, including Boris himself, feared it, and quite a few were plotting. Nikolai Glushkov, another man close to Berezovsky, feared it too. He was found dead in his London home in March 2018, so by the time Kodanev was released it was all over. Appointing someone from the KGB as the President of Russia, Boris did not stop warning, was 'to enter a vicious circle'.

'It is interesting to talk about Boris Berezovsky,' Petr Aven writes. '[He was] bright, fearless and never petty-minded. And he paid the full price.' Aven, a Russian billionaire with a Latvian passport believed to be a member of Putin's inner circle, did not explain exactly what Boris paid the full price for. He himself paid a price when Latvia decided to strip him of its highest state award for 'silent support to Russian aggression' against Ukraine.

Berezovsky was a professional mathematician before he became a businessman and then plunged into politics. In mathematics, twenty-three is a prime number. Because of their nature, many prime numbers but especially twenty-three are thought to have occult powers seen by many to have a mystical significance. Boris was born on January 23 and died on 23 March (William Shakespeare was born and died on 23 April). Litvinenko died on 23 November. The most famous and most quoted of the Psalms is number 23 (KJV): 'The Lord is my shepherd; I shall not want. He maketh me to lie down in green pastures; he leadeth me beside the still waters.' Each parent contributes twenty-three chromosomes to the start of human life and the average human physical biorhythm is twenty-three days. The Knights Templar, a Catholic military order which was among the wealthiest and most powerful, had twenty-three Grand Masters. On the night of 23 March, Russian emperor Paul I was murdered in his bedroom in the newly built St Michael's castle in Saint Petersburg by a group of his dismissed officers. He was succeeded by his son, the 23-year-old Alexander I.

I well remember Boris's omni-presence at Highgate Cemetery during the Litvinenko burial and later at the memorial ceremony, but Aven writes that Berezovsky hated to attend funerals and did not like visiting sick friends at hospital.

The first attempt on his life was on 7 June 1994. Berezovsky's first official company was a Soviet-Italian joint venture known as LogoVAZ, a combination of the Italian firm Logo Systems, an old partner of the AvtoVAZ, or Volga Automobile Plant, a Russian car manufacturer producing dismal vehicles of the Trabant class known in the West as Lada, and the Russian automaker. The joint venture was not a car dealership at the beginning, it was to adopt new automated processes to bring the production a little bit closer to the automotive industry standards of the time. Contracts for the Fiat, Mercedes, and Volvo brands came later. True to himself, Boris decided he needed an exclusive company headquarters in downtown Moscow and set up The Club (officially, the LogoVAZ Reception House), spending £1.5m to restore a rather modest turn-of-the-century merchant's house where he would entertain politicians, ministers, businessmen and guests from all over the world. On that sunny June afternoon, at 5.20 pm, Berezovsky's grey Mercedes 500 pulled out of the gates of The Club when a radio-controlled improvised explosive device placed in a blue Opel parked nearby exploded. The blast blew out windows in the eight-storey house across the street and wounded people passing by. The driver was killed instantly, but Berezovsky and his bodyguard suffered only minor injuries. Neither Boris's deputy for security matters nor the head of his personal protection detail could figure out how it could have happened. Both, as it turned out, were not security professionals. Fortunately, those who had placed the bomb were not professionals either.

Later, Litvinenko suggested it was someone at the Lada automaker who had put a contract on Boris – law enforcement agencies had no means to investigate at that time, so there were only wild guesses and rumours. Sasha thought it was because Berezovsky sent one of his lieutenants, Nikolai Glushkov, to act as a financial director at the car factory and someone feared his or her shadow deals with intermediary firms would become known. Litvinenko, then a senior officer at the FSB's Division of Operations against Criminal Organisations (URPO), suggested it was most likely the Kurgan Gang who specialised in contract killings. They had their own people in the Moscow police, he said, and even in the FSB. According to the Russian businessman Yuri Scheffler (Shefler), the owner of SPI Group who lives in London, Vladimir Rushailo, then head of the Serious and Organised Crime Command of the Moscow police and at the same time head of the Serious Organised Crime Directorate of the Interior Ministry (similar, but not identical to the British National Crime Agency) often visited his Moscow restaurant with leaders of the Kurgan Gang.[2]

Litvinenko's URPO was nothing else but a Special Tasks unit similar to that headed before and sometime after the war by Pavel Sudoplatov. Sudoplatov was a KGB general so secret that no one knew about him until he published his book *Special Tasks: The Memoirs of an Unwanted Witness* (1994) that instantly became an international bestseller and brought him world fame in spite of the book's multiple factual errors and a few inventions. But it was the first and remains the only serious publication about Soviet special secret ops in the West written by their principal organiser. Among several prominent victims who were done away with – such operations became collectively known in the West as 'wet jobs', essentially the wrong term – Sudoplatov was in charge of the operation to assassinate Trotsky in Mexico. He and his service became a role model for many secret KGB departments, including URPO. When Litvinenko was there, the division was commanded by General Khokholkov, whose claim to fame was his role in the assassination of the independent Chechen president Dzhokhar Dudayev.

In late December 1997, General Khokholkov's deputy told Sasha and several of his colleagues present at the meeting that it would be a good thing to get rid of Berezovsky permanently, just to snuff him out for old times' sake. Until recently, Berezovsky had been deputy secretary of the Security Council of Russia, a very important government figure. Putin was its Secretary in 1999 and for the past decade the Security Council had been headed by Nikolai Patrushev, former FSB director. In April 1998, Berezovsky would also be appointed Executive Secretary of the CIS, an intergovernmental organisation formed following the dissolution of the Soviet Union.

Naturally, Litvinenko and other URPO officers were not happy about this idea and informed Berezovsky who, in turn, informed the Kremlin. The next day, the deputy chief of the presidential administration summoned them to report, listened to all of them carefully until they had finished, and promised to do something about it. Until mid-April, nothing happened so several volunteers finally gathered at the Berezovsky dacha and recorded a video testimony. This video has never been shown to the public but after a meeting with the FSB director and a visit to the prosecutors, the whistle-blowers and their boss Khokholkov were suspended pending the outcome of the internal investigation.

One day in June 1998, Valentin Yumashev, a journalist who at the time headed the powerful presidential administration, summoned Boris to Staraya Square, an impressive Art Nouveau building at the centre of Moscow, formerly the seat of the Communist Party Central Committee. They knew each other well and for a while Berezovsky had even served as Yumashev's non-official political advisor, advising him on major government appointments. Among other things, Valya, as he was known to old friends, asked the tycoon for his opinion about his deputy, whom he wanted to put in charge of the Security Service. The name of the deputy was Vladimir Putin.

'Why?' Boris inquired.

'We are considering him for the FSB directorship. [Nikolai] Kovalyov is being dismissed because the president does not trust him.'

'Sure,' Boris said. 'I support Putin 100 per cent.'

Rumours had it that when Putin mismanaged Sobchak's re-election bid in August 1996, a criminal case was opened against him and he was desperate to move to Moscow. Anatoly Sobchak was the first democratically elected mayor of Leningrad (when he won the elections, the city voted to return to its historical name of St Petersburg) and a former professor of law at Leningrad State University (LGU). When Putin returned from his first and only foreign posting in Dresden and the KGB placed him at the LGU, Sobchak, then chairman of the Leningrad

City Council, invited him to join his staff. After Sobchak was elected mayor in June 1991, he appointed Putin to head the City Hall's committee for international relations and from 1994 he also held the post of deputy mayor of St Petersburg.

Badri claimed that he personally recommended Putin to Pavel Borodin, then head of the Administrative Directorate of the President (UDP) also in charge of the Presidential Property Management Department. Borodin, who had headed the UDP from 1993 to 2000, agreed to take the former Chekist as his deputy, appointing the former KGB officer with a career, albeit limited, in the foreign service to manage Russian property abroad. In March, Anatoly Chubais recommended that Putin should be transferred to the Main Control Directorate of the Presidential Administration, where he succeeded Alexey Kudrin, and in May 1998, Yumashev, much impressed by Putin's work performance, invited him to be his first deputy at the administration.

At the end of July, Putin was appointed FSB director. On that occasion, Berezovsky's life was saved. 'A process,' Goldfarb writes, 'instituted by Sasha's URPO whistle-blowers and steered behind the scenes by Boris plucked their future nemesis from obscurity and placed him in charge of one of the world's most powerful spy services.' This, of course, is not quite correct because the FSB is only a domestic security service and not a 'spy' organisation. But it was an important first step to real power and with Berezovsky's help and encouragement Putin successfully took all other steps to become the President of Russia. Which, without doubt, placed him in charge of one of the most powerful, cunning, and ruthless secret services in the world.

On 13 November 2000, Boris was having his usual breakfast at the Château de la Garoupe with a magnificent view of the Bay of Nice. In 1907, British MP Charles McLaren, 3rd Baron Aberconway, bought four acres at the point of the Cap d'Antibes. He hired an English architect to build the property. It features a long façade with half-moon windows and a long stairway leading to the sea. The garden, which was maintained by McLaren's wife, has a wonderful pergola with 12-metre-high rose bushes, irises and begonias. At times, the house was rented or visited by various celebrities including Pablo Picasso. The property passed to the owner's daughter Florence and her husband, Sir Henry Norman, a journalist and Liberal politician who became famous for his coverage of the Dreyfus Affair that divided French society for a decade. Norman expanded it and added an extra storey to the house. In 1999 this elegant French château, one of the few chateaux privés les plus chers au monde, was purchased by Berezovsky for 22 million euros.

Present at breakfast were also his life partner Elena Gorbunova and Alex Goldfarb. At one moment Boris announced that he was going to Moscow 'for a few hours' to answer the summons as a witness in the Aeroflot fraud case. It took some serious efforts to persuade him to stay and in the end Boris agreed and dictated his famous statement: 'They force me to choose between becoming a political prisoner or political émigré, and I am choosing the latter.' That was certainly a wise decision but it did not solve his problems in Russia. One of those problems was popular TV channel ORT, widely known as the Berezovsky channel.

According to its bylaws, major decisions in the company required approval of 75 per cent of the board of directors. At the time, Boris's loyalists – Konstantin Ernst, general director and executive producer; Tatyana Koshkariova, director of information programmes; Sergei Dorenko, her predecessor and later deputy general director and the main anchor; and Badri Patarkatsishvili, Boris's partner and ORT's Chief Operating Officer – controlled the board and with it the network. To gain full editorial control, one had to turn any or all of them.

Dorenko was summoned to the Kremlin but refused to take an offer. After some time, Ernst called Badri: 'I know that I am a piece of shit,' he said, 'but I will go with the winning side. It's pointless to resist. Sorry.'

In mid-December the Kremlin sent a messenger. Roman Abramovich flew from Moscow for a weekend. His villa was a ten-minute drive from Boris's château.

'You understand, of course,' he told Boris and Badri during a meeting, 'that if they wanted, they could take your share in ORT and you'd get nothing. But to make it easier, we agreed that I would buy your 49 per cent out.'[3]

By mid-January 2001 the transaction was completed. Ernst has remained its CEO and on his initiative the ORT was renamed the First Channel (they call it 'Channel One Russia'). Koshkariova was appointed editor-in-chief of *Nezavisimaya Gazeta* ('The Independent Gazette'). She later left journalism to become an administrator. Dorenko's television career was abruptly finished. Lately, he had been working for a Moscow radio station and in May 2019 suddenly died aged 59. In the summer of 2001, Badri fled to Georgia, making use of his Georgian citizenship. The principal owners of the channel as of 2020 were the state (38.9 per cent) and National Media Group (NMG, 29 per cent), a media holding chaired by Alina Kabayeva, a former MP and, according to information that she refuses to comment on and he denies, the mother of three of Putin's children. Other shareholders are VTB Capital (20 per cent), Russian news agency TASS (9.1 per cent) and Ostankino Technical Centre (3 per cent). In 2023, the channel's key person was still the same Konstantin Ernst, an Oscar-nominated film producer.

Since he had changed sides, Ernst had been known as Putin's chief image-maker also appointed to produce the opening and closing ceremonies of the 2014 Sochi Winter Olympics. Ernst would later say that the production was a task done for pleasure, not reward, a labour of love, but in what became known as the Pandora Papers project, confidential documents leaked to the journalists revealed that Ernst became a secret partner in a massive, state-funded privatisation deal. The International Consortium of Investigative Journalists found out that 'on the day of the Opening Ceremony a company was incorporated in the British Virgin Islands that would pave the way for Ernst's secret 23% stake in a state-funded privatization deal worth a billion dollars'. Ernst caught the eye of Berezovsky in 1995 and, about four years later, the oligarch appointed him CEO of the ORT television channel just as a new Russian president was taking power in what was seen by many as a new world order based on democracy, free-market capitalism and the Western lifestyle. But not by Putin and his cohort. In April 2005, in his annual state of the nation address, Putin called the collapse of the Soviet empire 'the greatest geopolitical catastrophe of the century'.

Berezovsky's new role as a symbol of Russian opposition to the Kremlin regime, albeit, like Trotsky, from exile, and a sponsor of all that was considered to be democratic in a non-democratic Russia, was announced by Elena Bonner at a press conference in Moscow. The conference was organised some two weeks after that memorable breakfast at the Château de la Garoupe on 30 November. Bonner, the 77-year-old widow of the Nobel Laureate who defied the Soviet system, said that she had accepted a $3 million grant from the New York-based Berezovsky Foundation (the future IFCL) as an endowment for the Sakharov Museum and Civic Centre in Moscow. Her husband, nuclear physicist Andrei Sakharov, who died two years earlier, was a well-known Russian dissident and activist for disarmament, peace, and human rights.

'For Boris and me,' Goldfarb, the director of the IFCL, says, 'awarding the first grant to Sakharov was a gesture ripe with symbolism. Elena Bonner had been the first among Russia's human rights activists to say that Putin represented "modernized Stalinism" at the time when Boris was still Putin's "brother". Three decades earlier Sakharov had become an emblematic figure, symbolising modern resistance to tyranny. The grant to the Sakharov Center was meant to underscore the continuity of Soviet oppression under Putin and the permanence of dissidents' resistance. From the outset it defined the colors of the new foundation.'[4]

By May 2001, the IFCL had awarded 160 more grants to various organisations across Russia that represented protest movements. Soon, a signal came from a group of democratic politicians who wanted to set up a new political party. The objective was to run in the 2003 election to the State Duma, the lower house of the Russian parliament, on an anti-Putin platform.

When Yushenkov, a veteran of Russia's democratic politics and Golovlev, another dissident MP, returned after visiting Berezovsky in France, Yushenkov announced the formation of a new political party, Liberal Russia, with Boris and himself as its leaders.

On 2 April, the newspapers reported: 'Russian oligarch Boris Berezovsky, fighting extradition to Russia on fraud charges, is released on £100,000 ($160,000) bail by Judge Timothy Workman, pending hearings scheduled for October. Speaking to reporters outside the Bow Street Magistrates' Court in London, Berezovsky dons a satirical mask of President Putin to underscore his claim that the case was a farce.'

Later that day, Berezovsky and Dubov were seen at the Le Meridien Hotel in Piccadilly giving a press conference after preliminary hearings at Bow Street Magistrates' Court.

'In early September,' Goldfarb writes, 'Judge Workman told Boris's lawyers that the extradition hearings would be moved from Bow Street to the Belmarsh Court, where high-security cases are usually heard, thanks for a request by the Metropolitan Police. They believed that there was a credible threat to Boris's life.' Quite unexpectedly for Berezovsky and his friends, the Home Office granted him political asylum without any explanation on 11 September. The next day, Judge

Workman threw out the extradition request, rightly asserting that it was now 'quite pointless'.

On 21 September, David Leppard commented in his article in *The Sunday Times*: 'An agent for the SVR, the former KGB, is said to have been sent to Britain to stab Boris Berezovsky, the Russian billionaire, with a pen filled with poison as he attended a London court hearing to contest his extradition on fraud charges.' David also mentioned that 'the Russian spy is said to have confessed that he had orders to smuggle a cigarette lighter filled with a lethal poison into London's Bow Street magistrates' court where Berezovsky was due to attend the extradition hearings'. In his article, Leppard quoted an unnamed Whitehall official who allegedly confirmed that 'MI5 had been approached by a man claiming he had been sent to Britain to murder the tycoon and they had referred the matter to the police'. 'The plot is understood to be under investigation by Scotland Yard,' the article stated.

After Boris was granted political asylum in September 2003, several Western media outlets controlled by Moscow started spreading rumours that the bogus SVR agent, whose name they found out was Vladimir Terlyuk, had been offered millions in cash for a false testimony and that Litvinenko had drugged the poor man and then video-recorded him 'confessing that he was dispatched by the FSB to kill Berezovsky' – a video, they maintained, that influenced the British government's decision on Berezovsky.

At the end of the day, these statements had their effect.

> London, House of Commons
> Boris Berezovsky
> Dr Julian Lewis [Conservative MP]: To ask the Secretary of State for the Home Department if he will make a statement on the outcome of police investigations into the claims made during the hearing of the extradition case against Boris Berezovsky that an assassin had been sent from Russia to attack him.
>
> Ms Hazel Anne Blears, MP, Labour Party [Minister of State for Policing, Security and Community Safety]: The Commissioner of Police of the Metropolis informs me that the Metropolitan Police Service was made aware of an alleged threat to Boris Berezovsky. Inquiries made were unable to either substantiate this information or find evidence of any criminal offences having been committed. Investigations into this matter have been concluded.[5]

Writing about journalism, Forsyth stressed that 'in a world that increasingly obsesses over the gods of power, money and fame, a journalist and a writer must remain detached, like a bird on a rail, watching, noting, probing, commenting but never joining'. Whatever David Leppard wrote in his article and, ironically, he published almost the same text ten years later describing a different case, Boris Berezovsky was granted political asylum in Britain not because of Terlyuk's supposed 'confessions', or Litvinenko's reports to the police. As the above quoted document shows, the decision was made regardless of external factors. As usual, the Russians underestimated and failed to understand the dominance of justice in the country they still refer to as Foggy Albion.

In any case, Litvinenko's assumptions and Leppard's writings made Boris feel completely baffled. 'Can you believe it,' he exclaimed, discussing the story with Goldfarb, 'that they would attack me with a chemical weapon? Volodya [Putin] must be really insane!' At the beginning of the new millennium, no one could imagine that Russian chemical, biological, radiological, or nuclear weapons (CBRN) would be used against individuals declared the Kremlin's enemies. In March 2018, in Salisbury, Wiltshire, and in August 2020, in Tomsk, Siberia, the victims' names were not Berezovsky or Patarkatsishvili, both of whom had long been out of anybody's reach by that time, but even after the chemical weapons attacks against the Skripals and Alexey Navalny, the world at large refused to believe that 'Volodya' was truly insane. The situation changed when, only a couple of years later, Putin began threatening the world with Russia's vast nuclear arsenal.

From his new home in King's Road, Chelsea, known as Stanley House, a fine seventeenth-century mansion with a large garden purchased by Boris in 2005, Berezovsky and his associates, who were labelled by the media 'the London Circle of Russian Exiles', launched a fierce propaganda campaign. Berezovsky publicly stated that he saw his political mission as bringing down Putin's regime either by force or by organising a 'bloodless revolt'. In April 2007, Boris told the *Guardian*: 'I am plotting a new Russian revolution.' British authorities reacted by launching an investigation into his remarks, immediately putting his political asylum status in serious jeopardy.

After Putin's army attacked Ukraine in February 2022, the British prime minister Boris Johnson made an official statement. 'Putin has made a grave miscalculation,' he said. 'The free world is united in its resolve to stand up to his barbarism... And I know that however long it takes, however arduous, Putin must fail.'

One day before Sasha Litvinenko died, on 22 November 2006, I wrote in the *Wall Street Journal* that whatever the truth, this poisoning also looked to be directed against Boris Berezovsky. How? Lord Timothy 'Tim' Bell, best known for his advisory role in Margaret Thatcher's three successful general elections campaigns and his co-founding and running of Bell Pottinger, a multinational public relations, reputation management and marketing company, a friend of Berezovsky who handled the Litvinenko poisoning affair with the media, explained.

'Boris,' he said, 'you have cast yourself as the archenemy of Putin: politically, personally, and ideologically. Reasonable people believe that you are on the good side in this crusade, even though they may question your motives. For the people at large, this is all pretty irrelevant because it's all about politics in a faraway land.' He paused for a second and then added, having in mind Sasha Litvinenko: 'But this time the situation is very different. A crime has been committed on British soil...'

A highly experienced professional described as Lady Thatcher's 'favourite spin doctor and confidante', Tim Bell was not able to correctly predict the reaction of the British public. 'The [Litvinenko] story,' he speculated, 'will reach many people, who will react intuitively. The problem is, most people will not want to believe it was Putin.' Lord Bell rightfully reasoned that members of the general public were instinctively averse to the idea of governments or presidents ordering murders. 'The more it seems obvious,' he said, 'the deeper they will go into denial. You [Boris] will be going against the tide, and you are the anti-Putin. If people don't want to think it was Putin, then they'll think it must be you. The louder you say it was him, the more this will happen.'[6]

What the experienced PR man actually said was very true about Russia, where those few people who still remembered the story would think that it had either been Berezovsky who poisoned Litvinenko or the British secret service – two versions actively promoted by Kremlin propaganda. During the Scotland Yard investigation and the Litvinenko Inquiry, Berezovsky's role in the case was meticulously studied and discussed with all pros and cons carefully weighed. At the end, Judge Sir Robert Owen had this to say: 'In summary, I am quite satisfied that Mr Berezovsky bore no responsibility for Mr Litvinenko's death.'

Bell Pottinger announced Lord Bell's departure as chairman in August 2016. A few months later, the company described as 'having the most controversial client list' in PR history suffered a huge reputational blow, a PR disaster which had a devastating impact on its performance. A scandal in its South African business quickly led to the firm's downfall. Lord Bell could predict a possible 'conflict of interests' but was not able to do anything about it. Five years earlier, he was also not able to help when Berezovsky brought a civil case against his former business partner Roman Abramovich in the High Court of Justice in London, accusing him of blackmail and breach of trust and seeking over £3 billion in damages. Like his friend and mentor later, Berezovsky suffered a reputational blow when, in her final conclusive remarks in August 2012, the High Court judge found Berezovsky 'an unimpressive, and inherently unreliable witness' and ruled against him.[7] Berezovsky condemned the ruling. 'Sometimes I have the impression that Putin himself wrote this judgement,' he said. Bell died at his home in London in August 2019.

In April 2007, Terlyuk suddenly appeared again, and again he was assigned the same role. The Russian television programme *Vesti Nedeli*, broadcast by the TV channel RTR Planeta, the equivalent of BBC Two's *Newsnight*, showed him 'in obscurity' and using the alias 'Petr', repeating word for word the story he told Martin Dewhirst of how Berezovsky offered him millions of pounds to pretend to be an assassin sent by Moscow to kill the oligarch. At the same time, 'Petr' claimed, Litvinenko had witnessed an attempt by Berezovsky to avoid extradition and get political asylum by obtaining false evidence from a Vladimir Terlyuk. He also suggested that Berezovsky was party to threats to Mr Terlyuk's life. That was the reason, 'Petr' claimed, for Berezovsky's receiving political asylum in Britain. Terlyuk denied at court that he himself was the person called 'Petr' and featured in silhouette in the TV programme, but the judge said he had 'no doubt'.

All these tales had already been rejected by the British authorities long before. This time, Berezovsky sued the broadcasting company VGTRK, but their defence lawyers asked the judge to refuse jurisdiction over the claim on the basis that the interviewee – Terlyuk, alias 'Petr' – was a Russian state-protected witness, part of the bigger case against Berezovsky. Nevertheless, Mr Justice Eady ruled that both RTR and Terlyuk were liable for the damages. The High Court awarded Berezovsky £150,000. In December 2011, two prominent British solicitors acting on behalf of Terlyuk tried to appeal this decision. After a most brilliant discussion and thorough consideration, Lord Justice Laws and Lady Justice Rafferty dismissed the appeal in relation to the grounds on which the defendant had permission to appeal and refused permission in relation to the remainder. The case was closed.

On 18 July 2007, I met Alex Goldfarb for a late breakfast at the Hilton Hotel on Park Lane. On that day, British media reported yet another story dealing with the attempt on Boris's life. The suspected assassin was only named as 'Mr A'. Alex explained that the man's name was Movladi Atlangeriev who had 'a long association with the FSB' and that the Metropolitan Police Service possessed intelligence that he had come to the UK to assassinate Berezovsky. He was detained on June 21 in the same Hilton, located conveniently round the corner from Boris's office where we were sitting, on suspicion of conspiracy to murder, but was released without charge to immigration officials two days later. No incriminating evidence was found, Alex said, and the suspected killer was quietly expelled to Moscow.

One day, Ahmed Zakayev invited Oleg Gordievsky and me for a long shashlik lunch at his home in Muswell Hill. Oleg arrived with Maureen and, because my wife was in London, she was also happy to join us. Shashlik or shashlyk is a popular dish of skewered and grilled cubes of meat, best of all marinated lamb, with pieces of onion and vegetables. Ahmed was a great master of making shashlik with his son Shamil helping him. He told us that Movladi Atlangeriev, known among his associates as Ruslan, born in 1954, was a childhood friend of a future Chechen president Akhmad Kadyrov, father of Ramzan Kadyrov. Ruslan began his criminal career in the 1970s with burglaries of rich foreign students' flats together with another Chechen by the name of Khozh-Ahmed Noukhaev, a future prominent Chechen politician. Noukhayev, a law student, was arrested and jailed, and after his release he and Atlangeriev became leaders of the Chechen organised crime group in Moscow. Russian media reported that eventually both were recruited by the KGB. In the 1990s, Atlangeriev and Noukhaev had dealings with Berezovsky, it was claimed, and in the 2000s collaborated with the FSB in their operations in the north Caucasus. Nikolai Patrushev, then head of the Security Service, reportedly valued Atlangeriev's services in Chechnya so much that he awarded him with an engraved pistol.

Paul Klebnikov (Pavel Khlebnikov), an American journalist who published a book about Berezovsky with a catchy but not quite appropriate title *The Godfather of the Kremlin* (2000), also published a book about Noukhayev, which he called

Conversation with a Barbarian (2003). Remarkably, the FSB first accused Berezovsky and then Noukhayev of murdering the American, who was shot dead in Moscow soon after his second book came out. Noukhayev disappeared without trace and after a while Russian investigators announced they no longer believed he had masterminded the murder. It remains unsolved to this day.

After his return from London, Atlangeriev, nicknamed 'Lord' and 'Lenin', was kidnapped in Moscow. He is widely believed to have been murdered in Chechnya. Mentioning him in the Litvinenko Inquiry Report, Sir Robert stressed that if the intelligence that the police were said to have received about Atlangeriev was true, this could serve as evidence that even at the time of Litvinenko's death Russian secret services were prepared 'to arrange the assassination of leading opponents of the Putin regime in London', meaning Berezovsky.

On Monday, 25 March 2013, the Press Bureau of the Thames Valley Police officially reported that a post-mortem examination was carried out on a 67-year-old Russian national, who was found dead at a residential property in Mill Lane, Ascot, on Saturday. The results of the post-mortem examination, carried out by a Home Office pathologist, have found the cause of death was consistent with hanging. It was not reported, however, that the body of the dead man was unequivocally identified as that of Boris Berezovsky (aka Platon Elenin). Police and forensic scientists concluded the man had committed suicide.

However, Bernd Brinkmann – doctor, professor, renowned medico-legal expert with international reputation – a German forensic scientist retained by members of the businessman's family, said that his examination of autopsy photographs had led him to conclude that the person in question had not killed himself. Professor Brinkmann submitted a report to the inquest that included the suggestion that the 67-year-old had been murdered by a group of assailants and then suspended by his scarf from the shower rail. 'The strangulation mark is completely different from the strangulation mark in hanging,' the expert wrote. The killers could have throttled their victim in a bedroom, he asserted.

The Berkshire coroner Peter Bedford said that after hearing evidence from such an eminent witness, he was not able to conclude that Berezovsky had taken his own life.

The police statement said:

> Thames Valley Police and the South East Counter Terrorism Unit carried out a thorough investigation into the unexplained death of Platon Elenin formerly known as Boris Berezovsky. This included the deployment of an experienced Home Office pathologist to examine the body in situ and conduct the subsequent post mortem. His findings were considered alongside examination of the ligature, detailed toxicology, physical evidence recovered from the scene and the deceased's medical history. The investigation could find nothing to support the hypothesis of third-party involvement.

Plain and simple, isn't it?

Nevertheless, after the two-day inquest at Windsor Guildhall in March 2014, the coroner recorded an open verdict.

Six weeks after being found dead on the bathroom floor of a house that belonged to Berezovsky's ex-wife, the body was laid to rest in a deliberately low-key ceremony in Brookwood cemetery near Woking, Surrey, just a few minutes' drive from my house. I was not there but saw video footage. The coffin remained closed for the funeral. The ceremony was a very private event, limited to around thirty mourners including Boris's children, former wives, close friends, and solicitors. The *Guardian* reported the service took place in a small brick chapel, overlooked by suitably Russian pines and silver birches, and under a dull, overcast sky. As Luke Harding noted, 'it was a strikingly understated send-off for a man who lived furiously in the public eye, both in Russia and in the UK.'

Boris Nemtsov, Russia's deputy prime minister during Yeltsin's second presidency, warned Berezovsky: 'He [Putin] will never forgive you for supporting him.' Nemtsov would be shot in Moscow in February 2015.

I know Alex Goldfarb believes in what the British police say. And he believes in the Old Testament: 'When Ahithophel [Absalom] saw that his advice had not been followed, he saddled his donkey and set out for his house in his hometown. He put his affairs in order and hanged himself.'[8]

'He was a friend. I miss him. I'm very grateful to Boris. Through him I felt the touch of history,' Goldfarb told the reporter. Five years later, Alex was suing two Russian propaganda TV outlets, Channel One and RT, that have publicly accused him of Litvinenko's murder. Alas, Boris and Tim Bell were not there to help.

Remarkably, Yuly Dubov, another friend, noted: 'The games that Boris used to play had to be interesting to him. The interest that he got when playing a game with an unpredictable result always complicating the conditions of this game – that was his main motive.' This is known as non-classical logic.

For me, the life of Boris Berezovsky, a businessman who turned to politics and started the New Cold War alone, could end in only one of two ways – either he must have been killed by Putin's men or simply disappeared to watch the collapse of the Putin's regime from a distance. In any case, the British government was not interested in making a lot of fuss about this particular death.

CHAPTER 3

The Escape

> And in a day, decades expire.
>
> Boris Pasternak, 'Single Days' (1959),
> translated by Andrey Kneller

Initially, Berezovsky had nothing to do with Sasha's escape from Russia and was not even informed of such plans. In May 2000, when Felshtinsky was in Moscow assisting Berezovsky and his team, he made his first and last attempt to negotiate with the FSB on behalf of Litvinenko. 'To see,' as Felshtinsky later wrote, 'if I could make some kind of deal with them and to obtain a guarantee of immunity for Alexander.' The American historian who left the country of 'developed socialism' under Leonid Brezhnev and arrived in the America of Jimmy Carter was unable to understand the mentality of the new Russian 'king's men' – former KGB officers with criminal minds who were now building capitalism with a Russian face. Felshtinsky naively believed that the nine months that Sasha had spent in jail were more than enough punishment for the press conference of November 1998. Whatever Yuri was prepared to offer them, the KGB (now FSB) dug their heels in and refused to deal. Their judgement: Litvinenko had committed the worst crime – he had gone against the system and this was something not permitted to anyone.

'Here's the story,' Felshtinsky told Sasha when they met. 'It's bad. You and Marina have to get out of here. You won't survive until the end of the year. In the best case, they'll put you back behind the bars, in the worst, you know…' Nothing was decided on that day but they returned to the problem a few months later, when Felshtinsky flew to Moscow again to discuss their future book with Litvinenko, who was surprisingly still at large.

On the night of 24 September, they went to Litvinenko's dacha outside of Moscow, made sure that they were not followed, left their cell phones in the house and went deep into the forest so that no one could eavesdrop on their conversation. 'The plan was extremely simple,' Yuri recalled. 'In the next two weeks, Alexander was to cross the border, and he would choose the place for the border-crossing by himself, without letting anyone know about it in advance, myself included. As soon as he crosses the border, I fly out to meet him, wherever he is, to make sure that everything is really in order, that he is really outside the country and not in the office of an FSB prosecutor [*sic*].' That was much easier said than done but the chaos of the early 2000s made a lot possible. Marina was unaware of what was going on and was advised to wait for a telephone call.

Although the Soviet Union had collapsed almost a decade before, it was still rather easy to cross its borders by going to a neighbouring country, especially when it was a former Soviet republic. Travel from Moscow to Minsk or Kiev was rather uncomplicated. It was even easier for those who lived in the border area. A short trip from Belarussian Grodno to Białystok, Poland, or from Russian Vyborg to Lappeenranta, Finland, was a usual thing. Litvinenko knew that without his passport valid for foreign travel, which he had to surrender, he could not travel abroad, so with his internal Russian passport he arrived in Sochi, the largest Russian resort and a seaport on the Black Sea, where a ten-dollar bribe secured him a free passage to the nearest port in Georgia on board an old Soviet ferry. It was a hydrofoil *Kometa*, which transported passengers between the ports of Sochi and Batumi. From there he moved to the Georgian capital Tbilisi and telephoned Felshtinsky. In the meantime, Marina was contacted and swiftly purchased a tour to Marbella for herself and their son Tolik, then aged six, still not knowing what was awaiting her.

Unlike Marina, Berezovsky, who by that time had moved to his house in Cap d'Antibes in the south of France, and Badri, locked in Tbilisi by the international arrest warrant issued by Russia's Prosecutor General's Office, were duly informed about all plans and developments. Boris asked Badri to help Sasha with a passport valid for travel abroad because it was clear that it was too dangerous to remain in Georgia. One can't escape the long arm of the secret service for long, whether it is KGB, CIA, or Mossad. In the meantime, Felshtinsky had in mind not one but two escape plans for Litvinenko and his family.

One plan he discussed with Vladimir Rezun, an old Soviet GRU defector who since 1978 had resided in Britain, looking more for professional advice than help. After his defection from the GRU station in Geneva, Rezun settled in the UK, occasionally consulting British and American secret services and writing books using the penname 'Viktor Suvorov'. And while his non-fiction works were mostly known to professionals, his fiction and military historical books became international bestsellers. Felshtinsky asked Suvorov whether in his opinion MI6 might be interested in accepting Litvinenko.

Suvorov is experienced and clever, even cunning, hiding behind the guise of a simpleton full of jokes and puns. We first met with him and his wife Tatiana in London in the spring of 1999. Everybody appeared to be in a good mood and we spent some time together working on a cover story about him and his book that Suvorov called *Self-Murder* (2000), which was later published in Moscow. We asked Patrick Lichfield, one of the UK's best-known photographers who at that time had started to specialise in digital photography, to photograph Suvorov for the article. After a long session at his studio, where he asked Suvorov to play Napoleon, Patrick took a gorgeous photo that made a superb magazine cover.

Suvorov is a convivial man, good company, but he is also very professional. And he did not need (and would not bother) to contact The Firm – as SIS is known in-house – to come out with an answer. No, he told Felshtinsky, the British were not interested in your FSB friend and would not accept him. No problem, Yuri said. He believed there were other options.

He thought that as a naturalised American, he could go to the US embassy in Tbilisi and arrange for asylum for the Litvinenko family, having in mind that Sasha was not an ordinary refugee, but a serving FSB colonel. Leaving behind their new Georgian bodyguard sent by Badri, one day they headed towards the embassy, with Felshtinsky going straight to the US citizens service and Sasha waiting on a park bench.

We discussed the episode several times. According to Felshtinsky, after that first visit there were several meetings, with at least one of them outside the city, which took a lot of time, but they all led to nothing. Finally, with Sasha's new passport ready, they departed to the airport where Boris's private jet was ready to pick them up. Without batting an eyelid, Litvinenko passed the passport control with a Georgian passport identifying him as 'Oleg Chernyshev', a Georgian citizen of Russian origin. Once on board and ready to depart, Boris called from France. He asked about the situation and where they were going.

It was now Felshtinsky's Plan 3. He reckoned that because Sasha's father was Walter, he probably had some German roots. Sasha's sister, as he had learnt, lived in Germany, so it would be natural for Litvinenko to try his luck in Germany. Knowing all details, I must say it was a risky plan and Berezovsky was probably of the same opinion because as soon as he heard about Germany, he said no. Felshtinsky tried to argue but because Boris had a controlling interest in this business and, accordingly, privileged voting rights, he quickly persuaded Sasha that they must go to Antalya, which Georgian and Russian citizens could visit as tourists without any visa or, rather, they can obtain a visa on arrival for twenty dollars. So, they flew to Turkey. While their jet was still taxiing to the runway, the US embassy called to say that the decision from Washington was still pending and suggested to meet later but the aircraft was already taking off and the connection broke up.

Berezovsky was footing the bill so in Antalya all three of them – Yuri, Sasha, and Badri's man – checked in at a five-star hotel as did the pilots. Just in case, Felshtinsky booked another hotel, this time in his own name, in another part of the city. The next day Felshtinsky flew to Malaga on the same jet, picked up Marina and Tolik, and returned to Antalya to witness a happy family reunion. Boris called again, inquiring about their plans, and Felshtinsky said they wanted to go to the American embassy as soon as possible. 'It was Thursday, 19 October,' Felshtinsky told me. 'I was not inclined to waste time and wanted Litvinenko to apply for asylum on Friday morning. "Don't go anywhere," Boris said. "Let me think it over." And he hung up.'

At the end of October 2000, a lot of Russians were spending their holidays in Turkey, many of them preferring Antalya, located on Anatolia's southwest coast, the largest Turkish city on the Mediterranean. Here, the Litvinenko family looked like typical Russian tourists and this was exactly what they actually were, with the fit paterfamilias taking his regular morning run on the beach, his wife getting a

The Escape

typical light brown tan and their mischievous six-year-old boy demanding constant attention from his parents. I am partly borrowing this description from Goldfarb, who would see them there in a week. Although relatively safe and with his family, Litvinenko was getting more and more nervous, peering at every new face around with suspicion. Felshtinsky tried to phone Boris to explain the situation but was not able to get through until one day Badri called from Tbilisi to explain that Berezovsky was busy. 'In the meantime,' he said, 'while Boris is not there, I am giving orders and I ask you all to remain calm and wait for the yacht which is already on the way to you.'

Felshtinsky panicked. He didn't want to get on any yacht, realising that as soon as they were at sea and in international waters, they would immediately become an easy target. Sasha was also not happy about the yacht. He became very suspicious, expecting Russian agents, perhaps even his former URPO colleagues, to arrive at any time, especially because Litvinenko's former second-in-command, FSB Major Andrey Ponkin, was calling quite often asking a lot of questions. 'I could not turn off my cell phone,' Felshtinsky explained, 'since it was my only connection to Alexander and Marina. Our only hope was that we would be faster than the flying squad of hired killers that Moscow would soon dispatch or might have already dispatched to Antalya.'[1] And they were. I immediately remembered Vladimir Voinovich, a famous Russian satirist and author of the dystopian *Moscow 2042* (1987). One day in Munich, where he lived in exile, Voinovich told me: 'I am not afraid of the KGB. Either their car will break when they decide to come and arrest me, or they run out of petrol on the way to my home, or they simply forget my address.'

Getting sick and tired of waiting without any purpose or perspective, and reluctant to get shot or drowned on a yacht floating in the middle of the Mediterranean Sea, Felshtinsky packed his bag and departed to Boston, previously calling Berezovsky and explaining the situation.

It was 12.00 noon in Cap d'Antibes when Berezovsky dialled a familiar number in New York. 'Hi,' he said, 'where are you?' Quite obviously, sitting in his beautiful house on the French Riviera between Cannes and Nice, Boris could not realise that there were still some 51 minutes before dawn in the Big Apple. And because it was a cell phone, he did not even think that he was calling the USA.

'Do you remember Sasha Litvinenko?' Boris asked, satisfied that a person on the other end of the line was not in Russia or any other former Soviet republic where their phone call could be intercepted.

What happened next is well known from many books, articles, films, and hundreds of interviews given by all participants of the Litvinenko drama and first of all by Alex Goldfarb, who picked up the phone in his New York home on that Wednesday morning, 25 October.

For me, the best way to travel from New York to Washington is by Amtrak, which takes you straight to the heart of the capital. Departing from New York Penn Station, conveniently located in Midtown Manhattan, passengers arrive to the beautifully refurbished and renovated WDC Union Station, a magnificent edifice with a domed ceiling opened in 1907.

A few hours after Boris's call, Goldfarb walked into the Eisenhower Executive Office Building, originally known as the State, War, and Navy building, located in Washington on 17th Street NW and occupied by the Executive Office of the President and Office of the Vice President of the United States. In about two weeks, the Republican candidate George W. Bush would win the election, defeating the Democratic candidate, the incumbent Vice President Al Gore, and a new team would soon occupy the offices of the huge government building just west of the White House. But in October, President Bill Clinton, whose friendship with the Russian president Boris Yeltsin had gone sour over the Kosovo War, was still in the White House.

Here, Alex arranged a meeting with an old friend, Mark C. Medish. Early in his career, Medish worked on Capitol Hill as a foreign policy staffer for Senator Edward M. Kennedy and at the time served in the Clinton administration as special assistant to the president and senior director for Russian, Ukrainian, and Eurasian Affairs on the National Security Council. His father, Vadim Medish, then 75, was an American University professor who specialised in the history of the Soviet Union.[2]

'I can give you ten minutes.' Mark was a busy man and could not afford to waste his time on trifles.

After listening to what Alex had to say, he summed up the discussion. 'As an official of the U.S. government,' he said, 'I have to tell you that we are not in the business of luring Russian agents into defections. And as your friend, I advise you not to get involved.' He probably added that a career diplomat, W. Robert Pearson, had just been appointed (14 June 2000) as the new US ambassador in Ankara and would not be happy if a Russian defector turned up at his embassy. Anyway, Medish smiled, in Turkey your friend would be dealing with the Consular Section officials whose job would be to keep people out of America.[3]

As a former Soviet dissident in Moscow who agitated against the Soviet regime when the dissidents regularly ended up in a lunatic asylum, Goldfarb decided not to follow his friend's advice.

When Berezovsky persuaded him to go to Turkey to help Litvinenko, one of the reasons was that Alex had the right connections in high places. Indeed, he had another phone number to call. This time, it was Thomas 'Tom' R. Pickering, Undersecretary of State for Political Affairs, the number three position at the State Department. Pickering was older than both Mark and Alex and had previously served as the US ambassador in Israel (1985–88) and Russia (1993–96). In 1996, Pickering was a top contender for the post of Secretary of State under President Clinton, but was ultimately passed over in favour of then-UN Ambassador Madeleine Albright.

Alex knew, of course, that in spite of his high position, Mr Pickering was not able to help the Litvinenkos and simply informed the diplomat that, disregarding his and Mark's advice, he was going to fly to Turkey and have a try at the US embassy.

'Should anything untoward happen in Ankara,' he asked, 'could I call you directly?'

The Escape

'Please do,' said Pickering, 'you can call me anytime.' And dictated his home number.

On Friday, 27 October, Goldfarb landed in London late at night and the next day flew to Antalya via Istanbul for a first rendezvous with Sasha and Marina. Although his wife Svetlana was not terribly enthusiastic, she decided to go with him. At his request, Joseph Sandoval, an American lawyer, was on his way to Ankara to meet Litvinenko and provide some legal help should that be necessary.

When Alex and Svetlana saw the Litvinenkos, they immediately realised that the fugitives were feeling quite at ease in Turkey. As soon as the muezzin recited the call to the midday prayer Salat Al Zuhr, and the distinctive sound of the adhan was pumped through loudspeakers installed on the minarets of the mosques, Tolik quickly asked Svetlana whether she knew the meaning of *Allahu akbar* (God is the greatest), well distinguishable among other words and phrases overlapping one another. 'It is the call to prayer,' the six-year-old boy explained, 'here they do it five times a day.'

'Do you think the Americans will accept us?' interrupted Sasha, turning to Alex.

'First we need to get to the embassy,' Goldfarb said, 'and then we shall see.'

They left Antalya on the same day in a rented car with Alex driving and Sasha telling stories from his KGB life to entertain him on the way, helping to stay alert and not to fall asleep behind the wheel. The traffic was normal and they covered the distance of almost 600 km in about seven hours, arriving at the five-star Sheraton Hotel conveniently located at the city centre in time to meet Joseph, an immigration and asylum attorney from New York. Because Boris was covering his expenses, Joseph kindly agreed to fly in for a few hours.

What Joseph told them they could easily find themselves on the State Department website or by researching other digital sources online. They would quickly find out that US embassies and consulates cannot process requests for such special legal protections as asylum or refugee status. That's because, under US law, asylum seekers can apply only if they are physically present in the United States (or at least at a US border or other point of entry). There is a common misconception that US embassies and consulates are basically the same as US soil. It is true that international law protects embassies and consulates from being destroyed, entered, or searched by the government agencies of the host country, but this does not give those embassies or consulates the full status of being part of their home nation's territory. Therefore, US law does not consider asylum seekers at US embassies and consulates to be 'physically present in the United States'.

However, Joseph explained, all this didn't mean that US embassy personnel could not offer any help at all to people who were in danger and sought protection. In exceptional circumstances, he said, US diplomatic missions could offer alternative forms of protection including a referral to the US Refugee Admissions Program (USRAP) managed by the Department of State in cooperation with other departments, or a request for parole to the Immigration and Naturalization Service (INS) of the US Department of Justice.

'Do you have a high-flier in the State Department?' he asked.

'Yes, I do, why?' Alex said, realising that his friend Tom Pickering, Madeleine Albright's deputy with the rank of Career Ambassador, the highest in the US Foreign Service, was now 69 and would probably retire next year after the elections.

'There's something known as INA,' Joseph explained, 'the Immigration and Nationality Act. Under the INA, a refugee is an alien who, generally, has experienced past persecution or has a well-founded fear of persecution on account of race, religion, nationality, membership in a particular social group, or political opinion. Individuals who meet this definition may be considered for either refugee status under Section 207 of the INA if they are outside the United States, or asylum status under Section 208 of the INA, if they are already in the United States.'

Anyway, he went on, 'I would recommend to register for USRAP to start the process because those admitted as refugees would be eligible for US government-funded resettlement assistance. But you need,' he looked at Alex, 'to pull strings in Washington because this may take a lot of time and effort. And I guess you do not have much time, right?'

'I do not want to stay in Turkey,' Marina promptly responded.

'We shall not stay here long,' Sasha said grimly. 'As soon as they know where we are, they come and snuff us out right in this bar.'

Alex turned to Joe. 'You are forgetting Sasha is not a Jewish immigrant, but a senior FSB officer. There must be a way.'

'Of course.' Joseph looked like he was revealing a great secret. 'There's still an option called "parole". Parole is a measure of last resort that allows people to enter and stay in the country "for a significant public benefit" to the United States. It is known as SPB parole. But first you have to decide: either you are fleeing persecution at the hands of an authoritarian regime or trading state secrets for US government protection and benefits. It is hard to combine the two.'

'Before leaving,' Goldfarb later recalled, 'Joseph gave Sasha one last advice. "In any case," he said, "if it comes to horse trading, be firm: your visa comes first, then you give them whatever they want."'[4] This only made sense if Sasha Litvinenko was able to give them what *they* wanted.

* * *

Only a year earlier, in September 1999, the intelligence world at large had been shaken by the publication in London of a book entitled *The Mitrokhin Archive*, which was a result of a three-and-a-half-year-long effort plus the talent and perseverance of the brilliant British intelligence historian Professor Christopher Andrew from Cambridge, based on copies of the most secret KGB files provided by a Soviet-Russian defector Vasili Mitrokhin. Despite extensive media coverage, Litvinenko knew nothing about it.[5] In his turn, Goldfarb only saw some press reports that did not provide any details.

In March 1992, a scruffy-looking old man boarded an overnight train in Moscow bound for the newly independent Baltic republic of Latvia. 'With him,' Andrew writes, 'he took a case on wheels, containing bread, sausages and drink for his journey on top, clothes underneath, and – at the bottom – samples of his notes.' Those 'notes' were handwritten and typed copies of several thousand classified documents from the archives of the KGB's First Chief Directorate, Soviet foreign intelligence, where Mitrokhin had been employed as a senior archivist. Next morning he arrived at the Consular Section of the US embassy at Remtes iela and asked to see a CIA officer. Following instructions, a junior consular official explained that the American diplomatic mission did not house CIA operatives and when Mitrokhin insisted, he advised him to return on a later date in order to talk to a more senior diplomat. Discouraged, he moved on to the British embassy, which was quite a way to go, on the other side of the Daugava and only minutes away from the Russian mission.

At the time, the small British embassy in Riga was located on the third floor of the imposing building in Elizabetes iela, which still houses several foreign embassies. A nice two-storey nineteenth-century villa at 5 Jura Alunana iela, acquired in 1930, which Britain had to relinquish when the Germans and then the Russians invaded Latvia in 1940 and 1941, was occupied by other tenants. Richard Samuel CMG CVO, the first British Ambassador in Riga after Latvia became independent of the Soviet Union, negotiated the return of the old British embassy back to HM government. Ambassador Samuel spent his National Service in the Royal Navy learning Russian, and in 1954 went on to study classics and modern languages at St John's College, Cambridge. An exceptional linguist, he spoke Russian, Polish, Italian, French, Chinese, Latvian, and German, and in his later years did a fair amount of translation, especially from Russian. The ambassador and his wife, the artist Frances Draper, left many friends in Riga after Samuel retired in 1993, and remained involved in Latvian affairs. He was appointed a Commander of the Latvian Order of the Three Stars and later became chairman of the British Latvian Association.

Inside the British embassy offices, Mitrokhin was met by a junior female diplomat introducing herself as Third Secretary, Consular and Management, who struck him as 'young, attractive and sympathetic'. As an extra bonus, she was fluent in Russian. He asked to 'speak to somebody in authority', explaining that he brought with him important documents from KGB files. While the tea was being served, she read some of his notes and asked questions. Mitrokhin told her they were part of a large personal archive which, among other things, contained substantial material on KGB operations in Britain. The young diplomat explained she needed to consult London and invited him to visit the embassy again a month later.

On Thursday morning, 9 April, in the same room, Mitrokhin identified himself to the SIS officers by producing his Soviet passport, Communist Party card, and KGB pension card. He also brought with him 2,000 typed pages from his archive that he had removed from a hiding place beneath his dacha near Moscow. Together they spent a day with them asking questions and making notes and him explaining about himself, his document collection, and how he had compiled it. At the end of the day it was agreed that he would visit the embassy two months later to discuss arrangements for a visit to Britain. By early May, the SIS Moscow station under John Scarlett (later Sir) was placed in charge of the operation. On 11 June, three months after his first visit, Mitrokhin arrived in the Baltic capital with a stack of papers from his archive staffed into a backpack. According to Andrew, 'most of his meeting with SIS officers was spent discussing plans for him to be debriefed in Britain during the following autumn.'

It was a truly extraordinary operation that had lasted for eight months. On 7 September, Mitrokhin secretly arrived in England for the first time. After initial debriefing in anonymous safe houses in London and the countryside, on 13 October he returned to Russia to make final arrangements for his departure.

Vasili Mitrokhin, together with his wife and their son, celebrated the seventy-fifth anniversary of the Bolshevik Revolution in the Baltic capital where he had first walked into the British embassy to offer his archive. On 7 November 1992, they were in Riga, but a few days later, the whole family were exfiltrated to begin a new life in Britain.

Three years after Mitrokhin landed in London never to return to his motherland, Professor Andrew was invited to the SIS head office at Vauxhall Cross to be debriefed on what had been unanimously accepted as one of the most remarkable intelligence coups of the late twentieth century. 'When I first saw Mitrokhin's archive a few weeks after the briefing,' Andrew recalls, 'both its scope [six large cases of top-secret material from the KGB's foreign intelligence archive] and secrecy took my breath away. It contained important new material on KGB operations around the world. The only European countries absent from the archive were the pocket states of Andorra, Monaco and Liechtenstein.'[6] Later, the FBI would describe the Mitrokhin files as 'the most complete and extensive intelligence ever received from any source'. But back in 1992, CIA officers working under diplomatic cover at the US embassy in Riga, perhaps without even consulting Washington, expressed their lack of interest in Mitrokhin documents. They seem to have thought he was either a street peddler, a hoax, or in the worst case a plant sent by the Russians, who was trying to mislead them.

***

They chose to visit the US embassy on Monday afternoon, 30 October, first, because it was necessary to make an appointment and give an advance notice that a potential defector would be coming, and secondly, because the US citizens service, which Goldfarb intended to use, was only open for visitors in the afternoon.

An advance notice was in the form of Svetlana who, with her US passport, came to the embassy in the morning to warn them about the upcoming visit. At 13.30, Alex led the Litvinenkos to the citizens' entrance, past the line of ordinary visitors patiently waiting along the embassy fence. In his book with Marina, Alex describes their visit in detail, so it makes no sense to reproduce it here except for a couple of details that may be pertinent to the Litvinenko case.

As expected, the meeting went on exactly as predicted by the asylum lawyer with a few minor exceptions. All four of them, Goldfarb, Sasha, Marina and Tolik, were escorted to the interview room guarded by a marine. Contrary to what they thought, it was not exactly 'the bubble, the type of soundproof room that appears in spy novels'. What Alex had in mind is known in the trade as a Sensitive Compartmented Information Facility abbreviated as SCIF, which is installed in every embassy and in several official US government buildings such as the Situation Room in the White House. In the embassy, access to SCIF is limited to the members of the CIA station and in other places to persons with appropriate security clearance.

When they settled, the consul introduced an officer from the political section. In his book, Goldfarb calls this officer 'Mark'. At that moment, Alex, Marina and the boy were asked to leave. 'I'd like to have a few words with Mr Litvinenko alone,' the officer said. And added in Russian, 'We won't need a translator.'

The interview lasted for about four hours.

'What took so long?' Alex asked when Sasha climbed into their car.

'It took them a while to crack me,' Litvinenko said, 'but they finally made me talk. They have set up a secure videoconference with Langley where they had a whole team standing by. And the guy on the other side was quite a character. Spoke Russian without an accent. After they figured out what I could know, for three hours he tried to pull out just one name out of me. I finally gave them something. I was sitting there and then I thought, what the hell. I have nothing to lose. That guy really jumped when I told him my titbit – it was one name. "Right, right, that's just what I need. Thank you very much." And he asked to write this name on a piece of paper.'

'Have they promised you anything at all?'

'No, nothing.'[7]

A couple of weeks before this meeting, the officer who interviewed Litvinenko in Ankara turned 44. Her name was Gina Cheri Walker Haspel, listed as Second Secretary in the diplomatic list. At 20, she married Jeff Haspel, who served in the US Army, and became Gina Haspel, but they were divorced by the time she joined the CIA in January 1985 as an officer in the Directorate of Operations, specialising in Russia. For two years before being sent to Turkey as deputy chief of station in Ankara, Ms Haspel had been deputy group chief, Russian operations, at the CIA's Central Eurasia Division, formerly the Soviet East-European Division, part of the clandestine service responsible for Russia and Eastern Europe. At the Agency, she learned Turkish and Russian and received extensive training as an operations officer.[8] Later, Ms Haspel developed a prominent career working as the CIA deputy director under Mike Pompeo during the early days of Donald Trump's presidency, before she was nominated to be the Director of the Central Intelligence Agency in March 2018, having served in this position until January 2021. She was the first woman to hold this post on a permanent basis. Former colleagues characterised her as 'smart, tough and effective'.

* * *

In the comfort of the Baur au Lac Terrace restaurant facing Zürichsee, I was having a dinner with a former high-ranking US government official. From 1990 to 1993, when Mitrokhin made his unlucky try at the American embassy, Jim had served at the National Security Council team under Brent Scowcroft as Senior Intelligence

Advisor to President George H. W. Bush. At the time when Gina Haspel's CIA career in the clandestine service was developing, between June 1999 and July 2004, he was Deputy Director for Operations (DDO), Haspel's boss, and as such certainly in a position to decide Litvinenko's fate in October 2000. Without revealing the name, I asked him what would be the first reaction at Langley if a Russian defector walked into a US embassy in a country like Turkey.

The first and immediate reaction would be mistrust, he explained. General wisdom would dictate that the man could be anything, from an SVR dangle to a violent lunatic, because defections are not done through the doors of the embassy. 'It is the policy of the United States,' he said, 'not to grant asylum at its units or installations within the territorial jurisdiction of a foreign state.' He recalled that Mitrokhin had been turned down in 1992 because the material that he offered – not genuine secret documents but hand-made copies, mostly of historic value – were not considered good enough to offer him and his family a government-protected shelter for life. Some defectors, Jim said, were only accepted because they proved they possessed information that was of a paramount importance to the US government at the time of their changing sides. With this, many, like for example Oleg Penkovsky, were not taken seriously for quite some time.

'It is also a matter of responsibility,' he said after a pause. 'What do the Russians do if an American who walks in turns out to be an empty shell?'

'How do I know? I think they can always send him back.'

'Here we are. And nothing ever happens to him. But the Agency cannot do that. There are many, many restrictions and obligations. A huge responsibility. And laws. If your friend were unable to tell us something really important, there was no way we could accept him.'

* * *

Alex didn't tell Sasha and Marina that his return flight to New York was booked for the next morning. He was not prepared to babysit the Litvinenkos and Boris had only asked him to bring Sasha to the US embassy, which he did. Now they simply had to wait, and Goldfarb had other important things to do, including trying to arrange a parole for them in Washington. But everything changed when, during a farewell dinner at the hotel, Litvinenko noticed that they were being followed. It was not real surveillance, but a man with a copy of the *Turkish Daily News* was quite certainly watching them. They did not think long and in five hours were in the most populous European city, lying both in Europe and Asia, once known as Constantinople, checking in at the spacious dark wood reception desk of the five-star Hilton Istanbul Bosphorus. Making full use of Berezovsky's expense account, Alex would later admit, they took the King Bosphorus Suite with fantastic views over the Bosphorus and the city from a private balcony. The suite was designed to accommodate four persons.

The next day, while Sasha was enjoying the view, Marina unpacking, and their son watching cartoons on the LED Flat Panel TV, Goldfarb dialled the US embassy number given to him in Ankara.

'I am sorry to say we cannot help you,' pronounced the voice on the other side of the line. 'You're on your own, I can't tell you why... I am really sorry. Goodbye.'

His first thought at that moment was: what should I do with them now?

One alternative was to agree to board the yacht that Badri had mentioned to Felshtinsky, which had been chartered in Greece to pick them up and sail into neutral waters. But they quickly realised that a yacht in the middle of the sea would be an excellent target for whoever might wish to get rid of them, and those unidentified culprits would be able to do it rather quickly without leaving any trace.

'And if not this, then what?' Alex asked when Berezovsky called to check what was going on. 'Sail forever, like the *Flying Dutchman*? You can get lost in a big city, but you can't hide on a yacht.'

Talking to Boris, Alex suddenly came up with a brilliant plan. It was too dangerous to share it with Berezovsky over an unprotected telephone line, so he didn't tell him.

'Where do you want to go?' he asked the family, who were looking at him expectantly.

'I don't care,' Sasha said, 'just as long as we get out of here as soon as possible.'

'I don't care either,' said Tolik.

'I want to go to France,' Marina said.

The next morning, 1 November, they arrived at Istanbul Airport, checking in at the Turkish Airlines counter for a flight to London, with a change at Heathrow to an Aeroflot flight to Moscow. The registration went smoothly except for a minor nuisance in the person of two plain-clothes Turkish officials who followed them to the aeroplane, making sure they got on.[9] In about four hours, they were in London.

***

'No one really want defectors,' a former MI6 officer who has long experience working against the KGB and later SVR told me. 'What you really want is an agent in place.' In Turkey, they were very lucky and Alex Goldfarb did not even have to apply to his high-level contacts in Washington, both of whom discouraged him from getting involved. Anyway, when the new 43rd US president George W. Bush moved to the White House in January 2001, they both retired from their high posts. By that time, Litvinenko and his family were already enjoying life in the world's best city.

With his exemplary government service record and high diplomatic rank, after his retirement Thomas Pickering was invited by the Boeing Company to serve as Senior Vice President for international relations. Prior to that, he was briefly the president of the Eurasia Foundation, a Washington-based organisation that makes small grants and loans in the states of the former Soviet Union. Remarkably, in 2009 Mr Pickering joined the Board of Directors of the Russian Steel Pipe Company TMK (also translated as Pipe Metallurgical Co.) with headquarters in Moscow, as one of its Independent Directors, remaining on the board until at least 2012. In 2012, he chaired the Benghazi Accountability Review Board at the State

Department and at the time of writing was affiliated with the International Crisis Group (ICG) as a board member. The ICG is an independent organisation 'working to prevent wars and shape policies that will build a more peaceful world', according to their Mission Statement.

After leaving the administration, Mark Medish was a partner in the multinational law firm Akin Gump Strauss Hauer & Feld LLP, headquartered in Washington DC, the largest lobbying firm in the United States.

In May 2005 Mark, together with his father, visited Krasnodar on vacation. Vadim Medish, Mark's father, was born in Minsk but grew up in Krasnodar, a Russian city close to the Black Sea. According to *The Washington Post*, during their stay they were arrested by Russian police and interrogated for eight hours. The police refused to tell the Medishes why they had been singled out for arrest. Both were released at the end of the day. Amazingly, the following August, Medish senior was awarded the Russian Order of Friendship during a ceremony at the Russian Embassy in Washington. The honour was bestowed on him by the Russian government for 'strengthening Russian-American friendly relations',[10] it was reported. At the same time, in 2006, Mark Medish joined the Carnegie Endowment for International Peace as its vice president for studies. When this book was sent to press, he was a partner with the Mosaiq Law Group PLLC, a small legal services firm based in Washington DC, and a member of the Council on Foreign Relations.

In June 2001, Felshtinsky flew to Zagreb, Croatia, to meet Yuri Shchekochikhin, deputy editor of the independent Moscow *Novaya Gazeta* and member of the Russian parliament. Felshtinky came a long way from Boston to hand over the manuscript of *Blowing Up Russia*, his book written together with Litvinenko, for serialisation in the newspaper. In August, several chapters from the book were published by *Novaya Gazeta* with a circulation of 500,000 copies.[11]

Shchekochikhin was a well-known journalist. He was one of the authors and host of an investigation programme on the ORT television channel controlled by Berezovsky. The programme was closed, he said, because of the episode called 'For Motherland! For Mafia!' which dealt with the Russia war in Chechia. It was aired in 1995 but the same contents would perfectly fit the war in Ukraine almost three decades later. Shchekochikhin was also investigating a major corruption scandal involving federal government bodies, criminal activities of FSB officers related to money laundering, and a former Russian minister who was later arrested in Switzerland on fraud charges. In June, Shchekochikhin contacted the FBI and was planning to fly to the United States to share information with law enforcement authorities. He was poisoned and died in Moscow on 3 July 2003. One of his last articles was 'Are We Russia or the KGB of the Soviet Union?'[12] In October 2022, there was little doubt that Russia had become much worse than the KGB of the defunct USSR.

'Borrowing from Adolf Hitler,' the *Financial Times* wrote shortly after Putin's invasion of Ukraine, 'he now refers to antiwar protesters as "national traitors" and threatens to "spit them out like a fly". Putin's regime has completed its reversion from a 21st-century spin dictatorship to a 20th-century dictatorship based on fear. Unfortunately, this is what Russia will look like until he is gone.'[13]

CHAPTER 4

A Coterie of Friends and Foes

'Our Service had not been involved in the Litvinenko affair,' Sergey Lebedev said in an interview for the Russian media in December 2006. A career intelligence officer, he was drafted into the army serving in the Kiev military district and after a short spell at the Komsomol regional committee in Chernigov (now Chernihiv, Ukraine, where Russian strikes killed scores of civilians in multiple attacks on the city in March 2022) was invited to join the KGB.

As usual, the young lieutenant was first sent to the KGB training course known as School No. 204 in Kiev, commanded by General Serafim Krikun who, before this appointment, had been serving as first deputy chairman of the Ukrainian KGB. The school prepared future KGB officers for counterintelligence work but in 1975 Lebedev was transferred to Moscow to the elite PGU – First Chief Directorate (foreign intelligence) after having spent another year at the Andropov Red Banner Institute. His service was mainly with the 4th department in charge of intelligence operations in Germany and Austria.

According to his official SVR biography, Lebedev, whose tour of duty in Berlin-Karlshorst KGB base coincided with Putin's posting in East Germany, also had field assignments in both West Germany and West Berlin. Both Lebedev and Putin later claimed they never met while in DDR, which is understandable because Lebedev was based in the East German capital while Putin was in Dresden, near the Czech border, and his position there was rather low. In Berlin, Putin reported to Colonel Yury Leshchev, his former boss from the Leningrad KGB. After a time at Yasenevo (also known as Moscow Centre or simply 'Forest'), where he headed one of the SVR directorates, Lebedev was sent to Washington, DC as the main resident in 1998. There, he had been liaising with the Central Intelligence Agency on unimportant issues while on the side running the most extensive network of spies his service ever had. In May 2000, Putin suddenly appointed him Director of the SVR. Now, after he was summoned to the presidential administration for a brief but highly confidential conference, he was back in the Forest, asking the head of the British Desk, former 3rd department, to come to his office at once.

Britain was not as important as America and housed fewer Russian spies, though 'our people' sat in the House of Commons and the House of Lords, major newspapers, the BBC, the biggest banks, and private banking institutions as well as in the London Stock Exchange. Lebedev surely smiled when he thought how quickly his service could trigger a mini-crisis on the ISLAND (that is Britain, in

Soviet intelligence reports) by launching an appropriate campaign in the British media.

At about that time, in April 2005, I flew in from Vienna to meet Litvinenko and Goldfarb to discuss a business project and settled in a bar in Mayfair. With me was Martin Dewhirst, a Russian speaker who often served as Sasha's interpreter during public events and who had offered to introduce us. Our visitors were late, so we spent our time discussing the news.

Goldfarb was in London, getting ready to take off for Kiev as Berezovsky's envoy to deliver, as he thought, some very hot material to the Ukrainian prosecutors. These were secret recordings from the office of Leonid Kuchma, who until recently had been President of Ukraine. They would become known as the 'Melnichenko tapes' or 'Kuchma tapes' and would inflame a scandal that broke out in 2002, which would be remembered in Ukraine and beyond as 'Kuchmagate'.

While waiting for Goldfarb and Litvinenko, my companion and I went through some details of this scandal, because it was related to the business that I intended to discuss with them.

Major Mykola Melnichenko, the central figure of the scandal, was one of the bodyguards of President Kuchma, the only politician in modern Ukraine who had served two consecutive terms in office. In about 1998, Melnichenko was ordered to start secretly recording all important conversations that took place in the Mariinsky Palace in Kiev. Litvinenko later told me the orders came from the office of Yevhen Marchuk, and Felshtinsky, the first member of the Berezovsky team whom Mykola contacted in America when he defected, confirmed that the whole operation was indeed supervised by Marchuk.

Marchuk, formerly a high-ranking Ukrainian KGB official, had occupied important government posts after the collapse of the Soviet Union. He had served as minister of national security and defence, prime minister, presidential candidate and, after Kuchma won, secretary of the National Security and Defence Council, the position he was holding when the bugging operation unrolled. Later Marchuk was reappointed Minister of Defence. He had earlier served in the 9th Directorate of the KGB, which provided close protection to the country's top leaders and visiting VIPs in Moscow and Kiev, from where he was transferred to the newly formed State Protection Directorate (UDO), the Ukrainian version of the Russian FSO.

In November 2000, when news about the tapping of the presidential offices began to circulate in Kiev, Melnichenko fled the country with his audio files. First, he went to the Czech Republic and then, the following April, was granted political asylum in the USA. This rash decision of the US authorities to accept a low-profile defector was prompted by Melnichenko's claims that his files contained crucially important political information.

The tapes would show, he claimed, that the Ukrainian president had authorised the sale of several sophisticated Kolchuga passive sensors to Saddam Hussein's Iraq in violation of the international agreements prohibiting such exports to a rogue regime. Kolchuga was an electronic support measures (ESM) system manufactured in Ukraine to detect and track aircraft. This greatly troubled the United States – the lives of American and British pilots tasked with flying sorties over Baghdad were at stake.

Of less importance for his US hosts was the fact that the recordings allegedly proved President Kuchma's personal involvement in the plot to murder the independent Ukrainian journalist Georgy Gongadze. This Georgian-Ukrainian journalist and film director had been kidnapped by local police officers and his beheaded body was later found not far away from Kiev. In September 2011, *The Telegraph* reported that four policemen had carried out the Gongadze murder on behalf of Kuchma. Three months later, a Ukrainian court ordered that criminal charges against the former president be dropped on the grounds that the evidence was insufficient. Although the actual murderers, police officers, were arrested and sentenced to various terms, those who gave orders remain unidentified.

After Melnichenko's testimony and the subsequent investigation by the combined US-UK expert team, the incriminating secret recordings were declared to be authentic by the US State Department. 'Foggy Bottom' had then suspended the $54 million dollar government-to-government aid to Ukraine, the fourth-largest recipient of US foreign aid at the time. In the autumn of 2001, NATO withdrew its invitation for Kuchma to attend the planned NATO Prague Summit. In December, the Italian prosecutor's office also accused Marchuk of violating the UN embargo on supplying arms to various parts of the world. In August 2008, already out of office, Kuchma happily and lavishly celebrated his seventieth birthday in Sardinia among friends and visiting dignitaries.

As it turned out, I came to London on 11 April 2005 in the middle of yet another scandal related to the former bodyguard.

When he arrived in Washington in early 2001, Melnichenko was a lost soul. The CIA did not need him, his command of English was almost zero, and he had no money. His only hope was that thanks to this scandal he would gain fame. He also thought that would secure him a triumphant return to Kiev, a place in the parliament and further favours from the opposition. It appeared that he wanted to become a sort of a celebrity, as he knew this status brought not only recognition but also quick money.

Melnichenko and his family had to find some way to make a living and (like everyone who followed political developments in the former USSR) he was aware of Boris Berezovsky's special interest in Ukraine and support of the opposition there. So exactly a year after his escape to the USA, in April 2002, Melnichenko visited Ilya Levkov, the head of Liberty Publishing House, a boutique New York publisher who were the first to bring out *The FSB Blows Up Russia* by Felshtinsky and Litvinenko in both Russian and English. Melnichenko asked to put him through to Felshtinsky in Boston. His idea was to use Yuri as an intermediary to contact Berezovsky and beg him for financial help.

Working on this book, I called Ilya in New York. For whatever reason, he preferred to speak English rather than his native Russian and immediately remembered Melnichenko's visit. Ilya said Melnichenko knew that both Liberty authors, Felshtinsky and Litvinenko, were from the Berezovsky circle and simply asked Mr Levkov to dial Felshtinsky's number for him because he had an interesting project to offer. Ilya complied.

Through the mediation of Felshtinsky who, like Goldfarb, was a close and trusted adviser to the former oligarch, Melnichenko received a $50,000 grant from the IFCL. In addition, Mykola demanded a monthly fee of $10,000 for his work of decrypting the tapes he had brought with him from a hiding place in Ostrava in addition to a nice office with a secretary and a comfortable apartment in New York.

An operation was set up under the command of Yuri Shvets, a former KGB major of the First Chief Directorate (foreign intelligence) who once spied on the USA under cover of a TASS correspondent in 1985–87 and later went to live there, having settled in Virginia, about 30 miles from Washington, DC. Berezovsky's foundation financed the decoding of the records by a hired team of SBU specialists who had laboured for several months, and their posting on the website 5element. net set up especially for this purpose. The site was shut down in January 2003 on Berezovsky's instruction. In the meantime, a leading US forensic laboratory Bek Tek controlled the authenticity of all records. To this project Melnichenko contributed all or at least a large part of his recordings (or, as Litvinenko suspected, their clones).

While the Ukrainian scandal was gaining force, Litvinenko and Vladimir Bukovsky, one of the most prominent Soviet dissidents who had spent twelve years in prison camps and psychiatric hospitals and whom Litvinenko had befriended in London, actively supported Melnichenko.

During a meeting at the National Union of Journalists at the end of February 2003, Mykola called Litvinenko 'a close friend'. Bukovsky told the meeting that the Melnichenko tapes provided a unique opportunity to look into the structure of the post-Soviet states and the catalogue of crimes committed from presidential offices. Russia, Ukraine, and other post-Soviet states, Bukovsky said, are ruled by 'a criminal clique, a merger of the underworld, security services and so-called business', which had become completely uncontrollable. The former dissident said that whereas in Soviet times dissidents could rely on support from the West, 'in post-Soviet times the West has decided that democracy has prevailed and no such support need be given.'

For his part, Litvinenko provided as much support as he could to the former major from Kiev. Melnichenko was a regular at the Litvinenkos' house and they spent plenty of time together. At the end, Melnichenko, a specialist in eavesdropping, began to tap their conversations and those in Berezovsky's office.

The Ukrainian media has long been reporting that in this complex operation – against Kuchma in Ukraine and against Berezovsky and his people in London – Melnichenko was acting as an agent of the Russian FSB. Most likely its Fifth Service started his recruitment in late 2002 after Mykola wrote a personal letter to Putin.[1] The Russian interest was evidently twofold: to get the original recordings so they could know what was really happening in the Ukrainian top echelons, and to infiltrate another of their informers into Berezovsky's court. At the end of October 2004, Putin made a live appearance on Ukrainian television to promote and support the pro-Kremlin candidate Viktor Yanukovich. Simultaneously, Lugovoy arrived in the UK, ostensibly to watch CSKA play Chelsea in Stamford Bridge (2-0 to Chelsea), but in reality, to contact Litvinenko. It was the first time the two men met in London.

As will later become known, Berezovsky's offices in Moscow as well as his London office at 7 Down Street in Mayfair had been well penetrated by agents working for different secret services and even private investigative firms. Especially the former KGB, now FSB and SVR, had planted as many moles as they could. The SVR New York station had also almost certainly taken over from the FSB and were in touch with Melnichenko in the United States. There is little doubt that during his visits to London, Melnichenko was given a secret telephone number to use in case of an urgent need.

It would, of course, be very unwise to contact a Russian diplomat at Kensington Palace Gardens and Melnichenko should have been advised not to try it. It is not a big secret that almost all Russian intelligence officers working in Britain are known to MI5. For example, when Melnichenko was in London, one of the Security Service's targets was Sergey Federyakov, a high-ranking diplomat who worked under the guise of an embassy counsellor posing as an arms control specialist. In reality, Federyakov, codenamed Comrade ALLEN, was an experienced intelligence officer, deputy head of the SVR London station, at the time headed by Lieutenant General Dmitry Epishin, also masquerading as a counsellor. Federyakov had previously served in New York, posing as Second Secretary of the Permanent Mission of the Russian Federation to the UN. When his cover was blown by a defector, he was recalled to Moscow and posted as a counsellor in the Department for Security & Disarmament Affairs at the Ministry of Foreign Affairs. In June 2022, I met Federyakov in Vienna, Austria. It turned out that since October 2019, he had been serving here as Alternate Permanent Representative to UNIDO, United Nations Industrial Development Organisation. It's a small world.

In Austria and some of its neighbours, the security services are not so vigilant as in Britain, but Ukrainian journalists were still able to obtain well-documented evidence of Melnichenko meeting SBU officials in May 2002 in Ostrava, then in Strasbourg and in the South Tyrol, then in February 2004 in Vienna, and later in August he was spotted with several known SVR and FSB officers in Moscow. Finally, it was arranged that a Ukrainian millionaire hiding from his country's prosecutors in Russia would purchase all master records. Those files, it was assumed, could contain a lot of compromising material on the Ukrainian officials close to Kuchma.

On 4 March 2005, one day before his 54th birthday, former Ukrainian Minister of the Interior Yuri Kravchenko was found dead in his dacha near Kiev. A prime suspect in the Gongadze murder case, after he was summoned to the prosecutor's office General Kravchenko chose a highly original way to avoid punishment: he shot two bullets, one after another, into his own head – first in the chin and then in the temple.

Almost immediately, Melnichenko, who was hiding in Warsaw, called Berezovsky in London insisting that his life was in danger and begging Boris to promptly send a private jet and bodyguards for him. Whatever else may be said about Boris, he was a generous person, especially to those he needed. Soon Mykola was in London checking into a hotel reserved for him by Boris's secretary. The idyll, however, did not last long as Melnichenko started to make public claims seriously undermining Berezovsky's standing with the future Ukrainian leadership and pouring mud on what he called 'an international criminal gang' with Berezovsky as its leader. The 'gang' members, in Mykola's version, were Goldfarb, Felshtinsky, Litvinenko and Shvets. In his letter addressed to the SBU chief, Melnichenko stressed that all his claims were documented by secret recordings of the talks between himself, Berezovsky, and Berezovsky's people. Perhaps that was exactly the role the SVR/FSB spymasters scripted for Mykola to play. Anyway, his claims were regularly reported to the then chief of the Ukrainian Security Service (SBU) Oleksandr Turchynov through diplomatic channels and were also leaked to the Russian and Ukrainian media.[2] In the meantime, Melnichenko announced his plans to meet newly elected President Yushchenko during the latter's official visit to the USA. The Ukrainian leader, however, had a different agenda.

Putin and his administration were clearly irritated because, despite all their efforts, they could not stop Berezovsky's anti-Kremlin and pro-Ukrainian campaign. In late February 2005, Boris, Russia's Enemy Number One, came to Latvia with a British-issued refugee document that allowed foreign travel in spite of the 'red notice' issued by Interpol at Russia's request. Just weeks before, the former oligarch had taken a short trip to Tbilisi and was planning a visit to Kiev. The Russian Foreign Ministry, using popular phraseology of the time, declared: 'Once they did nothing to arrest Berezovsky, official Riga ignored its responsibilities as an Interpol member and showed its unreliability as a partner in the struggle with organised crime. Latvia should realise that such actions couldn't stand.' In October, the young prime minister of Latvia Aigars Kalvītis capitulated, adding Berezovsky to the list of persons unwelcome in Latvia.

When Goldfarb and Litvinenko finally arrived and we settled around a small corner table in the bar, our talk quickly turned to recent events and the upcoming flight of Goldfarb and Felshtinsky to Kiev. Indeed, two days after our meeting, Alex said in an interview: 'We have brought the evidence in the cases of Gongadze, Elyashkevich and the sale of the weapons system Kolchuga to Kiev for consideration by the prosecutor's office.' Naturally, both Goldfarb and Felshtinsky acted on Berezovsky's instructions. 'These materials,' Goldfarb explained, 'include the masters in digital audio file format analysed by experts in the USA, the equipment that Melnichenko admitted he had used, and the original expert reports confirming the authenticity of the audio recordings. The evidence (recordings and equipment) is contained in bags sealed by the experts in 2001–2002 in the state of Virginia immediately after the analysis.'

Goldfarb and Felshtinsky told the journalists that Bek Tek had carried out the analysis and that the reports produced by this laboratory were widely used in legal proceedings in the USA. 'These materials are presented in a format required of the evidence by American courts,' Goldfarb said. 'Our legal experts believe that these

A Coterie of Friends and Foes

materials are sufficient to include 'Kuchma's conversations' in the criminal case file and use them as evidence.'

During their visit to Kiev, both Goldfarb and Felshtinsky testified as witnesses in the Gongadze case, which again had been arranged by Boris. Several weeks later, Litvinenko made his own statement to a Ukrainian prosecutor who had especially flown to London to interview him. In the meantime, shortly after the Ukrainian presidential election Shvets set up a new website on Berezovsky's request, which he called 5elementplus.com, and resumed publishing transcripts along with their sound recording and his comments.

I arranged a meeting with Sasha not knowing that Goldfarb might also be there. Together, they looked like a tutor and a student. It was a nice spring day at Carlos Place, no rain or drizzle, and everybody felt easy and relaxed. Sasha asked me whether I knew Oleg Gordievsky, a former KGB intelligence officer who had famously been exfiltrated from Russia by SIS and was now living in Britain. He also asked about Oleg Kalugin, another KGB legend, albeit of a different nature and calibre. Kalugin was the youngest general in KGB history and not a defector, although one day he moved to Washington and had resided there permanently ever since. Litvinenko communicated with him regularly.

At the end of the meeting Sasha asked about my book describing the case of Nikolai Khokhlov (codenamed WHISTLER), a Soviet defector reportedly poisoned by radioactive thallium-201 chloride salt in Frankfurt in 1957, which was due to be published in about a week. Although a former FSB officer, Litvinenko had little knowledge of Soviet intelligence history; during his years in the Russian security services he had been operating in the field and never outside Russia and hardly had or needed to have access to classified histories of the Soviet espionage regularly prepared 'for internal use only'. The Khokhlov story was important for him to assist his friends from *Novaya Gazeta* in Moscow in their investigation of the alleged poisoning of the famous reporter and a Russian parliament (Duma) member Yuri Shchekochikhin. Tons of papers have been written about Shchekochikhin's weird end, but his medical records and the autopsy report remain classified by the Russian government to this day. Six *Novaya Gazeta* journalists, including Shchekochikhin and Politkovskaya, have been murdered since 2001. Twenty years later, Dmitry Muratov, who co-founded the paper, won the Nobel Peace Prize. 'This award is to my colleagues from *Novaya Gazeta* who have lost their lives,' Muratov said in his Nobel Prize lecture. 'This award is also to the colleagues who are alive, to the professional community who perform their professional duty... We are the antidote against tyranny.' Following Russia's invasion of Ukraine, a court in Moscow stripped *Novaya Gazeta* of its print media licence banning the newspaper from operating inside Russia.

I promised to send the book as soon as it came out but it would help little in the Shchekochikhin case because even back in 2003, soon after Shchekochikhin died, foreign experts did not reach any definite conclusion about the cause of his demise.

We chatted and laughed, and well-trained and groomed waiters and waitresses did their job perfectly, never forgetting to take away empty glasses and cups and offer new drinks. I enjoyed my favourite cocktail and Sasha, not accustomed to such places, timidly asked Goldfarb to order him hot chocolate. Alex, who had a great advantage over Litvinenko because he spoke fluent English, was busy talking about his relative who had worked for the NKVD in Europe and the United States in the 1930s.

The relative's name was Grigory Heifetz (also sometimes transliterated as 'Kheifetz' and 'Kheifits'), widely known in professional literature as a rather successful Soviet spy handler at the time of the atomic bomb research and development that became known as the Manhattan Project.

The purpose of my visit to London, however, was not to spin old histories of Soviet spying. Since September 2004, I had been privately investigating the poisoning of Viktor Yushchenko, who had been treated in Vienna. By April, Yushchenko's personal doctor, Professor Nikolai Korpan, had collected enough evidence that his patient was deliberately poisoned and there was no doubt about who the perpetrator was. Korpan wanted to publish his findings and needed a grant to do the job because, besides his work as a practising surgeon, he was very busy doing research in hepatology and experimental cryosurgery and would have to cancel several engagements to start working on the material. I asked Goldfarb whether Berezovsky's IFCL could help. Litvinenko was very enthusiastic and immediately supported the idea. We agreed that they would have a word with Boris and let me know.

Martin, my English companion, and I saw the duo to Mount Street, from where they unhurriedly proceeded in the direction of Berezovsky's office nearby. The response never came.

According to Felshtinsky's estimates, Boris spent on the Kuchmagate about one million dollars. Was the game worth the candle?

***

Valery Okulov is a flight navigator by education. He is married to Elena Yeltsina, the elder daughter of Boris Yeltsin, the first president of Russia. The couple has four children: two daughters and two sons and, at the time of writing, several grandchildren.

It is hardly surprising that as soon as Yeltsin, the incumbent president, was elected for the second time in July 1996, his son-in-law became first deputy director general of Aeroflot, Russia's flag carrier and the largest airline. Earlier that year, in February, Berezovsky appointed his close friend Chief Commercial Officer of Aeroflot. Nikolai Glushkov took responsibility for the airline's commercial division in what concerned its overseas financial operations. According to the *Wall Street Journal*, Berezovsky owned an unknown quantity of Aeroflot stock but had reportedly held great sway over its management. Boris first hired Glushkov, a former Soviet foreign trade official, when he was establishing his first big company, LogoVAZ, where Glushkov was appointed commercial director and also took the purview of import and export contracts. For a period of time, Nikolai was

Berezovsky's closest friend and business associate; later this place was taken by Badri Patarkatsishvili. Skuratov, Prosecutor General of Russia, opened a criminal case against Glushkov and several other top managers of Aeroflot accusing them of embezzling millions of dollars from the company. In December 1999, Glushkov was arrested and spent four years in pre-trial custody, during which time Berezovsky and his lawyers did their best to get him out of jail. When Limarev came out of nowhere offering useful information, Goldfarb thought there could be a chance.

When we discussed the case in June 2022, Alex could not remember who introduced him, but in August 2002 Limarev appeared in London posing as a KGB/SVR defector now living under an assumed name in France. Goldfarb didn't pay much attention to the fact that this 'defector' was travelling with a new Russian passport issued by the Russian embassy in Geneva in May 2000.

What Goldfarb did remember was that he took Limarev to a firm of scrivener notaries where James Kerr Milligan, Notary Public, witnessed that Limarev personally signed his written testimony, doing it of his own volition. Limarev testified that in or about 1995, the SVR station in Geneva was instructed to watch Berezovsky, who was regularly visiting Switzerland. He said the SVR agents monitored Berezovsky's business and especially all deals going through his company Andava SA (established in February 1994 and registered in Lausanne at 7 Avenue de Rumine, only a short distance from Berezovsky's favourite hotel, Lausanne Palace, at Rue du Grand-Chêne). Limarev said this information was reported to Moscow and formed the basis of the so-called Aeroflot case (No. 18/277001-99) which led to the arrest of Glushkov.

Limarev also claimed that the SVR head of station in Geneva 'used to freely avail himself of Aeroflot cash for SVR business' before Glushkov was appointed. He described how one day a local Aeroflot representative, himself an SVR officer, reported to his intelligence chief that he no longer had access to the money. 'The station chief cursed Boris [Berezovsky] endlessly and said that if one of the guys took him out, he would do a great service to the Motherland,' Limarev related. He added that when Korzhakov visited, 'much of the time that they spent talking – and drinking – was devoted to the Aeroflot problem, and Boris.' General Alexander Korzhakov was Yeltsin's personal bodyguard and head of the Presidential Security Service. He was fired in June 1996.

Who was that young man who managed to so easily infiltrate the Berezovsky circle in London and to completely twist so many well-educated and professional but rather naïve people around his little finger for so long?

Evgeny ('Zhenya') Limarev was born on 19 July 1965 in the town of Frunze (now Bishkek), the capital of Kyrgyzstan, in the family of the KGB officer Lev Limarev and Maria Denisenko.

In 1974 in Morocco, where his father was stationed under diplomatic cover, Zhenya met and quickly befriended Misha, a fellow schoolboy and like himself the son of yet another KGB officer working undercover in Rabat, Vitaly Margelov. Both fathers worked out of the Soviet embassy in the capital, a city on the Atlantic coast with a municipal population of around two million people, both posing as middle-ranking Soviet diplomats. Margelov was handling agents and confidential contacts of what was known in the KGB as Line PR (political intelligence) while Limarev senior was taking care of 'illegals' as an officer of Line N. An important North African country, Morocco was of considerable interest to Soviet intelligence because a large number of Russian émigrés and so-called displaced persons moved there after the war. Besides, the anti-Soviet NTS (Narodno-Trudovoi Soyuz, for whatever reason known in English as National Alliance of Russian Solidarists) was quite active in Morocco as well as French and American intelligence services so the KGB station had their hands full with many different tasks. Their children attended the embassy school at 4 km Route de Zaiers (now Avenue Mohammed VI) in Souissi, Rabat's upscale neighbourhood, lined with splendid palm trees.

It is not surprising that when they were back in Moscow and the time came, both boys entered the Institute of Asian and African Countries (ISAA) affiliated to Moscow University. There, on Mokhovaya Street, Limarev studied Farsi while Mikhail sweated over Arabic. As mandatory part of the curriculum, both learned English and yet another language. This excellent institution near the Kremlin was under the patronage of the International Department of the Central Party Committee. The International Department controlled friendly Communist parties around the globe and decided how much to sponsor their work. And the institute was a known recruitment pool for future KGB and GRU officers.

In those days in 1988, Limarev, the son of a foreign intelligence officer, had rather limited career opportunities that largely depended on his father's position in the KGB. The young man could either enter a one-year course at the Andropov Institute to become an intelligence officer, or opt for post-graduate academic studies, or get a job as teacher or interpreter at one of the KGB institutions. Both Mikhail and Evgeny decided not to become intelligence officers. The former, due to his grandfather's and father's prominent careers within Soviet intelligence, joined the International Department as interpreter and the latter went to work in Balashikha, sixteen miles east of Moscow. It was actually not Balashikha itself, but the (in)famous Balashikha-2 where the much-feared Centre of Special Operations of the FSB is headquartered now.

From 1969 until the early 1990s, Balashikha-2 was a training base for Advanced Officers Courses (KUOS in Russian) of the KGB special forces. During a seven-month course, the students were taught the use of firearms, parachuting, mountain climbing, small-unit maritime operations, handling of explosives, topography, guerrilla warfare, and other energetic disciplines. Annually the course prepared about sixty special force commandos of the KGB to operate deep behind enemy lines. It is likely that the instructors of Balashikha-2 trained the Republican guards of Syria, Iraq and Iran, as well as other special forces units across the world. And a lot of terrorists. Limarev says that he was a language instructor there.

According to his own words, in 1990 Limarev was invited to undergo basic training as an intelligence operative at the KGB's Andropov Red Banner Institute (abbreviated as KI in Russian, former School No. 101) but, for whatever reason, probably due to *perestroika* when the future of Soviet spies became unclear, was advised not to start the course. Another reason could be that only four years earlier, in 1986, Lt. Colonel Vladimir Piguzov, the Communist Party secretary of the KI, was arrested, tried by court martial, and shot as a CIA agent because it turned out that for ten years he had been providing top-secret information about the staff and students of the Institute to his American handlers.

In 1991, a new foreign intelligence service (SVR), successor of the KGB's First Chief Directorate, was founded in Russia, and academician Yevgeny Primakov was appointed its chief. A new broom sweeps clean was not for Primakov, a veteran agent, so he made no changes in the organisation and Lev Limarev, Evgeny's father, was automatically transferred to this new service together with other officers of the former KGB's First Chief Directorate including Vitaly Margelov and those who would later be planning, supporting, and controlling the Litvinenko operation in London.

In 1991–92, Limarev junior spent about a year learning how to do international business. According to his written autobiography in the files of the Mitrokhin Commission of the Italian parliament, during this time he had regular contacts with his KGB handlers.

From 1992 until 1994 he worked as an interpreter at sugar refineries in Belgorod province. Russian media reported that during his work he had been involved in some shady deals that led to criminal prosecution, but the case never came to court. Whatever the truth, in 1995 he suddenly moved with his family to Geneva, Switzerland. In his statement under oath, Limarev claimed he had his permanent residence there between 1993 and 1999. In 1996 his father retired from the service and in December 2006 was working as an interpreter for a company located at Sheremetyevo International Airport.[3] According to all available sources, Lev Limarev had never been a general as Limarev junior asserted in a written, signed, and notarised statement at the police station of Avellino, Italy, in November 2004. I published a copy of this document in my book *The KGB's Poison Factory* (2009).

In Geneva, Limarev was busy setting up various SVR-backed trading and finance businesses, quite possibly pursuant to a secret order issued by the KGB chairman Kryuchkov in 1991. Kryuchkov, when it became clear that the old Soviet system was about to crumble, signed a secret decree authorising the KGB to create private businesses 'for the purpose of protecting state security' as well as using money from the Communist Party coffers. In 1998, Limarev junior became a vice president of the National Fund of the Stable Development of Russia (NFURR) registered in Geneva. This was almost certainly an SVR front. At the same time, in September, probably to enhance his profile and surely not without the SVR/FSB help, Limarev became an official adviser to the Communist Chairman of the State Duma Gennady Seleznev. After the CPSU was outlawed following the failed coup of August 1991, Seleznev joined the Communist Party of Russia under the old hardliner Zyuganov.

Later, when he was introduced to Mario Scaramella in an Alpine French hamlet and started collaborating with him actively, Limarev wrote in his curriculum vitae (verbatim):

> My relations with the SVR developed from its initial phase of information exchange. It became more active. My companies enjoyed the protection and support of the special services and my commercial activity was considerably integrated with SVR operations in Western Europe. I provided them with funding and carried out a large number of operative [sic] missions. The bulk of my activity for them concerned financial operations and gathering of economic and financial information regarding, mainly, Russian and CIS citizens.[4]

This looks like a confession and is a direct proof that he was informing on the Russian community in Geneva (the so-called Line EM of the SVR station). At the end of 1999, he moved to France.

As Limarev was quite proud to admit, during his sojourn in Switzerland he was personally run by Vitaly Margelov, the SVR head of station in Geneva under the guise of First Deputy Head of the Russian Mission to the UN. Vitaly Margelov was Misha's father and a fellow officer of Limarev senior. It is, however, extremely doubtful that this high-ranking diplomat and by that time SVR general would spend his time on such a small fish. More likely Limarev's handler was Colonel Vladimir Kozlov, another Asian and African specialist, who spoke French and was Margelov's deputy in charge of Line N ('illegals'). As soon as his assignment abroad ended, Kozlov was invited to the Anti-Terrorist Centre of the FSB as deputy chief of staff. Whoever was his case officer, Limarev could have met Margelov senior on several occasions because he knew his son.

Either Limarev was 'burned' or financial activities of his fund caused suspicion of the Swiss authorities (according to Limarev, his companies reached an annual turnover of US$60 million), or it was decided to give him another assignment – in or around August 2000 he suddenly moved to the small village of Cluses in France, just across the Swiss border between Geneva and Chamonix at the foot of Mont Blanc.

Having established himself in France, Limarev came to London and managed to contact Goldfarb who got quite interested in what Limarev had to say because of a pending Glushkov trial. It is possible that after Litvinenko's successful defection from Russia in 2000, Limarev was instructed to penetrate the Berezovsky entourage. He was quite successful in this mission and soon Berezovsky's Foundation for Civil Liberties gave him a grant to build and run a website named RusGlobus. The site was launched in 2002 with the help of Limarev's brother-in-law. Goldfarb planned to use this site to attract new contacts like, for example, Ramin Nagiyev, a former investigator of the Ministry of National Security of Azerbaijan who emigrated to France and was able to provide some useful information about the 1994 Baku

Metro bombings. As should have been expected, it also attracted the attention of the Russian intelligence services.

In May 2002, in what is known in the military as swarming when autonomous units attack an enemy from several different directions, yet another infiltration operation was mounted by the resourceful Moscow planners. They sent a former police officer, Oleg Sultanov, once an investigative journalist writing for *Novaya Gazeta*, to join Limarev in France pretending to work on an anti-Putin book. But when, after six months, Sultanov was invited to visit Boris's office in London, he panicked and insisted on being immediately recalled back to Moscow. There he published several anti-Berezovsky interviews portraying Limarev as the latter's chief adviser 'in charge of the propaganda operations in Western Europe'. All this seriously enhanced Limarev's status with Litvinenko and Goldfarb. Discussing his brief collaboration with Limarev with a Moscow journalist Alexander Hinstein upon his return to Moscow in December 2002, Sultanov admitted that it was a pre-planned operation and from the very beginning he acted as a 'mole' whose aim was to learn as much as possible about Berezovsky, his people and their plans.

A year later, Hinstein was elected to the State Duma and in January 2020 was appointed chairman of the Committee on Information Policy, Information Technologies and Communications. It goes without saying that he fully supported Putin's war in Ukraine. In early March 2022, soon after Russian forces crossed the border and started bombing Ukrainian cities killing women and children, Hinstein declared that the West had been engaged in unprecedented psychological warfare against Russia because, he said, 'we have too much of everything, we are too big and rich'.

In one of the interviews unrelated to Berezovsky and his people published in Moscow in April 2003, Sultanov admitted that he had been an agent of the KGB's First Chief Directorate, later SVR. He said that he also had 'an operational pseudonym known to only a few people' and that after a sudden meeting with SVR officers in Moscow who identified him by this pseudonym, he had to leave Russia and flew to Geneva.[5] Oleg Sultanov suddenly died in Moscow in December 2012.

***

At the same time as Sultanov, two more individuals moved into the sphere of Berezovsky. One was Nikita Chekulin and another known simply as 'Slava'.

Initially, I believed that perhaps Chekulin was not sent by the SVR or FSB from the very beginning. Berezovsky found him himself, I reckoned, and the Russian services used the opportunity later when Melnichenko casually pitched him in London in January 2003.

But then I thought better of it: the pattern, the goddamn pattern. As in many other cases, it was Shchekochikhin, an investigative journalist and liberal lawmaker, who incidentally brought Chekulin into Berezovsky's sight. In the autumn of 2001, Chekulin gave to the Duma deputy who was also a member of the Committee for Combating Corruption all documentary evidence of his institute's unlawful activities.

The Murder of Alexander Litvinenko: To Kill a Mockingbird

The arrival of Chekulin on 2 March was not accidental. For some time, Berezovsky, Litvinenko and Felshtinsky had been preparing a major press conference where the emphasis would be put on the FSB's role in the series of apartment-house bombings that took place in September 1999 in Moscow, Buinaksk and Volgodonsk and cost several hundred lives. The press conference was about presenting a new French documentary *Assassination of Russia* based in part on the findings from the book by Felshtinsky and Litvinenko, *The FSB Blows Up Russia* (2002). It aimed to provide an expert insight of why Putin, then the newly appointed prime minister, and the FSB, rather than Chechen terrorists, should be accused of these horrific bombings.

In 2000 Felshtinsky started researching the book on his own and when Litvinenko arrived in London in November, he joined in. Naturally, in this joint venture enterprise Felshtinsky played the leading role while Sasha made important contributions as an expert. He was convinced these terrorist acts had been orchestrated by the FSB in order to provoke the Second Chechen War. In April 2001, together with Felshtinsky, Sasha travelled to Georgia where they were supposed to meet an informant on the case. Their mission was aborted when their security was compromised and the driver was killed. In his witness statements to the Litvinenko Inquiry, Goldfarb described Sasha's role in this investigation.

Shortly after the first Russian-language edition of the book appeared, David Satter, an American journalist and scholar, wrote: 'The question of "who", however, is very significant. If, as the available evidence indicates, the bombings were carried out by the FSB, it means the present government of Russia is illegitimate. It also means that a tradition has been established in Russia that can only lead to the country's degeneration.'[6]

This is exactly what Berezovsky and his associates intended to prove. But a ten-minute version of the original fifty-two-minute-long TV documentary would not be explosive enough. They needed more facts. Thus, when Chekulin approached Pavel Voloshin, a reporter for *Novaya Gazeta* in Moscow, with his story and his documents that gave an unusual angle to the conspiracy, word reached London at once and Chekulin was invited to come to Foggy Albion, as Russians love to say, to show his evidence.

Straight from Heathrow he was chauffeured to Berezovsky. As a starter, Chekulin declared that he was a secret FSB agent recruited by Department T (Anti-Terrorist Division, where Kozlov, Limarev's handler, used to serve). Chekulin's affidavit with this statement, duly signed and notarised, is reproduced in my book *The KGB's Poison Factory* (2009). In May 2000, Chekulin was appointed acting director of the Russian Explosives Conversion Centre, a scientific research institute under the Ministry of Education. He explained and proved with documents that in 1999–2000, a large quantity of hexogen, the explosive believed to have been used in the apartment bombings, was purchased by the institute from various military units and then shipped to unknown places in various parts of the country. That was not yet a definite fingerprint, no 'gotcha, bastards', but everybody decided it was a 'go' and Berezovsky was sure he could persuade the audience of the same.

As it turned out, the press conference did not offer much that was new. Nonetheless, it was significant because it renewed discussion of an issue that had never really gone away. At the same time, a pamphlet novel by Alexander Prokhanov, a Russian nationalist, entitled *Mr Hexogen* (2002), was enjoying a wide circulation in Russia. The novel, based on information from sources in the intelligence agencies, described a conspiracy to unleash the Second Chechen War, exactly as Sasha stated.

Chekulin, who arrived in London with his 12-year-old son, was quickly accepted into Berezovsky's company of friends and associates and became a regular guest at Litvinenko's house. He was taken good care of and Berezovsky provided the newcomer with a lucrative monthly allowance. His son went to a good English school. Chekulin was helped with accommodation and everyday chores. Sasha and Marina trusted him completely and Sasha often used Chekulin as his interpreter during the meetings that he and his contacts did not consider confidential. And those meetings had absolutely nothing to do with Her Majesty's secret or security services, contrary to what Chekulin later claimed.

In his book *Bloody Oligarch and Russian Justice*, published in Moscow after his flight from London in April 2004, Chekulin names Martin Flint and calls him 'a representative of the British security service MI5'. In reality, until April 2010, Flint was one of four directors of the company Risk Analysis, a private entity, one of many in London, providing a discreet service 'of comprehensive business intelligence, investigation and security risk management services to its financial, legal and corporate clients around the world', as stated in the company brochure. At one point, Berezovsky used the services of Risk Analysis. When Litvinenko was granted political asylum in May 2001, George Menzies, the solicitor, introduced Sasha to Flint with the hope that Litvinenko's knowledge of Russia and Sasha's contacts in Moscow and elsewhere could help him (Litvinenko) to get consultancy commissions.

***

In early spring 2002, another Russian appeared in London who had been known to Berezovsky and Goldfarb as 'Slava Petrov'. In Russian, this is a kind of a placeholder name similar to the British 'John Smith', American 'John Doe', or 'Juan Perez' in the Spanish-speaking world. His real name was Vyacheslav Zharko and he said he was unemployed and needed money. This was, of course, almost a universal refrain used by people seeking Boris's help.

But a man from the street would not be able to approach the former oligarch and Zharko was no ordinary beggar. According to Goldfarb, he had served in special forces and later worked in the tax police directorate of St Petersburg, where he had spent seven years heading an investigation team and was promoted to major.

The Murder of Alexander Litvinenko: To Kill a Mockingbird

This is what Yuri Shchekochikhin, an MP and Politkovskaya's boss in *Novaya Gazeta*, wrote to Putin exactly one month before Zharko suddenly appeared in London:

> [In 1999] a young inspector of the tax police of St Petersburg, Vyacheslav Zharko, gave me some documents that proved that some ships had been regularly entering the harbours of the Russian Navy, Lebyazhy and Lomonosovo, without any border control or customs clearance. On the documents authorising such unlawful actions were several signatures, among them one of the then vice-premier [Oleg] Soskovets and one of yourself, Vladimir Vladimirovich...

Shchekochikhin, however, did not plan to discuss that old case with Putin. It turned out that his informer Zharko, who by this time had been transferred to the GRU Moscow headquarters, was detained at Sheremetyevo airport in December 2001 and charged with possessing a forged passport and illegal crossing of the state border. According to Shchekochikhin, Zharko was arrested and put in Lefortovo prison on the orders of the deputy general prosecutor of Russia, which was far too much, bearing in mind his alleged crimes. 'During his time in Lefortovo,' the journalist wrote, 'the FSB interrogators did their best trying to find out whether Zharko still had documents with your signature that had anything to do with those shipments. What especially astonished me was the fact that they were seeking his confession that he, Zharko, and myself continued to keep in touch with Berezovsky [in London].'[7]

During our long breakfast at the Hilton, among other things I asked Alex about Zharko. Goldfarb said he had seen Slava in Berezovsky's jet when they were visiting Karachay-Cherkessia, a republic and an electoral district in the north Caucasus that elected Berezovsky as their independent MP in 1999. Slava was a good guy, women liked him, Alex said, and he liked the former Spetsnaz man. At that time, people like Zharko and a former bodyguard Lugovoy as well as Litvinenko himself were part of the oligarch's protection and security team, often moonlighting for him while still employed by the government.

Both Zharko and Lugovoy were detained in 2001 but soon released. Russian prisons (for people sentenced or on remand) are places where no person in his right mind would think of spending even an hour, so they are generally considered to be ideal venues for KGB recruitment, especially regarding those who themselves were part of the *systema*. These former officers do not actually need to be recruited as they are in the reserve anyway. What is asked for first of all is repentance for keeping company with such 'enemies' as the former oligarch who had left Russia. Then an agreement that they will provide information on other 'enemies of the state' like Shchekochikhin, Patarkatsishvili, or Glushkov. And indeed, Zharko was close to Shchekochikhin up to the latter's tragic death in Moscow in 2003 and Lugovoy remained among those few whom the Georgian billionaire trusted, even after the Litvinenko operation, until Badri's last day in London in February 2008.

Unfortunately, all four (Berezovsky, Patarkatsishvili, Glushkov, and Shchekochikhin) had at least one dangerous feature in common: their assessment of people close to them was often wrong. Hence, none of them have survived. And while some British judicial officials may have expressed some doubts about the cause of death of the two oligarchs (unlike other ultra-high-net-worth individuals from Russia, Boris and Badri were true oligarchs), Glushkov and Shchekochikhin were quite definitely murdered.

A month before Zharko arrived in London to meet Berezovsky, Limarev started collaborating with Shchekochikhin, who came to visit him in France. For the MP, it was the project called 'Patriots of the GeBe' (mocking KGB, pronounced ke-ge-be in Russian), which he hoped to develop with Limarev's help. Limarev, using his website which pretended to be critical to the Putin's regime and his good contacts with people close to Berezovsky as proof of his trustworthiness, could not miss an opportunity to get as much out of Shchekochikhin as possible regarding his plans to reveal financial crimes of the FSB mandarins. As further developments proved, it was extremely important for Moscow generals to keep a constant watchful eye on the newspaper reporter turned legislator.

It is known that Limarev handed Shchekochikhin over to the Italian journalists Carlo Bonini and Giuseppe D'Avanzo of *La Repubblica*. Limarev had collaborated with this newspaper since 2000. It was *La Repubblica* that later published his 'revelations' directed against Litvinenko and Scaramella that were so useful to the Kremlin's propaganda campaign.

Zharko arrived in London shortly before the official release of a documentary *The Assassination of Russia* (director Jean-Charles Deniau, producer Charles Gazelle, 2002), on which Litvinenko and Felshtinsky acted as creative consultants. The screening of the film was arranged at RUSI on 5 March and the night before Felshtinsky spent several hours talking to Zharko whom he, like others, only knew as 'Slava Petrov' both in Moscow, where they occasionally met, and in London. Zharko was telling him stories about his military service in Venezuela with the GRU Spetsnaz and how devoted he was to Badri, even calling himself 'one of Badri's legionnaires'.

When Sasha met Zharko in London, his vigilance failed again. He was happy to have a secret service veteran, like himself or Melnichenko, as a friend and co-worker and immediately decided to do him a favour by introducing him to Martin Flint. The director of Risk Analysis did not forget Sasha's help in the liberation of Peter Shaw and gave Zharko a simple and routine assignment to collect some background information on a Russian telecoms company.

Such requests are common because foreign investors have been extremely careful when entering the Russian market, especially in the sensitive telecommunications industry which has been beset by scandals connected with major Russian telecoms ventures. All this activity stopped when Russia attacked Ukraine. In June 2022, leading newspapers announced that the British telecoms group Truphone, owned by Roman Abramovich and his business partners, was being bought for £1 by two European tech entrepreneurs.

It was obvious that Zharko was not able to deliver anything useful to Risk Analysis. According to his own words, he collected all his information from the internet. But, he said, the report was accepted and he was paid well. The Russian provocateur could not know that a similar assignment is usually given to several subs and that the company itself makes meticulous research from all public and quite often no-so-public sources in many languages so they knew perfectly well what his report was worth. But because Martin was so grateful to Sasha for his help, he let it go. Anyway, Zharko did not stay in London and returned to Russia.

According to Zharko, in April 2003, during one of his regular visits to the British capital, Litvinenko introduced him to 'Paul' and 'John', both Russian speakers and both, as he later said, from MI6. Because Sasha introduced Zharko as a GRU officer, they asked him whether he would be happy to help Her Majesty's Secret Service, to which Zharko habitually responded that for money he would do anything. 'Paul' and 'John' explained that because the Intelligence Services Act directs SIS to operate overseas, they would not meet in London but rather in some places abroad where the Russian could travel without any visa. The most convenient destination was Turkey, which invited all Russian tourists to spend holidays in the country visa-free, and thus the next meeting was arranged in Istanbul where 'John' arrived with Sasha. In the meantime, Slava's British visa was cancelled, as he later claimed.

'I needed money so when Litvinenko told me that I could earn easy cash by collaborating with British intelligence, I agreed,' Zharko, then 36, told Mark Franchetti of *The Sunday Times* in his first interview with a British newspaper in July 2007. Zharko also said that later he met his British handlers regularly in Turkey, Finland, and Cyprus and supplied them with analytical reports on Russia's economy and politics. Throughout the whole year of the presidential election in Ukraine, he said, they were also interested in an insider's view on the situation and he travelled to Kiev to get a first-hand impression of what was going on. In return, Zharko claimed, he was paid altogether about £60,000. Zharko said he turned himself in to the FSB at the end of June 2007, shortly after his last meeting with his British handlers in Turkey, and confessed to having worked for British intelligence for five years since 2002. The FSB reported that they identified 'Paul' as Pablo Miller and 'John' as John O'Callaghan. In 2004, according to the report, an official from the British Consulate General in Istanbul who introduced himself as 'Ken' was also present at their meetings. The FSB identified him as Quentin Phillips.[8] At one moment in 2003, 'Martin', who had served in Moscow and Vienna, substituted John as Zharko's case officer.

It is highly unlikely that Zharko, a former member of Spetsnaz, tax police major and GRU officer was acting on his own initiative. There is every reason to believe that he was instructed to infiltrate the Berezovsky camp in London as part of a wide-scale intelligence operation. Right up to his death, Litvinenko never learned the true role of his 'trusted friend Slava', which is known as a 'dangle' in the parlance of human intelligence. And that of his other 'good friends'.

***

In January 2003, Mykola Melnichenko was flying back to Washington and Chekulin was seeing him off to the airport. Two years earlier Mykola, who was part of President Kuchma's security detail for six years, had obtained political asylum in the US. 'Justice Department lawyers and officials of the Federal Bureau of Investigation have listened to some of the tapes and questioned Mr Melnichenko several times to determine whether charges are justified against other people from Ukraine,' Steve LeVine wrote in the WSJ. 'The figures under examination include current and former senior Ukraine state officials and their associates.'

On the way to Heathrow, the former KGB-SBU officer and presidential bodyguard explained to Chekulin that the latter's future with Berezovsky might be at risk because sooner or later the Russians would find a way to silence the tycoon. Mykola-the-tape-recorder suggested a simple way for Chekulin to bargain for immunity from prosecution in Russia. Buy a recording device, he said, and record all conversations with Berezovsky and his people as well as anything that could be of any use for the FSB. Of special value would be all Litvinenko's contacts and virtually anything to do with Berezovsky: his secretariate, friends and business associates, his tastes, his women, his security detail, in short, everything. Chekulin thought it over and soon acquired a light and compact digital voice recorder (using funds from Berezovsky's Foundation for Civil Liberties) with which he had made, as he later claimed, a hundred hours of secret recordings.

Chekulin even used some sort of trick in order not to be caught with a recorder switched on in his trouser pocket. Whenever he was invited to business meetings and picnics, Chekulin took his son, asking him to bring in a small bag where he had hidden the recorder in advance. The boy would not be searched, he reckoned. The trick worked flawlessly.

The spring months of 2003 were quite stressful for the tycoon. The previous August, Russian prosecutors opened a criminal case against Berezovsky and his two associates. In October, Russian prosecutors sent an extradition request. Boris was almost certain that the home secretary was not going to extradite him but at the end of March he and Yuli Dubov, his business partner and friend, a co-director and former chief executive of the LogoVAZ car company, were arrested and transported to the police station. They were each remanded on £100,000 bail and the episode left an unpleasant feeling for quite a while.

On 2 April, they were both giving a press conference in Le Meridien Hotel on Piccadilly after preliminary hearings at Bow Street Magistrates' Court, when a tall man approached Chekulin and started a conversation. The stranger's name was Vladimir Terlyuk.

***

Terlyuk is a mysterious figure. According to several published sources, he was allegedly born in Karaganda, Kazakhstan, on 8 April 1957, and resided in Velika Dimerka in the Kiev region of Ukraine on Gogolivska Street. Interestingly, even all-seeing and all-knowing Russian journalists in the country where virtually any information could be bought for a dime were unable to dig up anything on him. It was claimed that in May 2000 he applied for permission to travel abroad, received a Kazakh passport, and left for Germany.

This total lack of information on Terlyuk's almost five decades spent in the former Soviet Union and then Russia presents reasonable grounds for suspicion and speculation. In April 2018, two journalists from the BBC Russian Service entitled their article about him: '[Leonid] Brezhnev's driver, KGB agent, a victim of Berezovsky: who really is Vladimir Terlyuk?' And the continuous support by the Russian authorities of this stateless individual (whose name is often erroneously spelt as 'Terluk' in the official documents) certainly gives food for thought. The latest recorded move in his favour was an official statement by the Russian embassy in the USA dated 14 April 2018, which is another piece of supporting evidence of the Kremlin's unprecedented interest in asserting their version of events involving this man.

Vladimir Terlyuk was born on 4 October 1951 in a place called Duskaniya in Magadan Oblast of the Russian Far East. He arrived in the UK with his wife and son on 15 February 1999 and claimed political asylum. I can't imagine him being an agent of any sort. He simply doesn't fit the pattern. He is tall, attracts attention in the crowd, eagerly poses for the camera, and speaks poor English.

I met Terlyuk at a seminar at the London University of Westminster in February 2007 that it was seemingly not his business to attend and he uttered no sound as he towered in the front row as a silent and indifferent observer. An hour earlier, he invited Martin Dewhurst – a Russian speaker who often served as Sasha's interpreter during public events – to a café in Victoria Station, trying to persuade him that all that he had been saying to the media recently was nothing but the truth. And that Berezovsky had indeed offered him first 8 million and then 40 million dollars for supporting the story invented by Litvinenko. But he refused. It was a matter of principle for him, Terlyuk said, to never lie. He had been trying to impose this nonsense on poor Martin for three-quarters of an hour until they both had to go to the seminar.

Terlyuk approached Chekulin for the first time on 2 April 2003 when Berezovsky and his entourage were leaving Bow Street Magistrates' Court. He had already been noticed stalking the former oligarch at the London Economic Forum, where his presence could also not be explained.

Thus, when spotted again talking to Chekulin, a call was immediately placed to find out who he was. Terlyuk introduced himself as 'Vladimir Ivanovich' and said that he had been living in England for four years. He claimed his only reason for seeking Berezovsky's company was to do business with the billionaire.

As soon as he was told about Terlyuk, Litvinenko immediately suspected him of being a Russian agent – looking, speaking, and behaving like one, he said.

Perhaps Sasha knew better. There is something in the tradecraft called a 'passive probe' when someone, not necessarily a fully-fledged agent, is sent on an intelligence mission just to observe passively and record details about the target location or organisation. In Russia, they even made a movie about such people, calling them 'dilettantes', claiming that they can be extremely useful in intelligence work because they behave naturally not knowing the tricks of the trade, and therefore nobody suspects them. However, several Russian newspapers stated that Terlyuk had been recruited in the late 1970s when he worked in the special garage belonging to the 9th Directorate of the KGB (later FSO, Federal Protective Service). Of course, no proof had been offered.

Credit should be given to Berezovsky's security detail for spotting him. Amazingly, even after he had been quickly uncovered, Terlyuk sought to contact people close to Berezovsky. He attended all court hearings in 2003 before Boris was granted political asylum in Britain. He was omnipresent.

Chekulin, the first man he decided to approach, returned to Russia in April 2004 and after an obligatory repentance started actively collaborating with the FSB and the prosecutors. He then began accusing Berezovsky and all those who helped him in London of every possible sin. These included a cynical and impudent claim that Marina Litvinenko was involved in her husband's death and probably poisoned him herself. Chekulin also started to write books that were promptly published and widely promoted. Interviews were arranged with the author, who was placed on the 'protected witness programme' in Russia.

In his writings and public statements, Chekulin repeated the same old story that Berezovsky had allegedly offered Terlyuk millions in cash for a false testimony and that Litvinenko had drugged the poor man and then video-recorded him confessing that he had been dispatched by the FSB to kill Berezovsky. A video, he claimed, that influenced the decision to recognise Berezovsky as a political refugee and grant him an asylum in Great Britain.

Fifteen years after those events and more than a decade after the death of Sasha Litvinenko, in April 2018, the Russian embassy in the USA was instructed to make an official statement. As usual, the business at hand was murder.

CHAPTER 5

The Frenzied World of Private Spying

In Britain and the USA this is usually referred to as the private investigations business. Barry Meier, an award-winning journalist and writer, in his new book suggests that it is composed of 'a scattershot mix of people, drawn to the work by money, the opportunity for travel and adventure, and the heady rush of power that comes from spying on the lives of others'. Maybe he knows better. Some managers or employees of such companies, he writes, 'are ex-government spooks or retired investigators with the FBI or other law enforcement agencies, looking to extend their careers by selling private clients the skills they had acquired while serving the public. The business also attracts former prosecutors and attorneys who aren't interested in working within the confines of traditional law firms.' Indeed, on the staff of such companies are often former officers of intelligence or security services, Scotland Yard, the British or US Army, and people from banks and law firms. They also employ a considerable number of journalists and even academics. People of very different backgrounds are invited to join such businesses for obvious reasons but there is one thing these private companies never do. They never take the place of the secret services who work for the government.

As already mentioned, in one of his books published after he beat a hasty retreat to Moscow, Chekulin described Martin Flint as 'a representative of the British security service MI5'. As a matter of fact, he was not. Mr Flint had served as director of Risk Analysis (UK) Limited between September 1998 and March 2010. The company brochure stated that he, like many other private investigators, had extensive experience as a security consultant in the fields of corporate fraud investigation, asset tracing and recovery, investigation and litigation support, and due diligence enquiries. Although he had indeed spent twenty years working for the British Security Service, that was long ago, following ten years in the petrochemicals industry.

When George Menzies, the solicitor, introduced Sasha to Mr Flint, then one of the directors of Risk Analysis, he hoped that Litvinenko's knowledge of Russia and his contacts in Moscow and Tbilisi could help him to obtain consultancy commissions. Unfortunately, Sasha could provide only limited help to such companies because he lacked the necessary command of English and other special skills and knowledge that this work demands.

> Corporate investigative firms [Barry Meier explains], like most businesses, have hierarchies. There are the owners and bigger firms

often have a board of directors or advisors ... Senior investigators who oversee cases and interact with clients are often called managing directors to lend them a corporate air and regular investigators work under them. (People in the investigations industry don't like the term 'operative' because they feel it has negative connotations.) On the next rung down are researchers, who are known as analysts, and they dig out information from public filings, databases, and other records. At the bottom of the heap are freelance spies, or so-called contractors (who are also sometimes referred to as subcontractors or subs).[1]

It is usual for such firms to hire contractors or subcontractors on a temporary basis for specific assignments or even sometimes to employ people for some lucrative long-time projects. Alas, in spite of Litvinenko's excellent qualifications as a seasoned investigator in Russia, in such countries as Britain he could not be contracted even as a sub. However, the situation changed when on 18 June 2002 a British banker named Peter Shaw, when leaving his home in Tbilisi, Georgia, was bundled away from his car by a gang posing as police.

The British government applied great pressure but after two months Shaw was still not found. The Georgian authorities said seven men had been held in connection with the abduction, but no charges were laid against them so far while the banker remained in custody of the bandits. On 21 August, Martin Flint asked Berezovsky whether he could help in Shaw's case and Boris promised to use his contacts in Tbilisi to do whatever was possible. Without doubt Badri Patarkatsishvili, who by that time had moved to Georgia and was one of the richest and most influential persons in this former Soviet republic with a small army as his private security service, could do a lot.

A week later, Martin Flint and George Menzies met Litvinenko and Chekulin, who acted as interpreter, to discuss the situation. This was Litvinenko's turf. He was very familiar with the area, and investigating such crimes on the territory of what was formerly the Soviet Union was exactly the job that he loved and could do very well. Of course, from overseas, without seeing the crime scene and all the evidence, it was impossible to investigate properly, but Sasha offered his best advice.

It was considered valuable enough for Litvinenko to be put in touch after some time with David Douglas who headed the Hostage and Crisis Negotiation Unit at New Scotland Yard. (At the time of writing, David served as a director of TeamFusion, a London-based global security company. According to his company profile, the Foreign Office deployed David on its most challenging kidnap and extortion cases worldwide, from Azerbaijan to Sierra Leone and from Bangladesh and Iraq to the Yemen. Among other important assignments, David headed up the investigation into conspiracy theories surrounding the death in Paris of Diana, Princess of Wales.)

Sasha tried to be as useful as he could.

By October, Peter Shaw had still not been found and many people came to be involved in the rescue operation including Peter Hain (later Baron Hain), then minister of state at the Foreign and Commonwealth Office, who was undertaking diplomatic moves to secure the businessman's release.

During that month Litvinenko, again taking Chekulin along as a helping hand, met Flint in the lobby of the Park Lane Sheraton Hotel in Piccadilly to discuss all possible leads and suggest measures including his own trip to Georgia as by this time it was suspected (correctly) that the 57-year-old banker was being kept captive in the remote Pankisi Gorge area. The same place, the Sheraton lobby, would be later chosen by Lugovoy's handlers for a prearranged meeting with Litvinenko shortly before he was poisoned. Coincidence? Maybe.

On 6 November, Georgian television beamed the news that their special forces had successfully released Shaw following a complex police operation. Next day, the happy banker was already in London, tired and gaunt and dishevelled after 141 days in captivity. He told a news conference at the airport how he had feared that his kidnappers – who had demanded a ransom of $2m – were taking him out to be shot. He said he dived into a bush to escape and one of the kidnappers was shot by mistake instead. Shaw described his escape as a miracle and said he could not wait to get home to Wales, the BBC reported.

Martin Flint invited Litvinenko and Chekulin for lunch and was happy to hand over a letter addressed to Berezovsky expressing gratitude for whatever help he had provided to secure a successful outcome. Later, the Kremlin propaganda machine, based on Chekulin's 'revelations', would use this episode as one of the proofs that Berezovsky and Litvinenko were British agents.

In the meantime, a real British agent or rather a civil servant, 'a person in government', as he is described in the inquiry documents, materialised out of thin air. Chekulin never met him and knew nothing about him. When yet another independent business intelligence company appeared in London's frenzied market for private spying incorporated on 15 July 2004, its new director Dean Martin Attew received a discreet phone call inviting him for a business lunch. During a chat over a meal, it was explained to Mr Attew that Alex (whom he would later know as Sasha Litvinenko) had come from Russia and the government were helping him to integrate into the UK in view of settling Alex into British life. This was to ensure, he was told, that Alex had a commercial capability to become financially independent.

Titon International was established by two co-founders, John Holmes, ex-SAS, and Dean Attew, ex-investigator at Bernard Charles 'Bernie' Ecclestone's Formula One Management. Prior to Formula One, Attew was employed 'within the commercial security industry both in Britain and overseas', as he described it. The company was incorporated in July 2004 and both John Holmes and Dean Attew became its directors. Dean resigned in November 2011.

Major General John Taylor Holmes was a former commanding officer of the active service 22 SAS (as opposed to the part-time 23 SAS) and between 1999 and 2001 was Director Special Forces. The DSF comes under the Director of Military Operations who reports to the Chief of General Staff. Although members of the SIS and SAS have much in common, these are different organisations.

Titon International (now in Leominster, Herefordshire) was a subsidiary of Erinys International, a British private security company registered in the British Virgin Islands and headquartered in Dubai. It has branches and offices in different countries and one of them is Erinys (UK) Ltd, incorporated five days later than Titon, with General Holmes also serving as its director. Both companies had the same address at 25 Grosvenor Street in Mayfair with the offices on the fourth floor sharing a receptionist. Like its parent company, Erinys (UK), dissolved in July 2019, specialised in providing security guards in conflict zones including armed personnel and, specifically, physical security services to the oil industry.

Over the next three months Dean Attew, whose only second-in-command was a young IT guy called Danny, had three meetings with Litvinenko. 'It was too early,' he says, 'to know whether Sasha had any commercial value or could indeed be capable of working in the UK security arena.' It was therefore agreed that Litvinenko should first of all study English and familiarise himself with the specifics of the trade.

***

After his first reconnaissance visit to London in October 2004, where he met both Berezovsky and Litvinenko, Lugovoy was back in Moscow finding himself a modest job in the private company Lentus LLP, specialising in the production and installation of acrylic coatings for tennis courts. Very soon, however, he moved to the now-bankrupt Moscow commercial bank Metropol as head of security. This bank's former owner was shot dead by two FSB Alpha assassins. It was not a government assignment: the officers were off duty, acting as part of a large criminal gang.

How and when Lugovoy suddenly became a successful businessman remains a mystery. There were rumours actively supported by the Russian and friendly Western media that he had been involved in or even co-owned the company with a strange name 'Eugene Boujele Vine', also transcribed as 'Ejen Bujole Vain'. These are Russian transliterations of the French-English name in Latin characters – it should actually be Eugène Beaujolais Wine. The company, which produced popular Russian kvass of Pershin brand alongside other traditional beverages, filed for bankruptcy in 2009, while its two official shareholders were Irina Pershina and Principia Limited from British Virgin Islands. Irina is the wife of Eugene Pershin, who was reported to have been the real owner of the company. After changing owners several times, it was finally liquidated in June 2022. Other businesses erroneously or falsely attributed to Lugovoy were security companies 'Ninth Wave' and 'Capital-Shield'. Together with him, they also figure as minor shareholders of this 'Vine' company in the fake document (see INQ019377) given to the British authorities.

Questioned in Moscow, Lugovoy stated he was associated with three entities. In the company Eugène Beaujolais Wine, he said he acted as a member of the board of directors. The same position, according to his testimony, he had in Glavlizing, a leasing company providing physical assets like passenger and light or heavy-duty vehicles, equipment, and services for use by commercial clients or individuals exclusively on the Russian territory. Asked about his duties, Lugovoy said he was 'taking part in the meetings where strategic ways of developing those companies are determined'. But practically, he said, 'I am responsible for bringing into those companies foreign investment.' The third entity mentioned by Lugovoy was the commercial Metropol Bank, a limited liability company where he was 'advisor to the president' with his role limited to 'economic security', whatever that was supposed to mean. This bank's licence was revoked by the Central Bank of Russia in November 2016.

A simple due diligence report on Eugene Pershin will uncover a lot of interesting facts but suffice it to say that in April 2006 he founded a company named GazEnergoService, of which he had been a sole owner for seven years. The company quickly became one of the subcontractors of Gazprom, with multi-billion construction contracts. No wonder the kvass factory was quickly forgotten.

Whatever the story (Lugovoy was allegedly arrested for his role in the Glushkov escape affair, tried, and sentenced to one year and two months in March 2004, never serving time in jail, as had been claimed),[2] in the summer of 2004 he invited Glushkov to his impressive country house to celebrate. Glushkov later noted that Lugovoy would not be able to buy such a house and would not have money to invest in Boujele Vine. But he would be extremely well suited to penetrate the close circle of Berezovsky's friends and associates. And there were signs that he would perform well.

In the first half of 2005, Lugovoy was again in London. This time, he was invited by Boris and Badri and all three of them arrived in Israel to open a local representative office in Tel Aviv.

Since February 2005, Berezovsky's most trusted contact there was a young man named Misha Kotlik (aka Michael Cotlick), now a private wealth lawyer in London and a partner in a solid law firm with offices in Jermyn Street. Michael was born in Russia, where he lived until he moved to Israel in 1994. He was educated at the Hebrew University of Jerusalem, received his law degree in 1999, and since then had been serving as an advocate with the Israel Defence Forces (IDF) until Berezovsky picked him up. Initially Misha worked for the tycoon in Israel, running various errands for Boris and also travelling abroad as far as South Africa and Latin America. During that meeting in Israel in 2005, Lugovoy was introduced to Misha as Berezovsky's head of security. It seems that Litvinenko was not aware of that visit and it is hard to image what Boris and Badri needed Lugovoy for in Israel, where Michael was taking care of every little thing including security arrangements.

Sasha called Dean Attew again in mid-2005 and for the next few months, their meetings were mainly to improve Sasha's English skills and develop a requirement for him to work for the company. Later, their meetings would become much more regular and in a period of six months, that is, until their last short business meeting on 1 November 2006, Mr Attew met with Sasha about thirty to fifty times. During that period, he was tasking Litvinenko to provide different due diligence and risk assessment reports for the company's clients. He also learned that his new Russian friend was attending an English language school in Oxford Street.

Lugovoy telephoned Litvinenko from Moscow to arrange another meeting in November 2005. He arrived in the British capital later that month on a multiple-entry visa and Litvinenko immediately took him to RISC Management for a meeting with Garym Evans. Nine years later, Mr Evans could only vaguely remember the details of that meeting, only saying that during his work at RISC, he had met Litvinenko seven or eight times.[3]

***

It was Berezovsky who introduced Litvinenko to Keith Hunter – an appropriate name for the chief executive of a business intelligence company – who was the CEO of RISC Management Limited at the time when Litvinenko began working for them. After three years in London, both Sasha's mentors Berezovsky and Goldfarb strongly advised him to start earning money independently by getting a job. Say, as a subcontractor or even better an intern in one of the many private investigation companies. There are many of them in the British capital, they said. There's a sort of common wisdom that investigative firms sometimes serve as homes to misfits, oddballs, wannabes, and the occasional sociopath; at the same time it is also widely understood that private spies may have a considerable impact on politics, business, and even personal lives of some people. Berezovsky, without doubt, would be interested to have his man in one such firm.

As a former senior FSB officer and a friend of Boris, Sasha could not but realise that he was not sufficiently qualified to serve as Berezovsky's counterintelligence chief. Not that the tycoon was contemplating hiring someone for this job. But Sasha knew that when his patron needed information that was not easily available from public sources, he retained the services of Risk Analysis, RISC Management, and other similar firms. Also, some ultra-net worth Russian individuals living in London and Moscow like, for example, Oleg Deripaska, a man close to Putin, are known as power users of corporate investigative firms while their wives and mistresses often require the services of a troubleshooter, a reliable person who could solve problems for them and their children. Like in the Russian TV series *Londongrad* (2015), which came out long after Sasha's demise.

After eleven years with the Russian security service and some initial experience of collaboration with MI6, Litvinenko had reason to think that he might at least be useful to any of London's corporate investigative firms by collecting for them information from Russia. He could hardly do it himself but cherished great expectations for his newly formed friendships with Andrei Lugovoy and Vyacheslav Zharko, both of whom he saw as his possible intelligence sources in Russia. He was also in regular contact with Limarev, a self-employed consultant in France, though personally he had a low opinion of Limarev's skills and possibilities.

The Murder of Alexander Litvinenko: To Kill a Mockingbird

Keith Hunter's initial career in the Metropolitan Police Service involved investigating serious and organised crime on a national and international level while based at New Scotland Yard and the then Regional Crime Squad. He subsequently ventured into the private sector and successfully established a company specialising in corporate investigations for law firms, media, and medium- to large-size companies. RISC was a successor of ISC Global, a company established by Stephen Curtis and Nigel Brown, another former police officer, in 2000.

Curtis was a lawyer whose net worth clients in Russia included Boris Berezovsky, Mikhail Khodorkovsky, the CEO of the Yukos Oil Company, one of the world's largest private oil companies, and Vladimir Gusinsky, the owner of Media-Most, the largest media holding in Russia. Curtis died in a helicopter crash close to his palatial home in Dorset in March 2004 – a fortnight after he had gone to Scotland Yard saying that he had received death threats and feared that a hit team had been sent from Moscow to assassinate him. A Sky documentary *Once Upon a Time in Londongrad* (2022) is to a large extent devoted to investigating his story. 'If something untoward happens to me,' Curtis is reported to have said, 'it will not be an accident.'

Curtis introduced his Russian clients to ISC and after his death the company's business was split between Brown, who went to work in Israel, and Hunter, who rebranded London's ISC into RISC Management Limited. According to Hunter's witness statement, RISC Global was an anti-money laundering investigation company which at the end of 2005 was operated by the then managing and operation director Clifford 'Cliff' Knuckey, a Metropolitan Police veteran. Global was absorbed into RISC Management in the beginning of 2006 and Keith was appointed its CEO and Knuckey became the company's MD.

RISC Management offered a diverse range of services including security risk management, corporate investigations and litigation support, business intelligence, personal and corporate due diligence, and a lot of other professional services including whistle-blowing management. In April 2006, Lugovoy was again in London – one of a dozen visits over the course of a year. Accompanied by a female interpreter, to the best of my knowledge unidentified, they went to a meeting with some new managers of RISC Management which he visited with Litvinenko for the first time in November 2005. Now Lugovoy said he had some first-class material to offer, so they took a lift to the fifth floor and were soon escorted to the boardroom of RISC at the company's premises at 1 Cavendish Place in Marylebone.

Litvinenko had been here before. Soon after he settled in London, Berezovsky introduced him to Keith Hunter, speaking very highly of Sasha's investigative skills. Then he visited the company again when it became obvious that two Chechens had been attempting to extort money from Berezovsky, as a result of which the houses of Zakayev and Litvinenko, who both lived in Muswell Hill, were firebombed in October 2004. In July 2005, it was decided to use Sasha as a source and Knuckey, who first met Litvinenko during those tumultuous days of 2004, introduced Sasha to his first case manager at ISC Global. As already mentioned, the manager's name was Garym Evans and his job title was director of investigations.

Before getting involved in the commercial security business, Mr Evans had worked for the Metropolitan Police for about two decades, reaching the rank of detective constable before he left the Met in 1999 joining ISC Global two years later. When Litvinenko started working for them, the company employed about twenty free earners and support staff and was managed by Keith Hunter, Cliff Knuckey and Tony Brightwell.

In February 2006, Garym Evans moved to Fidelity Investments as head of fraud prevention and investigations. During that period, Evans and Litvinenko met seven or eight times but never for business because Sasha was unable to do even routine searches and compile reports in English. Before leaving the company, Evans introduced Sasha to his new case manager, Daniel Quirke, a former customs officer turned financial investigator. It was a brief meeting and they arranged how they would contact each other in the future. Daniel knew that the company was looking to build a working relationship with Berezovsky's lieutenant but was unaware whether Garym Evans paid anything to Litvinenko in 2005.

At that meeting in April 2006, both Cliff Knuckey and Dan Quirke were present in the boardroom. Litvinenko introduced his companion as Andrey, an associate of his from Moscow. Sasha said he had known him for a long time and that Andrey had a similar background as himself. He added he had worked with Andrey before and trusted him and that Andrey brought information that Sasha had been tasked to obtain.

The report they handed over was a document, as Mr Quirke recalled later, detailing the current structure, personnel, and organisation of several 'Russian organisations mainly concentrating on the FSB'.[4] It is hard to say what the two British investigators or their other colleagues might have needed this information for but they immediately realised that the report, which was in Russian, was not up to the standard they expected, as the information appeared to have been culled from Russian internet sites. Nevertheless, Lugovoy wanted 10,000 US dollars for his work – an incredibly high price – and Knuckey agreed to pay $7,500, just to secure further collaboration and, as he put it, in recognition of some other work Litvinenko had done for the company before. The money was transferred to Lugovoy's bank account in Cyprus shortly after the meeting and the document was destroyed because it was of no further use.

Ah, yes, note must be made of the first oddity of this strange April day, to paraphrase the great writer. Apart from Cliff Knuckey, Dan Quirke, Lugovoy, Litvinenko, and the interpreter, there was also another man present who was remembered, strange though it may seem, by only one person. Mr Knuckey later described him as 'a male aged mid-to-late 30s, dark hair, medium built and was similarly casually dressed as was Lugovoy on this day. I had not seen this other male before the meeting and I have not seen him since.'[5] There is little doubt that this was none other than Vladimir Valuyev, the fourth member of the team and the father of Alexey Valuyev. It was his second visit to London that year, although his son said he had only visited once. Then, in late February or early March, as Alexey said, he stayed at the Holiday Inn near Oxford Circus together with Lugovoy.

Litvinenko never mentioned Valuyev whom he had met for the first and last time at the office of RISC.

This second visit of Lugovoy and Valuyev was shortly before Easter, which in 2006 fell on 16 April. Lugovoy would remember it thanks to a little amorous adventure. During his previous stay London together with Vladimir, Lugovoy decided they should go to Soho. There, they dropped at a small bar fairly late, about midnight. At a table near the door were two girls drinking tequila and Scotch. After a while, the boys joined them, having introduced themselves as Andre and Vlad, while the girls were Briony, a medical doctor from Australia, and her friend Tara. Together, they spent about three hours in this bar, talking and drinking. Vlad said his son lived in London and he was visiting him while Andre explained he was a businessman travelling a lot around the world. When the bar was closing and they were leaving, Tara handed over to Andre her friend's private email address.

During the next few weeks, Andre (Lugovoy) sent her a few innocent emails saying he was travelling as usual but was planning to come to London soon. Indeed, he called just before Easter to say he was in London again and invited Briony for a dinner date. Soon she was in Knightsbridge and they settled in a fine seafood restaurant right in his hotel. It was a wonderful evening, they drank champagne, wine, and Scotch, and after dinner Andre ordered a cigar. Then they went to the hotel bar for another drink. In the morning, she left his room at about half past nine and took a cab because it was high time to be at her work at the Wellington Hospital. Briony later explained she felt wary about meeting up with Andre again. 'I had made up my mind I would not see him again and I have not since the meeting in the hotel,' she said.

Turning back to the meeting at RISC, Dan Quirke did not have the slightest trace of this third person in his memory but he recalled that at the end of the meeting and without Lugovoy's involvement, Litvinenko handed him a large CD-ROM disk with Cyrillic handwriting. Sasha said it was information just from him. The disk contained some business intelligence on the oil industry. Because Sasha stated it was very sensitive, it was given to a secure translator called Patrick Jost who was an associate of RISC. He assessed the information on the disk, explaining in his report that some of the information was good, some historic, and some readily available. His biggest criticism was that it had gone out of date with time.

Their next meeting was in early May and Litvinenko was again accompanied by Lugovoy. This time, Daniel Quirke was talking to them alone. According to his statement to DS Michael Hoban of SO15 counterterrorism unit, Litvinenko had not been tasked with any specific requirement. The visitors said they were investigating cases of corruption in the highest echelons of the Russian government, and specifically a person of interest was Alexey V. Gordeyev, then a Russian agriculture minister. Litvinenko and Lugovoy told Mr Quirke they could get some useful information on this man.

Daniel did not know that Keith Hunter had previously tasked Litvinenko with collecting information on Gordeyev and his associates for the client. The issue was Gordeyev's involvement in a long-term dispute between a Russian state-owned company and a private SPI Group, registered in Luxembourg, over the Stolichnaya vodka brand. Gordeyev would eventually become deputy prime minister of Russia and deputy chairman of the State Duma. In September 2021, Alexey Navalny's Anti-Corruption Foundation FBK revealed that the Gordeyev family actually owned real estate worth more than 1.5 billion roubles registered in the name of his wife, son, and daughter-in-law. Their investigation, still available online, was called 'Catch the billionaire! A thief from the United Russia party is striving hard to become an MP'. In March 2022, SPI Group officially changed the name of their Stolichnaya vodka to 'Stoli' because of Putin's ongoing war in Ukraine. Six years after the events, in his interview with DC Akshay Chibber, Daniel Quirke said he could only remember Litvinenko having been tasked with the Stolichnaya case and nothing else, and that the person of interest was 'Gordievsky'. It is little wonder that the name Gordeyev completely slipped his mind together with Valuyev.

***

General Holmes's assistant at Erinys (UK) was Timothy B. J. Reilly, also a former officer educated at the RMA Sandhurst. He was then commissioned into the Parachute Regiment, the airborne infantry regiment of the British Army, leaving the army as a captain. Reilly joined the company as Energy Projects Director in April 2006 and senior managers were very pleased to have him, rightly considering Tim 'the greatest new addition to the Erinys rooster'. This former officer had previously worked for Saatchi and Saatchi, Exxon, and Defence Systems Ltd as a joint venture manager with Russian Alpha in Kazakhstan and Moscow. Being fluent in Russian, a subject of his post-graduate diploma at Surrey University and a mini-MBA at the MGIMO, the elite Moscow State Institute of International Relations, he specialised in FSU markets after completing his MPhil at Cambridge in 'The Geopolitics of Oil and Gas in the Former Soviet Union'. Before joining Erinys, Mr Reilly had briefly worked for Kroll as managing director, energy and power, with special responsibilities for the CIS.

Before Dean Attew introduced Litvinenko to Tim Reilly, he was meeting him regularly but without actually tasking him with any assignment. According to his desk diary, although they had meetings in May, June and July, the first time Litvinenko was commissioned to provide a report on a Russian businessman for a client was in August 2006. 'I received a four-and-a-half-page report and supplement that contained excellent material,' Mr Attew later testified. 'It was so detailed it even stated what wine the subject liked to drink. My thoughts were that whoever had compiled the report was well versed in the English language.'[6] Mr Attew was unaware that to do the job properly, Sasha had asked Yuri Shvets for a favour. Shvets resigned from the KGB in September 1990 and moved to the USA permanently with his family in 1993, claiming political asylum. Here, in addition to his solid training in both English and French languages at the Patrice Lumumba People's Friendship University (RUDN) in Moscow, he learnt to speak and write sufficiently good English and was actively engaged with several US private investigative firms doing due diligence and risk assessment reports for them so he had been perfectly familiar with this work.

This first assignment was to prepare a due diligence report on Yevgeny A. Tugolukov, born in Sverdlovsk (now Yekaterinburg) in May 1970. Tugolukov was educated at the Urals State Technical University, after which he worked for the MDM Bank Group for almost ten years. In 2002, Tugolukov headed the investment company Rinaco and a year later bought the Public Joint Stock Company 'Taganrog Boiler Plant' Krasny Kotelshchik from the MDM, and then the Podolsk Machine Building Plant, on the base of which he created the EMAlliance power engineering holding. The new company was specialising, among other things, in the production of equipment for thermal and nuclear power plants. Shvets delivered the report on 23 August, which was followed by a supplement a few days later.

Before he received his first assignment from Titon, in April 2006 Sasha flew to Israel.

Misha, that is Michael Cotlick, had certainly heard about Litvinenko but only met him in person for the first time in Tel Aviv. Leaving aside other things that Sasha was eager to discuss with Mr Cotlick, the purpose of his trip to Israel was to meet with Leonid Nevzlin's lawyers in relation to a criminal case that was ongoing in Russia against Nevzlin, one of the top managers of the former Yukos business empire, until recently the biggest Russian oil company. During the same year, Alexey Pichugin, the former head of security of Yukos, was sentenced to twenty-four years in prison on trumped-up charges of carrying out murders allegedly commissioned by Nevzlin. Litvinenko also visited Nevzlin in Herzliya and handed him over what later became known as 'The Yukos Dossier'. In due course, Nevzlin passed the documents to Scotland Yard investigators. From Israel, Litvinenko flew to Spain, where he met a crusading anti-corruption prosecutor, José Grinda Gonzalez. And on May 11 he was in the office of Dean Attew.

Mr Attew introduced Tim to Sasha in early June 2006. He explained that Sasha was a defector from Russia and had been debriefed by MI6 who had finished with him. Like his senior colleague, Mr Reilly had a lot of meetings with Litvinenko in the few months, between ten and twenty-five informal meetings, he says, always at the Erinys office. Normally, Mr Reilly would tell Sasha what information he required and he would approach his contacts. Tim also explained to Sasha that the word Erinys originated from ancient Greek religion and mythology. According to Homer's *Iliad*, 'the Erinyes that under earth take vengeance of men, whosoever hath sworn a false oath'. On Earth, they are known as Furiae – a more familiar word to a Russian speaker. Tim explained all that in Russian and Sasha understood.

His initial impression of Sasha was that Litvinenko was quite laid back and surprisingly indiscreet as he would often mention people he had met and things he had done. At the same time, after several meetings, Tim realised that Sasha was intelligent and quite well read.[7] In the summer of 2006, Erinys was trying to establish contacts with Gazprom that before the war in Ukraine was the largest publicly listed natural gas company in the world. The company's CEO was Alexey Miller, who, like the chairman Alexey Zubkov, used to serve under Putin at the

Above: Lieutenant Alexander Litvinenko as platoon commander of the Dzerzhinsky division, Moscow, August 1986.

Right: Litvinenko and Tolik visiting Vladimir Bukovsky at Cambridge.

Interview at home by film director Andrey Nekrasov.

From left to right: Andrey Nekrasov, Vanessa Redgrave, Ahmed Zakayev, John Nicolas Rea (Lord Rea), Sasha Litvinenko. (© Martyn Hayhow/AFP)

Litvinenko, Berezovsky, Zakayev, and Felshtinsky at Berezovsky's 60th birthday party at Blenheim Palace, Oxfordshire, 23 January 2006. (Courtesy photo)

Above: Sir Charles Farr (left) and Christopher Steele. (Public domain)

Above: The papers of Vasili Mitrokhin, 33 archive boxes – Churchill Archives Centre at Churchill College, Cambridge. (Public domain)

Right: Mario Scaramella finally visited Cambridge to work with the Mitrokhin Archive years after the death of Litvinenko.

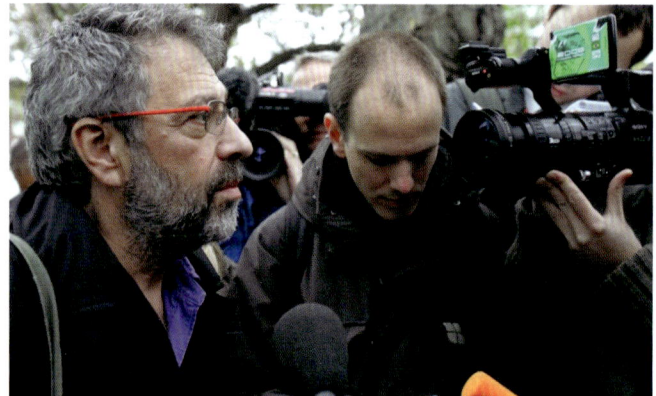

Alex Goldfarb interviewed by the world media at the UCLH 20 November 2006. (© Carl de Souza/AFP, Public domain)

Left: Marina Litvinenko speaking to the media at the Old Bailey.

Below: Madrid's office of Special Prosecutor Against Corruption and Organised Crime with whom Litvinenko collaborated in Spain.

Gennady Petrov, a leading Russian criminal figure, owned a stake at the Rossiya Bank where Putin once pompously opened his salary account. Arrested in Spain as part of Operation TROIKA. (Photo: Spanish police)

Inside the office of Special Prosecutor Against Corruption and Organised Crime. (Courtesy photo)

Jose Grinda Gonzalez is a Special Prosecutor for the Office of the Attorney General in Spain who was working with Litvinenko in Madrid. (Courtesy photo)

FSB General Yevgeny Khokholkov (ret.), former boss of Alexander Litvinenko at the Anti-Organised Crime Directorate (URPO), later used by the FSB leadership for 'special tasks' like beatings, krysha, and secret executions. (Public domain)

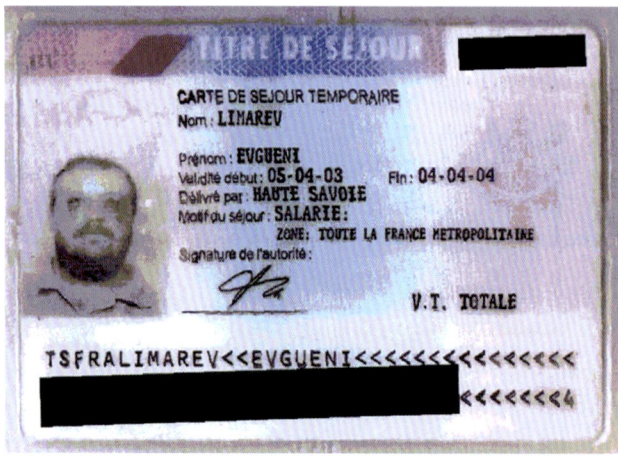

Above: Yegeny Limarev's ID as Adviser to the Chairman of the Russian Duma, and (*left*) his residence permit in France. (Litvinenko Investigation files)

Above: House in Cluses, France, the 'headquarters' of the RusGlobus site. (Litvinenko Investigation files)

Below: Sir Robert Owen, Chairman of the Litvinenko Inquiry (2015–16) – 'Calm, quiet judge who put Moscow in the dock', *The Times* wrote in January 2016. (John Stillwell/Getty Images, public domain)

Ben Emmerson QC, who represented Marina Litvinenko at the inquiry into the murder of her husband, was described by the media as 'one of the busiest, high-profile barristers in the London courts'.

Left: The Metropolitan Police SO15 team in Moscow. (Public domain)

Below: Berezovsky, wearing the mask of Putin, leaving Bow Street Magistrates Court with Vladimir Terlyuk in tow (far left). © Graeme Robertson. (Public domain)

Tea service at the London Sheraton Hotel, the fine silver teapot which Litvinenko confused with a simple white teapot at the Pine Bar. (Public domain)

Above left: Andrey Lugovoy and Dmitry Kovtun in Moscow, 2007, RIA Novosti. (Public domain)

Above right: Polonium salt can theoretically be transported as simple raw sugar – it is toxic and radioactive but not too dangerous.

Lugovoy, elected member of the Russian Duma after the Litvinenko operation, holding a copy of the Litvinenko Inquiry Report. (Public domain).

Left: Kovtun interviewed in Moscow by Egmont R. Koch for the documentary 'Spur nach Moskau' ('Traces Lead to Moscow', ZDF, 2015). (Courtesy photo)

Below: Litvinenko's friend and colleague, former FSB Lt. Colonel Mikhail Trepashkin, interviewed for the ZDF documentary 'Spur nach Moskau'. (Courtesy photo)

Young KGB officer Vladimir Putin (second left, standing) with senior KGB and East German Stasi officers in Dresden. (Stasi Archives, BStU)

The former KGB *rezidentura* (intelligence station) in Dresden where Putin was based from August 1985 until his recall to Leningrad shortly before the fall of the Berlin Wall in 1989. (Public domain)

Obedient servant. Igor Sechin, left, in winter 2022 still the powerful head (CEO) of Rosneft. In the 1990s, Sechin served first as chief of staff and then deputy to Putin, who was promoted to first deputy mayor of St Petersburg. (Public domain)

Boris Volodarsky at Check Point Charlie, West Berlin, on 9 November 1989, the day the Berlin Wall fell. (Author's archive)

Writer and historian Victor Suvorov (former GRU officer Vladimir Bogdanovich Rezun) at the London office of *Business Lunch* with Valentina (far left) and his wife Tatiana, 9 May 1999.

Above left and above right: Valery Velichko, a former KGB officer in charge of security matters during various assignments abroad. Limarev threatened Scaramella with 'Velichko's men', allegedly active as assassins in Europe. (Public domain)

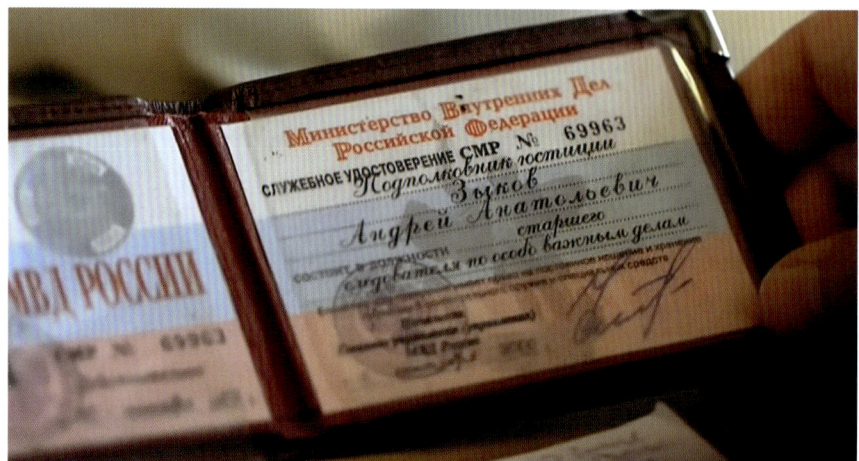

Police ID of Andrey Zykov, former senior investigator with Leningrad police who was in charge of investigating Putin's affairs in 1999–2001. Together with Grinda, Zykov took part in the Round Table 'Improving Cooperation between Enforcement Agencies and Civic Investigative Groups to Counter Transborder Corruption' in Sofia, Bulgaria in October 2017. (Public domain)

Tatyana Yumasheva (left), better known in Russia as Tatyana Dyachenko, the younger daughter of the former Russian President Boris Yeltsin, and her husband Valentin Yumashev, former Kremlin Chief of Staff and until recently Putin's adviser. The pair were granted Austrian citizenship together with their daughter in November 2009. According to the Russian media, Gunther F. Apfalter, President, Magna Europe and Asia, petitioned for the family, recalling their merits in the development of the Austrian automotive industry. Recently Russian investigative journalists found a luxury villa in Saint Barthelemy (usually abbreviated to St Barth in French, and St Barts in English), an overseas collectivity of France in the Caribbean. The 2,500 m^2 property was purchased for $15 million by the offshore company CDA, owned by Yumashev, who personally signed all documents.

Court Reference	Exhibit No	Title
Operation AVOCET	JJH/08a	Overhead view of the 3D model showing levels of radiation

KEY
- 1-300 cps
- 301-3,000 cps
- 3,001-10,000 cps
- > 10,000 cps
- **11** table number

METROPOLITAN POLICE — TOTAL POLICING

Notes: Pine Bar, Millennium Hotel, Grosvenor Square, Mayfair, London W1
Where differences in the shade of the colours shown in the key occur, this is due to the effect of lighting in the scene, not indicative of differences in the levels of surface contamination.

Computer Aided Modelling Bureau, Operational Support Group, Property Services | Ref: 1003-08 | MetSec: Restricted | Status: Final | Date: Nov 2014 | Surveyed

© Mayor's Office for Policing and Crime 2014

Court Reference:	Exhibit No.
Operation AVOCET	JJH/08a

Above: Overhead view showing the general levels of radiation found on furniture items around tables 1, 2, and 3.

Below: Overhead view showing the specific levels of radiation found on the items of furniture with the highest readings (table 2 and the chair located nearest to table 3 at the time the readings were taken).

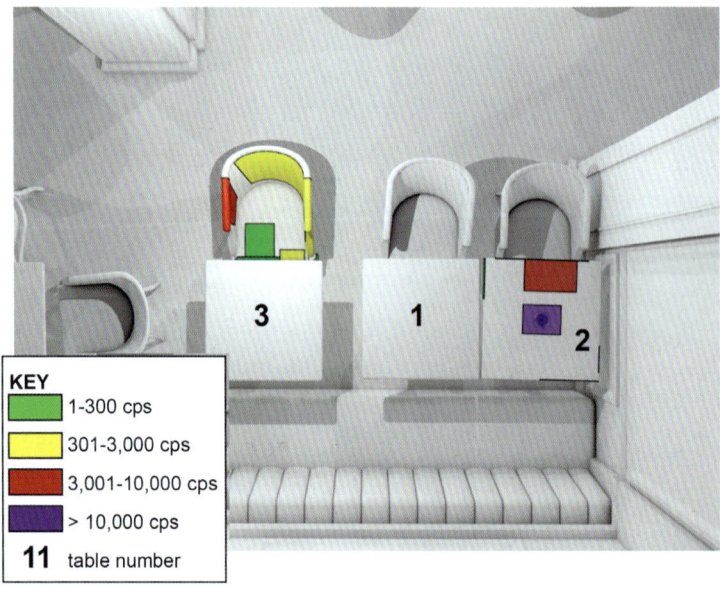

KEY
- 1-300 cps
- 301-3,000 cps
- 3,001-10,000 cps
- > 10,000 cps
- **11** table number

METROPOLITAN POLICE TOTAL POLICING

Notes: Pine Bar, Millennium Hotel, Grosvenor Square
Where differences in the shade of the colours shown in the key occurs, this is due to the effect of lighting in the scene, and not indicative of differences in the levels of surface contamination.

Computer Aided Modelling Bureau, Operational Support Group, Property Services | Ref: 1003-08 | MetSec: Restricted

© Mayor's Office for Policing and Crime 2014

Committee for External Relations of the St Petersburg Mayor's office. In June 2022, Navalny's FBK team published an investigation about Miller's $240 million private palace and Gazprom's little-known offshore activity. According to the joint investigation by FBK and Project, an independent Russian media specialising in in-depth journalism, a group of high-ranking ex-secret service officers hold $3 billion worth of assets for Miller. The investigators discovered that the money siphoned off from the state-owned gas company was used to build a business empire and purchase a series of luxurious real estate properties, all of them registered to nominees but actually used by Miller and sometimes by Putin.[8] But like many other Western companies back in 2006, Erinys did not care about such trifles.

At some point, after several meetings Litvinenko told Tim that he had a Russian partner called Lugovoy who was ex-FSB and had contacts with senior people in Gazprom. Lugovoy appeared in Erinys in July accompanied by Litvinenko. Talking to the police at the end of November 2006, Tim recalled that Lugovoy was very professional in appearance as opposed to Sasha, who was scruffy. Lugovoy explained that the security business was his bread and butter and he knew individuals in Gazprom Security. This was part of the legend fabricated for him by the operation planners.

In June 2006, Dean Attew of Titon, a sister company of Erinys, was looking to do work in Russia with artists. Sasha said he had an important friend that he wished to introduce Mr Attew to. He later testified:

> Sasha and I travelled to a coffee shop situated in Terminal One at Heathrow Airport. Lugovoy was in the process of travelling from Canada.[9] As far as I can recall, he was travelling to Moscow. Upon arrival at the airport, we had to wait whilst Lugovoy finished another meeting. I was led to believe by Lugovoy that the previous meeting was with a British banking official [while in reality it could have been an officer from the Russian embassy]. Lugovoy joined us at our table and gave me his business card. He said that he was ex-KGB and that he owned 3 security companies in Russia and still had very good connections. He made reference to doing 'old style' surveillance. I believe he was referring to the fact that he had the abilities to intercept telecommunications and place listening devices. He made it clear that for the right money he could perform any service. It is my view that Sasha seemed keen to impress Lugovoy. I also felt Lugovoy was possibly taking advantage of Sasha.

This meeting at Heathrow was on 30 June. Coincidentally, John Holmes, the Group Chief Executive, was on the same flight to Moscow. Unlike his junior colleague Reilly, Dean Attew stressed that he formed an instant dislike of Lugovoy. He said he did not have any desire to do business with him. 'I disliked him so much so that I did not want him in my office, quite frankly. Lugovoy is one of these people that you meet and take an instant disliking to, and he scared me,' Mr Attew recalled.[10]

Upon his return to London, he informed Tim Reilly that he thought Lugovoy was not to be trusted and advised Tim not to go near him. Unfortunately, Tim decided not to follow this wise advice.

Only some considerable time later did Dean Attew recall a strange episode that happened on 18 June, before the meeting at Heathrow. 'I got to the office at maybe 7.00 in the morning,' he testified during the Litvinenko Inquiry hearings, 'and the front door to 25 Grosvenor Street wasn't off its hinges, the large oak door had been split about 6 to 8 inches from the right-hand side and the locks, and it had been split straight down, so I was a little bit shocked. This was not a traditional break-in or burglary, that's how I viewed it.' He immediately went to the fourth floor to his office and saw that 'the door wasn't off, the whole frame had been moved and was pushed through'. It was quite obvious that somebody had broken into the first floor, then went straight to the Titon/Erinys's offices on the fourth floor, knocked the door out of the frame but did not take anything, and left after about five minutes. In his business, Mr Attew concluded, that was a reconnaissance, a recce.[11] And so it most probably was.

In September, there came a request from another client and Dean Attew again commissioned Sasha to write a due diligence report. Litvinenko duly passed over the job to Shvets, who agreed to pay him 20 per cent commission for such contacts. This time it was about Igor I. Shuvalov, born in January 1967, who was then working as personal assistant to President Putin (from March 2004 to May 2008). Shvets delivered his report on 18 September.

At the same time as the Shuvalov request, another assignment from another customer of Titon was to provide background information on Viktor Ivanov and the company passed it over to Sasha. Litvinenko decided to split the jobs and asked his friend Lugovoy to draft a report. This was almost an impossible task because Ivanov had been an old friend and confidante of Putin for many years and a high-ranking government official. Both Putin and Ivanov had served in the Leningrad KGB at the same time until Putin was sent to the Andropov Institute in Moscow in September 1984 while Ivanov continued at the Leningrad KGB directorate for the next ten years. From January 1980 until summer 1987 General Oleg Kalugin served as first deputy head of the Leningrad KGB and was Ivanov's and Putin's boss. After Kalugin's transfer back to Moscow, Ivanov was sent to Afghanistan. There he had spent a year as part of the Kaskad (Cascade) group, a KGB covert reconnaissance unit. Later, Ivanov headed the department of internal security of the FSB, then the department of economic security, and from May 2000 served as deputy chief of Putin's presidential administration, promoted to personal assistant to the president in March 2004. In the summer of 2005, Ivanov became the chairman of the board of directors of Aeroflot and two months later also headed the board of directors of Almaz-Antey – a company producing air defence systems. He continued to serve as Putin's personal aide until May 2008.

Accordingly, Lugovoy's controllers from the FSO, SVR or FSB could not even think about providing information about Ivanov other than that in the public domain, leaving Lugovoy no choice. After a while, he emailed Sasha less than half a page based largely on what was written about Ivanov on the Russian Wikipedia site. It goes without saying that he preferred not to mention the allegation published by Dissernet that Ivanov's doctoral dissertation contained large fragments of plagiarised text from four different works. Under the circumstances, Litvinenko had no option but to ask Shvets to compile a report, adding some facts about Ivanov and Putin that he had learnt from the Melnichenko tapes and from Kalugin.

During the Litvinenko Inquiry hearings, the eight-page report that Shvets delivered became public and was widely discussed in the media.[12] From the professional point of view, it is rather mediocre and not as 'damaging' as usually described. Ben Emmerson QC, the lawyer for Litvinenko's widow Marina, said the report contained 'staggeringly serious' allegations against both Ivanov and Putin, which even then could be seen as an obvious exaggeration. A valuable but nevertheless useless piece of information that Shvets inserted into the report was from his early work with the tapes. This was a reference to the information that the SBU chairman Leonid Derkach shared with President Kuchma in June 2000. Derkach claimed that his service obtained some documents from Germany showing that both Putin and Ivanov were involved in criminal business. Alas, there was nothing in the report to substantiate those claims.

According to Shvets, Ivanov, then head of the department (10th department of the Leningrad KGB Second Directorate in charge of the fight against smuggling and illegal hard currency transactions) was collaborating with the organised crime group Tambovskaya. The gang ran a lucrative operation of smuggling cocaine from Columbia to western Europe via the city's seaport. As evident from the Melnichenko tapes, the documents obtained by the SBU indicated that the German company SPAG (St Petersburg Immobilien und Bcteiligungs Aktiengesellschaft) was laundering money for the mafia by investing in real estate in St Petersburg. Putin had been a member of the SPAG advisory committee until March 2000. The case was thoroughly investigated by German and European law enforcement agencies.[13]

The report compiled by Shevts was delivered on 19 September. It was in English and Sasha was not able to read it, therefore was unfamiliar with its content. When it reached Titon, Dean Attew decided it was of very high quality, so Shvets and Litvinenko were, in the words of General Holmes, handsomely remunerated.

* * *

At their several meetings in September and October, Litvinenko and Reilly discussed various possibilities for making money in Russia, which seemed an endless source of business opportunities. Sasha was very serious about making money but, as Tim noticed, rather idealistic about the way of doing it. He was trying to understand the commercial aspect of acting as a broker, making a percentage of a deal, but the fact that such business required a lot of patience, integrity, dedication, and time irritated him. One example was ethanol, while Tim identified Ukraine as its possible producer.

Everyone knows that ethanol, or simple alcohol, is an organic chemical compound which is used as a renewable fuel made from various plant materials collectively known as 'biomass'. More than 98 per cent of US gasoline contains ethanol, typically E10 (10 per cent ethanol, 90 per cent gasoline), to oxygenate the fuel, which reduces air pollution. Tim explained that 80 per cent of vehicles in Brazil run on ethanol produced from sugar cane. Sasha was, as usual, extremely enthusiastic and they discussed the prospect of setting up a company that could broker deals between the producer of ethanol and the end buyer. Sasha thought it would be easy because he did not really understand the business, Tim explained to Detective Constable Zac Idun of the Metropolitan Police Counter Terrorism Command. Sasha even called a governor in Ukraine where they thought they could start their ethanol business and after five minutes reported that the governor would be willing to progress. Finally, they decided to make a conference call to Shvets.

Shvets identified twenty-seven producing plants in Ukraine and said the shipments could be done through Odessa. According to Tim, he seemed quite switched on. The three of them arranged some more conference calls discussing various details of the future business.

Then, in early October, Sasha learned that Anna Politkovskaya had been shot dead in Moscow. Anna was Russia's most famous journalist and a fierce critic of Putin. She was well known for her investigative reports on human rights abuses and high-level corruption in Russia. Litvinenko was very upset and angry, but not surprised. He told Tim that he had met her on a number of occasions in the UK and that she stayed with his family. Litvinenko was convinced that the order to kill Anna came directly from Putin. 'I asked him,' Mr Reilly recalled, 'if he felt any more vulnerable.' Sasha shrugged and said: of course.

Sometime in October, when the ethanol business seemed somehow to have lost all its attractiveness to Sasha, Litvinenko came to the office of Erinys with a letter that he had obtained from one of his sources. Whether he himself fished it out from Runet, the Russian-language community on the internet, or it was sent by Lugovoy was never established. The document, obviously printed out in an internet café, concerned some commercial structure through which medium-sized oil fields could be bought in Russia. Any person with minimal experience would immediately identify such a letter as a scam. Without any comment, Sasha handed the sheet of paper to Tim and left. 'I understand,' Tim later testified, 'that a significant person within the organisation mentioned in the letter, who was responsible for the marketing of those medium-sized oilfields, was recently murdered in Moscow.' That was it.

Litvinenko visited Erinys again, staying just for a little while because he had actually come to see Dean. Tim asked him about Gazprom and Sasha said Lugovoy was going to visit soon. The exact date depended on Lugovoy's arrival in the UK.

The visit was sooner than anybody expected but this seemingly unimportant episode was completely ignored by the police, although Robin Tam QC, one of the very capable legal advisers representing the Counsel to the Inquiry, spent considerable time asking Felshtinsky, the only witness, about his meetings on 12 October 2006.

On that day, Thursday, 12 October, Yuri Felshtinsky arrived in London in the evening travelling from Boston because he had agreed with Berezovsky to go with him to Israel. As he did not have enough cash, he decided to get some pounds from the ATM near Le Meridien on Piccadilly. Yuri checked in at the Athenaeum Hotel and Residences at the other end of the street, just round the corner from where Boris's offices were at the time, and decided to take a stroll along Piccadilly towards Piccadilly Circus, his favourite route, passing by the embassy of Japan with CCTV cameras. On the way to the Abbey National Bank ATM machine, Felshtinsky suddenly saw Lugovoy, accompanied by another person whom he had never seen before and would never see afterwards. Yuri remembered that while Lugovoy was friendly and smiling as usual, the man with him was tall and dark, had an intimidating, slightly hostile presence, and did not pronounce a word. Felshtinsky had a quick chat with Lugovoy and they parted, proceeding in different directions. A few minutes later, Felshtinsky came face to face with Goldfarb.

On that particular evening, Berezovsky, Goldfarb and Yuli Dubov went to the theatre to watch *King Lear* directed by Lev Dodin, the performance that the MDT from St Petersburg brought to London for only one night. After the theatre, Boris went to a restaurant with some Russian guests and Goldfarb was on the way home when they met. On the next day, 13 October, Felshtinsky attended the memorial service for Anna Politkovskaya at Westminster, where he saw Litvinenko for the last time, and late at night flew with Berezovsky to Israel. They returned to London on 16 October.

Investigating the episode, the SO15 officers decided that Felshtinsky confused the dates and the meeting was actually on 16 October. Because it was established that Lugovoy arrived in London with Kovtun on the morning of 16 October and not before, everybody thought the man accompanying Lugovoy was Kovtun, although in his witness statement to the police, Felshtinsky said:

> I have since seen media coverage of Lugovoy when he made an appearance on Russian television. In this coverage, Lugovoy is accompanied by another Russian male called Dmitri Kovtun. Having seen Kovtun on television, I am not sure he was the man I had seen on 12 October 2006 in company with Lugovoy in Piccadilly, although similar appearance the man I saw was noticeably taller and thinner than Lugovoy. Kovtun did not appear to be taller or thinner in the television images ... If he is not taller or thinner, I would say that I have seen somebody else.[14]

There was no evidence that Lugovoy visited London on that day and he himself vehemently denied it, so the matter was dropped. However, there is little doubt that unbeknownst to anybody, Lugovoy was indeed in London on that day, together with Vladimir Valuyev, the fourth member of the team directly involved in the Litvinenko operation. Saying that in 2006 his father only visited London once with Lugovoy in April, Valuyev's son Alexey either did not know about the October visit or somehow forgot about it, or was instructed not to mention it at all. Vladimir Valuyev would later serve as a Moscow coordinator of the activities involving Lugovoy, Kovtun and Sokolenko in London on 1 November, so his incognito visit with Lugovoy both using false Latvian, Polish, Ukrainian, or any other passports on assumed names about two weeks before the final stage of the operation could be easily explained. This may also explain why Sasha, in his last interviews in hospital, confused Lugovoy's partners, each of whom he saw only once, calling a tall man with dark hair, the eyes of a killer and sharp features either Vladimir or Vadim. Valuyev senior is Vladimir, and Dima, which sounds similar to Vadim, is short for Dmitry, Kovtun's first name.

Litvinenko told Dean Attew he would be overseas for one week during October but Dean could not recall where and when he was planning to go. According to Shvets, during October he was in contact with Litvinenko daily and Sasha did not go anywhere. His next visit to Dean Attew at 25 Grosvenor Street was on 31 October at around 4.30 pm. They scheduled their next meeting on Wednesday, 1 November 2006.

CHAPTER 6

Italy

- What does it mean, 'talking though your hat'?
- That means to talk about something without understanding what you are talking about.

Whether it was a fatal or a fateful meeting is impossible to say, but soon after a brief encounter with Sasha Litvinenko in London on 1 November 2006, Mario Scaramella became very famous. Like in Bulgakov's *The Master and Margarita*, 'Where there's one of us, straightaway there will be the other! Whenever I am remembered, you will at once be remembered, too!' As it happens, Mario could never predict such turn of events after Litvinenko first visited him in Naples together with his half-brother Maxim about two years earlier.

In late January 2004, the Italian lawyer Mario Scaramella was 33. His career in the previous decade included a bachelor's degree in jurisprudence from the University of Naples Federico II, the oldest public university in the world listing Giordano Bruno among its notable alumni, and his follow-up work at the same university where, according to his words, Mario had received an academic appointment. This had been disputed by many authors and journalists who were not in the know. And because only a few of them understood the meaning of the term 'Professor Jean Monnet', those who did not openly mocked Scaramella for using the title. During the Litvinenko Inquiry hearings, it took the chairman, solicitors, and counsel a lot of time to figure out whether Mario did have certified qualifications and titles that he had claimed he had. Although questions and detailed answers cover thirty pages (Day 27, 18 March 2015), it remained somewhat a mystery because it was clear that on one hand, right after law school, when he was not even a doctor (PhD), Scaramella could not have become a professor, which is the highest rank for a university academic, while on the other, he produced all necessary documents to prove that it was indeed the case, so the inquiry just dropped it.

In reality, as part of its Lifelong Learning Program, the European Commission adopted what became known as Jean Monnet Learning EU initiatives for schools and VET providers (VET stands for 'vocational education and training'). Simply put, it is education and training in specific job-related and technical skills. In its initial version, the programme existed for twenty years from 1991 to 2011, during which time the EC financed 3,700 educational projects in seventy-two countries. The idea was for various educational institutions to establish teaching of a specific EU-based subject(s). According to the plan, activities were to be taught during the school year and should have included 'project weeks, study visits, and other immersive activities' while providers were to create learning experiences themselves with the support of higher education institutions or other relevant organisations. Among other expected outcomes, the programme was supposed to have strengthened EU literacy, leaving students better equipped to become active European citizens.

Until 2013, there were three levels of the programme known as Jean Monnet Modules, Jean Monnet Chairs, and Jean Monnet *ad personam* (that is, on an individual basis) each with a different EC grant. The second programme for higher education institutions, Jean Monnet Chairs, awarded the temporary title of 'Professor Jean Monnet'. It was supposed to last for three years and had a minimum duration of ninety teaching hours per academic year in the field of European Union Studies. The maximum grant for three years was €45,000, representing 75 per cent of the total cost of the teaching programme or course. The document that Scaramella sent to the Litvinenko Inquiry (INQ020905) was a copy of the confirmation, signed by Professor Gian Maria Piccinelli, head of the Faculty of Political Studies, that Dottore Scaramella had been appointed lecturer ('Professor Jean Monnet') at the Jean Monnet Chair, which existed from July 1999 to March 2001. He was subsequently named Coordinator of the Centre on Civil Defence and Foreign Security Policy Studies of the EC ('Centro Studi sulla Difesa Civile e sulla Politica Estera di Sicurezza Comune Europea'). In June 2002, the Centre was further transformed into a faculty of the university and Scaramella's employment was terminated.

But even before Mario received his JD (Juris Doctor) diploma, he created a unit within the university's faculty of law which he called the 'environmental crime prevention programme' that served as the basis for the future ECPP, the organisation with the same name that he founded together with his partner in 1997. Later, the ECPP website described its mission as 'providing environmental protection and security through technology on a global basis, particularly for developing nations'. He later managed to raise its status to the international level, promoting his ECPP as 'a permanent intergovernmental conference focusing on environmental crime with rotating presidencies'.

Unable to realise his dream – becoming an officer or agent of a secret service – Mario created his own private secret service. Years later, in his witness statement he described it to the SO15 officers as 'an international organisation which deals with all kinds of environment crime, environment terrorism to the dumping of nuclear substances'.[1] Using the opportunity provided by the Jean Monnet Chair at his university and his newly acquired status there, he established contacts with different institutions including Stanford University, one of the world's leading universities in Stanford, California. One day, Scaramella was asked to assist a guest from Italy on an official visit to Stanford. This was Dr Lorenzo Matassa, deputy public prosecutor at the court of Palermo, who was so much impressed by the young lawyer that he recommended him to be accepted as a consultant to the recently established Mitrokhin Commission of the Italian parliament.

For a young man captured and carried away by James Bond-inspired adventures and spy games, academic contacts and international recognition were not enough and Scaramella started to establish personal relations with former and acting intelligence officers. One of his few public appearances at a security-related conference in 2002 was, among others, with Georgetown University Professor John Gannon, a former high-ranking CIA official.[2] The Italian-born security consultant Filippo Marino, who is said to have been a co-founder of the ECPP, introduced Mario to Robert Seldon Lady, a former CIA station chief in Milan, as well as to Louis F. Palumbo, who had served for twenty-two years with the Agency specialising in sensitive investigations. Among Scaramella's new friends there was also Vladimir B. Rezun, a former GRU mayor. Rezun, later widely known as writer and self-made military historian publishing under the pen name Viktor Suvorov, was part of the legal residency of Soviet military intelligence in Geneva under the cover of the Permanent Mission of the USSR at the United Nations Office at Geneva, who defected to the British in June 1978.

After having been recommended by Dr Matassa, one of the principal legal consultants of the commission, Mario was invited to Rome for a personal interview with the commission's president or chairman, well-known Italian journalist, writer, and then senator Paolo Guzzanti.

In all available sources, including Wikipedia and, remarkably, even in Scaramella's own testimony to the Litvinenko investigation and later inquiry, the purpose of the commission is explained incorrectly. According to Scaramella, 'this was a commission that had been set up primarily to investigate the links between the KGB and Italian political figures during the Cold War on the basis of a dossier which had been sent by the British Services to the Italian Services'.[3] Wikipedia articles (both in English and Italian) claim that the commission was set up 'to investigate alleged KGB ties of some Italian politicians ... its focus was on alleged KGB ties to opposition figures in Italian politics, basing itself on the controversial [?!] Mitrokhin Archive'. The archive, which has long since been deposited at the Churchill Archives Centre of Churchill College in Cambridge and is open to the public, may contain some minor errors but it is certainly not 'controversial' and has been universally accepted as a unique and reliable source. This, however, is not the main point.

The parliamentary 'Commission of Inquiry concerning the "Mitrokhin dossier" and the Italian intelligence activity' (the official title) was established with the law no. 90 of 7 May 2002. Its mission was formulated in fifteen paragraphs, most important of them being (a) the investigation of all aspects of the acquisition, safekeeping, and further use or non-use of the documents from the so-called Mitrokhin Archive provided to the Italian SISMI by the British SIS in the period between 1995 and 1999, as well as of when and how the Italian government was informed about the dossier and its contents; (b) possible direct or indirect financing by the KGB of Italian political parties, political groups and currents, and/or Italian mass media, plus the actual status of persons mentioned in the documents; (c) activities of the Rome residency of the KGB;

and (d) the search of the caches secretly deposited by the KGB and/or its agents on Italian territory that may contain arms and ammunition, explosives, radio transmitters, and other material. At the end of October 2022, I re-checked it again and the former president of the commission, Signor Guzzanti, assured me that the main concern of the commission members was not to investigate the allegations contained in the Mitrokhin papers but to review the activities of the SISMI in relation to the secret files received from London. The only exception was to establish whether, in the time period covered by the documents, any Italian political party, movement, or media was a beneficiary of direct or indirect financing from the Soviet KGB.

At the same time, the Litvinenko investigation and later inquiry clearly demonstrated that Mario Scaramella, who was a good young fellow but incompetent, inexperienced, ambitious, and with zero knowledge of the KGB in terms of its history, structure, and organisation, had considerably exceeded his authority as a consultant, also trying to use information obtained under the auspices of the commission for personal purposes. He was also faint-hearted, which is usually interpreted as cowardly, lacking courage or resolution, which was immediately noticed and used by the KGB (by this time SVR) not only to involve him in the Litvinenko affair but also to compromise him, which subsequently led to Mario's arrest and imprisonment on trumped-up charges.

The so-called contribution of Litvinenko to the work of the Italian Mitrokhin Commission may be disregarded because a long and detailed report compiled by Scaramella (with the help of the private detective from Naples named Fulvio Mucibello and interpreter Andrey Ganchev) covering all topics discussed in the course of their two-year collaboration contains precious little of interest and value. Anyway, all of it has already been included in three books published in the West.[4] For there is nothing hidden that will not be disclosed, and nothing concealed that will not be known or brought out into the open (Luke 8:17). And Sasha Litvinenko was not the kind of person who could keep secrets for long.

Likewise, the contents of the secret 'Litvinenko file' confiscated from the personal safe of the commission's president by the carabinieri sent by Bologna prosecutors in the spring of 2006 with Sasha's allegations that Romano Prodi was the 'KGB's man in Italy' have long been known and dismissed as false. Preparing for the inquiry hearings, members of the counsel correctly decided not to use this material which covered a wide variety of topics from the Italian Red Brigades (1970s), to the US businessman Paul Tatum, gunned down in Moscow in November 1996, to the 9/11 attacks when Litvinenko was already in London, and to Ayman al-Zawahiri, an Egyptian-born terrorist and al-Qaeda leader (killed by a CIA drone strike in a Kabul neighbourhood in 2022) allegedly trained by the FSB. With this, most of the facts reported by Litvinenko had little or nothing to do with Italy. Nevertheless, Robin Tam QC, who interviewed Scaramella after having read all 128 pages of his interviews, was very kind and understanding:

Q. This all appears to be about Soviet or Russian intelligence and similar operations around the world. Is that right?

A. Yes, sir.

Q. This is what he was talking about?

A. Yes.

Q. So this is definitely Mitrokhin Commission territory, isn't it?

A. Yes.

Q. That was the basis on which you were talking to him?

A. Yes, exactly.[5]

For an intelligence historian who might think about writing a book like, for example, *The KGB in Italy*, a lot of excellent primary and secondary sources are available,[6] but Mario preferred an easy way of Q&A. Then, in January 2004, the construction 'Prodi and the KGB', the most sensitive part of the Litvinenko file, was discussed by Scaramella and Litvinenko for the first time.

'We are interested in international organisations, most of all in the European organisations,' Scaramella started his interview, 'and most of all in the involvement of Italians in the intelligence work inside European organisations.'[7] Answering this question, Litvinenko mentioned Prodi for the first time.

It is a well-known fact, and Sasha obviously heard about it during his KGB training, that the far-left terrorist group, the Italian Brigate Rosse (Red Brigades), ambushed a car with the leader of the Christian Democrats, former prime minister Aldo Moro, in the centre of Rome on 16 March 1978. The politician was bundled into a waiting car and for the next fifty-four days held prisoner in a secret hiding place. There were persistent rumours that some leading figures of the Italian Communist Party (PCI) were not only well informed that the Red Brigades were supported by the Czechoslovak StB (who worked under the strict control of the KGB), but were also associated with certain individuals involved with the Red Brigades. Some of the Communist leaders, acting through the long-term Soviet ambassador in Rome Nikita Ryzhov, even tried to persuade Andropov to stop the Czechs. According to Mitrokhin's notes, on 4 May Giorgio Amendola of the PCI Central Committee warned the Czechoslovak ambassador that if Moro's kidnappers were caught and put on trial, the StB's assistance 'could all come out'.[8] The Italian police failed to discover the hiding place where Moro had been kept prisoner. He was murdered on 9 May, widely celebrated in Russia as a Victory Day, and his body left in the boot of a car in via Michelangelo Caetani in the vicinity of the PCI headquarters.

Before the shock of this tragedy rattled the country, on 2 April Prodi with a couple of his colleagues from the University of Bologna informed the police that during a séance with a Ouija board the word 'gradoli' was revealed to them in relation to a place where Red Brigades possibly kept the former prime minister. Instead of concentrating their efforts on the Italian capital, the police under

Francesco Cossiga, the interior minister, began searching in Gradoli, a municipality about 100 km northwest of Rome. It was later discovered that the safe house where the Red Brigades kept their victim was at 96 via Gradoli in Rome, so the mysterious spirit directing the Ouija board was right after all.

Prodi, who was appointed minister of industry in November that same year, was summoned by the Italian parliamentary commission on terrorism to give evidence about the case in 1981. In the commission documents the séance was described as a fake used to hide the true source of the information, which had never been properly identified. In August 1979, Cossiga became the prime minister, then president of the Senate and later president of Italy. Prodi became the prime minister of Italy in May 1996, President of the European Commission in September 1999, and again the prime minister in May 2006.

Answering Scaramella's question about KGB agents' penetration of European organisations, Litvinenko delivered a long lecture. 'For example,' he explained, 'with regards to the murder of Moro. The fact that Prodi knew the place where this crime, this murder took place ... If a person claims he knows the address where a serious crime was committed, the officer who carries out the investigation must establish where he knows this from ... Then this officer must establish the status of this person, he can, [this] person can be a suspect or a witness.'

After listening to Litvinenko's arguments, Scaramella deliberated over what Sasha had just said: 'Prodi knew of the base of the Red Brigades, therefore Prodi is a KGB agent,' he concluded. 'But it is not known to us that the Red Brigades depended from [*sic*] the KGB.'

Mario quickly found out it was not so easy to baffle his new Russian friend. 'First of all,' Litvinenko responded, 'I must declare that I am not a witness, I am an expert and on the basis of the material that I have seen, I have to state that there are all the indications that this person [Prodi] really could be collaborating with the secret services, with the KGB, because first of all he participated in the organisation [probably meaning the BR] that received money from the KGB and in the organisation that the KGB used for its crimes.' To prove his point, Sasha said he had documents confirming that the KGB killed people and continue doing it. 'I know,' he said, 'that the KGB gives this kind of information [meaning the address in via Gradoli] to politicians before pushing them over [*sic*, helping rise through the ranks]. I know this from examples of other politicians.'

And about the Red Brigades Litvinenko added, 'About the Red Brigades I know the following: The KGB was giving money directly to the Italian Communist party but in the Italian Communist party an armed wing was created, it was called the Red Brigades.'[9] Thus, in January 2004 there was no talk about General Anatoly Trofimov who allegedly revealed a secret about Romano Prodi and the KGB to Litvinenko. No, a myth about Trofimov's role was created later, after he was assassinated in Moscow in April 2005.

During the same session Litvinenko first mentioned Limarev as an 'ex-officer of the foreign exploration [*sic*, intelligence] service'. 'This Limarev was doing the special courses in the operational training centre (OUTs)', he explained, meaning the

FSB training facility in Balashikha-2 known as the Special Forces Centre (abbreviated in Russian as TsSN). Limarev's father, Litvinenko added, used to be the controller of a Soviet spy ring in Morocco. Soon Scaramella contacted Limarev in France, making him another expert on the KGB but, unlike Sasha who did not take money for his consultations, a well-paid expert, with Scaramella using him in a dual role as an information provider for the Mitrokhin Commission and a source for the ECPP.

One of the first questions that Scaramella asked Limarev was about Prodi. In his usual peremptory manner, Limarev responded that his contacts informed him about a KGB officer by the name Felix Konopikhin ('K') who was accredited in Italy using the cover of a TASS correspondent. This officer allegedly attended Moro's lectures and left the country immediately after the abduction. According to Limarev's report, this 'K' confirmed 'that information on where to look after A. Moro was passed to R. Prodi by KGB'.[10] For Scaramella, this completed the circle.

Limarev was duly interviewed by the French police with three Scotland Yard officers present and grilled at length during the Litvinenko Inquiry hearings. There was no doubt that he was brazenly lying and inventing things. When driven into a corner by Mr Tam's questions and documents that were shown to him, Limarev simply pretended not to remember anything. When confronted by his threatening emails to Scaramella with his own handwritten notes and explanations, he countered this argument with: 'I will not believe any paper or word which will be coming from him.'

'Do you remember writing these paragraphs?'

'No, I don't remember.'

However, it was established without any doubt that all email messages and reports on his file had indeed been compiled and sent by Limarev.

One of such emails arrived as early as 10 February 2006. In it, Limarev maintained that the SVR was monitoring and closely followed all activities of the Mitrokhin Commission both from Moscow and from its station in Rome. All daily movements of Senator Guzzanti, the commission's president, he claimed, were controlled and SVR agents were even following him during his meetings, especially because of his closeness to the prime minister Silvio Berlusconi. Even Putin himself ('biggest Russian friend') advised Berlusconi to stay away from Guzzanti, he wrote. According to Limarev, to know more about the commission's president, a Romeo agent was sent to his daughter Sabina. Male 'Romeo' agents, better known in the trade as ravens, are involved in sexpionage using romance or seduction to obtain classified information. '[He] now appears to be her friendly and (relatively) close contact, whom she meets regularly and shares personal, family and other confidential information,' Limarev reported. He also warned Scaramella about possible risks if he decided to travel to Russia but reassured him that so far no 'active/impact measures' had been planned against any commission members or staff.[11] However, when Limarev learned that at the end of October Scaramella was going to London, the tone of his messages changed.

At about 2.00 pm on Monday, 30 October 2006, Limarev informed Scaramella by email that his contacts had assured him that Russian intelligence officers were considering MS (Scaramella) and PG (Guzzanti) as having formed 'stable criminal group which serve interests of the most conservative/rightist wings of special services of Italy, USA and UK ... seeking to profit from SISMI, FBI and CIA'. In Limarev's words, the most troubling and dangerous development was that a former KGB General Valery Velichko and his people were involved, as he put it, 'into planning of actions against PG and MS'.[12] 'Velichko's agents,' Limarev went on frightening Mario, 'are presumably involved in the assassination of Anna Politkovskaya in October 2006 as well as in elaboration of other similar assassination plans in Russia and Baltic states – by order and on behalf of FSB/SVR.' At the end of his message, adding to the fear and mystery, he warned of the real threat to life claiming that one of the Russian operatives had already been in the Naples for over a month following all movements of PG and MS, having a local network of KGB agents at his disposal and preparing a 'final act' like a serious provocation or even assassination attempt.[13]

The above message was entitled 'Urgent! Security-2' and on Tuesday, 31 October a new, even more threatening email arrived in Mario's mailbox before noon.

This likewise urgent message, marked 'Security-3', from Limarev now provided the name of the would-be assassin. It was one Igor Anatolievich Vlasov, Limarev wrote, 'a spetsnaz (SEAL) acting officer of Balashikha-2, specialises in preparation of subversive operations'. As if that was not enough, he added that 'Vlasov is also known as boss of several criminals – professional killers in Saint-Petersburg'. And then, 'It's very unlikely he would act (for example, will try to assassinate) himself, but he is recognised organiser of any kind of "active operations" and is perfect coordinator of any kind of "special operation" [sic]. He is likely to come to Italy by car from Nice (France).'[14]

All those threats pushed poor Mario to seek an urgent meeting with Litvinenko in London on the morning of 1 November. Sasha was busy so they agreed to meet at 3.00 pm at their usual place on Piccadilly Circus. In the evening, Scaramella reported to Limarev that he had met Litvinenko, asking for his advice. It was obvious that Mario was very scared and in panic. He stressed that it was necessary to speak with competent authorities as soon as possible. 'Judiciary, police or secret services must be informed about all the details,' he insisted, 'it's too big for me.'[15] Mario Scaramella could never imagine how big a problem awaited him because of his meeting with Litvinenko on that November day. A meeting that was arranged by him exclusively to discuss Limarev's false threats.

Paolo Guzzanti never had the slightest doubt that somebody was leaking information collected by his commission to the Italian newspapers, judicial authorities, secret services, and perhaps even to the Russians. Obviously, no one had ever been caught red-handed. In May 2003, there was a micro conflict involving Andrea Papini MP, a vice president of the commission, but it was quickly sorted out by Guzzanti. During the Litvinenko Inquiry hearings, Scaramella accused Limarev of leaking information to *La Republicca*, the Italian newspaper that was trying to discredit the work of the Mitrokhin Commission and attack Scaramella personally, but again it was only his personal opinion. Anyway, with forty full members of the commission, twenty Senators and twenty Representatives, supported by a group of consultants, advisers, researchers and clerical staff, Russian intelligence services should have been sufficiently well informed of all information passing through the commission. No doubt the involvement of Litvinenko in its work had been duly noticed.

As mentioned, almost everything that Sasha told Mario he had already exposed in detail in his two books, articles and interviews but there must have been reasonable grounds to suspect that he had more to say. For example, his 'special assignment' while serving as a captain in one of the Dzerzhinsky division units was mentioned only in passing while the full story told to Scaramella must have irritated Sasha's former colleagues who could have interpreted it as high treason.

The Dzerzhinsky division where Litvinenko served in 1985–88 was an Independent Special Purpose Motorised Rifle Division of the Internal Troops of the Soviet Interior Ministry. Since its formation in February 1918, its primary task was guarding the soviet and party leaders and providing them with special cars. Later, it was expanded to guarding the Kremlin and its dwellers and ensuring the security of particularly important installations in the Russian capital. All these activities were carried out in collaboration with the KGB and, in answering Mario's questions, Litvinenko was able to add some fascinating details.

One of the special units of the division was dealing exclusively with the evacuation of the families of the top party functionaries in case of war or other imminent and present danger, saving their precious lives by all means. But Litvinenko's special unit was tasked with something no less valuable. It was responsible for collecting gold, precious metals, diamonds and works of art in various parts of the Soviet Union and transporting all that treasure to the special top-secret depository near the city of Miass located about 100 km west of Chelyabinsk on the slopes of the Ural Mountains. After 1986 it was only Litvinenko's unit entrusted with this special task and in the year between 1987 and 1988, he said, 'almost every month we went to St Petersburg and took 2 or 4 containers, each container weighing 23 tonnes, and transported them to Miass'.

'Each time forty-six or ninety-two tonnes of gold?'

'Yes, almost every month.'

'And where did this gold come from?' Mario asked.

'From Germany. Our containers always arrived by civilian vessels. They were loaded at the bottom of the ship so we had to wait till the rest of the cargo is unloaded and then we took them.'

According to the common wisdom, a secret Russian (former CPSU) gold depository is located somewhere under the Kremlin but the Gokhran, a state institution responsible for the State Fund of Precious Metals, Precious Stones and Diamonds, established in 1920, has other depositories. One of them, Object 304, was built by the Soviet GULAG internees during WWII in the southern Urals. The story goes that prisoners had hollowed out one of the mountains of the Ilmensky ridge from the inside. And there, behind massive doors, treasures are being stored until this day.

The Murder of Alexander Litvinenko: To Kill a Mockingbird

Why Miass? In the nineteenth century, the richest gold deposits in the Urals were discovered in this area, which initially was a copper mining facility. Initially, the average extraction was about 1,400 lb (about 640 kg) but later the production slowed down. After the war, the Makeyev Design Bureau, the main Russian designer of submarine-launched ballistic missiles (SLBM), was relocated to Miass from another city in Chelyabinsk Oblast. Initially, the project was developed by the German engineers at the end of the war. On 13 September 1946, the USSR Council of Ministers issued decree No. 2163-880s, 'On removal of hardware from the German military enterprises'. The document officially launched the process of transfer of German rocket production potential to the USSR. In October, the best German specialists who worked for the secret missile programme were ordered on the trains and together with their families sent to various locations in the USSR to assist in the organisation of missile production and design. By the beginning of the next year, the Soviets had completed the transfer of all works on rocket technology from Germany into secret locations in the USSR. The top-secret Soviet plan to deport thousands of German specialists into the USSR was codenamed Operation OSOAVIAKHIM.

Telling the story, Litvinenko could not remember the exact address of the secret depository, only recalling it was somewhere near Lake Chebarkul. Indeed, the settlement known as the village of Ozerny could not be found on any map of the region until quite recently. Getting there is not easy and at least until 2006 all driveways and passages to the village were cut off by road signs saying 'No entry'.

And Sasha would not be Sasha if he did not tell Mario about his adventures in Turkey in October 2000, especially because he knew that Goldfarb had already related the story in their book *LPG*, published two years earlier. However, Alex deliberately omitted a few details of the interview at the US embassy that Litvinenko was now willing to share with Scaramella and his two ECPP colleagues.

'It was a woman,' Litvinenko said, 'a second secretary. They organised a videoconference with America for me but the CIA was only interested in one thing – who was that person who helped to steal the equipment to point a rocket on the cell phone.' What Litvinenko had in mind was the RIS operation sanctioned by President Yeltsin against Dzhokhar Dudayev, a former Soviet Air Force general and Chechen separatist leader who was the first president of the Chechen Republic of Ichkeria from 1991 until his assassination five years later. It was a joint operation of the GRU, FSB, and the army. According to Litvinenko, in charge of the operation on behalf of the FSB was his former boss Khokholkov. Sasha claimed to have learnt the details from General Khokholkov himself and from Dudayev's widow Alla, whom he interviewed in Nalchik shortly after her husband's demise.

Litvnenko explained that the success of the operation depended on the Russian secret services' ability to track Dudayev's phone to accurately pinpoint his position. As soon as the phone was located, a guided air-to-surface missile was directed to eliminate the target. It is known that American GPS satellites provide services to civilian and military users. While civilian services are for public use, military services are only available to US and allied armed forces as well as to approved government agencies. Sasha claimed that the FSB acquired the technology from an agent within the FBI. When the US embassy in Ankara established a video link with Langley, their only question was the name of this agent.

'And I gave it to them,' he said. 'It was Paul Griffiths of the FBI who was also working for the FSB.'

'After that, did they accept you?'

'No. I emigrated to England where I received political asylum.'

Scaramella was well aware that Litvinenko travelled to Italy using a British passport in the name 'Edwin Redwald Carter'. He also knew that in January 2004, when they first met, Litvinenko was not a British citizen, so to establish his bona fides Mario couldn't help but ask whether, after his arrival to the UK, Sasha had been collaborating with Western secret services who, he reasoned, could provide him with a travel document.

At this moment, Litvinenko's inner voice held him back a bit. 'No,' he said, 'I am not a collaborator of any Western secret service.' It was not true. By that time he was already a fully-fledged agent of the British SIS but correctly decided it would be prudent not to disclose his contacts with British intelligence at least at this early stage.

Fifteen years after the operation against Dudayev, information was leaked to the Russian media purportedly revealing what really happened near the Chechen village of Gekhi-Chu on 21 April 1996. Two GRU colonels, Vladimir Yakovlev and Yuri Aksenov, who took part in the operation, stated that the exact location where Dudayev had arranged to make a phone call from his (Iridium) satellite phone was betrayed to them by a Judas from Dudayev's close circle, who had been paid one million dollars for his betrayal. To estimate a mobile unit's location, Doppler navigation from the satellite was used, the satellite phone tracker technology already available to the Russians. Because a piece of wasteland from where the call was scheduled to be made had been known in advance, a military aircraft with an ASM was already airborne. As a result of the attack, Dudayev was killed but his wife, who was only some twenty metres away from him, survived unscathed.

***

Even if all Sasha's revelations reached Moscow in real time, it was irritating but certainly not sufficient to sanction an assassination on foreign soil, especially during Putin's first term as the President of Russia. But unexpected developments in Vienna, Austria, could very much influence Putin's plans for Italy, where Silvio Berlusconi, an old friend of the Soviet Union, became the prime minister for the second time in June 2001. Shortly before, he invited Paolo Guzzanti, a well-known journalist and long-time member of Berlusconi's Forza Italia party, to stand for the Senate, the upper house of the Italian parliament and, when elected, head the Mitrokhin Commission. Litvinenko's collaboration with the commission could interfere with Putin's efforts to restore Russia's influence in Europe.

The preliminary talks to establish a new gas pipeline from Turkey to Austria to diversify natural gas suppliers and delivery routes for Europe started in February

2002 between the Austrian ÖMV and Turkish BOTAŞ. While BOTAŞ is BOTAŞ Petroleum Pipeline Corporation, a state-owned crude oil and natural gas pipeline and trading company, the Austrian group Österreichische Mineralölverwaltung AG emerged from the Sowjetischen Mineralölverwaltung (SMV, Soviet Mineral Oil Administration) controlled by the Soviet occupation force until 1955. In June 2002, representatives of five countries gathered in Vienna to sign a protocol of intentions between ÖMV (Austria), MOL Group (Hungary), Bulgargaz (Bulgaria), Transgaz (Romania), and BOTAŞ (Turkey) to construct the new pipeline. In the evening, the delegates were invited to the Vienna State Opera where the Italian opera *Nabucco* by Giuseppe Verdi was performed. The protocol signed during that meeting was followed by the cooperation agreement in October and the project was named Nabucco. It goes without saying that Moscow learned about all these developments immediately not only because it was a European project of strategic importance also backed by the United States but first of all because its idea was to lessen European dependence on Russian energy supplies.

Russian reaction followed without delay. In December, Centrex Europe Energy & Gas AG (CEEG) was registered in Vienna at 17 Wiedner Hauptstrasse, with Gazprom Export LLC as a sole shareholder. Its Supervisory Board consisted of three private persons, all Russian, and the aim of the company was, according to Gazprom's website, 'to operate in the energy sector of liberalized European markets'. As usual, a network of other business entities was formed as part of Centrex Group, registered in Cyprus, including Centrex Beteiligungs GmbH at the same address, as well as Centrex Energy Italien [*sic*] Gas Holding GmbH (CEIGH), its 100 per cent subsidiary. A Vienna lawyer Marco Szucsich was registered as its managing director. Magister Szucsich, whose law firm is located at Kärntner Ring opposite the State Opera, studied law at the Moscow State University. It was later established that a close friend of Berlusconi, an Italian businessman called Bruno Mentasti-Granelli, owned 33 per cent of CEIGH through two companies, Hexagon Prima and Hexagon Seconda, registered in Milan.

Like in Spain, where prosecutors had been investigating dirty business schemes and money laundering of the Russian organised crime groups since the 1990s but were only able to trace their contacts to the Kremlin and Russian intelligence services thanks to Litvinenko's tips, his involvement with the Mitrokhin Commission could reveal hidden links between Italian officials and businessmen and Russia, where, since Putin came to power, the former KGB had been playing a leading role in state affairs. Starting from 2005, this had been exacerbated by the fact that Litvinenko began to collaborate with different corporate investigations firms whose job was to look into Russian business dealings in various countries.

In May 2005 Eni, an Italian multinational energy company headquartered in Rome, signed an agreement that would have allowed Gazpromexport to participate in selling Russian gas to Italian domestic consumers. Gazpromexport was headed by Alexander Medvedev, Deputy Chairman of the Gazprom Management Committee. Between 2002 and 2005, Gazpromexport was known as Gazexport, Gazprom's most strategic unit which controlled all the state gas giant's exports. Medvedev had spent many years in Vienna as director of IMAG Investment Management and Advisory Group, set up by Andrey Akimov, Director General of the Soviet-controlled Donau Bank in Vienna, where Medvedev had been his deputy. 'Together,' Catherine Belton writes, 'they oversaw the billions of dollars that were transferred from Gazprom's coffers to RosUkrEnergo, as it began independently exporting excess gas from Ukraine into Europe.' Their contact was 'a man named Dmitry Firtash, [in 2005] a forty-year-old Ukrainian gas trader who secretly, with the Kremlin's blessing, held most of the other 50 per cent stake in RosUkrEnergo'. According to Belton, a former *Financial Times* correspondent in Moscow, 'London became a particular target: Firtash took up a place at the heart of the city's establishment, and his chief London minion funnelled hefty donations to Conservative Party grandees.'[16]

Almost immediately after the contract between Eni and Gazpromexport had been signed, it came under scrutiny by a commission of the Italian parliament, Bloomberg reported in October 2005. The parliamentary commission discovered that CEIGH, a part of Centrex Group, was to play a major role in this lucrative business deal. Italian lawmakers promptly blocked the agreement, accusing Berlusconi of having a personal interest in this deal through his friend Granelli's participation.[17]

After Litvinenko's death, several journalists, business analysts, and private investigators in different countries began to dig up proof of shadow business schemes involving Italian companies and Russia. In September 2007, the German *Stern* magazine came out with a long and detailed analysis under the title 'A tale of *gazoviki*, money and greed', describing Gazprom managers building a network of front companies over Europe. In late 2008, Roman Kupchinsky published a series of articles in *Eurasia Daily Monitor* revealing 'the shadowy side of Gazprom's expanding Central European hub', and in September 2010, Gidi Weitz, in a detailed *Haaretz* report described how the former Stasi officers and agents from Dresden lived and did business in Vienna, bringing together Austrian politicians, Italian entrepreneurs, and Russian oil and gas business.

In his article about Berlusconi, Centrex, Hexagon, and Gasprom, Roman Kupchinsky writes: 'The official Centrex subsidiary in Italy is Centrex Energy Italia S.P.A. based in Milan. The Centrex Group website, however, does not provide any indications that its branch is in any was affiliated with Gazprom. The subterfuge suggests that [Berlusconi, then the Italian prime minister] is deeply indebted to Moscow and will play the role of a loyal puppet, similar to that played by former German Chancellor Gerhard Schroeder and former EU Commissioner [and another former Italian prime minister] Romano Prodi, who have been promoting the Kremlin's energy, and possibly other interests in their home countries and in the EU in any way they can.'

In Vienna, only a few people had ever heard of Martin Schlaff, a billionaire with a penchant for Cuban cigars born to a family of Jewish Second World War refugees. In Austria, Mr Schlaff had long been identified with the SPÖ, the Social Democratic Party, founded as Social Democratic Workers' Party and later transformed into the Socialist Party (the Reds), with friends like the former chancellor Alfred Gusenbauer and former chancellors Viktor Klima and Franz Vranitzky ranking among his associates. I have asked Gert-René Polli, founder and former head of the Austrian Federal Office for the Protection of the Constitution and Counterterrorism (BVT), whether he knew anything about Schlaff's former affiliation with the Stasi, the East German secret police. Herr Polli gave a somewhat evasive answer stating that the BVT, dissolved in 2021, was a police organisation and not the security service. In the meantime, Western researchers had long since found out that Schlaff was the main agent in Vienna of the Stasi's scientific-technical espionage arm (SWT). In March 1986, Schlaff had a meeting in Zagreb with three high-ranking SWT and HVA (foreign intelligence) officers, after which he was given the code name LANDGRAF and the registration number XV 3883/86, listing him as a secret Stasi confidential contact (IM/KP).[18]

In May 1998, a Bundestag committee of inquiry published a report mentioning one of Schlaff's real estate deals in Dresden while in Austria the Stasi entrusted all their real estate business to another agent, Rudolfine Steindling, the legendary 'Red Fini'. Known for providing well-paid positions to senior Austrian politicians after their retirement, Schlaff also employed a good number of former Stasi officers in his business empire. The Bundestag committee noted that after the secret services of the DDR (MfS/AfNS) were disbanded in late 1989, the Schlaff group had supported their former employees by creating for them new companies and jobs.

Like shortly before and right after the collapse of the Soviet Union, when the KGB officers were moving money abroad, the Stasi's foreign intelligence division (HVA) was instrumental in transferring large sums into the West through a web of companies to enable them to finance operations after the fall of the Berlin Wall. Dresden, where Putin had served as a senior case officer of the local KGB station, was a central hub for these preparations. Colonel Herbert Köhler, one of Putin's contacts as head of Department XV (intelligence) in Dresden BV from August 1987 to March 1990, was closely involved in the creation of front companies whose bank accounts could be used for hiding the Stasi's 'black cash'.[19] Köhler worked closely with Schlaff who later employed him in one of his group's businesses in Vienna.

Schlaff was not directly involved in Centrex but his close confidant and business partner Michael Hason held a number of important positions in Centrex Group and another partner, Viennese entrepreneur Robert Nowikovsky, reportedly held 20 per cent of shares in Centrex Energy & Gas until March 2006. Centrex, Schlaff and Nowikovsky even shared the same press office in Vienna, *Stern* reported.

Mayor Mathias Waring was a Stasi officer who in 1989 was sent to Dresden as head of the SWT's Department XV/3 (intelligence/rocket science & technology) at Bautzner Straße. Here his job was to collaborate with the local KGB station in recruiting agents for the KGB's operations in the West. Waring's cell, one of a few that Putin helped to set up after the fall of the Berlin Wall, operated under the guise of a business consultancy. In March 1990, after enrolling for management training at Dresdner Bank, Waring was hired at their Berlin offices, telling the HR officials that he had worked for the East German Ministry for Economics.

In 1990, Putin returned from his tour of duty in East Germany and in June 1991, after a short spell at Leningrad University, was promoted to head the

City Hall's external relations committee, becoming the primary contact for Western businesses in Russia's former imperial capital. In the same year, Waring was sent to St Petersburg to open a new operation. The office was opened in December, and by 2002 he had become head of Dresdner Bank's Russian division.[20]

With all people, companies, banks, and money in place, it took the Putin government almost five years to prepare an alternative deal after they first learnt about Nabucco. In November 2006, Gazprom and Eni signed an agreement which opened the way for direct Russian gas exports to Italy. In June 2007, a year after the Mitrokhin Commission was dissolved, Scaramella arrested and Litvinenko poisoned, Eni and Gazprom agreed to build a controversial US$10 billion South Stream pipeline, which was to deliver gas via Bulgaria to Austria, Slovenia and Italy. 'Under the memorandum on establishing the South Stream, Gazprom and Eni will each hold 50% in the company,' Paolo Scaroni, Eni's CEO said, and on 23 November Associated Press reported that an agreement was signed setting up a 50–50 joint venture to develop a marketing and feasibility study for the South Stream pipeline.

From the very beginning international experts doubted that South Stream was a viable project. It was estimated to cost at least twice as much as Nabucco, while its only purpose was to divert some gas exported through Ukraine. 'It is a political pipeline designed to counter Nabucco,' Alan Riley, Professor of Law at City, University of London was quoted as saying. In spring 2008 Romano Prodi, then the prime minister of Italy, received an offer from the Russian government to become the chairman of South Stream AG. It was reported that 'Prodi was extremely flattered, but reiterated that he wants to take some time off to ponder after leaving Italian politics.' In 2014, after Russia invaded and subsequently annexed the Crimean Peninsula from Ukraine, Gazprom cancelled the South Stream project.

Because I did not find this information in his book, I called Paolo Guzzanti in Rome asking whether his commission ever investigated KGB activities in Italy in 2002–6 and whether he knew anything about the Centrex Group. The former senator said the Mitrokhin Commission was never authorised to investigate KGB agents in Italy or KGB operations anywhere and that he never heard about Centrex.

In the meantime, several Centrex Group companies in Austria and Italy had been liquidated, with some others still remaining active. IMAG Investment Management & Advisory Group moved from Austria to Switzerland, and Russian Lukoil's new headquarters at Schwarzenbergplatz in Vienna had been completed by 2023. One day *Haaretz* reported that Martin Schlaff had financially helped Avigdor Lieberman in Israel to finance his party; then that Lieberman, at the time the Israeli Foreign Minister, said during his visit to Moscow that Russian elections were 'absolutely fair, free and democratic'; and then, as Finance Minister, admitted that in every aspect of Russia's invasion of Ukraine he foremost supported Israel's interests.[21] Commenting on the prime minister's words calling the scenes of dead civilians in the Ukrainian town of Bucha a war crime, Liberman said these were 'mutual accusations'… Well, nothing is new. Nothing is new under the sun.

CHAPTER 7

Storm Clouds are Gathering

> We wanted the best, but it turned out as always.
>
> One of the famous 'Inspiring Quotes and
Sayings' by Viktor Chernomyrdin,
a former Russian prime minister

On 14 April 2018, the Russian Foreign Ministry instructed their embassy in Washington DC to make the following statement:

> Anti-Russia campaign launched by the British authorities over the alleged poisoning of former officer of the Main Intelligence Directorate [GRU] Sergey Skripal and his daughter has been following the pattern that was already used to groundlessly accuse the Russian Federation in connection with the alleged attempted murder of Boris Berezovsky in London in summer 2003 and the death of Alexander Litvinenko in the UK in November 2006.

Less than four years after this exercise in frustration produced by the Kremlin propaganda machine, the whole world would learn that the Russian Foreign Ministry is a cesspit full of liars, the most distrustful, awful, and hypocritical foreign policy institution without any moral values. As a result of this sudden revelation, new to only a few, the West would impose personal sanctions against Sergey Lavrov, Russian foreign minister, and his ministry's spokesperson Maria Zakharova in addition to many other individuals. And, according to *Politico*, since the Russian attack on Ukraine, Ambassador Antonov is Washington's least popular man.

On that April day in 2018, the text distributed by the Russian embassy worked as a time machine, bringing me back to the events of 2006.

In July 2006, the Russian embassy's 'statement of facts' asserted, the Prosecutor General's Office of the Russian Federation received a written application from Vladimir Terlyuk, 'a stateless person originating from Kazakhstan who had resided with his family in the United Kingdom' for seven years. As stated in the application, prosecutors said, between May and September 2003, Boris Berezovsky, Alexander

✂ DISCOVER MORE ABOUT PEN & SWORD BOOKS

Pen & Sword Books have over 4000 books currently available, our imprints include: Aviation, Naval, Military, Archaeology, Transport, Frontline, Seaforth and the Battleground series, and we cover all periods of history on land, sea and air.

Can we stay in touch? From time to time we'd like to send you our latest catalogues, promotions and special offers by post. If you would prefer not to receive these, please tick this box. ☐

We also think you'd enjoy some of the latest products and offers by post from our trusted partners: companies operating in the clothing, collectables, food & wine, gardening, gadgets & entertainment, health & beauty, household goods, and home interiors categories. If you would like to receive these by post, please tick this box. ☐

We respect your privacy. We use personal information you provide us with to send you information about our products, maintain records and for marketing purposes. For more information explaining how we use your information please see our privacy policy at www.pen-and-sword.co.uk/privacy. You can opt out of our mailing list at any time via our website or by calling 01226 734422.

Mr/Mrs/Ms ....

Address..

Postcode .... Email address..

Website: www.pen-and-sword.co.uk Email: enquiries@pen-and-sword.co.uk
Telephone: 01226 734555   Fax: 01226 734438
Stay in touch: facebook.com/penandswordbooks or follow us on Twitter @penswordbooks

Freepost Plus RTKE-RGRJ-KTTX
Pen & Sword Books Ltd
47 Church Street
BARNSLEY
S70 2AS

Litvinenko, Alexander Goldfarb and their British lawyers, 'in order to create fictitious grounds for Boris Berezovsky's asylum application, tried to threaten and bribe him [Terlyuk] to make a false statement to British law enforcement agencies confessing that he was a member of Russian special services and was involved in preparing an assassination of Boris Berezovsky'.

As a fit and proper person, they further stated, Terlyuk refused to bear this false witness, after which Litvinenko and Goldfarb, acting under Berezovsky's instructions, submitted on 31 July 2003 and 4 August 2003 respectively to the competent British authorities knowingly false information alleging that Terlyuk was a Russian special services agent tasked to kill Berezovsky using a poisonous substance. And the most interesting part:

> As part of this investigation, in September 2003 Scotland Yard officers Simon Rose and David Cadman questioned Terluk [*sic*] if he belonged to the Russian special services and had the task to kill Berezovsky with a poisonous substance. Terluk categorically rejected these groundless statements and described in detail the whole scenario of Berezovsky's staging of the attempt on his life in order to obtain asylum in the UK as well as the actions of Litvinenko, Goldfarb and other persons involved in staging this provocation.

This is a typical example of 'active measures' which is an important part of the political warfare conducted by the Kremlin since the 1920s. Active measures include disinformation, propaganda, deception, false statements, wild guesses and inventions aimed to discredit, deceive or at least sow doubt, all this supporting the foreign policy priorities of Russia.

When this book was being researched, I was not able to contact Terlyuk but Alex Goldfarb was at his home in Washington and therefore easy to reach. I have been acquainted with Alex for almost twenty years and have no reason not to trust him. Goldfarb explained that he never regarded Terlyuk as a direct threat. In fact, he said, his assessment was that Terlyuk was an insignificant figure used by Russian intelligence. Terlyuk did not make any written statement in 2003, although Alex and Sasha encouraged him to do so. There is, nonetheless, a brief written record of Terlyuk's account of events. It is a purely internal police report dated 26 November 2003.

In London, I met David Leppard, the author of the article 'Russian spies plot to kill tycoon in Britain' published in *The Sunday Times* on 21 September 2003. At the time David was a staff writer, assistant editor (home affairs) who, I immediately noticed, was inclined to produce sensationalist, sometimes inaccurate accounts without properly checking the facts. Nevertheless, after his article appeared, two police officers, Detective Sergeant Rose and Detective Constable Cadman, were sent to interview Terlyuk. Their record, consistent with what Goldfarb and Litvinenko were saying, was included as part of the evidence in the High Court of Justice (Queen's Bench Division) during the trial *Berezovsky vs. RT&RBC and Terlyuk* on 10 March 2010.

According to Terlyuk's interview with Special Branch, Terlyuk stated that shortly after he arrived in the UK, he was walking near a park in Camden Town. There he met two men, both speaking Russian, one of whom introduced himself as Alexander Smirnov, employed by the Russian Trade Delegation in the UK. The diplomat left his business card with his telephone and his office address at 33 Highgate West Hill, N6. Soon he and Terlyuk started to meet. One day, according to Terlyuk, they agreed to attend the extradition hearings of Berezovsky and Dubov at Bow Street Magistrates Court in Central London but, for whatever reason, Smirnov did not appear and Terlyuk went alone. As recorded in the above-mentioned police report, 'they met again after the hearing and Terlyuk stated that Smirnoff [sic] asked lots of questions in minute detail about what went on in the hearing'. Terlyuk stated that Smirnov 'asked about the layout of the building, Berezovsky's security detail, the general security and how members of the public were shown in and out'. After that, Terlyuk attended another three hearings, always alone. He explained that Smirnov always phoned to make apologies at the last moment. After his last visit, Smirnov asked how people were searched when they entered, if the court guards used metal detectors or checked inside folders, and if they examined pens.

Terlyuk told the Special Branch officers that he realised that Smirnov 'worked for the Russian Security Services' (meaning the former KGB) and that he was being used by him. Terlyuk stated that Berezovsky's legal team had subsequently badgered him for a statement, which would be used to bolster Berezovsky's asylum application, in return offering him legal help with his own asylum application, which was still pending. He said he refused. That report ends with a note that

> Mr Terlyuk is a former KGB/FSB and is a very sharp-minded and intelligent man. He has stated that he accepted taskings from the Russian Security Service and he has passed this information on to Berezovsky's team. He denies taking any payment for any of this but does not work and lives in a well-appointed semi-detached house.

The judge noted that there was no record of the defendant making any complaints to the police officers of the bullying and bribery attempts that he later raised in his litigation. Nor did he mention anything about being given psychotropic substances or anything of the sort. The judge concluded that there should be judgement in favour of Berezovsky and that an appropriate award in respect of two joint tortfeasors – the TV company and Terlyuk – must be £150,000. I do not know whether this sum covered Boris's legal expenses, but it was a fair decision.

In September that year, Berezovsky was granted political asylum by Britain not because of Terlyuk's supposed 'confessions', although this case probably helped. There is no doubt that both the Home Office and the Foreign Office were well aware of the threat to his life as well as of the fact that since his departure from Russia, he had become Enemy Number One to the Kremlin and Putin personally.

And although Boris despised his enemies and despised danger, he was not able to mitigate the threats when he had to face them. As it turned out, fears for his life were well justified. Unfortunately.

* * *

The basic problem of the Russian secret services is absence of modern, unconventional thinking. It an infirmity inducing conformity which, contrary to common assumptions, is a scourge for all Soviet dictators from Lenin to Putin and all their intelligence chiefs. Perhaps, alongside caution, this is a common feature of all intelligence chiefs, I don't know. If we take Putin's long period in power in Russia, they have been as bad and unprofessional as all their predecessors. While Patrushev is portrayed as a hawk, Bortnikov as a schemer, Zolotov as a dumb ox, and Naryshkin as a weakling, and taken individually they do not represent any serious threat, in a multilevel intelligence operation in London – first against Litvinenko and then Berezovsky – they seem to have been acting in unison and that secured an apparent success, again contrary to what has been stated in virtually every published source dealing with the subject.

Another serious drawback is that in what concerns Russian intelligence operations abroad, everything is done by the book. One might think this is an advantage, but the problem is their book has long been out of date. Therefore, all their 'covert' actions are perfectly predictable, one should only take a good account of the trade, that is, of Soviet intelligence history. Alas, Western intelligence analysts are bad historians. And while British intelligence historians are by far the best in the world, Her Majesty's intelligence officers, as Sir John Scarlett once admitted, do not like to read books. Like 007, they are rather action heroes.

Already in 2003, there was one of the first attempts to compromise Litvinenko in London. On 12 October, Scotland Yard detectives arrested former FSB Major Andrei Ponkin and businessman Aleksey Aliokhin, both travelling to the UK on tourist visas.[1] Ponkin was Sasha's second-in-command in the 7th department of URPO, the notorious and corrupt 'special tasks' unit of the FSB headed by Colonel Gusak, whose name is translated into English as 'gander', a male goose.

There are several, sometimes quite extraordinary, versions of what happened that October in London with Litvinenko playing 'a large supporting role', as they say in the theatre. A brief bibliographical essay will include a good number of conflicting sources.

As claimed in the article 'UK plot to kill President Putin', published by David Leppard in *The Sunday Times* on 19 October and on the same day picked up by CNN, 'the alleged plot "in which Putin was to be shot dead by a sniper while on a foreign trip" was uncovered by the [Scotland] Yard nine days ago'.

> Detectives from the Yard's anti-terrorist branch SO13 arrested the former KGB major, said to be a trained hitman, and a second Russian after a tip-off last weekend ... Police were alerted after they received

a detailed legal statement from Alexander Litvinenko, a former intelligence officer in Russia's FSB.

An unnamed police spokeswoman confirmed to the CNN reporter that two men aged 40 and 36 were indeed arrested by officers from SO13 'on the morning of Sunday, October 12 in Central London following allegations of offences under the Terrorism Act 2000'. She also added that the officers received details from Litvinenko 'after he had been contacted by the alleged plotter'.

Alan Cowell in his book *The Terminal Spy* (2008) offers a version promoted by Andrey Soldatov, one of the editors of the Russian internet site agentura.ru. According to Cowell, Litvinenko explained to Soldatov during their meeting at Piccadilly Circus that Ponkin had put out word that he wanted to meet with Berezovsky to discuss the financing of an operation against Putin. Litvinenko, according to Soldatov's story, 'arranged to meet Ponkin in a hotel room bugged by MI5 operatives who then arrested the two visiting Russians and deported them'.

Luke Harding, a *Guardian* foreign correspondent, comes up with yet another story.[2] Ponkin flew to London with a Russian businessman 'and Litvinenko agreed to meet them at the Piccadilly branch of Wagamama, a Japanese noodle bar. [In reality, Wagamama is a restaurant chain serving Asian food. It was founded by Alan Yau, who later opened such famous London Chinese restaurants as Hakkasan and Yauatcha.] Ponkin had a suggestion: Litvinenko should assassinate Putin!' Ponkin allegedly told Litvinenko he had a friend in the Federal Protection Service, General Yuri Kalugin (and senior FSO officer Vadim Medvedev), who could provide details of Putin's movements two weeks in advance. All Litvinenko needed to do was to ask Berezovsky and Zakayev to arrange a hit.

This version, also distributed by the Russian media, had as usual a twofold agenda which immediately betrayed a clumsy FSB plan: to accuse Berezovsky and his people of planning to kill Putin, and to compromise Litvinenko.

Ponkin and Aliokhin were instructed to pretend that they initially decided not to respond to any interview requests but in the end succumbed to the pleas of *Komsomolskaya Pravda* (acronymised as KP, which literally means 'Pravda of the Young Communist League'), a popular daily Russian tabloid with some links to Gazprom. As should have been expected, they made up a bizarre story.

To begin with, Aliokhin accused Litvinenko of racketeering and extortion even after he left Russia. According to this legend, in order to help his friend to resolve the problem, Ponkin suggested he fly to London and talk to Litvinenko. Having arrived in the British capital on 5 October, they immediately called Litvinenko and arranged a meeting at Piccadilly Circus on the next day.

When Litvinenko finally arrived, according to Ponkin, he was somewhat nervous and their meeting ended in haste with Sasha suggesting a rendezvous with Berezovsky 'to discuss one important problem'. However, at about 11.00 pm of the same day, both Ponkin and Aliokhin were detained right in their room at the Hilton. At 5.30 am, they were released after both refused to sign any document, according to KP.

When Litvinenko telephoned them again, they asked him not to disturb them any more, having decided to complain on Litvinenko's behaviour directly to Berezovsky. Three days later, two plain-clothes Scotland Yard officers visited them again in their hotel room. One introduced himself as DS Simon Rose (remember the Terlyuk case). Detective Sergeant Rose said they simply wanted to discuss Litvinenko's recent book *The Lubyanka Organised Crime Group*, also asking questions about the Russian mafia, racket, krysha, as well as about Berezovsky's relationship with Putin. At the end, they invited Ponkin to join the staff of the Special Branch as an experienced former FSB officer – an offer, he said, he declined.

After three more days in London, so the KP story went, on 12 October their hotel door was broken by a large group of officers from the counterterrorism police force. Ponkin and Aliokhin were both detained and brought to the police station, where they were charged with conspiracy to murder President Putin. When they demanded to see a Russian consul, they were informed that the Russian embassy officials refused to come. 'In spite of repeated interrogations that followed,' Ponkin said, 'I did not confess to anything.' On Friday, they were escorted to the airport.

'We had to spend six days in prison without any reason,' Ponkin explained to the KP correspondent, 'and only at the airport I guessed who had been behind this affair. On the tickets I noticed the name of the payer: Secret Intelligence Service.'

'Back in Moscow, did they summon you to the competent organs [in Russia, a euphemism for the FSB] to ask what really happened in London?'

'Of course, but they said they understood everything and had no problems with us.'

Amazingly, instead of studying appropriate police documents pertinent to this case, during the Litvinenko Inquiry the coroner decided to hear evidence from Marina Litvinenko. She recounted how Ponkin came to London and tried to involve her husband in a plot to kill President Putin. She testified that Sasha 'quickly came to the view that this was a provocation orchestrated by the FSB, and reported the matter to the British police'.[3] Ponkin and another man, with whom he was travelling, were deported, Marina said.

In their turn, the Met felt obliged to make an official statement. 'If Scotland Yard get an allegation of this kind, it has to investigate if there's any truth in it. It seems like there wasn't in this case,' a police source told Reuters.

'They were released without charge on 17 October,' Scotland Yard Press Secretary Paul Clark told a popular Moscow newspaper. 'They returned to Russia at their own will. We are not entitled to confirm or deny any other information.'

On 17 October, Boris Berezovsky accompanied by his lawyers visited Scotland Yard. He was told that the police had indeed informed the Russian embassy of the arrest of two Russians reportedly planning the assassination of President Putin. Later, Berezovsky was on record as saying: 'The police were very surprised that there was no reaction to this from the Russian diplomats.'

In October 2004, Andrey Lugovoy, a former major in the GUO (Protection Command), made a telephone call from Moscow to Sasha's mobile number in London suggesting a meeting. He said he was coming to the British capital to cheer for his team in a CSKA v. Chelsea match. It would be the first time the two men met after Litvinenko managed to escape from Russia.

In the meantime, the first round of presidential elections in Ukraine was held on 31 October. As no candidate managed to get 50 or more per cent of the votes, a run-off ballot between the two leading candidates, Viktor Yanukovich and Viktor Yushchenko, was scheduled for 21 November. The Russian newspaper *Kommersant* reported that the first units of Russian special forces were transferred to Ukraine on 23 November. The first aircraft with Russian soldiers onboard asked for permission for transit flight over Kiev at 1.32 am. Another aircraft reached Kiev two hours later. Both landed at Hostomel Airport, Kiev Oblast, which would become internationally known after severe battles took place here between February and March 2022, during the Russian invasion of Ukraine. When this book was sent to press, the media described abandoned Hostomel Airport standing as a monument to Ukraine's struggle against by now badly battered Russian forces.

Back in November 2004, soldiers of the Russian special operations forces unit Vityaz ('Knight'), active during the First Chechen War, were on the planes. They were taken to the nearby base of the special forces brigade of the Ministry of Internal Affairs of Ukraine and dressed in the uniforms of Ukrainian militia. On the same day, it was announced that the run-off election – rigged, according to many international observers – was won by Yanukovich. The subsequent events led to a political crisis in Ukraine, which developed into what became known as the Orange Revolution. People called for a re-run of the second round and the Supreme Court appointed the re-run for 26 December.

A year later, the International Foundation for Civil Liberties (IFCL), headed by Goldfarb and funded by Berezovsky, quit the tape scandal. Goldfarb made a statement that the Foundation 'from today is not going to pursue the public debate on the so-called "Melnichenko tapes"'. It was after the incumbent prime minister Yanukovich, Putin's favourite candidate also supported by the Ukrainian government, lost the election in the final run-off ballot. Kuchma solicited Putin's support since relations with the West had deteriorated in the wake of the Kuchmagate crisis. The GlobalSecurity.org site in their long comment stressed that Putin and Russia held the key to the 2004 transition to a post-Kuchma era. Yanukovych's Russian-inspired electoral platform called on Ukrainians to abandon their aspirations for NATO and EU membership, promising to make Russian the second official language, which had always been a sensitive issue for Putin's regime.

In January 2006, Lugovoy was among the numerous guests whom Boris had invited to celebrate his 60th birthday, an extravagant and very formal black-tie event at Blenheim Palace in Woodstock, Oxfordshire. Together with the others coming from Russia, Lugovoy arrived in a specially rented private jet. During the reception, he was seated at the same table as Nikolai Glushkov (according to another version, at the same table with Litvinenko and Goldfarb), whom Berezovsky had planned to rescue from prison by selling his and Badri's interests in ORT, Russian Public Television.

Storm Clouds are Gathering

Four weeks before Litvinenko was granted political asylum, on 11 April 2001 Berezovsky's long-term business partner Glushkov, officially in custody for channelling Aeroflot money to Andava S. A. in Lausanne, Forus Leasing S. A. in Bern and Andava Finance Ltd, was taken to Lefortovo prison. As a matter of fact, there was nothing unlawful in what he did – as soon as Glushkov was appointed Aeroflot deputy general director, he closed all 450 bank accounts controlled by 100 Aeroflot offices worldwide and transferred all money to Switzerland where Andava, as a fiduciary services company, became a kind of Aeroflot's treasurer abroad. This is a common practice, explained Glushkov to prosecutors. For example, Volvo Group Treasury operates its branches in different countries. In the Aeroflot case, this was done to reduce taxes, coordinate funding strategy and facilitate leasing payments.

On that day, Glushkov left his Moscow hospital ward wearing only his gown and slippers. He had been arrested by Russian authorities on fraud charges in December the year before, shortly after Berezovsky established his permanent residence in London where he moved from his French property, the Château de la Garoupe on Cap d'Antibes (Côte d'Azur).

Formally under arrest, Glushkov had been hospitalised at Moscow's Scientific Haematological Centre for a blood condition. That evening, he was going home as usual for an overnight stay. A former Aeroflot colleague was waiting at the gate. As Glushkov was about to get into the car, a squad of plain-clothes FSB officers appeared out of nowhere, arrested both men, and charged them with 'attempted escape from custody'. On the next day, the former head of the ORT security, Andrei Lugovoy, was detained and charged with organising the alleged escape while Badri Patarkatsishvili, Berezovsky's closest friend, had to flee to his native Georgia to avoid arrest.

When Goldfarb interviewed Glushkov for his book years later in London, the former physicist turned businessman who once noticed that 3,000 people out of the total workforce of 14,000 in Aeroflot were Russian intelligence officers on active duty, offered a different version of the events of that evening. 'He believed,' Goldfarb says, 'that he had been set up and insisted that he had no intent to escape. He wanted the Aeroflot case to be tried because he knew he was innocent. In fact, he was under the impression that he would be released pending the trial "through a secret high-level deal", as his lawyers had hinted to him.'

Although Glushkov was absolutely innocent, Berezovsky was indeed contemplating an exfiltration operation to get him out of Russia, Felshtinsky recalls.[4] The escape route was planned via Ukraine and Felshtinsky readily offered his services, but Boris declined saying that he already had a reliable person in Moscow to take care of his old friend. It seems he had in mind Lugovoy.

In Blenheim Palace, 'a string quartet was playing as 200 guests sipped pink champagne by a magnificent fire', writes a BuzzFeed reporter. 'Among them were all the key players in the oligarch's global chess game.' Sasha, Marina, Goldfarb, Felshtinsky, Akhmed Zakayev, and Zakayev's aide Yasha (Yaragi Abdullayev) were seated at one table and did not stand out among other prominent and less prominent personalities whom Boris invited to his birthday party. I met all those six guests, including Berezovsky, after Sasha's death to discuss every detail of what I call Operation VLADIMIR, a codename for the plan to poison Litvinenko and send him to a slow, excruciating death.

This was 23 January 2006, a day and night of joy and exuberant celebration. It shall possibly also be remembered as the date when not only the fate of Litvinenko but also of Patarkatsishvili, Berezovsky and Glushkov was sealed. No one was able to foresee or control unexpected and unfortunate developments that were to take place at the end of the year and then again in February 2008, March 2013 and March 2018, with precise five-year intervals. And if the circumstances of Berezovsky's and Patarkatsishvili's demise remain unexplained, Glushkov was strangled to death by what is professionally known as a rear naked choke (RNC), a martial arts technique applied from an opponent's back. And Sasha was poisoned.

All this, however, will happen later, although active preparations for the final stage of Operation VLADIMIR aimed at silencing Litvinenko began on that January night. Today, one can say with complete certainty that this radiation poisoning was a very Russian murder. But contrary to many other similar operations, this one was meticulously planned and professionally executed.

***

The last ten months of his short life, between January and October 2006, were perhaps the most difficult and at the same time most fruitful period for Alexander Litvinenko. In February, he went to Italy where, with the help of Mario Scaramella, he recorded a sensational video testimony openly accusing Romano Prodi, who would soon be prime minister again after defeating Silvio Berlusconi, a friend of Putin, in the April election. Sasha was careful enough not to say that Prodi was a Russian agent, rather, he accused him of being 'a KGB man'. This was the last help Sasha could provide to the Mitrokhin Commission of the Italian parliament because, at the end of March, its mandate expired. When Scaramella made those accusations public, Prodi threatened to sue but named no one in particular.

The final planning of Operation VLADIMIR began when four active participants – Lugovoy, Kovtun, Sokolenko, and Valuyev – were summoned to a conference in the Russian spa resort area known as the Caucasian Mineral Waters (KMV). All of them took the same regular flight from Moscow Vnukovo to Mineralnye Vody Airport on 10 March 2006, spending five days there. The local FSB chief, Colonel Sergey Kirillov, was instructed to arrange a meeting and discreet transfer to one of the FSB dachas.

In the meantime in London, Litvinenko's articles for the Chechenpress separatist site linked to Zakayev, head of the Chechen government in exile and his followers, became fierce and crushing recalling the style of Anna Politkovskaya, a *Novaya Gazeta* journalist whom Sasha greatly respected. His work for the Chechen commission preparing evidence for the International Criminal Court became more organised and systematic. He had already visited Georgia using his new British identity issued by MI6 in an attempt to find the key witness of the 1999 Russian apartment bombings that he and Felshtinsky were investigating. Since his meeting with the Spanish anti-corruption prosecutor José Grinda Sasha was actively assisting security services and law enforcement agencies in Europe and Israel to arrest Russian mafia bosses many of whom, he knew, were linked not only to the SVR, FSB and GRU but also to the Russian government and even to the Kremlin.

One day in July 2006, when Marina and Tolik were on holiday at a camp with other children and their parents and Sasha was 'home alone', Lugovoy suddenly arrived in London with his wife saying that he wanted to buy a home in the UK. Litvinenko invited them to his house being happy to show how a real English house looked. Like many other similar buildings, the residential property at 140 Osier Crescent was no architectural gem, but functional. This modest dwelling was of course rather far from what is usually known as a Typical British Home, but Sasha was very proud and happy anyway. He felt it natural to help his friend establish himself in Great Britain and started looking for an appropriate property. In their covert operation, Moscow planners were trying to lull any possible suspicions that Sasha, as former FSB operative, might have.

Shortly before or right after Lugovoy's sudden visit, Litvinenko accused Putin of being a paedophile. In early July, the Chechenpress website published Litvinenko's article 'The Kremlin Pedophile'. Putin was walking in the Kremlin grounds, Sasha wrote, when he stopped to chat with the tourists, among them a 4- or 5-year-old boy. The president lifted the boy's shirt and kissed his stomach. The incident was covered by the Russian and international media. The *Daily Mail* website quoted Litvinenko: 'The world public is shocked. Nobody can understand why the Russian president did such a strange thing as kissing the stomach of an unfamiliar small boy.'[5] Sasha went further by claiming – which he could never have known – that after graduating from the Andropov Institute in 1985, Putin was not duly promoted, that is, sent to one of the West European countries, because the authorities found out that he was a paedophile. So, he concluded, they exiled him to provincial Dresden. There, he was not involved in any intelligence work but was only liaising with the Stasi and reporting to Karlshorst.

But Sasha did not stop here. When the future Russian president became the FSB director, Litvinenko stated that 'among other things, Putin found videotapes in the FSB Internal Security directorate, which showed him having sex with some underage boys.' Carefully evaluating all reasons that could finally push Putin to give orders to get rid of this mockingbird who became a real everyday nuisance, the Litvinenko Inquiry chairman Sir Robert Owen wrote in his report: 'It hardly needs saying that the allegations made by Mr Litvinenko against President Putin in this article were of the most serious nature.'

Putin joined the KGB when he was 23 and still a Komsomol member. Little was known so far about 'Comrade Platov', his Andropov Institute pseudonym, from a single declassified carefully selected evaluation of the young KGB major written by his course supervisor Colonel Mikhail Frolov. When the Family was only promoting Putin to be nominated a candidate for president, the old colonel added a few words of his personal impressions for the book *First Person* (published shortly after Putin's election in May 2000). Mark Galeotti summarised all available information writing that Putin was the meticulous, dedicated young man, not an A-lister but a strong B, who got into the First Chief Directorate (foreign intelligence) on the basis of not brilliance but determination. In the twenty-plus years of Putin's presidency, he had always managed to combine this lack of intellectual brilliance with the strong determination of a KGB thug. After Putin started a war in Ukraine, there was hardly any media outlet in the world except those of new Russian allies like Iran and North Korea, which would not compare him to Stalin or Hitler, both mass-murderers.

On 6 September, Sasha met Peter B. Reddaway, professor emeritus of political science at George Washington University and former director of the Kennan Institute for Advanced Russian Studies, for a seven-hour-long interview. They discussed Litvinenko's relations with Berezovsky and his take on other oligarchs, Sasha's life and work after he stopped being a regular employee of Boris, the Terlyuk affair, and an array of other topics including Russian organised crime. In particular, Litvinenko told Reddaway that Sergey Lalakin, nicknamed 'Luchok', the leader of the Podolsk organised crime group, had recently hired Vyacheslav Ivankov, nicknamed Yaponchik, a notorious mobster with convictions in both the former Soviet Union and the United States, to control and orchestrate organised crime groups that were closely associated with Gazprom, the giant Russian gas monopoly. Now 'Luchok' is a respected Russian businessman.[6] Ivankov was shot dead in Moscow in July 2009.

A week after their meeting, on 13 September the deputy head of the Central Bank of Russia Andrei Kozlov was murdered in Moscow. Men wielding pistols walked up to the banker in the parking lot of a soccer stadium and shot him in the head.

Natalia Morar wrote in *The New Times*, a liberal Moscow magazine:

> According to the MVD [the Interior Ministry], the examination uncovered a unitary scheme for sending abroad the money of officials close to the oil companies controlled by the Kremlin and lieutenant-general Alexander Bortnikov, deputy director and head of the Economic Security Service of the FSB. Bortnikov is known for his close relations with the deputy head of the presidential administration Igor Sechin and with Vladimir Putin's assistant Viktor Ivanov. According to the sources of *The New Times*, Bortnikov supposedly oversaw the outflow of the money of various commercial structures engaged in the sale of electronics in Russia.[7]

Two weeks before his murder, Kozlov had been cooperating closely with the Austrian authorities on the money laundering case, a detail made public in a report posted on the website of the Austrian Ministry of Interior. It said the Austrian police could not rule out 'official corruption' in Russia as a motive for murder.

Sasha could clear up the puzzle. He would explain that for almost thirty years (1975–2004), Bortnikov, a Brezhnev-era functionary, worked in the Leningrad KGB and before his transfer to Moscow in February 2004 headed the St Petersburg and Leningrad district directorate of its successor organisation, FSB. Putin had been his pupil all along. On 12 May 2008, General Bortnikov was appointed director of the FSB.

The officers of Scotland Yard's SO15 asked Keith Hunter whether he was familiar with the report 'Main characteristics of Russian Organised Crime 2003–5' which, without doubt, was found among Sasha's papers. Keith said he never saw the document and never tasked Litvinenko to compile it. The police did not know that Litvinenko meticulously collected all information that had anything to do with Russian organised crime, corruption, and the Kremlin/FSB links to the criminal underworld.

While Litvinenko was helping *Novaya Gazeta* in their investigation into the poisoning of Yuri Schekochihin, its deputy editor – one of the topics of our discussion in London in 2005 – bad news came from Moscow. On 7 October 2006, Putin's birthday, Anna Politkovskaya was shot in the elevator of her block of flats in Moscow. Like Berezovsky, Litvinenko and Nemtsov, Anna was one of the most outspoken critics of Putin. She wrote:

> Why do I so dislike Putin? This is precisely why. I dislike him for matter-of-factness worth than felony, for his cynicism, for his racism, for his lies, for the gas he used in the Nord-Ost siege, for the massacre of the innocents, which went on throughout his term as President ...
> His outlook is the narrow, provincial one his rank would suggest; he has the unprepossessing personality of a lieutenant colonel who never made it to colonel, the manner of a Soviet secret policeman who habitually snoops on his own colleagues. And he is vindictive.

For whatever reason, Professor Reddaway decided her death was 'in retribution for her reports on abuses and atrocities in Chechnya'. In reality, neither Putin nor his clique cared about the reports of a female journalist who was perhaps known and admired in the West but could not make a big impact on the Russian media space. The real problem was that Anna was publicly mocking Putin and, as a very vindictive person, Putin would not tolerate this.

In Reddaway's opinion, on 27 October Putin tried to mitigate the damage caused by Politkovskaya's murder by giving a big reception at his Novo-Ogaryovo residence for Western businessmen, bankers, and lawyers, wooing them to step up their investments in the Russian economy. The Kremlin website showed him at the reception flanked by Igor Sechin, Putin's confidante since the early 1990s and chairman of the board of directors of Rosneft, which swallowed up the asserts of Yukos, and Petr Aven of the Alfa-Bank, like Sechin, a member of Putin's inner circle. After some deliberation, Peter Reddaway concludes that 'the murder of Politkovskaya (on Putin's birthday) was carried out by the hardliners without

Putin's agreement'. It seems a long session with Litvinenko could not persuade the American professor that Putin was quite certainly personally behind this murder, irrespective of whether he directly commanded his henchmen to do it or not. 'I have some rules of my own,' Putin said in one of the earlier interviews. 'One of them is never to regret anything.'[8]

In the Frontline Club near Paddington Station, where I interviewed Alex Goldfarb for the BBC *Panorama* documentary *How to Poison a Spy* a few weeks later, Sasha, speaking through an interpreter, addressed the gathering:

> The question was asked here who killed Anna Politkovskaya. I can give an answer. It was Vladimir Putin, the President of Russia. After her book *Putin's Russia* was published in the West, Politkovskaya started to receive threats from the Kremlin. Only one person in Russia could kill a journalist of her standing, only one person could sanction her death. And this person is Putin.

The executive phase of the Litvinenko operation started in London days after the death of Politkovskaya. As reconstructed later by the Scotland Yard investigators, it began with a puzzle.

For several weeks, members of a Russian surveillance team who arrived from Moscow and St Petersburg under various guises followed Sasha in London. They studied, analysed, and cross-checked all his movements and regular places of meeting his contacts and recorded his telephone calls using the eavesdropping listening station installed at the top floor of the Russian embassy. But while in Moscow and the whole of Russia, and even on the territory of the FSU, physical surveillance was the job of the FSB, as was clearly established in the cases of Politkovskaya, Nemtsov and Navalny, it was not so easy on the enemy's turf. An educated guess based on experience will suggest that only officers of the Presidential Security Service (SBP) are sufficiently trained and able to do this job because, as part of protective intelligence measures, their work, which includes advance threat assessments in place, starts long before the president lands in this or that foreign territory. But with all their professionalism and training, they probably missed or at least overlooked one important fact: in October Alexander Litvinenko and his family were granted British citizenship.

On Friday, 13 October, Sasha, Marina and their son attended their citizenship ceremony at Haringey Civic Centre in Wood Green making an oath of allegiance and a pledge promising to respect the rights, freedoms, and laws of the UK. At the end of the ceremony, they were presented with their certificates of British citizenship and a welcome pack, and Sasha was quick to inform everyone about it. But because on that day they did not receive their British passports and because Sasha was always inventing and fantasising so much, few people believed him.

'We were thrilled,' Marina recalled. 'We thought it was particularly important for Anatoly to be British given that he had lived in the UK since he was six years old. Sasha said that we had given our son his future and this was very special.' There was, of course, a darker side to this moment and after the ceremony Sasha and Tolik went to a memorial service for Anna Politkovskaya, organised by supporters just outside Westminster Abbey.

One of the reasons Sasha was so pleased to be granted British citizenship was that it made him feel safer. In the crowd, not far from Anna's niece who was holding her large portrait, Sasha noticed Felshtinsky who was attending the service. He immediately approached Yuri, saying, 'You know, I have just received my citizenship. Now they will not be able to touch me.' Ironically, this was the last time Felshtinsky saw Sasha Litvinenko.

As expected, Bukovsky was also there. 'Did he say anything to you that day about his own safety and security?' Robin Tam QC, Counsel to the Inquiry, asked the old dissident during the Litvinenko hearings. Bukovsky remembered that Sasha was very pleased with getting British citizenship. 'He asked me: it makes me more secure, right? It protects me? And I had to smile and say: well, not much, not really.'

CHAPTER 8

To Kill a Mockingbird – Part 1

Gordievsky, his life companion Maureen and I got out of the cab at the designated place on Swain's Lane by the entrance to Highgate Cemetery West, which was surrounded by hundreds of television cameras and photographers who were being kept at a distance by the police. We moved forward, crossed the courtyard, and were greeted by a solemn and rather small group of mourners gathered under the roof of the retaining wall anticipating rain.

The group included Berezovsky and Zakayev, both of whom I met in person here at Highgate for the first time; Alex Goldfarb, Marina Litvinenko and Boris's girlfriend Elena Gorbunova, mother of his two children; Walter and Maxim Litvinenko, Sasha's father and his younger half-brother who had just arrived from Italy, as well as Andrei Nekrasov, a film director whom I immediately liked and who would soon become famous for his documentaries about his friend's life and death. I did not notice then that Bukovsky was also there. After he settled in Britain, Bukovsky became a senior fellow at the Cato Institute in Washington, DC, a public policy research organisation and a thinktank dedicated 'to the principles of individual liberty, limited government, free markets and peace'. It turned out that at Highgate he was in the company of Pavel Stroilov, who introduced himself as Bukovsky's personal aide, and Gerard Batten, then a UKIP member of the European Parliament. They were together with Litvinenko's first wife and her two children. Later I learned that there were also two Norwegians – Maria Fuglevaag Warsinska, a documentary filmmaker from Oslo, and Ivar Amundsen Minneside, a Norwegian investment banker and businessman also serving as the Honorary Consul of the Chechen Republic of Ichkeria in his country and Director of the Chechnya Peace Forum in London.

Not surprisingly, given the occasion and the ill-assorted group of people gathered on that tragic day at the cemetery, a political discussion broke out and was only interrupted by a signal that the burial was about to start. It was already raining heavily when we entered a muddy road to accompany Sasha to his final destination, but the real storm would start later.

When we were all standing near the grave, Walter Litvinenko said in barely audible Russian: 'Sasha was killed for telling the truth by those who are afraid of what he had to say.' These words were somehow recorded by *The Telegraph* correspondent, reproduced in his report from the funeral and would be used by the Russian propaganda machine a decade later.

After it was all over and Sasha Litvinenko was laid to rest among the Victorian ivy-clad monuments near the poet Christina Rossetti, scientist Michael Faraday, and the graves of Mary Anne Evans better known by her pen name George Eliot, and Karl Marx at the opposite, eastern side, we were all given small white security passes and transported to Lauderdale House in Highgate where a sumptuous memorial service had been arranged.

As soon as the choir finished the first song ('There is a Green Hill Far Away' by Pitts), Boris Berezovsky made the first address. I remember he was very articulate and an excellent speaker. Boris was aware of his authority and strength, especially in this company and situation. Bukovsky, Zakayev, Amundsen, Goldfarb, and Sasha's friend David Kudykov – all spoke well but none as impressively and with such great force and feeling as Berezovsky.

After the ceremony we were seated in waiting buses and transported to the Italian restaurant Santini on Ebury Street in Belgravia, where a dinner was served and everyone remembered Sasha. Though it was both the wrong place and the wrong time, I used the opportunity to speak to Boris and Marina and got their agreement to be interviewed for the BBC *Panorama* documentary. Those were their first ever interviews after Sasha's death and Boris quickly introduced me to Misha Cotlick, his personal assistant who was also there, for further contacts and coordination. I also managed to discuss some details with Kudykov, a rather controversial character as it turned out. David appeared to be very garrulous and immediately handed me a business card with his profile neatly embossed on it above private numbers. Later, Nicolas Rea (Lord Rea) appeared at the party and apologised that he had not been able to attend the funeral. We all ate, drank, and talked a lot and I had a strange feeling that this evening symbolised the beginning rather than the end of something.

In early 2006, Goldfarb had discussed with Litvinenko his financial situation with regard to the funds that Sasha was receiving from Berezovsky's foundation IFCL. Berezovsky asked Goldfarb, the IFCL director, to review the budget for 2006. Litvinenko admitted that he was occasionally receiving 'some money' from various private and government organisations but 'that was not enough to live on' so he could not forgo Berezovsky's support altogether. As a result, Sasha's support from the IFCL was reduced by half – from about US$60,000 a year to $30,000, which was a very considerable reduction indeed. In a rough calculation, also having in mind the exchange rate, that meant instead of approximately £3,400 a month Litvinenko was now receiving from Berezovsky about £1,380.

During the Litvinenko hearings, one of his account managers at RISC Management, Daniel Quirke, was asked about his impressions of Sasha's financial means at the time they were working together, that is, between February and November 2006. 'He was trying to establish a business,' Mr Quirke recalled, 'he was working hard, I think he was short of money. I think monies that he'd previously got from – as like a retainer from Mr Berezovsky, had ceased and that left a hole in his finances.'[1] This question was asked again and again, and Michael Cotlick was among those who had to answer.

Hugh Davies OBE QC (Counsel to the Inquiry): You go on to say: 'I had a phone conversation with Alexander in late summer or early autumn 2006, I was in Israel at the time, he was upset that Boris had apparently cut his salary that for a number of years he had been given...' So whose decision was it that there would be a reduction?

Michael Cotlick: What Alexander told me, that his salary was reduced. I don't know whether there was a discussion between him and Mr Berezovsky, whether the reason to this was the amount of work that Mr Berezovsky had given to Mr Litvinenko was reduced, I don't know what was the reason behind it.

Q. What was your sense of the effect on the relationship between the two men of this reduction in salary in 2006?

A. I can't say that he [Alexander] was pleased with the fact that his salary was reduced, but nobody would probably. At the same time, I have never heard from him a bad word about Mr Berezovsky.

Q. You have never heard a bad word from him about Mr Berezovsky?

A. No.[2]

Even with this substantial reduction, Litvinenko did not have to worry about the family because Berezovsky's foundation continued to pay his son's school fees and the house in Muswell Hill where they moved in February 2003 did not cost them anything except that he and Marina had to take care of utility bills themselves. This they could easily deduct from £2,000 that had been regularly transferred to their joint bank account from an unspecified donor at the end of each month. Both knew where this money came from and sometimes Sasha looked at the ziggurat on the other side of the Thames at Vauxhall Cross with envy and a bit of regret. He thought that Gordievsky had certainly been inside this Legoland many times while he had never had a chance to visit. He consoled himself with the thought that most people did not have a clue about what kind of species inhabit this phantom world behind triple-glazed windows, let alone what they do.

After the Litvinenkos made an application, Marina was not surprised that they only had to wait for three months until a positive decision of the Home Office duly arrived in their post box. It was a pure formality. On Friday, 13 October 2006, the whole family attended their citizenship ceremony making an oath of allegiance and a pledge: 'I, Edwin Redwald Carter and I, Marie Anne Carter, sincerely and truly declare and affirm that on becoming a British citizen, each of us will be faithful and bear true allegiance to Her Majesty Queen Elizabeth the Second, Her Heirs and Successors, according to law.' Their son Tolik, who was also there, did not have to remember the text because he was too small at the time. Years later, he would fully realise how grateful he must be to his parents. And to 'Uncle Boris'. His apparent good luck is a true testament to their dedication, perseverance and love.

Their new British passports arrived in December.

***

On 16 October the commercial Transaero flight UN333 from Moscow landed on schedule at London Gatwick, then still a rather small airport, at 10.48 am. The registration number of the aircraft that made the flight that morning was EI-DDK. Passengers in the South Terminal proceeded to the immigration hall downstairs to join the crowd waiting in the line of passport control officers. Two Russian men in their early forties, each carrying an attaché case, were immediately noticed. 'Both individuals were coming off a flight from Russia,' Detective Constable Spencer Scott, who was on duty on that day, later testified. 'I identified them as – I thought they were of interest and basically as they came through immigration controls, I stopped them and questioned them.' The CCTV camera automatically recording the stop and taking pictures gave the time as 11:34:50 am.

The pair looked somewhat suspicious and DC Scott started to ask questions. He quickly found out that Mr Kovtun, one of the two passengers, did not speak any English while Mr Lugovoy, his senior partner, was ready to give answers.

DC Scott's minimum background investigation (MBI) on the spot showed that two rooms were booked for the Russians via the London travel agent Gullivers Travel Associates (GTA) at the Best Western Shaftsbury Hotel at Shaftsbury Avenue for two nights, from 16 to 18 October, and that on that day they were supposed to fly back to Moscow from Gatwick aboard Transaero flight UN444. So far, everything checked out and looked all right.

However, as soon as DC Scott started to ask questions, he immediately found out that the Russians 'were very evasive as to why they were coming into the UK'.

'They were very evasive?'

'Yes.'

'Can you amplify upon that assertion?'

'Well, as I asked them questions, they weren't coming out with the answers that I wanted to hear or expected to hear.'

As it was later established, Lugovoy was brazenly lying to the policeman. He said he owned a company called Global Projects, which did not exist, and introduced his old mate Kovtun as a member of the finance department of the Metropol Bank (DC Scott recorded it as 'Bank Metropolises in Russia'), which he was not. Kovtun never worked in that bank and Lugovoy was placed there briefly before the Litvinenko operation as security advisor. Lugovoy further claimed that they had travelled to London for 'business purposes', and those purposes were all with the company called Continental Petroleum Limited (CPL) whose director, he said, was one Alexander Shadrin (phonetically recorded by DC Scott as 'Shadray'). The vigilant detective constable called the number provided by

Lugovoy and the voice on the other end confirmed that two Russians were indeed visiting this address but the company's name was Eco3 Capital, a sister company of CPL.

Spencer Scott was quite obviously a very good policeman and he did not stop here. He went as far as doing searches 'on our systems', that is, the police database and the internet to check whether those companies existed and were registered in the UK, and found out that they were not. Actually, they were properly registered but were entities composed by Russians with Russian personnel. It would not be a problem to find out that Shadrin also served as director of Laurasia Resources Ltd, registered at the same address, as well as of Ecological Finance BV, also sitting here but registered in Rotterdam. Its secretaries were, unsurprisingly, Laurasia Resources and Eco3 Capital. Later, Overseas Resources Ltd with Shadrin as director would also be placed here. By the time of the Litvinenko Inquiry hearings all of them would be duly dissolved. The last one, Interguarantee Limited, incorporated in August 2000, was waiting to be struck off as of spring 2023.

'On what basis did you permit them to continue [their travel] if you'd found them somewhat evasive in their responses to you?'

'I was given advice that I should allow them to go forward, to leave…'

'You were given advice that you should allow them to go forward?'

'Yes, I was given advice that I should let them leave the airport on the facts that I'd found.'

'Thank you very much, Mr Scott.'[3]

There were no more questions. And no one cared to ask who gave the advice to just let them go.

As soon as Lugovoy was left alone, he immediately called Shadrin (the call was registered at 11:45:34 am) to say that he had passed. That means that the time the pair spent with DC Scott was less than fifteen minutes. Almost immediately after, Lugovoy dialled Litvinenko's secret mobile number reserved for their private communications only, and said that he had safely arrived and would now be moving to the hotel in Central London. Because the call lasted for over seven minutes, they probably also discussed their planned visit to Erinys.

After he heard that Lugovoy had arrived and everything was all right, Litvinenko called Tim Reilly to arrange their meeting at 25 Grosvenor Street for 3.00 pm. The call lasted for twenty-six seconds. Sasha said that Lugovoy had arrived, just called him from the airport, and confirmed the meeting in the afternoon for the same day. Because of this call, when he was later giving evidence during the inquest hearings, Tim said that the meeting with the Russians on that day was in the morning.[4] There is nothing unusual in this.

The police failed to establish the means by which Lugovoy and Kovtun travelled from Gatwick to Central London and subsequently to the Best Western Premier Shaftesbury Hotel in Shaftesbury Avenue (now the Piccadilly London West End), some 300 metres from Piccadilly Circus where Sasha used to arrange all his meetings. Lugovoy later said from Gatwick they came to London by train. It seemed obvious and no one cared to recheck.

On 5 December, the investigating officers from SO15 interviewed the house manager of the hotel, one Goran Krgo from the former Yugoslavia. He provided statements to the police first on 24 November 2006, then 5 December, and finally on 26 October 2007. Alas, only his December statement is available. As should have been expected, seven weeks after the events the evidence of Mr Krgo was absolutely unreliable. He said the Russian guests arrived about 9.30 am when he was working at the front desk, which was wrong because at that time they were still in the air. He also said he immediately recognised Lugovoy as a former bodyguard of the Russian premier Yegor Gaidar (name misspelt in the witness statement). In reality, Mr Krgo had no way of knowing it before the Litvinenko case attracted the attention of the world media. He added that Lugovoy 'had made a considerable amount of money and was quite a notable figure in Russia from the media', by far a too far-fetched claim for a first meeting with a stranger.[5] Naturally, all this information Goran got later from the British television and newspapers that went berserk about the Litvinenko story after his death. I had been in London since 22 November, working for BBC *Panorama* and was a first-hand witness of what was going on in the press and TV.

It is, however, important how the pair reached London. Provided that neither Lugovoy nor Kovtun were carrying, as it was later described, an 'extremely dangerous radioactive substance' with them, their chances to get it before a planned meeting with Litvinenko later that day were rather limited. If they were travelling from Gatwick by a private car or a limousine service arranged for them, the driver could have given them what I shall call a container, which could have been just a very small package. Another opportunity was when they left the hotel because their rooms were not ready by the time they arrived and they had to hang out somewhere before coming back and checking into one of the rooms, specifically room 107 allocated to Lugovoy. Before getting a key, his credit card was pre-authorised to cover any incidental costs for two rooms and two nights, therefore the investigation could later establish the time was 12.51 pm. And it is quite certain that before this time none of them touched that 'radioactive substance'.

Because the second room was still not ready, both guests took their luggage and went up to room 107 where they changed and reappeared in the lobby again sometime later more smartly dressed, according to the house manager Mr Krgo, although his evidence cannot always be taken for granted.[6] Passing by the reception, Lugovoy made several telephone calls as seen from his call logs and Mr Krgo's witness statement. First, he telephoned Litvinenko again (the call was registered at 13:22:48) confirming their meeting in front of the Nike shop on Piccadilly Circus at about 3.00 pm. Then Moscow called him (13:34:55). Starting from 16 October, two direct channels of communication with Moscow were set up for Lugovoy: via his so-called private secretary Angelina Idrisova, and via Vladimir Valuyev who was instructed to be on the alert 24/7 through the duration of the operation.

For Angelina, it was her first working day in a new company named EVP-Holding Ltd. She was seated in a hastily rented office space at the Radisson Slavyanskaya Business Centre and had never seen Lugovoy because when she came, he had already left for London. She didn't know anything. We shall deal with her later. That telephone call on behalf of Angelina was probably placed to check whether things were going according to the plan.[7] When the formalities were completed, Lugovoy and Kovtun went shopping in the iconic West End shopping area. Actually, it was Lugovoy who did the shopping because for Kovtun it was his first visit to the British capital. He was a simple man with very limited funds and experience so Leicester Square, Piccadilly Circus and Regent Street, plus London architecture in addition to just everyone walking on whichever side of the sidewalk they please should have been culture shocks he could not have experienced before.

Before leaving the hotel, they had spent at least half an hour in room 107. Based on the expert's opinion, who in turn based her judgement on the tests conducted by the Atomic Weapons Establishment (AWE), then Health Protection Agency (HPA) and finally the forensic management team from the Metropolitan Police (MPS) starting on 30 November and not concluding until 22 December – more than two months after Lugovoy and Kovtun checked in there – the coroner made a number of conclusions.

To begin with, it was established that Kovtun was allocated room 308. According to the expert, room 107 was more heavily contaminated than room 308 although both rooms had radioactive traces as well as a few other rooms in the hotel (that were much less contaminated). The most significant result of the testing was the discovery of what the expert judged to be primary contamination in the U-bend of the sink in the bathroom of room 107. As the Inquiry Report has put it, 'in a nutshell [the expert's] A1 view was that the contamination in the U-bend was consistent with polonium being poured down the sink plughole'. This, of course, is a very imprecise and a hugely misleading conclusion suggesting that a rare and highly radioactive metal with the symbol Po and atomic number 84 (or one of its isotopes) was flushed down the sink. As shall be seen, this was quite certainly not the case.

A decade later, answering his own rhetorical question of how the polonium came to be in the U-bend of room 107, the chairman Sir Robert Owen reached an equally sweeping and dubious conclusion that 'it [!?] was poured down the sink by Mr Lugovoy and/or Mr Kovtun either in the act of preparing a solution to be used in an attempt to poison Mr Litvinenko at the Erinys meeting, or in disposing of the remainder of the solution later in the day', promising to assess the strength of that inference in due course.[8] Because his initial impression was based on inaccurate input data, Sir Robert's final assessment was also incorrect. With the advantage of hindsight, it is now possible to refine it. But first of all, it's high time to establish what poison was actually used against Sasha Litvinenko which no one, except a handful of polonium specialists, seems to understand, leading to serious errors of judgement.

Interlude: A short treatise on Polonium-210 and high-school chemistry

Every day, hundreds of millions of people use sodium chloride with their meals and are quite happy about it. Sodium chloride is better known as table salt. It is an ionic compound of sodium ions and chloride ions. There is one sodium cation for one chloride anion so the chemical formular is NaCl, where sodium is a chemical element with a symbol Na (from Latin *Natrium*) and atomic number 11. Like other alkali metals (lithium=Li, potassium/in Latin *Kalium*=K, rubidium=Rb, caesium=Cs, and francium=Fr), it is a soft, silvery-white, highly reactive metal. Natrium (sodium) as a free metal does not occur in nature and must be prepared from compounds. All this to make a pinch of salt that we use every day.

Like all other elements in Group 16 (VIa) of the periodic table, polonium is a chalcogen. It is a rare and highly radioactive metal with no stable isotopes. Polonium-210 (^{210}Po or Po-210) is one of the isotopes of Po. It is generated in a series of radioactive decays (known as the decay chain) of, for example, uranium-238 and radium-226, or radon-222 gas (therefore it can be found in the atmosphere) and undergoes alpha decay, that is, emits an alpha particle to stable lead (^{206}Pb).

Polonium-210 is a prominent contaminant in the environment, mostly affecting seafood and tobacco. The average daily intake of naturally occurring Po-210 for people following a typical European diet is estimated to be 37 – 370 millibecquerels (1 mBq = 0,001 Bq). Populations that consume marine food, such as crustaceans and shellfish, can have a much higher intake of Po-210. Elevated body burdens of this specific isotope, according to the experts, are also observed in humans that consume large amounts of reindeer meat.[9] The lethal dose (LD) of Po-210 for humans ranges from 60 MBq to 400 MBq (megabecquerels), which corresponds to a mass of 0.2μg (microgram, one millionth of a gram) to 2.4μg after penetration into the body. Therefore, police and intelligence officers, journalists, writers, lawyers, judges, and even politicians in this or that way involved in the Litvinenko case rushed to nuclear reactors and scientific research papers of Marie and Pierre Curie, Willy Marckwald and Ernest Rutherford in order to understand what happened to Sasha Litvinenko. First, the UCLH doctors and later MPS investigators applied for help to the Atomic Weapons Establishment, a research facility of the UK Ministry of Defence, as well as to the International Atomic Energy Agency in Vienna, and the results were later used in the final police report for the Crown Prosecution Service. They were also reviewed during the Inquiry hearings and included in the Litvinenko Inquiry Report.

The only problem is that it is impossible to use Po or its isotope polonium-210 as a poison in a covert operation. For a number of reasons. First and probably most important – Po-210 is a highly radioactive metal and emits so many alpha particles each second that the energy released from one gram is 140 watts, and a capsule containing about half a gram will spontaneously reach a temperature of 500°C. Those who work with Po-210 also emphasise its extraordinary ability to 'wander'. As renowned expert on polonium Professor Dr Bogdan Skwarzec of the University of Gdańsk explained, if it is left in an open vessel, it 'crawls out' after a short time and can be found in a completely different place.[10] In other words, Po-210 becomes airborne very quickly through the process of sublimation. Besides, Po-210 is very dangerous to handle in even microgram amounts, and special equipment plus specific safety requirements are necessary to transport it.

To cut a long story short, what poisoned Sasha Litvinenko was... a salt. Actually, quite similar to the table salt used by all of us in our everyday life. It also has a similar chemical formular ($PoCl_4$) where polonium stands instead of natrium (sodium). Scientifically it is known as polonium tetrachloride, which is a hydroscopic bright yellow crystalline salt solid at room temperature. Theoretically, which is less likely, it could have also been polonium dibromide $PoBr_2$ or polonium tetrabromide $PoBr_4$, also a salt with purple-brown to dark red crystals, likewise solid at room temperature. All these chemical compounds are highly radioactive, alpha emitters and belong to hazardous agents (only if they get into the body). Like that of metallic polonium-210, their half-life is also 138.376 ± 0.002 days.

It is important to notice, as all specialists stressed during interviews, that emitted alpha particles do not travel very far – no more than a few centimetres – and are stopped by a sheet of paper (for example, if a tiny amount of $PoCl_4$ is packed in a brown sugar sachet) or by a layer of outer skin on a human body. Therefore, external exposure is not a concern and the compounds do not represent a risk to human health as long as the chemical agent remains outside the body. Most traces of it can be eliminated by careful hand washing with soap.

Working on the BBC *Panorama* documentary in December 2006, I interviewed Nicholas 'Nick' Priest, then Professor of Environmental Toxicology at London Middlesex University and, after August 2017, a consultant at Oxford. Nick explained that although Po-210 is an alpha emitter, once in about 100,000 decays it lets out a gamma ray. During the following years, there were meetings and discussions with other international experts and polonium specialists like Professor John Harrison at Oxford Brookes University, who kindly sent me his academic research article on this poisoning case together with his comments on the autoradiography of hair samples.[11] Prof. Dr Bogdan Skwarzec at the University of Gdańsk and Dr Peter Steier at Vienna University, both of whom I consulted at length, agreed that the best container for transporting the polonium salt would be a sealed glass vial, although other packaging was also possible. For me this meant that those who had sent this deadly vial to London could not rely on its passing through the airport undetected and would certainly not risk placing such a toxic piece of evidence into Lugovoy's or Kovtun's suitcases. It is well known that stringent security measures are in place in all UK airports and the system includes baggage scanning, X-ray screening, and radiation detection. Especially after what became known as the 2006 transatlantic aircraft plot to detonate explosives aboard airliners with twenty-four people arrested in London and elsewhere in Britain in August.

That leaves three alternative routes of bringing a container to London, which are the VOLNA,[12] a diplomatic bag, or a courier arriving in the UK by car or ferry. In Eurostar, the security measures are similar to airports, so it must be excluded.

In all three above-mentioned transportation methods, the packaging could be sufficiently protective to exclude any possible detection of radiation. As soon as the container was in Britain, all the rest would not be a problem.

***

The question now is: what happened in room 107 between 12.51 and 13.22? According to the Litvinenko Inquiry Report, Lugovoy and Kovtun were either preparing a solution to be used in an attempt to poison Litvinenko at the Erinys meeting planned for three o'clock, or disposing of the remainder of the solution later in the day.[13] For a good number of reasons, however, neither looks like a very plausible scenario.

First of all, there is no doubt that both suspected poisoners were *not* told about the kind of devilish substance the KGB's poison factory had prepared for them to use. (The exact name and affiliation of the secret research facility in Russia doesn't make any difference.) They quite certainly did *not* take any protective measures while handling the highly radioactive compound simply because they had no idea what substance they were dealing with and therefore were not cautious or scared. And even if they were instructed to try poisoning Sasha in the office of Erinys, which seems like a very unprofessional plan with only a few pros but many cons, Lugovoy and Kovtun would not need 'to prepare a solution'. The only thing they would have to do would be to open a container and remove a package with a few small coloured crystals inside. Which Kovtun most probably did, getting immediately exposed to radiation initially through skin contact. After that, he started to leave polonium traces everywhere. As Professor Priest said, at the moment the seal was broken, the spider of contamination started to spin its web of 'soiling'. The first release of minute traces of polonium would be dancing around Central London and elsewhere – and then be possible to follow.

It was most likely their first contact with the real radioactive substance, as all preparatory training in Russia that seem to have begun in March should have been conducted with harmless yellow or brown rock salt or raw sugar crystals that look very similar to polonium salts. Therefore, in his room at the Best Western hotel, Lugovoy could have suggested dissolving a couple of poison crystals in water to see how it would work in a real-life situation which was going to present itself soon. Again, it was probably Kovtun who made a try. Both were satisfied and disposed of the solution by pouring it down the sink plughole, although, according to the available tests results, the contamination within the U-bend was not too excessive, about KBq 108. Analysing the evidence presented by the Met on my request, Professor Skwarzec pointed out that if the activities with highly active polonium solution were performed in the hotel room, its traces would remain in the sink near the plug, in the U-bend and on all glass and porcelain surfaces where the polonium absorption is greater, and levels of contamination would be high. Whatever those activities were, the Russians did not need to take the solution with them because a simple small sachet with polonium salt crystals would be just right.

There's of course another possibility. Stopped and questioned at considerable length and detail while passing through immigration control at the airport, and not simply by a border official but a police officer, if not a traumatic but obviously a nervous experience, one or both of them could have suffered a minor breakdown. Most likely it would be Kovtun, who was nervous travelling to the UK for the first time. Suspicious that the true purpose of their visit might have somehow become known to the British security service (MI5), the first thought that would come to their mind should logically be to immediately destroy all compromising material that was now in their possession. With a view of Ponkin's failure in London while dealing with Litvinenko, they were obviously instructed what to do in emergency but had themselves seen in the movies how a drug dealer might flush his goods down the toilet rather than be arrested red-handed. If they decided to get rid of the poison before the imaginary MI5 mousetrap slummed shut, they would dispose of it by simply pouring those few coloured crystals into the sink and then flushing it with water. Back in Moscow, they could always say (and probably did say) the conditions were unsuitable.

As we know, after leaving the hotel they went shopping. At 14.54 Lugovoy called Litvinenko and said they were ready to meet him at Piccadilly Circus to go to Erinys.

* * *

The meeting between Tim Reilly, Litvinenko, Lugovoy and Kovtun at the boardroom on the fourth floor at 25 Grosvenor Street took place at about 3.00 pm. For obvious reasons, Mr Reilly did not remember the meeting too well but Hugh Davies QC, Counsel to the Inquiry, did his best to squeeze every detail from the former energy projects director of Erinys. As summarised by the Inquiry chairman, 'the purpose of the meeting was for Mr Reilly to discuss with Mr Lugovoy Erinys' proposed business with Gazprom'.

The seating arrangements around the boardroom table in this small room were of special interest to the Inquiry. It was established that Litvinenko was sitting at the head of the table, Reilly to his right facing Lugovoy, and Kovtun next to Lugovoy.

Tim recalled that he himself did not eat or drink anything during the meeting but left the room rather often going to the gents because he drank a lot of water that morning. He also said that his guests insisted that tea must be served and he provided them with either tea or coffee. During the investigation, evidence of high-level surface contamination was discovered in the room, in particular on two of the chairs and a section of the green baize that covered the table. Although the overhead view of the 3D model of the room (Exhibit no. JJH/04a) turned out to be a false, horizontally flipped reproduction, Reilly recognised the room from a photo. Based on his testimony, one may conclude that the chair and place where Litvinenko was sitting were not contaminated or, rather, as many other objects in this room were contaminated very lightly, nevertheless the investigation concluded and Sir Robert Owen agreed that Sasha was poisoned on that very day and in this particular room.

This inference was reached on the basis of evidence and reasoning by the female nuclear forensic scientist formerly employed by AWE and codenamed A1 in the investigation and inquiry documents. A1's evidence was that the small patch of contamination on the baize cloth represented primary contamination, that is, it was caused by a primary source of polonium. The rest was secondary contamination, she said. Hence it was decided that Litvinenko must have been poisoned here.

As usual, regarding this conclusion, there may be some pros but rather more cons. Among the evidence in favour of the poisoning theory is the fact that several experts calculated, judging by the autoradiography of hair samples, that the first intake of radioactive poison should have been between 14 and 23 October. Another positive sign for them was the place at the boardroom table where Lugovoy was allegedly sitting, showing full-scale deflection when the room was first tested more than a month after the meeting. And one more indirect evidence in favour of the poisoning attempt in this very room could be a June break-in when the intruders were able to make a detailed plan of the room and find out that there was no video recording equipment or listening devices secretly installed in hidden places, so the site was 'clean'.

At the same time, there are several solid arguments against this version. Dr Black estimated that the earlier intake – if we take it for granted that there was indeed an earlier intake – happened between 14 and 18 October while Dr Harrison, Dr Gent, and A1 concluded that the earlier intake probably took place between 18 and 23 October.[14] Until the afternoon of 1 November, Litvinenko was not leaving any traces of polonium and was feeling quite well (his brief indigestion and nausea before the meeting he himself explained by food poisoning). Besides, because the 3D model of the boardroom was done incorrectly, it is not only possible but almost certain that the most contaminated place at table was the one where Kovtun was sitting. All experts agree that people who are externally contaminated with radioactive material can contaminate other people or surfaces that they touch. And Kovtun, as we shall see, *was* externally contaminated when dealing with poison about two hours earlier in room 107 of the Best Western hotel.

When they met on Piccadilly Circus before going to Erinys, Sasha did not expect to see his friend with anybody else but was not too surprised or suspicious when Lugovoy introduced his companion as Dmitry or Dima, a businessman who, in Lugovoy's words, had recently joined his company and was now serving as director of their Global Project venture. They studied, he explained, at the same military command academy in Moscow and had been friends since childhood. Kovtun had never served in the KGB or FSK or FSB but was a former army officer stationed in Germany before the collapse of the USSR and disappearance of the DDR.

It was the second new person whom Lugovoy had suddenly brought to their meetings, but Sasha did not attach too much importance to it because he trusted Lugovoy. After the meeting with Reilly, where Kovtun did not pronounce a single word, Sasha invited his guests to the Itsu in Piccadilly. It was his favourite Japanese eatery. Because he did not feel well the previous day, Litvinenko did not order anything but Lugovoy did order and paid with his credit card. Later, the police found out the payment was processed at 4.22 pm. Unfortunately, it was not possible to establish at which table they were sitting.

It seems that during their visit to Itsu, the most important thing for Lugovoy was to contact Alexander Shadrin, a Russian who at the time was registered as secretary of Continental Petroleum Limited (and not the CEO, as he claimed). CPL was a typical shell company incorporated in June 2005 in Bristol, whose aim was to serve as cover for bogus business activities. Unfortunately, the books, financial reports, and bank accounts of CPL had never been checked. By sheer coincidence, the CPL/Eco3 offices at 58 Grosvenor Street were exactly opposite the Titon/Erinys offices at no. 25 on the same street.

On that day Lugovoy telephoned Shadrin five times: in the morning when they arrived (11:45:34), before they finished at Itsu (16:19:46), twenty-five minutes after he paid at Itsu (16:47:38), then again about two hours later (18:54:41), and finally at 8.00 pm (20:01:02). Questioned by Hugh Davies QC, Counsel to the Inquiry, Shadrin was not able to comment on those calls. Remarkably, the telephone call logs directly contradicted his claims that Lugovoy and Kovtun came to his office in late afternoon and stayed there for several hours discussing business, after which they all went to the restaurant suggested by Shadrin. Darya Davison (whom Shadrin calls 'Ms Pridmore'), the company's administrative assistant, was on holiday conveniently between 10 and 30 October and therefore was not able to give evidence about the events.

It seems the last call was to invite Shadrin to the restaurant because shortly before that, at 7.55 pm, Lugovoy called Briony, an Australian therapist then working at a London hospital, with whom he previously had a drunken one-night stand. He probably wanted to invite her too. Briony later explained she was not interested in seeing him anymore.

It is not exactly established when they split up with Litvinenko, but shortly after six he boarded his bus at Tottenham Court Road going home to Muswell Hill. The bus was checked and screened and found to be clean.[15] Who decided that Litvinenko was poisoned that day?

Lugovoy, Kovtun and Shadrin went to the Pescatori on Dover Street, just off Piccadilly – an Italian seafood restaurant with black leather banquettes, a grand fireplace and wood panelling. Later, Shadrin was not able to remember the time they went in there (it was about 8.30 pm), when they finished, and what exactly he did after dinner. The police records show that Lugovoy paid with his credit card at 10.39 pm. From there, the two Russians moved to Dar Makkaresh, a Moroccan restaurant and shisha lounge at the Trocadero complex with a rear entrance on Shaftesbury Avenue. From there Lugovoy tried calling Briony again (22:56:21) without success.[16] They spent less than half an hour at the lounge, paid at 11.05 pm and returned to their hotel after mooching around the strip joints, sex shops, and video booths and even taking a special rickshaw ride through night-time Soho.

* * *

The following day, 17 October, Lugovoy and Kovtun checked out of the Best Western hotel at half past one without asking for a refund for the second night that had been booked, fully prepaid but not used. They took a black cab that transported them to Knightsbridge and checked into the upmarket Parkes Hotel (now transformed into one of the most prestigious apartment developments in London). In 2006, the Parkes Hotel, featuring grand brick façades and large arched windows, was a luxury establishment located in a tree-lined cul-de-sac in Beaufort Gardens, just a short stroll away from Harrods. By design or simply by chance, their elegant new lodgings were conveniently located near the Lanesborough Hotel, Berezovsky's favourite meeting place.

Early in the morning, still in his room at the Best Western hotel Lugovoy was woken up by an avalanche of telephone calls from Moscow. The first call was from Valuyev (08:28:05), probably telling him – without explaining why – they would need to move to another hotel as soon as possible. Should anybody care to ask about the reason for such an early call, Lugovoy could always explain that Valuyev wanted to remind him about his son Alexey, to whom Lugovoy had been asked to hand over money to pay for his driving licence. Five minutes later (08:32:52), Angelina called. Then Lugovoy called Valuyev twice (09:24:17 and 09:25:49), probably not being able to get through the first time, then Angelina called Lugovoy in ten minutes (09:35:22), and then again (09:59:34) with instructions about the new hotel.

All telephone calls 'from Angelina' must be understood as communications from the control centre in Moscow. Finally, Lugovoy telephoned Litvinenko, asking to arrange a meeting with Daniel Quirke at RISC Management for late afternoon, and Litvinenko immediately called Dan. At midday, still from his room at the Best Western, Lugovoy first called Berezovsky, probably asking about tickets for the football match on 1 November, and then Berezovsky's associate Vladimir Voronov, who also figures as 'Voronoff' in the Inquiry documents, causing a lot of confusion. In May 2006, Voronov/Voronoff, a British subject with a Russian passport, was appointed as a new director of CPL while Shadrin was registered as its secretary. It did not matter very much because all their business was a sham.

It seems that as soon as news about their activities with poison in room 107 reached Moscow, an urgent decision was taken to move them to another hotel. It took almost no time and at 3.07 pm on 16 October two rooms were booked at the Parkes through its website, allegedly by Tatiana Lugovaya, Lugovoy's stepdaughter. At that time, Lugovoy, Kovtun and Litvinenko were entering the offices of Erinys.

It is difficult to assess why Tatiana was chosen (at least, the reservation was made from her computer). Probably somebody decided it would be better if the bookings were done by Lugovoy's closest next of kin. She was not interviewed, and no one investigated such a minor detail. Lugovoy checked in to room 23, a deluxe double (£295 plus VAT) at 13.50 on Tuesday, 17 October. Kovtun's room, a standard double, was number 25 (£199), both rooms next to each other.

The Murder of Alexander Litvinenko: To Kill a Mockingbird

According to the Inquiry documents, an hour later they arrived at the offices of CPL/Eco3 Capital vis-à-vis Erinys, where they remained until 5.30 pm.

In the part devoted to this meeting, the Litvinenko Inquiry Report refers to the testimony of Detective Inspector Craig Mascall who, confirming the meeting details, could only rely on the Visitors' Book entry, which is highly unreliable, and then quotes from Shadrin's and Darya Pridmore-Davison's witness statements.

> Hugh Davies OBE QC (Counsel to the Inquiry): We can see for the 17th, they're [Lugovoy and Kovtun] shown as visiting 58 Grosvenor Street between 15.00 and 17.30 hours.
>
> Shadrin: Yes.
>
> Davies: Do you remember meeting them?
>
> Shadrin: I don't.
>
> Davies: Was Mr Voronoff any part of any of this?
>
> Shadrin: No, none.
>
> Davies: It looks like a two and a half hour meeting.
>
> Shadrin: Yes.
>
> Davies: Who else was present?
>
> Shadrin: Well, Dariya, if she was in the office, but it was myself, Lugovoy and Kovtun.[17]

It may be remembered that Darya was on holiday between 10 and 30 October. Although Shadrin tried hard, or so it seemed, he could not remember any detail of that very long meeting.

An interview with Dan Quirke conducted by Hugh Davies QC on 16 February 2015 was, as always, the work of a master. Printed as a hard copy, it covers ninety-nine pages. Mr Quirke testified that 'the meeting at RISC's headquarters in Cavendish Place on 17 October was at about 4.00 pm. Alexander [Litvinenko] and Andrei [Lugovoy] arrived with a third man who I had never seen before. The meeting was supposed to have taken place early in the afternoon but I received a call from Alexander telling me they were running late.'

When they finally arrived, they were taken to the boardroom and offered tea. Cliff Knuckey was not in the office, so there were four of them, with Litvinenko acting as interpreter. Sasha said they had brought all required information and the third man – it was Kovtun – produced a minidisk. On the disk was their report on what they called Project G, which was a due diligence check on Alexey Gordeyev, then deputy prime minister and minister of agriculture, for a client. The assignment related to the Stolichnaya vodka dispute between the Russian state and the private SPI Group chartered in Luxembourg. Lugovoy had previously demanded $10,000 for this work and Cliff Knuckey authorised the payment, which had been transferred to Lugovoy's account in Cyprus prior to the meeting on 17 October. Dan Quirke explained that Litvinenko had told him they would not attend without the payment.

There was nothing particularly interesting at this meeting except for a total confusion regarding its timing which has never been duly clarified. According to Quirke, the meeting started at 4.00 pm and took fifty to fifty-five minutes, under an hour. Lugovoy received a text message or an alert shortly before 5.00 pm, he explained, and they were anxious to get away to another meeting. Questioned by Hugh Davies QC, Counsel to the Inquiry, Dan recalled that when Lugovoy received that message, he said, 'One nil.' Everybody decided this was related to a football match in Moscow between CSKA and Arsenal.

There was only one goal scored in the match and it was in the twenty-fourth minute of the game. 'Andrei appeared happy,' Dan said. But the game, Mr Davies noted, kicked off at 5.30 pm. The twenty-fourth minute of the game would take us to 17.54 hours.

'So what time do you estimate it [the meeting] finished, if that's a text message received?'

'Shortly before 5.00...'[18]

Lugovoy was planning to come back to London at the end of October, but both Quirke and Knuckey were busy travelling abroad, so their next meeting was scheduled for 1 November 2006.

***

On that very day, the meeting with Alexey Valuyev must have been so important that it took Lugovoy ten (!) telephone calls to arrange it. He first called Alexey in the morning after nine o'clock (09:24:17) but because no one picked up the phone decided to leave a voice message (09:25:49) asking him to call back. Lugovoy entered his room at the Parkes at about two o'clock and was back at the reception within about ten minutes.[19] From there, while chatting with the front office manager about where he and Kovtun could pick up girls 'for fun and good time',[20] he called Alexey again (14:30:45), then again (15:00:11) and again half an hour later (15:29:17). In between, at about three o'clock (15:05:22), Vladimir Valuyev called Lugovoy from Moscow. When Alexey got back from school, he listened to the voicemail and dialled Lugovoy's number (15:42:43). It may be remembered that they first met when his father, together with Lugovoy, visited London in March. Lugovoy told Alexey to come to Knightsbridge but said he still had some business to attend and would give him a ring as soon as he was free. Indeed, he telephoned him twice (at 18:38:35 and 18:46:57) asking him to come to the Parkes. As soon as he was in Beaufort Gardens, Alexey called (18:51:47) to say he was already there and waiting. Soon, a black taxi arrived containing Lugovoy, Kovtun and Litvinenko. According to Alexey Valuyev,

> Lugovoy, Kovtun and myself went upstairs to Lugovoy's room. We tried to find the [CSKA-Arsenal] game on the TV because there was

still about 15 to 20 minutes left. There was no channel with the game available. Lugovoy called my dad to ask the score and I had a bit of a chat with him. Kovtun gave me an envelope with [$1,000] US dollars in it and asked me to count it which I did and placed in my pocket. Lugovoy and Kovtun had a whisky, I had a Red Bull from the minibar, we drank these and went downstairs. Litvinenko was sat [sic] in the lounge and we joined him. I am not sure if there was anyone else there. I cannot remember. Lugovoy was still on the phone about the game. I made small talk with all of them. The game ended with a one nil win to Moscow.[21]

On the surface, that sounds plausible, except there was not a single telephone call registered at that period of time or later between Vladimir Valuyev and Lugovoy. According to the police records, they did not call each other but then again, not all Lugovoy's phone calls were logged.

The unsolved puzzle remains: it has not been established with 100 per cent certainty whether they indeed visited the offices of CPL/Eco3 and met Shadrin that day and if 'yes', when and how long they stayed. According to Lugovoy, after breakfast at the Best Western hotel, he and Kovtun took a stroll around the area and did some shopping in Mayfair, coming to Eco3 Capital Limited about eleven or twelve o'clock. At the reception, they were met by Alexander Shadrin, he said, who took them into the company's office. Lugovoy recalled that there they met Shadrin's secretary Darya and his assistant Nikolai (Gorokhov). 'We left Shadrin at about 1400 hours,' he said, 'returned to the hotel, packed our luggage and moved to another hotel... We were there at about 1500 hours... At about 1800 hours, Kovtun and I arrived at the offices of RISC Management.'[22]

There's a small problem with this version. Gorokhov had no memory at all of that visit and Darya was on holiday, not coming to the office until the end of the month.

Regarding the meeting at RISC, it is clear that the meeting took place but there is a conflict in the evidence as to precisely when the Russian visitors arrived and at what time they left. Finally, based on these two uncertainties, it is difficult to say whether Sasha was right or wrong when he stated that before going to RISC they first met Alexey Valuyev to give him some money from his father 'and arrived at Global Risk [RISC Management] at approximately 6:00 pm'.[23] One should also have in mind that the witness statement of Valuyev junior quoted above may be as unreliable as anybody else's.

***

Litvinenko felt quite at ease in this company. From the elegant Beaufort Gardens, he and his guests returned to Soho, the right place for them to be, and had a late dinner at the Golden Dragon, a popular Cantonese and Peking restaurant in London's Chinatown. Again, Lugovoy paid the bill, which amounted to £126.70, with his Mastercard. The transaction time was 9.49 pm.

From there, they moved on to a modest bistro named Café Boheme at the corner of Old Compton Street and Greek Street – Litvinenko did not like the place, left them there and went home by bus. Later in the evening Lugovoy and Kovtun, who had drunk sake in Chinatown, proceeded to the Hey Jo 'erotic nightclub' in fashionable Jermyn Street, then a recently opened *établissement* much favoured by the 'new Russians', where they stayed until the early hours, coming back to the Parkes after 3.00 am. Dave West, the notorious owner, who also opened an adjoining 150-seater Russian-themed restaurant called Abracadabra (a reviewer wrote that dining at Abracadabra was like eating in 'an overpriced McDonald's in a brothel') later claimed that Litvinenko was also there that night, which was not true.

On Wednesday, 18 October, they checked out and travelled to Victoria Station by taxi which the hotel porter called for them, and from there to Gatwick by train. It seems the formalities at the airport took little time because at about half past ten they were already sitting at the Caviar House & Prunier bar, conveniently located at the exit from the duty-free shopping section to the main halls with fine boutiques, restaurants, and small eateries as well as the ubiquitous Boots and WHSmith. After a half bottle of champagne that they emptied before leaving the hotel, at Gatwick they treated themselves to a posh breakfast. At 11.19 Lugovoy paid with his card (£82.50) and they proceeded to the gates. It was Transaero flight UN444, landing at Domodedovo at 20.00 hours Moscow time. There is no doubt that they were duly met, transported to a safe house, and reports collected from both at once.

***

Lugovoy was back in London one week later. According to the police report, he flew from Domodedovo by British Airways flight BA875 business class on 25 October. For whatever reason, on that Wednesday there was a considerable delay and the machine landed at Heathrow at 10.54 pm. This time he was alone and it was clear that the decision to fly to London on that day was made in haste. At least, the Crown Prosecution Service and later the Inquiry were presented with documentary evidence that on that occasion, Lugovoy's flight and hotel bookings were both made only one day before the trip.

At Heathrow, all passengers who were not catching a connecting flight proceeded to the immigration hall for the passport control. There were two queues – one for European Union, European Economic Area, British and Swiss nationals, and a second for all other nationalities. Above this large space and to one side, a mirrored wall contained a two-way mirror and a room behind it. Matthew Butterworth, Intelligence Manager with Heathrow Airport Police in charge of the airport security, whom his friends called simply Matt, stood in that room looking down at the crowd. He saw Lugovoy and decided the guy must be either from the army or the Home Office. This time the Russian did not cause any suspicion, collected his luggage and got out, taking a black cab to Central London.

Here he checked into the Sheraton Park Lane Hotel in Piccadilly, a celebrated Art Deco property, now Sheraton Grand London Park Lane, where he was given room 848. Because it was rather late, just after midnight (which was 3.10 am in Moscow), he probably went straight to bed.

The next day, Thursday, 26 October, seems to have been rather important for Lugovoy because in his interview in Moscow with Detective Superintendent Alan Slater he sought to avoid a lot of details presenting it as a rather relaxed country meeting with his old acquaintance Badri Patarkatsishvili. 'We talked about business,' Lugovoy said. 'I tried to bring him in as an investor in Ejen Bojole Vine' (translator's spelling). In reality, it was a rather long and by every measure very stressful day for him.

From the very beginning, Lugovoy started his story with a small lie. He said that after breakfast, he left the hotel at about 9.30 am and went to the offices of CPL/Eco3, where he met Shadrin in the street at the entrance to their office building and they exchanged some important documents. At about 10.00 or 11.00 hours, according to Lugovoy, he took a taxi and went to visit Badri at the Downside Manor in Leatherhead, Surrey, that belonged to his wife. In reality, at 9.30 am he was at his hotel's reception desk negotiating with the concierge the price for a limousine service to take him to Leatherhead and back. An hour before (08:29:27), he tried to call Shadrin but no one picked up the phone. Lugovoy repeated the call at ten (10:13:30), left a voicemail message, then called again (10:13:31) and then again (10:30:54). In the meantime, the price was agreed upon and the grey Mercedes E200 arrived to pick him up from the door leading to Brick Str. Lugovoy was in the car at 10.45 having with him nothing except two mobile telephones, at least one of which was unknown to the SO15 detectives who later tried to reconstruct his every move on that day.

Normally, if you know the way, it is a rather short trip but the driver, who was a subcontractor working for the company London Chauffeur Drive, did not and it took them quite a while to get there. While they were moving, Lugovoy made and received several telephone calls from his both mobile phones, the number of only one of which would later become known to the police. Shadrin called him back at half past twelve (12:32:38), left a message, and Lugovoy retuned the call later (13:47:40), when he was already sitting with Badri on the patio overlooking the sprawling, manicured lawns of the $20 million estate.[24] Besides Lugovoy, the meeting had been attended by Vladimir Voronoff (Voronov), the director of CPL, and Martin 'Marty' Pompadur (correct spelling), then Chairman of News Corporation Europe. Mr Pompadur's previous career was associated with the American Broadcasting Company (ABC), where he had been employed for seventeen years rising to vice president. According to his own words, in his decade with News Corporation he was instrumental in managing three successful businesses: a television station group in several emerging countries; a radio station group in Russia and Bulgaria; and News Outdoor, the leading outdoor advertising company in Russia.

Badri thought it was Voronov who suggested a meeting and the idea was to discuss outdoor advertising in Moscow. He said he specifically invited Lugovoy along to advise Voronov about a security problem News Corporation allegedly had in Russia. He did not specify what kind of problem there was and how he had learnt about it. Years later, one may say that at the end of 2006 outdoor advertising was of rather doubtful priority for Badri, who at that time started to be actively involved in Georgian politics. But that advertising business as well as problems with security in Moscow could have been a good enough reason to arrange that particular visit. Remarkably, according to Badri's recollections, the meeting lasted for about one or two hours while Lugovoy said it took a good five hours. Five hours to discuss an investment in a kvass company in Russia?

There are many other controversies and conflicts in the evidence that the Inquiry preferred to ignore. For example, Lugovoy claimed that he arrived at Leatherhead at one o'clock, while in reality it was some time before twelve. At the hearings, Mr Tam grilled Voronov on the details of the meeting but the former Soviet diplomat managed to deflect all difficult questions. In the meantime, the limousine driver testified that Voronov arrived in a silver BMW5 shortly after 12.30 pm and that it was a chauffeured car with three passengers: a tall Russian and two Americans, not one. Mario Bonetti, the limousine driver, took the BMW chauffeur to the nearby snack bar for breakfast, but while he was eating his mobile telephone rang and he said he now had to take one of the Americans to London, which he did, returning to the estate about 5.30 pm. The BMW driver told Mr Bonetti that before they arrived at Downside Manor he had picked up one American at Heathrow and another American (Pompadur) and a tall Russian (Voronov) in London. According to his witness statement, Voronov and Pompadur left at about 5.30. The BMW chauffeur picked them up. Lugovoy left after 6.00 pm and they were back at the Sheraton at 7.30.

Interviewed in Moscow by DS Slater, Lugovoy never mentioned that Voronov, Pompadur, or anybody else was present during his meeting with Badri. He said he had arrived at about one o'clock and left around five or six. Patarkatsishvili testified that 'Voronoff and Pompadur arrived together shortly before the meeting started in a two-seater car'. He said nothing about the second American. Interviewed by DC Nathan Taylor in September 2012 and asked whether he had any knowledge about a meeting that took place at the home of Arkady Patarkatsishvili (it was actually his wife's home) in late October, involving Messrs Lugovoy and Pompadur, Voronov said: 'I can confirm that I have no recollection of any such meeting... I cannot ever recall being there with Mr Lugovoy. This is not to say that this particular meeting did not take place however, as previously stated I have no recollection of it.'[25] 'It all sounds plausible,' he later said, answering the same question during the Inquiry hearings, 'except one thing: I wouldn't have arrived with two Americans because my car was a two-seater.'[26] A puzzle.

Following the presumption of innocence principle, even if somebody looks like a KGB agent, speaks like a KGB agent, and behaves like a KGB agent and, in addition to all that, is installed at the Russian embassy as a first, second, or third secretary, which is a standard KGB slot, it is still impossible to say that he or she is a KGB agent. At least, until this person's personal file from the KGB archive showing his affiliation becomes available or the individual confesses. Thus, Alexander Lebedev, who had been working for the KGB and then SVR in London under the cover of the Third Secretary of the Russian embassy in Kensington

Palace Gardens between 1987 and 1992, publicly admitted that he was sent to the UK on an intelligence assignment as a spy.

In October 1993 Voronov, who had been posted to London since July 1991 as a Russian diplomat, first Second and later First Secretary of the Russian embassy, left diplomatic service but remained in the UK. A year later, he got acquainted with Berezovsky during the latter's visit to London and started working for the oligarch. In 1995, Boris introduced him to Badri and in 1997 Voronov introduced Boris to Rupert Murdoch, who owned News Corporation, a multinational mass media corporation headquartered in New York City. Murdoch and Berezovsky got along well with each other and established LogoVAZ News Corporation that soon became News Media, a large media holding that Voronov headed. Together with Boris, Badri was one of the shareholders of the joint venture bringing into the holding, which controlled Russian radio stations Our Radio, Best FM, and Ultra, his IMEDI Television and Radio that Badri party owned with News Corporation. Even more ambitious plans were to include the most important Russian television channel ORT, controlled by Berezovsky, to create Russia's largest media corporation. This plan was not accomplished because Berezovsky had to leave Russia in 2000 and later that year was pressured to sell his stake in ORT to the Kremlin-chosen buyer and his former business partner, Roman Abramovich.

In February 2008, a month after he came third in the Georgian presidential election, Badri suddenly died, aged 52, having unexpectedly collapsed in his bedroom after a family dinner. Voronov says he remained Badri's close friend until the last day and was present at a dinner in New York when Badri secretly signed his will in November 2007 where Boris, Badri's closest friend and business partner, was not even mentioned. Berezovsky was once quoted as saying, 'Badri had almost everybody become his friend, even my enemies.'

In November 2008, Mr Pompadur stepped down as a top manager of News Corporation to pursue other business interests.

All this would not be important if a very high level of contamination were not found in room 848, occupied by Lugovoy, in the Sheraton Hotel between 25 and 28 October. The Litvinenko Inquiry radiation expert, A1, was very confident that the readings there were undisputable evidence of primary contamination. As established by the police, Lugovoy's schedule for those days was rather full and he hardly had any time for meetings with Litvinenko. This does not explain why the highest readings of the radioactive poison's activity were found in the bathroom bin of his hotel room as well as on two towels, but it certainly raises doubts that Litvinenko was the intended victim, at least during that particular visit. As before, how polonium salt reached Lugovoy in London remains a mystery. What he did with it in the hotel room and on what particular day, only Lugovoy could explain. Although he got slightly contaminated, at least externally, he would probably never tell anybody.

In addition to what had already been mentioned, there was an extensive telephone exchange on that day, only part of which became known to the investigators. Litvinenko telephoned Daniel Quirke (10:17:28), who was in Marseille not able to pick up the phone. After a while, Sasha called Tim Reilly (11:55:22) telling him he would drop by. He soon arrived and Tim thought Litvinenko was in their office to meet Dean Attew. Nevertheless, they talked for some twenty minutes discussing Gazprom and Lugovoy's progress there. Sasha said his friend was due to visit London again in mid-to-late November (he knew he had invited Lugovoy to fly with him to Spain to give evidence to the Spanish authorities about the Russian mafia). Then Litvinenko left, as always in good spirits.

Sasha called Lugovoy after one o'clock (13:27:35) but Andrey was with Badri and others and was unable to talk. He, however, returned the call shortly after two (14:10:07) explaining he had been very busy. Then Sasha called Daniel again, and again no one answered. Later, he tried to reach Lugovoy two more times (at 16:30:42 and 17:08:07) leaving voice messages. Lugovoy finally telephoned him (17:13:53) to say he was almost ready and would be back in London in the evening. Sasha said he'd be happy to wait at the Sheraton. At six, Attew called to inquire about the reason for Sasha's visit that day, and Litvinenko called him back (18:05:30) to explain there was nothing urgent. He then called Daniel (18:07:12) and a minute later telephoned Lugovoy (at 18:08:23 and again at 18:13:44), every time leaving voice messages.

Travelling back to London by the same limousine, Lugovoy phoned Litvinenko twice (at 18:20:47 and 18:21:44) but then suddenly Vladimir Valuyev called him (18:53:30) from Moscow. Whether Lugovoy had to report about his meeting with Badri or received some new instructions would not be established but while he was still in the car, Sokolenko called (19:10:07). As soon as he arrived at the hotel, Lugovoy dialled Litvinenko (19:35:14) to say he was there. The available cell site data show that Litvinenko was in the vicinity of the Sheraton already before 7.00 pm.

They met at the Palm Court, an iconic Art Deco bar with tapestries, marble floor, and ceiling details dating back to 1927 when it was completed. It is possible that Lugovoy intended to end their meeting rather sooner than later because by 7.50 pm he had already paid. The bill showed that he ordered three glasses of red Burgundy wine, two teas, and a fine Cuban Punch Punch cigar, which clearly shows that after he paid they remained in the Palm Court for some time. It was the same place where Sasha had been discussing ways of helping the English banker, Peter Shaw, with Martin Flint, then one of the directors of Risk Analysis. A coincidence? Perhaps.

Sometime later, Valuyev called Lugovoy from Moscow (19:54:42) using his mother's telephone. There was obviously something to discuss because Lugovoy managed to arrange a meeting with Berezovsky for the next day.[27] While still at the bar, Sasha called Daniel Quirke twice (at 20:08:03 and 21:10:15) and was only able to get through after nine. He explained to Daniel that his translator had let him down, so their planned meeting with Lugovoy would have to be delayed a few days. That was hardly the case because Sasha's English translator, Martin Dewhirst, was always there, happy to help. Litvinenko left the bar after 9.40 that evening and went home by bus. Lugovoy retired to his room and immediately called Badri's mobile from his hotel phone.

He dialled Valuyev's number at exactly 00:00 that night. The phone call lasted six seconds...

CHAPTER 9

To Kill a Mockingbird – Part II

On the morrow, Lugovoy opted for a continental breakfast at the Bracewells Restaurant in the Sheraton and went shopping at about half past nine, starting from Hawes & Curtis at Jermyn Street. From there he went along this half-kilometre stretch with the highest concentration of the best gentlemen's clothiers in London until he turned left and was soon in Regent Street. His next venue was Uniqlo, a Japanese casual wear designer not far from Piccadilly Circus. Here, Lugovoy bought something for his children, and at 10.34 he disappeared from the screen. But not before Shadrin telephoned him while he was still inside the shop at 10.32. According to Lugovoy's version, an hour later, at about 11.30, he was at Continental Petroleum.

With untypical attention to small details, this time Lugovoy recalled that all visitors to Shadrin's first-floor office were logged in a book which was held by the administrator at the entrance of the building, and that during their meeting Shadrin's assistant (Nikolai Gorokhov) and his secretary (Darya Pridmore-Davison) from time to time came into the room. Confirming this version of events, the Inquiry Report refers to the testimonies of Craig Mascall of the Metropolitan Police (whose information is only based on the Visitors' Book entry), as well as on Shadrin's and Darya's witness statements.[1] But alas, those rather refute than confirm Lugovoy's story.

> Q. Was there a visitor's book maintained for the reception area?
>
> Dariya Davison: Yes, there was the reception area, they kept the record of all the visitors who came to the offices … I think there was a time there was nobody there, especially if it was after certain time … After probably 5.30, 6.00 in the evening, so – and of course lunchtime, sometimes they didn't have no cover [*sic*], so there was no people at the reception.
>
> Q. Would the visitor's book be left out for people to sign?
>
> Dariya: It would be left out.[2]

As had already been established, according to the official company documents, Alexander Shadrin was neither the CEO of CPL, as he himself claimed, nor the 'Chief Investment Officer' of Eco3 Capital, as Gorokhov maintained. Shadrin was registered as director of Eco3 Capital from its incorporation in August 2000 and until the company was finally wound up in July 2013 and dissolved in April 2016. In the meantime, Charles Balfour was appointed director of Eco3 in December 2004 resigning in May 2007. As is well known, in offshore or shell companies, positions of 'director' and 'secretary' are nominal. Nikolai Gorokhov was not an 'assistant' at CPL but a 'project manager' employed by Eco3 who only joined the company in mid-October 2006, one or two days before Lugovoy and Kovtun visited the office at 58 Grosvenor Street. 'This company,' Gorokhov explained, 'looks for opportunities to invest in projects for clients throughout the world.' His boss Shadrin was appointed to the position of CPL secretary in October 2005 and likewise formally resigned in June 2007. During that period, the director of CPL was Voronov aka Voronoff. His two 'close friends', Berezovsky and Patarkatsishvili, were entirely unaware of this fact and never heard about either CPL or Eco3.

Gorokhov was questioned twice, the first time by DC Nicholas Fell and DS Lisa Harman of SO15 in early January 2007, and then again by Hugh Davies QC, Counsel to the Inquiry, in February 2015. Both times, he firmly stated that he only met Lugovoy (and Kovtun) once, on 31 October 2006. Shadrin informed him, he said, 'that both these males knew wealthy Russian clients that wished to invest money in the UK and in London in particular'. 'This was the first time,' Gorokhov added, 'that I had heard the names of Lugavoy [sic] and Kovtun.'[3] Provided that Kovtun was in Hamburg on 31 October, only coming to London the next morning, this witness's value is nil.

About Lugovoy's remark that Darya was 'coming to the room from time to time' during his visit to CPL on 27 October, Darya, who had worked as executive assistant of Eco3 Capital from September 2005, testified, 'I'm unable to provide any more details about this visit as I was on holiday between the 10th October and the 30th October 2006'.[4] Which essentially leaves only Shadrin as a witness.

> Q. The visitor's book on the 27th shows Mr Lugovoy arriving at your premises at about 11.30.
>
> Shadrin: Right.
>
> Q. Are you able to help with apparent visit on the 27th to your premises, and there are other calls to you from Mr Lugovoy on the 26th, what if any was Mr Voronoff's role in relation to that trip?
>
> Shadrin: I have no idea.
>
> Q. Were you dealing with him in the office, discussing any of these projects with him directly or not?
>
> Shadrin: With Voronoff, no.
>
> Q. Was he in the office around this time?
>
> Shadrin: No.
>
> ...

Q. What was Mr Voronoff's position in Continental Petroleum by this time?

Shadrin: In 2006 –

Q. 27 October.

Shadrin: He was – I think he was an adviser. He became a board member in spring 2007.

Q. Right. If he was an adviser, it doesn't sound as if he was advising you.

Shadrin: No.

Q. Or that you were seeking his advice.

Shadrin: No, no.[5]

After studying all evidence and witness testimonies regarding the proposed meeting at the CPL/Eco3 offices on 27 October 2006, Sir Robert Owen had to conclude: 'When he gave evidence before me, Dr Shadrin was unable to assist as to whether or not he had seen Mr Lugovoy at his office on that day.'[6]

Lugovoy claimed that he arrived at 58 Grosvenor Street at 11.30 and left at about 18.00. 'The meeting,' he said, 'went on for 3–4 hours.' Pretty strange arithmetic, one might say, but okay. While there, he telephoned his 'old acquaintance' Ruslan Fomichev and they agreed to meet 'at 16 hrs 00 min at the Hilton Park Lane'. It seems that Lugovoy wanted to say that the meeting with Shadrin was until about 4.00 pm and then he rushed to the Hilton to see Fomichev.

Ruslan Fomichev is an interesting personality. According to the media, he had worked for Berezovsky in various capacities from about 1995 to 2008 and in Russia represented Berezovsky's interests in a bank, two television channels, and one newspaper. His trading company Anstead Holdings Inc., registered in Novorossiysk, which he owned with a business partner and which was exporting low-quality heavy fuel oil (known in Russia as mazut) from Bashkiria, received a loan from Berezovsky in 2003 but defaulted on a total amount or part of it. Berezovsky's lawyers filed a lawsuit and won a $52.6 million judgement in June 2010. Fomichev first moved to London in 2001 'looking like a Polish construction worker', according to a former colleague. But after mixing with the likes of Stephen Curtis and Scott Young, by 2007 he was adorning the society pages of *Tatler* alongside his beautiful and intelligent wife. Mark Hollingsworth and Stewart Lansley write in *Londongrad* (2009) that in 2008, Ruslan and Katya were listed as the thirteenth most invited couple in the British capital but people close to Berezovsky say they never liked Fomichev, calling him a 'nasty type'. Litvinenko was also quite suspicious about the man, largely due to the fact that Fomichev's father was a KGB general.

Lugovoy said he had a short half-hour meeting with Fomichev in one of the Hilton's restaurants and from there went to the office of Berezovsky. They talked about the political situation in Moscow and Boris requested that Lugovoy arrange personal guards and provide security for his daughter as well as for the journalist Yelena Tregubova. Tregubova became famous in Russia for her book *The Tales of a Kremlin Digger*, published in October 2003, but after the murder of Politkovskaya she began to fear for her life. According to Lugovoy, the meeting with Berezovsky lasted for no more than ten to fifteen minutes 'either in his office, I don't remember, or in the hall', and then from Down Street he proceeded to his hotel, where they agreed with Sasha to meet at the bar.

'This time I came first,' Lugovoy recalls, 'Litvinenko came about 15–20 minutes later. The two of us talked for about 40 minutes. After the meeting Litvinenko left the hotel and I met with my friend Vladimir Voronin [*sic*]. He is a member of the board of directors of Continental Petroleum Co. Ltd.' In reality, there had never been any 'board of directors' at CPL and saying 'Voronin', Lugovoy apparently meant 'Vladimir Lvovich Voronov' although there was also Vladimir Voronkov, who was Berezovsky's office manager. Whether it was simply a slip of the tongue or he was deliberately misleading the investigation would now be impossible to figure out. Anyway, Vladimir Voronov, aka Voronoff, Vladimir Voronin, Vladimir Voronkov, and Vladimir Valuyev is a little bit too much all together.

During the Litvinenko Inquiry hearings, Robin Tam QC, Counsel to the Inquiry, asked Craig Mascall whether the suggested schedule of Litvinenko's and Lugovoy's movements on that day tied with the locations of the cell phones compiled by the police and the detective inspector answered in the affirmative. This, of course, only concerned the cell phones known to the police and referred to some limited parts of the day. There are still questions to be answered.

The timetable of telephone calls that morning (the cell site map for the first part of the day on Friday, 27 October is missing) shows that starting from 10.44 am, Lugovoy kept on calling Berezovsky's office before and after he was supposed to be conferring with Shadrin.[7] After 2.00 pm (14:21:49), Litvinenko called Lugovoy and while still supposedly in the Shadrin's office, Lugovoy called Voronov (15:18:22) and then again Berezovsky (15:24:39). Shortly after, he received another call from Litvinenko (15:38:07) and himself called Vladimir Valuyev in Moscow (15:42:34) but no one answered. Valuyev called him back in two minutes (15:44:40). No wonder Shadrin was unable to say anything plausible about their meeting, if any, that Friday.

After he supposedly left CPL, Lugovoy called Berezovsky's office again (16:29:25) and this time probably told the secretary that he would be expecting Boris's call as soon as Berezovsky might be back in the office. Then he dialled Voronov's number (16:31:34) and Voronov called him back at once (16:34:39). After that, he exchanged a few telephone calls with Litvinenko probably asking him to buy a couple of extra SIM cards on the way to the Sheraton.[8] It is rather doubtful that Lugovoy visited Berezovsky on that day, as he claimed, because at about five o'clock, Berezovsky personally telephoned him twice (16:59:47 and 17:00:03). That would hardly happen if they were sitting in the same room. Provided that Lugovoy can *a priori* not be trusted, one should rather agree with Berezovsky and Glushkov that the meeting with Lugovoy at 7 Down Street was in fact several days later, on 1 November.[9] It was impossible to recheck because not too long after the events both of Putin's critics were found strangled in their English homes.

At 5.06 pm Sasha bought two SIM cards and at that moment somebody called him (17:07:56). For whatever reason, the police preferred not to mention the caller in any document. That means that they either could not identify the number or it was from Sasha's MI6 minder. At the time of the call, as the cell sites map shows, Litvinenko was close to Claridge's, one of the best luxury hotels in the world on Brook Street, not too far away from Piccadilly. The next registered call from Lugovoy to Litvinenko was shortly after five o'clock (17:09:54). Sasha had probably not reached the Sheraton yet when Sokolenko called Lugovoy (17:16:47) and soon after him Voronov was on the line (17:19:03). Lugovoy seems to have been in great demand that afternoon.

It is quite obvious that when Voronov called, Lugovoy had already been at the Sheraton's Palm Court bar because a waiter came up and he placed his order at 17.21. The bill shows that Lugovoy ordered two glasses of excellent Auchentoshan Three Wood Single Malt Scotch with a little spring water – gently shaken, not stirred – and his favourite Punch Punch Cuban cigar that has lots of creamy vanilla wood flavour. Just like James Bond, no? Lugovoy must have been still talking to his Moscow friend so Voronov left a message and in ten minutes called again (17:29:33). He finally reached Lugovoy at 17.34. When Litvinenko arrived, Lugovoy also ordered two pots of afternoon tea, for which this place was and still is so famous. They say their tea is served with intricate pastries and delectable savoury treats inspired by the 1920s, with a contemporary twist. And – attention – they have silver metal teapots there!

Lugovoy and Litvinenko spent slightly over an hour in the bar. At the end, Lugovoy asked Sasha to book a table at the Pescatori, the same Italian seafood restaurant he had visited earlier that month with Shadrin and Kovtun, now explaining to Sasha he still had a late business meeting to attend.[10] They parted soon after. At 6.36 pm Litvinenko travelled home by tube.

Lugovoy signed the bill at the Palm Court at 19.50 and went to join Voronov at the restaurant which is only a few minutes' walk from the Sheraton. He later said it was a dinner for two and he and Voronov finished about half past nine. No one checked. But, as usual, what he said was not completely true.

At 21.00, Lugovoy was at the Palm Court again, alone or not, and he repeated his previous order, only this time without tea. That is, it was again two glasses of Auchentoshan Three Wood whisky and one Punch Punch cigar. When Sasha left earlier that evening, Lugovoy again tried to call Briony, obviously having in mind inviting her to join him at the Sheraton, but she did not pick up the phone. Lugovoy signed the bill at 22.08 and almost certainly retired to his room until the next day. Whether he indeed met Voronov that evening, as he claimed, it could have only been between 20.00 and 20.40 and there is not a single trace of that meeting in the Inquiry papers. It is quite possible that he indeed had a business meeting but in some other place like, for example, a safe house or a park bench.

A small part of his next day *is* in the case file. Lugovoy rose early in the morning on Saturday, 28 October at the Sheraton Park Lane Hotel room 848, where he had stayed for three nights. Hotel records indicate that he checked out at 5.30 am. He travelled to Heathrow and caught the BA flight 872 to Moscow Domodedovo, which took off that morning at 9.10 am. The aircraft was the same G-BNWX on which he had flown to London from Moscow three days earlier.[11] It was tested for contamination at Heathrow a month later, but the result was inconclusive.

As expected, after their initial contact with radioactive poison on 16 October, Lugovoy and Kovtun were leaving radioactive traces everywhere they went. On his next visit, as soon as he boarded the British Airways machine in Moscow, Lugovoy, as meticulously documented by the police, contaminated all places that he used or visited in London and of course his hotel room at the Sheraton. The Inquiry Report stressed that the readings taken in room 848 were the highest found in the entire investigation. During the hearings in March 2015, A1 gave her expert opinion as to the interpretation of those results.[12] She noted that relatively wide dispersal of secondary contamination was registered within Lugovoy's room and even beyond this room. There is not the slightest doubt that at one moment Lugovoy had a contact with poison in his hotel room probably getting rid of it and was himself externally contaminated, 'soiled' with radioactive material. However, there is no evidence that he had ever tried to use it against anybody – like Berezovsky or members of his close circle, including Litvinenko – with whom he met during that late October visit. Perhaps, at the last moment he gave up on the idea of following the order and poisoning a potential victim, opting to report that the circumstances were inappropriate. It is possible that using a lot of soap and water while washing his hands and then wiping them with a wet towel, he was able to considerably decontaminate himself (not even knowing that he had been contaminated) before flying back home.

Lugovoy, the main protagonist of this long secret operation, was to return to the British capital within three days, on Tuesday, 31 October 2006. The cover legend for the trip was to attend another match, watching Arsenal's attempt to avenge the defeat inflicted on them by CSKA Moscow two weeks before. On that important mission Lugovoy was accompanied by almost his whole family, all of whom, exactly like himself, were unaware that he was dealing with deadly radioactive substance. Two members of his operational group, Kovtun and Sokolenko, were also in place accompanied by a large support team. Posing as football fans, all of them had a solid pretext to come to London on that day. With Vladimir Valuyev coordinating in Moscow, plus an unknown number of Russian intelligence officers and agents operating in London under various covers, whose task was to passively observe being ready to intervene, if necessary, I would be very surprised if the whole party was less than twenty people.

***

In the course of the frenzied preparations for the operation, Kovtun flew to Hamburg on the same day, 28 October, by Aeroflot. A day before, a ticket was purchased to him for a return flight London–Moscow on 3 November. His short visit to Germany seems to have been a clumsy attempt to mislead the investigation that everyone knew would almost certainly follow by pretending he had to renew his residence permit, which probably seemed a good enough pretext for the operation planners. Kovtun acted almost completely 'in the dark', having been advised to rely on his established pattern and visit his former family with whom he maintained surprisingly good relations. His German ex-wife Marina Wall, who many years after their divorce still found Kovtun to be very charming, picked him up from the airport in a BMW and drove to Erzbergerstrasse 4, a nice old house in a quiet side street in Hamburg's Ottensen neighbourhood, where she shared an apartment with her Polish boyfriend Radoslaw and their two children. Kovtun then went to town to buy new trousers at Massimo Dutti and spent the night on a sofa in the same apartment.

On Sunday, 29 October, Marina booked him an early-morning flight to London for November 1, paying with her boyfriend's credit card because Kovtun did not have his own. In the afternoon, his ex-mother-in-law, Dr Eleonora Wall, picked him up. They drove to her house in Haselau outside of Hamburg, which she had been sharing with her partner and where Kovtun spent his second night in Germany. Dr Wall is neurologist, specialist in psychiatry and psychotherapy, with German as her mother tongue and Russian being her native language. Not that it matters much in this case.

Interlude: 'Those arseholes have probably poisoned us all!'

Dmitry Kovtun would not merit a separate entry if he did not pass away on 4 June 2022. Based on the Russian TASS news agency report, Western media like the BBC, *Der Spiegel*, and Wikipedia stated that Kovtun had died of Covid in a Moscow hospital while the real cause of his demise was almost certainly cancer associated with high dose radiation exposure, in other words, polonium poisoning.

Working on this book, I noticed that Kovtun completely disappeared from the news in 2015 and his name had not popped up anywhere in social or public media. I asked my research assistant to send an email to Marina Wall in Hamburg and inquire about her ex-husband. On 15 March 2022 Marina responded that she had been in regular contact with Dmitrij [*sic*] and 'he is alive and well and we communicate'. It was useless to ask any further questions because shortly after the death of Alexander Litvinenko in London, Marina was interviewed by the German criminal police (LKA) in Hamburg together with many other people who knew or met Kovtun in Germany, and spoke at length about her former husband. There was certainly nothing else that she could add.

Kovtun was born in Moscow on 25 September 1965 to the family of a Soviet army officer. His father, who reached the rank of colonel, died in 1995. Dmitry attended the Moscow Higher Military Command School together with Vladimir Valuyev and Andrey Lugovoy. Lugovoy, exactly one year younger, was Kovtun's childhood and military school friend. Sokolenko, born in 1969, finished the same military school and joined the company later. Except Kovtun, all of them served in the former Ninth Directorate of the KGB which in 1991, after the collapse of the Soviet Union, became the Chief Directorate for Protection (GUO) and later the Federal Protective Service (FSO) of Russia. After leaving government service, all three had been in the private security business, with Lugovoy and Valuyev also serving as personal guards to Berezovsky and Patarkatsishvili.

As a son of an army colonel, Kovtun was sent to the Soviet military contingent in East Germany, which was viewed as great luck. His regiment was part of the Western Group of Forces (WGF) based in the vicinity of the airport Schwerin-Parchim.

In 1990, already an army captain, Kovtun was in the USSR on vacation and at a private party in a Moscow hotel met Inessa 'Inna' Davletova (after her first marriage Yamatina), a divorcee with a small daughter called Anna, whom he started to date and married a year later. All three of them moved to East Germany and settled in the officers' barracks.

After about two months, Dmitry received a letter informing him that his unit was being transferred to Chechnya. For obvious reasons, neither Inna nor Dmitry wanted to go there and they decided to desert. One dark night in early 1992, they made their way through the fence, took a taxi and asked the driver to go straight to Hamburg, which was less than 150 km away in West Germany. By that time, the border between the two Germanies had ceased to exist and they easily reached the nearest West German police station, asking for asylum. They were then placed in the hostel for asylum seekers at Björnsonweg in Blankensee, Hamburg. Very soon they separated and three years later divorced. In the meantime, in 1994, Inna met Frank Höhne and by the end of the same year Kovtun met Marina Wall at a Christmas party at a friend's house.

Like Inna and Frank, Kovtun and Marina started living together, both couples getting married in 1996. In August, Inna moved away from Hamburg with her new husband and broke off all contact with Dmitry. She knew that he had a mother, a brother, and an aunt in Russia but never met them. He had also introduced her to Marina. Following a MLAT request from London, Inna was interviewed by the German police.

> Q. How did Dmitrij spend his time at Björnsonweg?
>
> Inna: He drank a lot, which was eventually the reason for our separation and in addition he hung about in Hamburg and on the Reeperbahn ... Dmitrij wanted to be a porno star.
>
> Q. How do you regard Dmitrij and his lifestyle?
>
> Inna: Dmitrij was not particularly down to earth, more a man about town. He had all sorts of dreams and plans, none of which he realised ... I have now read his interview in *Spiegel* and have read

that there was trade with gas and with oil.[13] I can only say that this has absolutely nothing to do with Dmitrij.

Q. Can you imagine that Dmitrij works for the Russian secret service FSB or any other secret service?

Inna: No, I cannot imagine that.

Q. Can you tell us anything else about Dmitrij Kovtun?

Inna: No, I cannot say anything further ... I cannot imagine how Dmitrij got involved in this affair, he is not really the type for this.[14]

Marina and Kovtun separated at the end of 2002 but still shared the same flat for about a year. Having spent six years of her life with jobless Kovtun, Marina wanted at least to have children but it somehow didn't work. By the time Dmitry left for Moscow in 2003, she was already pregnant with the first child by her new Polish boyfriend. Because Kovtun did not have any documents, the German authorities issued him the border crossing paper to travel to Russia.

In Moscow, Kovtun lived with his mother for three months during which time he obtained a passport allowing him to travel abroad, and came back to Hamburg. Now he got his working permit, settled with Marina at her flat but did not find any work. He left the flat in November 2003, stayed somewhere in the city for a while, and then left for Moscow again.

According to Marina, in Moscow Kovtun lived with his mother where Marina could always reach him. He could not find any work there either, although the amnesty freed him of any legal responsibility for his desertion, and kept in touch with his ex-wife. 'We have remained very good friends,' Marina says, 'and regularly spoke to one another on the phone. Every woman finds Dmitrij charming, it is just he does not fancy working and is not a family man.' He visited Hamburg again in November 2005 staying at the house of his former mother-in-law over the weekend.[15] In or about March 2006, Kovtun told Marina he was going to start some business with Lugovoy who, he said, had a firm for protecting people and property.

Dmitry and Marina officially separated in August 2006. He was not able to attend a final divorce hearing because his German residence permit as well as his Russian passport had expired, so he asked her to arrange an appointment at the Aliens' Authority. He said because now he would have a new passport, he hoped to get a new residence permit. The appointment was fixed for 30 October. Marina said he arrived by plane on Friday, 27 October, at around midday.

In reality, Kovtun flew from Moscow to Hamburg on Saturday, 28 October, on the Aeroflot aircraft RA85663. At the request of the British colleagues, the German police sought later to test this machine for radiation but because they had already been forewarned, the Russian aircraft did not turn up as expected. There is little doubt, however, that the traces of polonium were to be found exactly where Kovtun was sitting during the flight, as every other place that he visited on and after 16 October had been exposed to ionising radiation or was contaminated with radioactive material. At least twice in the period of two weeks, various locations in London where Kovtun was together with Lugovoy tested positive for primary radioactive contamination, which means that each of them touched radioactive material with his hands at least once. However, out of the two, only Kovtun has died so far.

Back in early December 2006, Kovtun called his former mother-in-law from his hospital ward in Moscow. 'He sounded ill,' she recalled. 'He sounded full of despair.'

* * *

After meeting her ex-husband at the newly opened Terminal 1, the whole party, which included Marina, her boyfriend, and their two children moved by car to their home at Erzbergerstrasse. Kovtun unpacked his Samsonite, which was Marina's old suitcase, and produced a box of chocolates for his former wife, a bottle of vodka for Radoslaw, and pickled mushrooms in a glass jar. They spent the evening talking, eating, and drinking. At one moment, Kovtun said he wanted to go to a football match in London and asked her to buy him an air ticket as he wanted to fly on 1 or 2 November.[16] If Marina was not mistaken about the dates, this would suggest he was not too much in a hurry to get to London on November 1. Nevertheless, a ticket was purchased for him for the Germanwings flight 4U 7342, departure time from Hamburg International on 1 November at 6.40 am.

Contrary to what the German police suspected and the Litvinenko Inquiry chairman suggested based on some formal indicators, Kovtun's stay in Hamburg was uneventful. His only night in his friend's small room from Monday to Tuesday, 30 to 31 October 2006, was nothing special, exactly as this Italian waiter-cook described in his first witness statement to the Hamburg police.[17] His later evidence is an obvious invention and should be ignored. The story involving the Albanian cook in London (Witness C2) is a legend invented to mislead the investigation.

What must not be neglected is the reason why Kovtun chose to stay in a small uncomfortable flat where he had to share a bed with an old but not close friend instead of spending his last night in Hamburg in the good company of his ex-wife or ex-mother-in-law? Kovtun knew this man, who figures in the Inquiry documents as Witness D3, from 1996 to 1998 when they worked together at Il Porto, an Italian restaurant in the heart of Hamburg's waterfront area overlooking the Elbe. After 1998, they were only in contact occasionally – 'sometimes he phoned, sometimes I phoned him', D3 says. The answer is quite simple: because Kovtun's last day in Hamburg, Tuesday, 31 October, was largely devoted to the coordination of the London activities for the next day, so he had to have a free hand, stay on his own, and have enough time to do what he needed to do without anybody bothering him.

At about ten o'clock on that Tuesday morning, Kovtun started calling Moscow. The first four calls were to Vladimir Valuyev (09:52:34, 09:55:12, 11:14:34, and 11:14:55), who was acting as a coordinator in this operation initially planned to be clandestine but suddenly turned to be covert, albeit not very effectively. These terms, both meaning 'secret' or 'hidden', are usually confusing to most people. A covert operation is an operation that is planned and executed so that the identity of the agency or the organisation sponsoring the operation remains unknown or deniable, while in a clandestine operation, even the operation itself must not be noticed. After Valuyev, in less than twenty minutes (between 12:19:49 and 12:36:06) Kovtun called Angelina Idrisova, declared to the inquiry as Lugovoy's assistant. Four minutes after the last call to Moscow, Kovtun spoke to Valuyev again (12:40:45) and then again called Angelina's phone number twice. At one o'clock (13:00:49), he stopped calling Moscow, fully briefed on his tomorrow's programme, and returned to his final Hamburg chores.

As mentioned, the German police later found traces of secondary polonium contamination at every place that Kovtun visited but ironically not on the plane that took him to London. 'I do not believe that he knew when he visited us,' Eleonora Wall said, 'that he was giving off radioactivity. He was just as he always was. He would not have come to us, if he had known that.'

**

In the early morning of 31 October 2006, Tatiana Lugovaya, then aged 20, and Maxim Begak who features in the Inquiry documents as her boyfriend, flew from Moscow to London on the British Airways flight BA 881 arriving at Heathrow at 7.11 am. According to the Report, the BA machine left Domodedovo at 5.43 Moscow time (2.43 GMT), which means that Tatiana and Maxim were to be at the airport at about three o'clock in the morning and had no chance to sleep that night.

As evident from the available inquiry and investigation documents, it has never been established where they went or what they did after they arrived in Central London except that she called her father at eleven o'clock (11:06:06). It could of course have been Maxim or somebody else using her phone. It is also unclear at what time Maxim checked into room 404 at the Regency Hotel in South Kensington, only about twenty minutes' walk from the Russian embassy. What little became known, however, is that Tatiana Lugovaya – it was almost certainly her first visit to London – checked in at the Millennium Hotel alone at 4.36 pm, that is, nine hours after her arrival in the British capital. She was allocated room 284.

On that last day in October, hours before the poisoning of Sasha Litvinenko, several less important events attracted attention of the investigating police officers and the Inquiry.

One such minor event was Sasha's visit to Titon International at 25 Grosvenor Street, where the Inquiry suggests he visited Dean Attew at an unknown time. There's a copy of Mr Attew's diary for that day with a note 'Sasha R' referring to about 4.00 pm. Litvinenko almost certainly did visit Titon on 31 October because he had to deliver a report – therefore 'Sasha R' – compiled by Yuri Shevts on Attew's request concerning one Kirill Shubsky. During the day, Shvets emailed his report to an email account especially set up by him for Litvinenko for such assignments and in the evening (London time), Sasha wrote that he duly delivered it to Titon.[18]

Kirill Shubsky, born in Moscow in January 1964, was a Russian businessman, president of the closed joint stock company with a strange name Consent-Alliance. According to the official Russian sources, the company had been engaged in a variety of businesses such as the mining of precious metals, cargo services, and consulting. It was also said to be acting as a holding which owned shares of several large companies. At the time when Mr Attew placed his order to compile a due diligence report on Shubsky, the businessman was a member of the board of directors of the Atlant-Soyuz Airlines (later Moscow Airlines). Atlant-Soyuz, founded in 1993, initially used Soviet-built aircraft for its passenger and cargo flights but in 2006 added the first Boeing to its fleet. The company was partly owned by private investors (75 per cent) and the City of Moscow (25 per cent). Together with leasing a Boeing, there were plans to form a joint venture with the US-based cargo airline Evergreen.

Evergreen International Airlines was a charter and cargo airline based in McMinnville, Oregon. It had long been suspected of having close ties to the CIA, operating contract freight services as well as charters and scheduled flights. Naturally, Evergreen handled more than military or intelligence community work. As was reported, its supertankers put out fires from Israel to Mexico, its unmanned systems division flew drone flights over disaster zones, and NASA hired it to operate its flying infrared observatory. The company even started a vineyard and a hazelnut farm.

In Russia, Shubsky became widely known as the widower of a famous Russian actress who died in Baden-Baden, Germany, in August 2017. The report probably also contained information about his private life, his mistress, and her husband – a former FSB general – and mentioned that after his celebrity wedding to the actress, the family settled in Switzerland.

For whatever reason, during his interview with DI Brent Hyatt from the Specialist Crime Directorate of the Metropolitan Police in his hospital bed, Sasha preferred not to mention his visit to Titon, saying that he only met one person on that day.[19] Sasha was very reluctant to say anything else about that person and their meeting, suggesting the officers call him and find out themselves.

That rendezvous was arranged in advance and took place at Waterstones in Piccadilly. Many people visit this famous bookshop, London's biggest, but only a few take the lift as far as the fifth floor to the aptly-named 5th View bar and restaurant. Unlike the Travellers Club, a historic venue in Pall Mall, or the SFC in Knightsbridge, neither this inconspicuous eatery nor the coffee shop on the lower ground floor had been known as a secret den where intelligence officers meet contacts and hold discreet conversations. Nevertheless, Sasha met his SIS contact here and over hot chocolate and homemade cakes they most likely discussed his planned visit to Spain in about a week's time. Right after the meeting (16:33:05), Sasha called Berezovsky's private number. He either visited Titon before or after that meeting at Waterstones.

The Murder of Alexander Litvinenko: To Kill a Mockingbird

Another event of that day that attracted the attention of investigators was the arrival of Lugovoy and his family. Their British Airways machine left Moscow at 17.00 local time (14.00 GMT), landing at Heathrow at 18.35 in the evening. The later tests conducted by the scientists from the Atomic Weapons Establishment demonstrated that the place where Lugovoy was sitting during this BA 873 flight, seat 23D, showed the highest level of contamination by polonium.

Lugovoy, his then wife Svetlana, stepdaughter Galina, 19, and son Yegor, 8, accompanied by Vyacheslav Sokolenko, showed up at the Millennium Hotel on Grosvenor Square shortly after 8.00 pm. According to Lugovoy, Tatiana had already been waiting for them in the lobby (which contradicts what a CCTV camera recorded). While Galina, who was wearing a dark polo neck top, jeans, and a belt, did most of the talking with the staff at the reception desk, a man and a woman walked down the steps into the reception area, approached the desk, and paused behind Sokolenko – he turned, shook hands with the man, and they started a conversation. Sokolenko later said that he didn't know those people. While standing at the reception desk, Lugovoy appeared to use his mobile phone (20:23:00) but this call was not registered.

Sokolenko was allocated room 382. Both the police and the inquiry counsel remained completely unimpressed by the fact that during his flight from Moscow, within only one hour between 16.43 and 17.40, Sokolenko made seven (!) telephone calls to the company referred to in the Inquiry's Telephone Call Schedule file as 'Risk Advisory Group PLC'. This PLC had existed as a publicly traded corporation between December 2005 and April 2017. Before and after, it was called Risk Advisory Group Limited, incorporated under a different name in October 1997. The group advertised itself as 'a leading independent global risk management consultancy that provides intelligence, investigations and security services'. They say they have offices in Washington, New York, London, Dubai, Moscow, Hong Kong, and Singapore. All Sokolenko's calls to their registered London number remained unanswered and this topic was dropped. We will come back to it because he repeated the exercise the next day.

There was considerable confusion at the Millennium because the receptionists took Tatiana Lugovaya, who had arrived at the hotel some four hours earlier than the rest of the group, for Lugovoy's wife and allotted her a double room (no. 284). After the mistake was cleared, she was issued entry cards for room 121, which was twenty minutes later swapped for room 101. Both Lugovoy's daughters, Tatiana and Galina, went up to room 101 while room 284, initially occupied by Tatiana, was cancelled at 20.26.[20] Finally, Lugovoy, his wife and their son Yegor checked into double room 441, but the room change exercise did not end here.

'On that day I did not speak to anybody on the phone,' Lugovoy claimed later, answering the question of DS Alan Slater. '[I] did not inform anyone of my arrival although Litvinenko was aware of the date and time of the flight and the hotel in which I planned to stay.'[21] As should have been expected, he was lying.

The CDR (Call Detail Records) schedule for that day covers two pages. First Tatiana telephoned her father from London (about four hours after her landing at

Heathrow), then Lugovoy called Berezovsky's office several times and they called him, and then a series of telephone calls followed when Lugovoy was already in London. Some of them can be explained, others not. For example, Tatiana calling him first at about seven (18:53:04) and then half an hour later (19:33:54) was probably about checking their arrival and transfer to the hotel. Then he called Tatiana (but never her sister) when she was supposed to be already in her room (20:38:56 and 20:39:16) and she promptly called back (20:48:26). After that, Lugovoy made a call to Alexey Valuyev. A possible inference is he may have been ringing Valuyev junior to tell him that the party had arrived, also saying he had some money for him from his father and suggesting a meeting on the next day. He then called Shadrin twice (20:57:45 and 21:00:36) and Tatiana (21:01:05) once again. During those two days, 31 October and 1 November, there were so many calls to Tatiana, often at odd times of the day and night, that it may be reasonable to suggest that her mobile phone was being used by somebody else. For example, Maxim Begak, whose role in this operation remains uninvestigated but who was inconspicuously omnipresent in all important places at all times.

Lugovoy made his single call to Litvinenko shortly after nine (21:03:18). A bit later, he called Tatiana three times within twenty-five minutes and that was his last registered telephone activity of that day. With this, plenty of telephone calls made by Lugovoy, Sokolenko, Galina and Tatiana remained unregistered and therefore unchecked.

That evening Sokolenko did not hurry to retreat to his room and get a proper sleep before the operation. He actually hung around until almost half past eleven, waiting at the reception area, when a woman with blonde hair wearing a black and white coat with zigzag horizontal stripes walked into the lift. Sokolenko offered his hand to her, she accepted, and he bent to kiss it. He then got out on the third floor alone and proceeded to his room while she went up to the seventh floor. The woman remained unidentified. 'On that day,' Lugovoy claimed later, 'neither I, members of my family nor Sokolenko left the hotel. On that day I did not speak to anybody on the phone...'

***

Less than two weeks later, on 11 December, Lugovoy was questioned in Moscow in the presence of several Russian officials. 'In the morning of 01.11.2006,' he said, 'at about 10hrs 00min I, members of my family, Sokolenko and Kovtun left the hotel. I and Kovtun went for a meeting with Shadrin whereas Sokolenko and members of my family took the double-decker tourist bus and went on a sightseeing tour of London.'[22] Previously, Lugovoy had asked Berezovsky and his then son-in-law Georgy 'Egor' Schuppe to help with the tickets to the football match between CSKA and Arsenal at London's Emirates Stadium and on Boris's instruction the secretariat arranged eight tickets that were delivered to the office in Down Street. From 1997 to 2012, Schuppe had been married to Berezovsky's daughter Ekaterina and since 2004 had resided in London.

The Murder of Alexander Litvinenko: To Kill a Mockingbird

To begin with, on 1 November Kovtun arrived at Gatwick on a low-cost Germanwings flight from Hamburg at about 7.25 am, took a taxi and went to the Millennium Hotel. The taxi was later found to have been contaminated but the German authorities stated that the aeroplane was clean. What Kovtun later claimed was of course irrelevant:

> I have declared repeatedly and publicly that I arrived in London by chance on 1 November because ... I was anticipating complications with having a 'residence permit' inserted into the new passport and was prepared for the fact that I might have to stay in Germany for 2–3 weeks and deal with residence and insurance matters, registration of the company or employment.[23]

There was no company to register, no employment to think about, and on his first evening in Hamburg Kovtun mentioned that he would need to fly to England soon to attend a football match (after dinner in London, he was sent to rest at the hotel and Alexey Valuyev went to the stadium instead of him). As early as the morning of 29 October, the day after his arrival, Kovtun bought a ticket. All this activity was before he was due to visit the Beziksamt Altona at Platz der Republik to personally apply for an extension of his residence document. The only true thing is that he indeed arrived in London by chance on 1 November – should there be no tickets for this date, he asked for a flight for 2 November. A return ticket London–Moscow for Friday, 3 November, was purchased for him even earlier, on 27 October, a day before he left for Hamburg. Again, it is true that he had nothing at all to do in London, as he initially admitted... except playing a support role in the Litvinenko operation.

For Lugovoy, that Wednesday began at eight o'clock in the morning (08:22:53) London time by calling the telephone number of his friend Vladimir Valuyev in Moscow. Exactly the same happened on 17 October at more or less the same time. The call lasted two minutes and seven seconds. It is possible that Lugovoy made a preliminary report to the control centre that he and his team had arrived all right and asked for further instructions. There is a degree of overlap between Lugovoy's call to Moscow and Kovtun's arrival at the hotel, where he was caught by a CCTV camera shortly after 8.33.[24] Kovtun is seen sending a message and making or at least trying to make a telephone call and then looking down at his mobile phone so one may assume that he had somehow managed to inform Lugovoy about his safe landing at Gatwick an hour earlier. Andrew O'Connor QC, Counsel to the Inquiry, didn't miss an opportunity to discuss this small telephone mystery with DI Mascall and was advised that a possibility that some telephone communications remained out of control could not be ruled out.

Vladimir Valuyev was born in April 1965 and went to the same military command academy as Lugovoy, Kovtun, and Sokolenko. Like Lugovoy and Sokolenko, Valuyev had served in the Chief Directorate for Protection charged with protecting the nation's leaders and security of government buildings. The Service was a successor to the Ninth Directorate of the KGB (close protection, government bodyguards) and existed until August 1996 when the FSO was established. Valuyev figures in various databases as the founder of several private security companies, sometimes with Sokolenko (Ninth Wave – Security, Quantor, Rusich, Gardé X, and even a restaurant with an Italian name, La Terrazza) – some of them closed down long ago but some still active as this book went to press.

Like Valuyev, Vyacheslav Sokolenko was undeservedly neglected by the British police and the Litvinenko Inquiry. From the military academy he was invited to the KGB and until 1995 had served in the Ninth Directorate and its successor agencies. After two years in private security companies, Lugovoy, who at the time had been head of the security service of the ORT television, invited Sokolenko to be his deputy. They had both served there until 2001. Following the scandal related to Glushkov and his alleged attempt to escape from hospital, which was presented by the FSB as having been organised by Lugovoy on the orders of Patarkatsishvili, Sokolenko moved to Gardé X and Stolitsa-Shchit (Capital-Shield), a private security firm which he had headed from 2004 to 2007 and was its deputy managing director between 2008 and 2013. According to Russian sources, at one time he had also been working for Renaissance Capital, an investment bank founded in Russia in the nineties that employed many former senior KGB-FSB officers in leading positions.[25] When Lugovoy became a member of the State Duma and was subsequently promoted to first deputy chairman of its Security Committee, he appointed Sokolenko his personal assistant. It goes without saying that for the Litvinenko operation in London, Lugovoy could only choose a person he fully trusted to take care of his family's security and wellbeing.

At about ten o'clock in the morning, Sokolenko and Kovtun were waiting in the lobby in front of the reception when Lugovoy, his wife Svetlana, daughter Galina and son Yegor came down. Some time before, Sokolenko and Kovtun visited Lugovoy in his room on the fourth floor and here the first oddity of this dreadful November day should be noted. On their way back to the lift, Kovtun appeared to be holding something small in his hands. On the third floor Sokolenko left and went in the direction of room 382 that he occupied together with Kovtun while Kovtun got out at the ground floor, crossed the lobby and settled down on the sofa. Minutes later, Sokolenko got out of the lift at the ground floor. He walked past Kovtun sitting on the sofa, went up the stairs and crossed the courtyard towards the back entrance leading to Adam's Row. He returned to the lobby after a minute or so, joining Kovtun. All this activity remained unexplained.

Lugovoy, Svetlana and their son Yegor got out of the lift on the ground floor shortly before ten. In a few moments Galina joined them. At the reception desk, Sokolenko, Galina and Lugovoy started discussing something when Sokolenko produced his mobile phone and handed it over to Galina. It is unclear whether somebody called her or she made a call, but after talking to an unknown person she returned the phone to Sokolenko and they both joined the rest of the family while Lugovoy remained at the reception desk. Standing there, he used his mobile phone (at 10:01:20) and, like that of his daughter, this call too remained unregistered.

Finally, Tatiana joined them and the whole group left the hotel at 10.10 am, crossing the courtyard in the direction of Adam's Row. On the way (10:09:35), Sokolenko made his first call – or perhaps sent a message – to Risk Advisory Group PLC.

The whole party headed north and some twenty minutes later, at Marble Arch, they purchased four adult tickets for Svetlana, Sokolenko and the girls plus one for Yegor for a sightseeing tour around London and five entrance tickets for the London Dungeon.[26] By all indications, they went sightseeing. Between ten o'clock in the morning and five o'clock in the afternoon, Sokolenko called or most likely texted Risk Advisory Group twenty-one times (?!). All calls were registered but there seem to have been no conversations. One of the last calls was at 16.40 from the Millennium Hotel – minutes after Litvinenko was poisoned – and the very last at 17.01 when the main group, that is, Lugovoy, Kovtun and Sokolenko accompanied by Svetlana with Yegor in tow was leaving the hotel after the successful operation, habitually moving towards Adam's Row. But we are getting ahead of ourselves.

Sokolenko's extremely strange and suspicious telephone activity was later discussed – very superficially – during the hearings:

> Mr O'Connor (Counsel to the Inquiry): A body called Risk Advisory Group plc, trying to make calls [*sic*], it would seem, to Mr Sokolenko. There are a number of these calls, aren't there, I won't take you to them but they go on into the next day, 1 November, don't they?
>
> Mr Mascall (Metropolitan Police): Yes.
>
> Q. None of them appear to have had any duration?
>
> A. No.
>
> …
>
> Q. Did you investigate what relationship that company may have had with Mr Sokolenko?
>
> A. We have tried, but we've not got very far.[27]

And that was the end of it.

The company Risk Advisory Group had existed under this name since November 1997. One Oleg Babinov, who claimed that in the nineties he had served as Associate Director for Kroll, said he played an active role in establishing the Moscow office of Risk Advisory, later serving as its director. Mr Babinov also says he had been serving as Head of Russia, Eastern Europe and Eurasia Practice at Risk from September 2004 to April 2019. The documents show he had been employed at Risk Advisory as director between January 2012 and December 2018. As part of the Inquiry proceedings, it seems no one came to the idea of interviewing him. Anyway, it would be a waste of time.

Another former employee of Risk Advisory Group is Evgeny Tarasov, a graduate of the Institute of Asian and African Studies of Moscow State University, where Limarev also studied. According to some reports, Tarasov became the Risk Advisory Group's head of the Moscow office, succeeding Babinov in July 2004. The available company documents show that exactly like Babinov, he had also served as the company's director from January 2012 to December 2018 and in October–November 2006 they were part of Risk Advisory staff. Even with all this in mind, it was impossible to establish any connection between Sokolenko and Risk Advisory Group and anyway, this was of little interest to the police detectives who were investigating the murder. In Moscow, DC Mark Greenough of SO15, who was assigned to question Sokolenko in December 2006, was unable to squeeze any information from this former FSO officer. However, talking about the night of their arrival in the UK, Sokolenko suddenly remembered, contrary to what Lugovoy stated, that he went 'to the bar or pub to explore Downtown London' on the night of 31 October.[28] He recalled there were Oleg and Oleg, two Olegs, but said he didn't know their surnames and did not remember the name of the bar.

* * *

Lugovoy testified: 'On 01.11.2006 having sent my family with Sokolenko on a tour of London I telephoned Berezovsky's office again whereby it was confirmed to me that the tickets are with them and that I can take them. For that I and Kovtun went to Berezovsky's office. I came to the office between 10 and 11 o'clock. I went up into the office, took the tickets, went down to the street where Kovtun was waiting for me … From Berezovsky's office we went for a short walk in the Piccadilly area.'[29]

Remarkably, no one else remembered that episode.

It is, however, established that at about 10.40 am (10:42:41) Lugovoy did not visit but rather called Berezovsky's office and some fifteen minutes later (10:57:59) sent a message to Kovtun from another cell phone or using another SIM card, which means that at that moment they were not together. The same call was repeated seconds later (10:58:07), again without any conversation. Half an hour later (11:33:20), during which time Sokolenko managed to contact Risk Advisory Group twice, allegedly from the Big Bus tour, repeating calling or texting them non-stop for the next few hours, a telephone call was made to the former acquaintance of Kovtun codenamed 'Witness C2' in the inquiry documents. That was an Albanian cook who used to work in Hamburg and was now in England, and the call was made from the same cell phone (Lugovoy's) that was used to contact Berezovsky's office. It lasted for slightly over a minute and the caller was later identified by C2 as Kovtun.

Litvinenko, at the time still at home, dialled Lugovoy's number shortly before twelve (11:41:14). They agreed to meet later, after which Lugovoy called Shadrin again (11:47:48, the call lasted for nineteen seconds). Then Tatiana called Lugovoy (12:14:41). A reasonable inference would be that either – within the time space of one minute and twenty-one seconds – she was anxious to tell her father how well her London tour was going or, more likely, somebody else was using her cell phone.

There was some kind of pause in Lugovoy's barrage of telephone calls and text messages between 12.15 and 14.30. Naturally, the available records only reflect the activity of his known phone numbers. For those that were not identified, the cell site analysis and CDRs do not exist.[30]

At half past two (14:32:20), Litvinenko called Lugovoy, then called again twenty minutes later (14:55:21) in between trying to reach Shamil Zakayev, the son of Akhmed. At three o'clock (15:05:12), Lugovoy called Angelina's number, allegedly at her Moscow office, and a Radisson PBX automatically redirected his call to the control centre. Questioned in Moscow by DC Philip Booth of SO15, Angelina was completely unaware of those phone calls. Shortly after (15:19:43), Lugovoy dialled the number of Alexey Valuyev, probably confirming that Alexey must go to the football match with the group. One mysterious telephone call that Litvinenko placed from Burlington Arcade, having just left Itsu at 15.35, was duly registered but not explained. Finally, at about 15.40, Litvinenko telephoned Lugovoy (15:38:53) and Dean Attew called Sasha (15:43:49). By that time, Lugovoy and Kovtun had already reached the reception area of the Millennium Hotel entering from Adam's Row, and Lugovoy even managed to visit a men's restroom.

Knowing all these details, would anyone believe, as Sir Robert Owen did, that during three and a half hours, from 12.00 to 15.30, Lugovoy and Kovtun were 'discussing business' with Shadrin at the offices of CPL/Eco3? At least some of Shadrin's documents, later classified (like, for example, INQ021180-87), were available to Sir Robert and from them he could easily deduct that in reality the declared business between them was a sham. Even more incredible would be to think that after this 'business meeting' they went straight to the hotel and poisoned Litvinenko.

Berezovsky said that Lugovoy came to his offices at 7 Down Street on 31 October. 'I had asked him to visit me,' Boris explained, 'so that I could thank him for arranging my daughter's security in St Petersburg. He looked well. We had a drink of wine in my office ... I also remember that he turned up to collect the Arsenal v CSK [sic] Moscow football tickets.'[31] In another document filed by the investigation (INQ016371), Berezovsky stated that this meeting was on 1 November.

Berezovsky's personal secretary Vladimir Voronkov was also unable to recall whether he saw Lugovoy in the office on 1 November or the day before. 'I can't remember, probably not,' he said, 'but I saw him before that.' In his turn, Nikolai Glushkov testified that on the afternoon of 1 November, Boris invited him to his private office and he was very surprised to see Lugovoy there.

It was not a pleasant surprise. Glushkov had a grudge against Lugovoy but nevertheless shook his hand. He said he refused to have a drink with them but still served them some white wine and left. And, he added, 'if you speak about the meeting on the 1st [of November], it was a little bit earlier [than previously suggested], I would say before 4.00.'[32] Glushkov insisted that contrary to what Lugovoy was claiming, that memorable meeting at the Berezovsky office was quite certainly not on 27 October but on 1 November. This is an important detail.

During his questioning by the British police in Moscow, Lugovoy further stated that from Down Street he and Kovtun went for a stroll along Piccadilly and from there walked to Shadrin's office. 'We reached there between 11 and 12 o'clock,' he said. 'As previously we were met by Shadrin and [he] took us to the same hall. The three of us talked, i.e. I, Kovtun and Shadrin. Sometimes, during the conversation, into the hall came Shadrin's assistant [Gorokhov] and the secretary [Darya] whom I mentioned earlier on. Our conversation went on until about 15 hrs 30 min.'[33] In other words, what he meant to say was they had so much 'business' to accomplish on that particular day that it took them considerable time to discuss all outstanding issues.

Remarkably, Sir Robert decided to accept Lugovoy's version of events in spite of an obvious inconsistency between the latter's story, witness evidence, and established facts. Referring to the testimonies of Shadrin, Gorokhov and Darya Pridmore-Davison, the inquiry chairman could not but say that 'the strong impression that I gained from the evidence of these three witnesses was that there was little real business, and certainly no urgent or important business done that day'. Nevertheless, in his final Inquiry Report, Sir Robert stated:

> It is quite clear that Mr Lugovoy and Mr Kovtun did attend the CPL offices at some point on the morning of 1 November. I have already referred to the evidence of the Visitors' Book and the cell siting. The Visitors' Book does not record a time of arrival. Mrs Davison's evidence was that the two men arrived between 11.00am and noon, which is broadly consistent with DI Mascall's understanding of the cell site evidence.[34]

Taking each point separately, the Visitors' Book does not record the time of arrival and is often left unattended. Regarding Mrs Davison's evidence, she was interviewed by the police three times. Unfortunately, her first witness statement is missing from the files. There she said Lugovoy and Kovtun arrived between 11.00 and 12.00. But a couple of weeks later, interviewed again, she specified that on that day, 1 November, she went to buy a bottle of Evian water to the nearby post office. 'When their meeting started,' she said, 'I went to another room on the 1st floor which we also use as an office'.[35] During the Litvinenko Inquiry Hearings, Hugh Davies QC, Counsel to the Inquiry, questioned Darya:

> Q. On 27 November 2006 you were asked to give a time for when Mr Lugovoy and Mr Kovtun arrived. What time did you give?
>
> A. When they arrived, I can't remember like this.
>
> Q. How good is your memory of these events, Mrs. Davison, eight years on without your statement?
>
> A. Bad. Obviously, I am just – on the times, I wouldn't be able to tell exactly the times that...

Q. We understand. What then do you remember, prompted by your statement, as to the men's arrival, whether you'd met them before?

A. Obviously, I've never met them before, and it was something unexpected...

Q. Had you seen Mr Lugovoy before?

A. No.

Finally, regarding Craig Mascall's 'understanding of the cell site evidence' referred to by Sir Robert, there was in fact no cell site evidence regarding this time period and this particular cell phone.[36] So, no understanding.

Alexander Shadrin, allegedly the host of the meeting which they say went on for three and a half hours, suffered from unusual forgetfulness regarding that day.

Q. Can you remember the timing of that meeting?

A. No.

Q. Even approximately?

A. Well, I think as far as I am aware, it was either the – I think it was the match between Arsenal and CSKA.

Q. Did the meeting take place in the same room that you've identified?

A. Yes, but frankly I don't remember that we actually discussed anything...

Q. Was Mr Kovtun present?

A. I don't remember, actually. And openly I just quitted the meeting...

Q. Can you remember your meeting being disturbed in any way by phone calls to Mr Lugovoy from anybody else?

A. No.

Q. Did Mr Lugovoy at any point leave your meeting to take phone calls from anybody else?

A. No, I can't remember, I'm sorry.[37]

Sasha Litvinenko switched on his mobile phone at 8.53 am near his home at 140 Osier Cresent on the way back from his usual early-morning run. At about eleven, Marina was ready to leave. It was agreed that they both had a lot to do that day and would together celebrate their sixth anniversary in London in the evening. Sasha wished her a good day and Marina left. Litvinenko stayed at home a little longer and then dashed off to town.

According to several sources, he had a light breakfast at eleven, then telephoned or texted Lugovoy (there was no conversation), and left home at 12.15. On the way, he called Shamil Zakayev and, according to his Oyster card data report, boarded bus 234 on Wilton Road at 12.29. From there he also made a call to Marina, then to Dan Quirke at RISC Management and to Dean Attew at Titon International, entering East Finchley Underground station to catch the Northern Line at 1.10 pm. Londoners know that from the Northern Line one cannot get directly to Oxford Circus so in order to travel there he had to change at Warren Street. He most likely did change to the Victoria Line, getting out at Oxford Circus at 1.34 pm. The camera looking down onto Regent Street at Oxford Circus saw him crossing the street. Litvinenko then turned left at New Bond Street and at 13.59 the camera saw him walking west from New Bond Street on the north side of Grosvenor Street in the direction of Grosvenor Square.

Although the evidence provided by Dean Attew was inconsistent and contradictory, his diary reminded him that on 1 November he arranged a meeting in his office between Malcolm McNally, then director of Amicus Mentor Limited, a private security company (dissolved in April 2017) and Neil Barnett, a journalist. Neil and Sasha had met before and the journalist recalled his encounter with Litvinenko in 'a hotel off a main square in a central European capital' back in 2002 in his article published by *The Spectator* twice (the first time it came out was two days after Sasha died). According to Attew, after the meeting with Malcolm and Neil, he talked to Sasha but could not remember what they discussed, only saying it was a short visit.

The reason for Litvinenko's coming to Titon on that day was not such a big mystery. A day before, on 31 October, Sasha delivered the Shubsky report compiled by Shvets to Attew and now returned to pick up another assignment.

It was indeed a rather short visit because by 2.25 pm, he had already left Titon International and was walking east towards New Bond Street. It may be worth recalling that Titon's offices were at 25 Grosvenor Street, right opposite number 58 where Lugovoy and Kovtun were allegedly discussing business all that time. From Grosvenor Street Litvinenko turned right heading towards Piccadilly and on the way called Lugovoy. The time was 14.32 and he still had a few minutes to drop by a Russian souvenir stall at the churchyard in front of St James's church on Piccadilly known as St James's market before a planned meeting on Piccadilly Circus.

A young man from Belarus by the name of Alexander Tabunov used to sell Russian matryoshka dolls, lacquer boxes, Soviet militaria and similar treasures for tourists at this small market employed by a company called Russian Troyka. Once Litvinenko turned up there, he found a compatriot who agreed to be a patient listener to his endless stories, and he began to visit the place regularly whenever he was in the vicinity of the church. The officers from SO15 came here on 22 November, when Sasha was still alive, and Tabunov was one of the first to provide witness evidence, although he had nothing particularly interesting or important to say. What the police and – nine years later – the inquiry learned was that during those short encounters Sasha used to tell his namesake a lot of things about himself.

From the churchyard Sasha moved towards Piccadilly Circus where Mario Scaramella was impatiently waiting with Limarev's emails that worried him a lot. He was standing just a few metres away from the Shaftesbury Memorial Fountain, popularly but incorrectly known as 'Eros', watching live videos and ads. The new huge screen featuring recognition technology was not yet installed. He had been standing there for less than ten minutes when Sasha approached him unnoticed.

Litvinenko was wearing blue jeans and a matching denim jacket with a khaki T-shirt underneath, very casual. Mario was probably the only friend who never called him Sasha, always Alexander or Alex, and they greeted each other warmly, with Litvinenko giving him a kiss on the cheek. Mario leaned to another side and gave Sasha a second kiss, saying, 'In Italy we give two,' which is indeed a standard friendly greeting, especially in Naples where Mario came from. They hugged each other and Mario also patted his friend on the shoulder. Although Scaramella spoke quite decent English, which I can vouch for, Sasha's was still rather bad so they communicated more with gestures than words. Then Litvinenko pronounced his traditional 'there is a good restaurant, they have very good fish at a very low price' and invited Mario to Itsu on Piccadilly, his favourite Asian eatery which they had already visited on a previous occasion. At 15.10 a CCTV camera saw them heading from Piccadilly Circus in the direction of Itsu. Quite by chance, the moment Litvinenko approached Scaramella at Piccadilly Circus Lugovoy called Angelina's number in Moscow. The conversation lasted two minutes and six seconds.

As usual, while they were walking, Litvinenko was the one who talked. Sasha told Mario that he wanted to start a new business trading with natural resources. He explained that in Russia all state companies that dealt with natural resources were compelled to do exactly what the Russian secret services told them to do. 'He told me,' Mario later testified, 'that he had a friend in the secret services, who knew the president of one of these companies and therefore he could supply any product at a very low price. He told me that he was closing or had closed a deal with a load of copper. He concluded his explanation by saying "Millions, Mario, millions!" Because of his English, I did not understand what he meant and asked him to repeat what he said.'[38]

And Litvinenko, as best as he could, explained it again.

Questioned by the police several weeks later, Dean Attew recalled that one day Sasha came to his office asking whether he knew somebody who could buy and sell metal copper. By chance, a man named Graham Neil Cormac was in the office. He was an engineer with broad contacts who was involved in several companies and said he just had the right commodities dealer in mind. After a while, Dean received a request from Graham on behalf of that dealer and some days later Sasha gave him a document detailing the chemical composition of the offered copper. 'That was the only occasion,' Dean said, 'Sasha has mentioned being involved in a business deal.' When the Metropolitan Police attended Titon offices at the end of November, the document was still lying in Dean's diary.

On the way to Itsu Sasha also told Mario that he was looking for a new job because he could no longer work for Berezovsky. He stressed that Berezovsky was still a good friend who had been paying for the house where the Litvinenkos lived, also covering his son's school fees. Sasha did not mention that he had actually never been employed by Berezovsky or any of his business ventures.

At Itsu, Litvinenko chose his meal, Mario took a bottle of water, paid for both, and they headed downstairs, turning right at the bottom of the steps. There were three tables adjacent to the wall and Sasha opted for the one in the middle. As part of Operation AVOCET, photographs, pictures, plans, drawings and 3D models were produced showing the basement and that particular table from all perspectives.[39] Some traces of light secondary alpha contamination were found on the table and settees Mario said they were using, but then plenty of other places and objects in Itsu were also showing minor traces of polonium so at the end of November it was closed and only opened for business (after expansion planned well before the incident, the owner said), in April 2007.

While Litvinenko was eating, he was still talking about the article written by Paolo Guzzanti, president of the Mitrokhin Commission of the Italian parliament and, as such, Mario's boss. The articled mentioned Litvinenko and Politkovskaya, shot to death in Moscow on Putin's birthday, 7 October. Mario also had a copy with him but said it was time to concentrate on more important things. He produced two emails from Limarev and handed them over to Litvinenko.

The text was in English and Sasha only glanced at the pages not willing to read them because he could hardly understand what was written there. When Mario said the documents were very important because they contained information, allegedly from secret sources in Moscow, that the lives of Senator Guzzanti, Scaramella, Berezovsky and Litvinenko were in mortal danger, Sasha asked who sent those messages. When Mario revealed they came from Limarev, Litvinenko said: Limarev wants to appear as an intelligence officer, a spy, but he had only worked at the FSB Special Purpose Centre training facility in Balashikha. Do not believe him. Sasha went on, telling a story how Limarev asked Berezovsky to pay him 20,000 euros to demonstrate official income to the French authorities. Anyway, he promised to check Limarev's information, probably having in mind Lugovoy or Zharko because they were his only sources in Moscow.

At the end of the meeting Litvinenko also suggested introducing Mario to Gerard Batten, with whom he discussed his allegations about Romano Prodi. Since May, Prodi had again been serving as prime minister of Italy having previously been President of the European Commission. Litvinenko claimed that Prodi had been a KGB agent all along. In early April, Batten, based on Sasha's information, told the European Parliament that, according to Litvinenko, Prodi had been the KGB's 'man in Italy' and demanded an inquiry into the allegations. At the end of April Batten repeated his call for a parliamentary inquiry, stating that apart from Litvinenko 'former senior members of the KGB are willing to testify', meaning Gordievsky and Shvets. Nothing came out of it but twelve years later, in April 2018, Batten was elected unopposed as the leader of his political party, UKIP, of which he was a founding member.

Litvinenko tried to call him from Itsu but Batten's mobile was switched off. Remarkably, his consolidated telephone call data report does not show this call. When they were leaving Itsu, Mario again told Sasha how seriously he took Limarev's warnings. Sasha, please understand it is me, my babies, my security, and my life, not a trifle, he pleaded. Take it seriously, please. And Litvinenko replied, Mario, you are a friend, don't you worry. 'At this point we separated and I don't remember in which direction Alexander went,' Scaramella said to Nicoletta, the Italian interpreter who was taking down his statement to the Metropolitan Police in a separate ward at the Haematology Department of UCLH on 5 December 2006. A very frightened Scaramella had been placed there by the Health Protection Agency (HPA) several days earlier when preliminary results showed he had been exposed to radioactive polonium.

After he parted with Mario Scaramella, Litvinenko crossed Piccadilly and headed north via Berkeley Street and Berkeley Square where one of the most elegant and famous clubs in the world is situated, of which Sasha was not aware. He also could not know that some three years earlier, Her Majesty Queen Elizabeth II visited the club, almost certainly the only nightclub she had ever visited, and this was only because it had been one of the very few London haunts frequented by Princes William and Harry. When he reached the junction of Davies and Grosvenor streets, Dean Attew called him, which Dean had completely forgotten. They discussed the new assignment and Sasha immediately telephoned Yuri Shvets in Washington to assure him that a new job would be forthcoming. He then dialled Attew's number just to make sure. Before coming to Grosvenor Square, Litvinenko made six more telephone calls including Berezovsky's personal number and at exactly two minutes to 4.00 pm was standing in the lobby of the Millennium Hotel.

CHAPTER 10

The Third Man

The word itsu, written in proper kana, is mostly used to mean 'when' in Japanese. 'When' becomes a key word when dealing with everything that happened in and around the Millennium Hotel on that fateful day because several CCTV cameras and even the bar till were showing the wrong time. Therefore, all timings here are approximate.

At about 15.29, as Litvinenko began walking away from Itsu to the Millennium Hotel, Lugovoy and Kovtun entered the reception area. A CCTV camera saw them passing by the seating sofas where all their company gathered in the morning and then disappearing from view. From there they entered the Pine Bar where there were no cameras not only inside but also outside, and Lugovoy paused at the door examining the guests. Then he approached a waiter, asking for a Cuban cigar.

On 1 November 2006 Noberto Andrade, a 69-year-old head barman who had been working at the Millennium for a quarter of a century, started his working day at 11.00, hoping to finish about 19.30 in the evening. He had placed a young man, Jacob, behind the bar to mix cocktails while serving numerous guests himself as a waiter. They were only two on that day and the bar was unusually busy, very busy because there was a property auction in the ballroom plus a lot of Russian guests had arrived to attend a football match. Many of them were sitting at tables and others at the bar, occupying all five stools. Andrade was moving fast, trying to sit everybody down at a table at the same time taking orders and serving drinks to the customers.

They spoke English but the Italian said he quickly realised that this clean shaven and good-looking gentleman had a Russian accent. Lugovoy, for it was him, asked for his favourite Punch Punch but from the Cuban cigar brands Andrade could only offer a mild Romeo y Julieta No. 1, which comes in a tube. In all cases it was an excellent choice. When Andrade asked whether he also wanted to order drinks, Lugovoy said he was waiting for other guests to arrive, so they would order later. 'The bar at that time was very busy,' Mr Andrade would later testify, 'and all of the tables were occupied.'[1] Both men then took table 1, which appeared to be free and very conveniently moved together with table 2 next to it, making it one long table, and table 3 in the same section seemed also to be still available, no doubt quite by chance.

Noberto Andrade had worked at this place long enough to start thinking about his retirement, which would be in two years. At the time, his son Richard with his fiancée and Noberto's grandchildren stayed with him and his wife a lot at home and his other son, Paul, was also living there with his girlfriend. Andrade had to think about his family after his retirement and because of that and his age he had become a bit careless and absent-minded and could occasionally be forgetful and easily distracted. Thus, on 29 October he forgot to change the bar till to winter time (following the clocks going back) and it was now running one hour late. Due to his age, Noberto was not very computer literate and employed somebody to do computer work for him. Besides, about a week before he had lost his swipe card needed to process purchases at the bar and had to borrow one from another barman, David. Using this swipe card, at 15.33 he opened up a bill for table 1, where Lugovoy and Kovtun now sat down with Lugovoy sitting on a settee conveniently located in the corner so that he was seeing the entrance door and the whole bar.

Minutes later while Kovtun remained at table, Lugovoy, who was wearing a yellow pullover and a dark jacket, approached a member of the staff at the reception and asked how to get to the gents. At about 15.35, another camera caught him descending a set of steps back down into the reception area. He took his phone, listened to the voice messages, and as soon as he finished Litvinenko called him (15:38:53) to say he was on the way to the hotel.

At about 15.47 a CCTV camera saw Kovtun coming to the reception desk and repeating all movements in the same order as Lugovoy. That is, he approached a male member of staff, asked to direct him to the gents, and a couple of minutes later another camera got him returning to the reception area.

When Andrade approached table 1 again (moved together with the adjoining table 2 to make a longer table and thus more space for a party of guests), Lugovoy was sitting with two men. At that moment, he ordered three teas with lemon and honey and three gin and tonics. Later, Lugovoy also ordered the same Gordon's dry gin but without tonic and one champagne cocktail. The waiter recalled that two of Lugovoy's companions seemed younger than him and both had darker hair but was unable to recall anything else.[2] While he was serving other guests, the three of them were sitting, drinking, and talking. Although Andrade noted that 'in total there were 3 or 4 men at table', in reality there were always only three. One doesn't need to employ Tony and Jonna Mendez to perform this simple trick.[3] It is known in the trade as substitution or identity swap, which means putting one person in the place of another.

Analysing the actions of the whole group of 'actors' and all arrangements on the stage, one must also give a credit to the operation planners and controllers as everything in this secret operation seems to have been well coordinated like in a good theatre production. A perfect *mise-en-scène*, a critic might say. At 15.51 another operator, Maxim Begak, moved into position. He appeared to be walking from Adam's Row towards the hotel entrance followed closely by a member of the hotel staff. Begak walked down a set of steps into the reception area looking into the Brian Turner Bar to the left of the steps before turning away and walking across the reception area. Moving behind the seating area, he was seen using his mobile phone, then turning again and finally entering the Brian Turner Bar, which was smaller than the Pine Bar on the opposite side of the reception area close to the restaurant, and disappearing from view. Begak's phone and movements were not registered and remained unchecked throughout the whole operation and after. The time was approximately 15.53.

Camera 14 was screening the reception area between 15:57:25 and 16:00:24 as Litvinenko walked into full view behind the sofas and moved towards the Brian Turner Bar. At that moment he called a private number of Berezovsky to tell him about the emails that he had received from Scaramella. The call lasted for twenty-six seconds, during which time he probably managed to say what he wanted to say but because Boris was flying abroad that evening, Sasha was told to come to the office. He then called Lugovoy (15:59:04) but the line was busy because Lugovoy was talking to Moscow. In the investigation file it was logged as a call to Angelina. That was a rather short conversation, slightly less than two minutes, but when Sasha dialled Lugovoy's number again, the line was busy again because at that moment Lugovoy was calling... Vladimir Voronov. With Litvinenko waiting in the reception area, only a few moments before he would be poisoned in a complex operation involving a large group of people and a most unusual radioactive poison later compared by some to a mini nuke, Lugovoy, after having consulted with Moscow, was calling a nominal director of CPL and their conversation lasted for six full minutes. What was so terribly urgent and important to discuss at that moment?

While Lugovoy was on the phone and Litvinenko was looking for him and waiting, a slight movement began in the bar. This technique is called the mobility of holes, the term borrowed from physics, and is used when a covert operation in carried out in a location like a small restaurant, club, or bar. Ideally, four groups should be involved, where one is staking out the location, another is there to distract attention, there's of course a team or an authorised individual for what is termed an 'executive action' (a euphemism for shooting, poisoning, or any other way of disposing of a person), plus a specialist unit called cleaners. If the 'cleaning' is not required, three groups or even three individual operators may be enough for a successful hit. Alas, there are many tricks in the spy trade of which the police may not be aware. Espionage is not their business. As a result, a professional intelligence operation rather than a simple murder by poison had not even been discussed. Because the barmen's vision was blocked by the people sitting at the bar while the waiter, Noberto Andrade, was busy serving thirteen tables alone, the operators chosen for the mission had a free hand to move unobtrusively.

At one moment Kovtun disappeared from the room. It is of course possible that he somehow managed to escape without anybody, including CCTV cameras, seeing him but this was, strictly speaking, not necessary. He could simply move to another table while a trained professional from that table moved to his place at table 1. As Mr Andrade had noticed, Kovtun and the third man looked very much alike and this was perhaps one of the reasons why Kovtun was needed in London on that day. Nobody would notice the substitution.

Now, as soon as this third man settled at their table, there was a whole variety of options. He could either bring a teapot prepared in advance with him, or if he wanted to avoid making too much fuss about it he could just sit down and insert a few crystals of polonium salt into the spout of the teapot already standing on the table close to where Sasha was going to be seated. Remarkably, the teapot – if one believes it was the same teapot that Litvinenko poured his polonium-laced tea from – had only been slightly contaminated from inside and the only heavily contaminated part was the spout. The AWE experts who had worked with it marked it as 'full-scale deflection' meaning Geiger counter readings of alpha radiation. From outside, it had a few heavily contaminated drops underneath the spout and only one small place on the side.[4] After quietly finishing his work, a specialist – the Third Man – moved to another place at another table prepared for him. The whole exercise would only take a few seconds.

At about 16.06 Lugovoy came out of the bar, saw Litvinenko waiting in the reception area, and invited him to come with him. He went in first with Sasha in tow following Lugovoy to the second set of tables located in the far corner. The table marked as 'table 1' in the investigation documents (a combination of tables 1 and 2) was indeed at the corner on the right side from the entrance after the first set of tables (tables 4 and 5). There was also table 3 close to tables 1 and 2, about whose occupants or lack of such there is no mention in the files. When they entered, all three tables were not occupied. Lugovoy sat down on the settee in the corner and Litvinenko wanted to sit just in front of him but was offered to take a chair positioned diagonally to Lugovoy and closer to the nearby table. As mentioned, there was nobody else in this part of the bar but otherwise the place was full of customers, most of them Russians.

Several teacups, empty glasses, and a teapot were still on the table. Only one teapot, which Sasha later described as 'silver in colour, made of silver, not silver, the legs... expensive metal – it's a rich hotel'. This teapot was just in front of him. Almost certainly the memory did not serve him right when he later described the scene to two police officers who visited him at hospital and he mistook a beautiful vintage silver metal teapot from the Palm Court – a bar at the Sheraton – in which he was served his green tea during his meeting with Lugovoy a couple of days ago for a simple white tea pot from the Pine Bar.

When Litvinenko took a seat, the waiter silently approached from behind, asking whether he would like to order anything because it was teatime. Sasha said, 'No, thank you,' and Lugovoy said something like 'Okay, well, we are going to leave now anyway.' But turning to Litvinenko, he proposed, 'There is some [green] tea left here – if you want you can have some', at the same time asking Andrade – there was no other waiter in the bar – to bring a fresh cup, which was promptly served in spite of the busy hour. Sasha poured himself some tea out of that teapot and it turned out there was little left. It made just half a cup. It was Sasha's favourite green tea with no sugar and it was not hot, almost cold. But then an expert would say it is advisable to consume green tea at a lukewarm temperature to reap maximum benefits. Those who had prepared this teapot were well versed in *sadō*, the Japanese tea ceremony. In addition to their main speciality: toxicology.

As soon as Lugovoy and Litvinenko disappeared inside the Pine Bar, a CCTV camera noticed Begak (16:08:32) walking into the hotel lobby from the Brian Turner Bar doors on the opposite side and moving towards the seating area. He sat down facing the Pine Bar door and remained motionless for about twenty minutes, paying no attention to other guests.

Interlude: Poisoning as a means of state assassination

Poisoning is a traditional method of state assassination and it is mentioned at length in many authoritative sources, some of them dating back to ancient times. One such source is *Corpus juris Civilis*, a compendium of juristic writings on Roman law compiled by order of the emperor Justinian I in the fifth century AD. One of its four parts, *The Institutes*, explains Lex Cornelia on assassinations, specifically stressing that 'this statute also inflicts punishment of death on poisoners, who kill men by their hateful arts of poison and magic, or who publicly sell deadly drugs'.

Lenin, the Bolshevik leader with sadistic personality disorder, was fascinated by rare and lethal substances used throughout the centuries to murder people. The first Soviet poison laboratory was established directly in his secretariat and was called the 'Special Room'. From the very beginning its 'products' were to be used against the enemies of the people. This was an understatement. What the Soviet bigwigs always meant by 'enemies of the people' or 'national traitors' were in reality Kremlin critics. But the worst enemies were those who disagreed with and were opposed to the national leader himself. Lenin ordered them to be shot on the spot. Stalin's favourites were mass executions, slow deaths in the forced labour camps of the GULAG, and forced resettlements. Brezhnev sent dissidents to mental hospitals and then forcibly expelled them from the Soviet Union. And Putin – in full conformity with the time-honoured KGB practice – preferred targeted killings in and outside the country for some of his enemies and long prison terms for others.

Specific research activities in toxicology, the study of poisons and their effects had been carried out in Russia since the early 1920s. Academic institutes, scientific laboratories and centres are being involved in this work with hundreds of scientists getting paid, promoted, and decorated for the development of new toxic substances. Yet another group of highly educated and motivated men and women has been working on improving old ways and developing new ways of murdering people by means and methods more sophisticated than before and, as humorously defined by *Scientific American*, preferably without 'such effects as those produced by a small quantity of lead entering the body at high velocity'.

Early in their careers, acquiring the skill and tools of the trade, a set of rules or standard operating procedures known as 'tradecraft', they have already learnt that a good assassination plan will ensure that the result looks like a death by natural causes. 'When successfully executed,' they had been taught, 'the death will cause little excitement and will only be casually investigated'. Indeed, a high-profile murder must be carefully planned, well prepared, and simple to put into practice in order to look like a suicide, heart attack, or acute indigestion. Students of intelligence studies also learn that the aim of every executive action, whether it is poisoning, drowning, or strangulation, is to kill the target. Not to threaten, send a message, or demonstrate, but to permanently dispose of a certain person.

Having taken the decision that an individual must be liquidated, the powers that be – in the Russia of 2006, just like in 2023, it was Putin's presidential administration following his tacit approval – would authorise an intelligence agency or an individual to carry out the task. In a few particular cases, for example, when Stalin was the Master of the House, it was Trotsky – his Enemy Number One plus all his relatives, secretaries and associates – whose assassination the dictator personally ordered. And with Putin as the Kremlin leader there had been his own Enemy Number One, Berezovsky, plus members of his close circle whom he sought 'to wipe out in the shithouse', exactly like Stalin calling them a gang of terrorists and extremists. In such rare cases it is the ruler himself who would issue an explicit instruction authorising an executive action. Such 'personalist rulers', the analysis suggests, having purged all voices who could challenge them, quickly find themselves isolated and out of touch. 'They are more likely to pursue nuclear weapons, repress their citizens and rely on corruption to maintain their rule.'[5] Their regimes are dictatorships of dread. And they never hesitate in granting a licence to kill.

The Presidential Administration of Russia is somewhat similar to but at the same time different from the Executive Office of the President of the United States – a group of offices and agencies at the centre of the executive branch of the federal government. In Putin's Russia, the presidential administration is a command-and-control centre of the regime. The chief of the presidential administration who oversees its work, his deputies, heads of main directorates and services as well as their deputies are appointed and serve at the pleasure of the president who can dismiss them at will without anybody's approval. Other staff are appointed by the chief of the administration, himself a senior Kremlin figure. At the time of writing the incumbent Kremlin Chief of Staff of the Presidential Administration was Anton Vaino, the grandson of the former First Secretary of the Communist Party of Estonia, appointed in August 2016. Exactly like in Stalin's Soviet Union, in Putin's Russia the PA, like in the US known as the Presidential Executive Office, is a secretive institution having everything under its control including the army, secret services, media, and even some Russian masonic organisations. In other words, the PA is where power truly lies in this system.

About a year after the events described in this chapter, a Russian defector living under deep cover in the Washington area agreed to talk to an American journalist who was working on a book about Russian espionage in America. Among other things, I remember his story about Yevgeny Murov, then General of the Army and Director of the Federal Protective Service (FSO), and Viktor Zolotov, then Major General and chief of Putin's personal security detail, which he transformed into the most powerful and secret government agency of Russia – the Presidential Security Service (SBP), Putin's Praetorian Guard. In the Roman Empire, the Praetorian

Guard was a special unit serving as personal bodyguards and intelligence agents for the emperors. Similar to it, in addition to Putin's personal bodyguards (*líchniki*), the SPB has its own intelligence branch with an obscure name, the Department of Psychological Security, assisted by a panel of experts seconded from all other secret services of Russia.

According to the defector, himself a high-ranking Russian intelligence officer, Murov and Zolotov 'decided to make a list of politicians and other influential Muscovites whom they would need to assassinate to give Putin unchecked power'. It took them quite a while and in the meantime the list had grown to several hundred. 'There are too many,' Zolotov said pensively after they finished, 'it is too many to kill – even for us.' Fifteen years have passed since those days but the Kremlin's kill list, as the world has seen, exists and grows faster than before. Before Russia started killing in earnest after having invaded Ukraine in February 2022, the most prominent victim was Alexey Navalny, a Russian opposition leader who miraculously survived a poisoning attempt. As later established by several specialised Western laboratories, it was acute poisoning by an unidentified organophosphorus compound.[6] In such cases the cause of death is usually respiratory paralysis but Navalny survived thanks to the timely evacuation and efforts of the German doctors, his family, and members of his team.

In May 2016 Murov retired and was immediately appointed chairman of the board of directors of Zarubezhneft, a Russian state-controlled oil company based in Moscow. But Zolotov remained in place, was promoted to General of the Army and placed in charge of Rosgvardiya, the National Guard of Russia, a formidable force of about 340,000 personnel located in eighty-four units across Russia. The only person to whom Putin could entrust such highly sensitive assignments as the assassination of Politkovskaya, Litvinenko, Berezovsky, and Nemtsov would be Zolotov.

Apart from mutual trust and his years-long closeness to Putin (Zolotov had served as Putin's personal bodyguard back in the 1990s), essential elements in such sensitive matters, there is another reason why only Zolotov could have been placed in charge of the Litvinenko operation. The affair was a consolidated effort of the MVD, FSB, SVR and even GRU, but first of all it was the FSO that provided its officers as frontmen. In place, that is in London, the leading actor was without doubt Lugovoy, a former GUO/FSO major assisted by two other officers: Sokolenko and Valuyev. Lugovoy also involved his childhood friend Kovtun, a former captain of the Soviet army who proved to be a convenient partner, especially when it was decided that Valuyev should stay in Moscow. Besides, Kovtun possessed that quality so beloved of spymasters. He was quite dispensable.

The foreign intelligence service (SVR) provided a legal cover using its shell companies while its officers and agents resident in London and masquerading under various covers, acted in support roles to principal operators. In their turn, the FSB supplied agents who were infiltrated for short-term assignments penetrating the offices of Berezovsky and his inner circle. Most likely the FSO also provided a surveillance team because FSB watchers who are very good in Russia would look awkward or clumsy conducting surveillance in London. And, of course, the poisoner (the Third Man) must have been a specialist from the SVR's Directorate S.[7] There is little doubt that the Third Man was present in the Pine Bar on 1 November and not only because they ordered three gin and tonics, three teas with lemon and honey, and three cups as soon as they settled at the table and before Litvinenko arrived at the hotel (when Sasha was invited to come to the bar, Lugovoy was there alone).

The waiter Andrade remembered that there were always three (he even said four) men at that table. But most importantly, only a trained specialist can guarantee the success of such mission. At least in two previous cases both Kovtun and Lugovoy acting alone failed to use the poison, at the same time leaving a lot of traces. Reasons why it happened could be easily explained, having in mind that none of them was a trained murderer or special operations officer. As a result, Kovtun was exposed to large amounts of radiation which caused ARS, Acute Radiation Syndrome.[8] Although the dose was external, it subsequently led to his demise.

Generally, the mechanics of assassination are fairly simple. 'Once a decision has been taken,' Barry Davies writes, 'the project is then handed over to the appropriate organisation for action. Those responsible for carrying out [the operation] will plan, organise and execute their orders.'

As soon as the executive action or, as it is known in Russia, direct action had been authorised, the responsible PA official was addressed to approve the method and the means by which the target should be eliminated. In the case of a potentially high-profile poisoning, the method would always be clandestine. That is, the aim is for the operation not to be noticed at all. And because the means was determined to be a special poison which was not to be easily identified by standard equipment and would also guarantee a long and excruciating death, a specialised research facility was commissioned to provide such a poison. As one reliable spycraft manual puts it, those who control and direct covert operations at the service level will then meticulously plan it together with the team, and decide on the best course of action depending on the target location and profile.

While the location was known and easy to inconspicuously infiltrate by any number of operators due to such an excellent pretext as a football match, Lugovoy and the support team had spent a year establishing the whereabouts of a target (or possibly targets), the pattern of usual movements, and perceived strengths and weaknesses. Much of this information had already been available from the local agents and the London SVR station (rezidentura). The file, known in the old KGB as 'liternoe delo' with some denigrating nickname on the cover (for example, when Gordievsky defected, he was nicknamed GNAT), also included photographs of a target, his family and his home, detailed maps of the London boroughs like the City of Westminster and Haringey where the target had been spending most of his time as well as that of Central London. There should have also been bus and Underground routes, photographs and plans of buildings regularly visited by the target, his mobile phone numbers, eating and drinking habits – in short, everything that made the target's profile, the most important aspect of any executive action.

The Third Man

There is also one golden rule that applies to any murder whether by shooting, poisoning, road accident or, say, defenestration: it is all about getting the target into a position where the planned operation can take place. The location and the time when a potential victim is going to be there must be known well in advance.

Thus, the Pine Bar and the polonium salt, contrary to what many journalists and writers claimed, were quite obviously a perfect location and an ideal poison. The bar had several entrances and exits but no CCTV cameras inside or outside; it was one of the two bars both conveniently situated on the ground floor of an elegant four-star hotel – not too luxurious but positioned right near the well-guarded US embassy at the heart of Westminster, which provided a feeling of extra security. Radioactive polonium compounds like polonium tetrachloride ($PoCl_4$) or tetrabromide ($PoBr_4$) look like normal salt crystals, are comparatively harmless to skin but lethally toxic if inhaled or swallowed. In addition, they are alpha emitters and alpha radiation detection is notoriously time consuming and difficult to carry out due to the short range of alpha particles in the air. From every side, the operation might have been an ideal murder... if Berezovsky, his money, and his team did not start to act, and act quickly. Their efforts almost turned this well-planned covert operation into a complete failure.

***

University College London Hospital, Department of Haematology, Ward T16, 18 November 2006, Litvinenko speaking:

> Andrey said I go to Millennium, left side bar. Andrey I asked [by phone where to come]. Andrey, 'Oh, Alexander, I'm sit here.' Please. Invite me. Andrey sit only one on the table. It is on [the right]. I sit opposite him, maybe, its big table. I sit here. Andrey, 'Sorry, its Vajim table, Vajim chair, Vajim back... come back and will be back.'[9] I sit with chair. It's nothing eat. Andrey, 'Do you like tea?' 'Umm, yes.' They told me, 'Please, this er...' Jug? Jug. This jug it's not, its maybe fifteen centimetres in jug, from metal. From, maybe its silver. A fifteen-centimetre-high jug? Yeah. It's a very expensive cup [sic, jug]... Maybe waiter bring me new cup. I pour. Its little bit tea. It's finish. Tea is not hot, it's warm, its green tea. China tea. After this arrive Vadim. Vadim said, 'I am very, very tired... I'm go through Hamburg. I'm not sleep.' And Vadim maybe five minutes sit with me with Andrey. Andrey's wife downstairs, 'Oh, hello.' Andrey go to, for her. And meet me with his son, and show me his daughter. Andrey go to football club. Vadim down, upstairs to his room sleeping. I go to Boris Berezovsky's office. This meeting I drinking only tea.[10]

The next day, and now with an interpreter present, Litvinenko recalled another detail. 'Well, we were sitting there for about twenty minutes on the whole. Yes, also, before Volodya came, some Russian male came up, a tall one, I could not see him from behind. No, Volodya was already sitting.[11] Then some tall Russian came up, I only glanced at him from behind, wearing some dark cardigan. And he said something to Andrey and he said yes, yes, all right, he said, go on, I will speak to you later.'[12]

This was probably Sokolenko telling Lugovoy that they had returned from the city tour and were gathering at the Brian Turner Bar, as previously agreed. But it could have been someone else as well.

During his interviews at hospital with Metropolitan Police officers Detective Inspector (DI) Brent Hyatt and Detective Sergeant (DS) Chris Hoar, Sasha wittingly or unwittingly missed several important details, which was not that crucial but might be worth mentioning. At one moment, after Litvinenko took a few sips of tea, Lugovoy dialled Vladimir Valuyev's number again (16:26:12) right at the table. The call was rather short, only one minute and eight seconds, but it was more than enough to say two words like, for example, mission accomplished.

Until that moment, Begak remained in his place on the sofas at the reception area. While he was there, a woman with a child sat nearby for a few minutes before getting up and leaving – he did not appear to acknowledge them and did not even move. Could she be part of the team? She could, of course, but no one checked. As soon as Lugovoy finished talking to Valuyev on the phone (16:27:15), Begak got up from his seat and returned to the Brian Turner Bar behind him passing from view. Less than five minutes later, Svetlana Lugovaya with small Yegor, as well as both Lugovoy's daughters, Tatiana and Galina, entered the reception area accompanied by Sokolenko. The same CCTV camera saw them moving towards the Brian Turner Bar on the right side of the hotel entrance. As described in the police file, 'over the next few minutes various group members walk from the bar area and out into the reception area before returning'.[13] What conclusion can be drawn from this? One may argue that the job of the police was not to analyse cell movements but to investigate the murder and find the killer. Maybe. We shall come to it in the next chapter.

Recalling the final moments of his meeting with Lugovoy and Kovtun, Litvinenko explained: 'In the end [Lugovoy] looked at his watch, he said, "My wife is about to come". There in the hall Andrey's wife turned up, she was waving her hand and he said, "That's it, let's go". So, Volodya [*sic*, Dmitry Kovtun] and I stayed, the two of us, and he stood up, approached his wife, Andrey, and then he brought his son, 8 years old. He is such a boy, eight years old, wearing a jacket, he said, 'This is Uncle Sasha, shake his hand'. We shook hands, and he went ... So, then we came out and then Volodya and I were left on our own.'[14]

The whole company seems to have gathered at the Brian Turner Bar and after leaving Litvinenko Lugovoy walked straight there. A CCTV camera caught him passing the reception area and entering the bar at 16.33. He reappeared with the family one minute later.

***

The Third Man

After he left the Millennium Hotel, Litvinenko walked in the direction of Berezovsky's offices at 7 Down Street, where Boris's company named FSL Solutions Ltd was registered, calling Ahmed Zakayev on the way. At this moment, while already in the Brian Turner Bar, Sokolenko dialled the number of or sent a text message to Risk Advisory Group (16:51:08). As if following some prearranged plan, he called them again exactly ten minutes later (17:01:10) and after no one answered, demonstrating enviable perseverance, made another three attempts at intervals of a few seconds.

While this strange and so far unexplained telephone activity was in progress, Begak left the bar, crossed the reception area and went to the gents. Two CCTV cameras followed him there and back in approximately ninety seconds and saw him coming to the bar door, then turning and retracing his steps before passing from view while making a telephone call (not registered). He was soon seen again in the reception area, where he spoke with a member of staff and walked towards the bar. A few moments later, another camera caught him entering the lift that took him to the first floor. There, he spent no more than five minutes. Between about 16.47 and 16.55, he is shown walking on the first floor away from the camera, then returning to the same place and taking a lift going to the ground floor. In the meantime, the system registered Tatiana's call to Lugovoy (16:53:08), which lasted for one and a half minutes. This telephone call found Lugovoy walking towards a set of steps and the hotel exit doors leading to Adam's Row. He was accompanied by Sokolenko, Kovtun, Svetlana, and small Yegor.

Call logs show there was another phone call from Tatiana's mobile to Lugovoy twenty minutes later (17:11:55) lasting, as previously, one and a half minutes. By that time the whole party including Tatiana had gathered at the Angus Steak House in Coventry Street where they enjoyed a substantial dinner with soup, shish kebab (which is a Mediterranean cuisine version of the shashlik popular in the Caucasus and much loved by many Russians), chicken Kiev, and a dessert of fresh strawberries. The atmosphere was festive and jolly. It is difficult to imagine a person poisoning somebody with radioactive polonium and then laughing and telling jokes while having a sumptuous feast with family and friends before going to a football match. All the people at the table – Sokolenko, Kovtun, Begak, Alexey Valuyev, Lugovoy, his wife and two daughters – were completely at ease. Only minutes before, encouraged by his father, Lugovoy's eight-year-old son was shaking hands with 'Uncle Sasha' back at the hotel after the fatal tea party. Two months later, a specialised team of AWE experts were following their steps wearing disposable protective suits and masks for ionising radiation equipped with dosimeters and respirators.

Remarkably, no contamination was found in the restaurant.

After paying the bill (£244.50) at 18.28 and leaving the tip for their Polish waitress on the table, the whole group except Kovtun departed to the Arsenal stadium some two hours before the football match was due to begin. Before leaving the steak house, Lugovoy called Shadrin (18:01:08). At 18.57 CCTV camera 7, installed in the lift, saw Kovtun stepping in and moments later getting out on the third floor. He then proceeded to Sokolenko's room 382 and almost certainly went to bed after a sleepless night. Later, the expert team found a pillow on the bed that he had used and a chair seat contaminated considerably more than other objects in this room with traces of primary polonium contamination found in the bathroom. The bathroom traces looked very much like those in the Best Western hotel where Kovtun and Lugovoy had stayed two weeks earlier.

At 20.42, when the match had already begun, Lugovoy dialled Tatiana's telephone number again, although she was supposed to be sitting nearby.

Lugovoy, his wife and son returned to the hotel at 22.23 and went directly to their room. Information about the movements of the girls and Begak is not in the files.

It turned out that Sokolenko did not return to the hotel that evening and spent the night elsewhere. Questioned in Moscow in mid-December, he said he went with other football fans to their hotel where they were all drinking beer, after which he fell asleep and slept the whole night in somebody's room. He neither knew the surnames of his convives, nor could he remember the name of the hotel in which they stayed. In the morning of 2 November, a CCTV camera saw him at 9.33 coming back to the Millennium and going straight to Lugovoy's room. On that day, Risk Advisory Group did not interest him anymore.

* * *

Late in the afternoon of the same day, Wednesday, 1 November 2006, Litvinenko was seen at the offices of Berezovsky at about 5.00 pm copying the emails that Scaramella had brought to their meeting. Sasha wanted by all means to give them to Boris who on that evening was leaving for South Africa. He was flying to Cape Town on the invitation of Frederik Willem de Klerk, a former president. Two years earlier, in 2004, de Klerk had established the Global Leadership Foundation (GLF) as a network of former national leaders to advise newly democratic countries on issues of governance and stability. Boris supported the GLF, among the initial members of which was Václav Havel, a former dissident who became the first president of the Czech Republic, and was happy to accept the invitation.

Berezovsky later testified that for whatever reason the CCTV system at his office was not working that evening. When he saw Sasha in the print room using a copy machine, he could not spare him any time because he was in a hurry and when Litvinenko handed him several sheets of paper, Boris asked Dubov to take care of them until his return. Sasha presented the papers in his usual manner, stressing that they were absolutely confidential, to which Berezovsky responded that he trusted his old friend Dubov completely.[15] With this, Litvinenko left and Berezovsky returned to his computer because he still had a lot to do before departure.

At half past five Litvinenko called Akhmed Zakayev and they agreed that Zakayev who was nearby would pick him up. Ten minutes later Sasha was already in Zakayev's Mercedes S-Class, comfortably settled on the back seat. Ahmed was driving. On the way to Muswell Hill, where he and Sasha were neighbours,

The Third Man

Ahmed's assistant Yaragi ('Yasha') Abdulayev sitting in the front passenger seat was reading Scaramella's emails that Litvinenko had just copied for Berezovsky. Yasha told me later that all was as usual and Litvinenko was in excellent mood. Several weeks later, investigators found transferred radioactive contamination on the back seat of the Mercedes.

At home, he and Marina had a modest dinner celebrating their sixth anniversary of arrival in London. Those were an exciting six years and all three of them – Alexander, Marina and Anatoly, now naturalised British citizens Edwin, Marie Anne and young Anthony Carter – should have been tremendously proud and happy. They were still quite young, looking forward to an interesting and rewarding future for themselves.

At half past ten Litvinenko telephoned Yuri Shvets in Washington. His last registered phone call that evening was to Marina's mobile at 22.37.

At about 23.10, Sasha Litvinenko began to die.

CHAPTER 11

The Litvinenko Inquiry

> We don't have innocents here, only those who haven't been caught yet.
>
> KGB adage

It was a visit that only a few people remember. First Putin arrived in Brussels where Albert II, King of the Belgians, invited him for breakfast at the Royal Palace of Laeken, his official residence. They discussed possible transportation of Russian gas to Britain via Belgium, the construction of the North Stream pipeline under the Baltic Sea from Russia to Germany, and economic relations between Russia and the European Union. On the same day, 4 October 2005, Putin left for London to take part in the Russia–EU summit.

The overall command of security plans for Putin's three-day visit to the British capital was entrusted to Andy Hayman, Assistant Commissioner for Specialist Operations, Metropolitan Police, who had been directly responsible for the investigation into the 7/7 bomb attack as well as the 21/7 London bombings, both of which had happened earlier that year. During the first suicide attack on 7 July, fifty-two UK residents were killed with more than 700 injured. Fortunately, two weeks later, on 21 July, four attempted bomb attacks by Islamist extremists failed. It seemed natural that the Russian leader wanted a full briefing on both the intelligence and operational sides of these anti-terrorist operations only weeks ago. In addition, his office specified, the Russian president would like to know – should there be a major crime happening in London in the near future, how would the Security Service (MI5) and the Metropolitan Police handle the situation?

On Wednesday morning, October 5, the secretaries of Eliza Manningham-Buller, DG of MI5, and the deputy of Andy Hayman alerted their bosses that on that day they were both scheduled to have a top-secret briefing with the Russians at the COBRA crisis management bunker. It was the first time a foreign leader had been allowed into this 'underground cellar in the bowels of Whitehall', as Hayman described it in his book years later. He and the MI5 Director General met at her austere, wood-panelled office at Thames House, Millbank, to work out the briefing tactics. It was decided that she would handle intelligence – what was known about the terrorists, their possible international links, those pulling the strings, and so on. In his turn, the SO chief would describe the operational side, presenting the forensic details that helped to piece together the picture of what had happened on those two devastating days in July. They also agreed on how their input would complement each other.

On 5 October, *The Guardian* reported Putin was given a tour of COBRA during a meeting with Tony Blair 'on increased cooperation over counter-terrorism'. Andy Hayman later recalled: 'I read that as a sign of the prime minister's commitment to a close partnership and even friendship with the Russians. I felt privileged to be part of it.'[1]

The meeting at COBRA was opened by Tony Blair with his view on the security situation, then both the security chief and the police chief had their say. After thirty or forty minutes, Hayman noted that the Russians were impassive, dispassionate, and 'Putin was deadpan as he asked a series of questions'. No one could imagine that the former KGB spy and FSB director, with Viktor Zolotov standing behind him and carefully listening to everything that the interpreters did their best to translate as accurately as possible, was setting the stage for the coming covert operation. A joint statement put out at the end of the visit emphasised that the two sides would continue their partnership 'in particular by increasing practical co-operation between our security agencies'. Unexpectedly and quite soon, both Eliza Manningham-Buller and Andy Hayman would find themselves in charge not of 'an old-fashioned Cold War-style stand-off' as they thought, but of a large-scale counterintelligence operation for which neither of them were quite prepared.

The first alarm was sounded by Marina Litvinenko. Even she initially refused to believe that her husband had been poisoned but very soon realised that something was seriously wrong. Then the BBC Russian Service had an exclusive interview with Sasha at Barnet General Hospital on 11 November, where he described himself as being in 'very bad shape' after a 'serious poisoning'. At that time, Litvinenko, a very healthy young man, believed he would recover soon in spite of such a gloomy self-assessment. A week later he was transferred to University College Hospital (UCLH) where Goldfarb, accompanied by Marina, visited him. 'He looks like a ghost. He lost all his hair, he has a kind of a red mouth because he has an inflammation in his mouth,' Alex reported. 'He looks like a cancer patient who went through heavy chemotherapy. And just a month ago he was a fit, young, handsome guy.' Suffice it to say that three days before he was poisoned, Litvinenko ran 10 kilometres in forty-four minutes. Still, the police didn't have any reason to interfere because, Hayman would say later, 'he was ill, that was all'. Finally, the doctors suggested that Litvinenko was poisoned with highly toxic thallium.

In fact, like polonium, thallium is a metal that is not found free in nature and cannot be used as a poison. When speaking about thallium poisoning, experts mean the odourless and tasteless thallium sulphate (Tl_2SO_4), the sulphate salt of thallium once widely used as rat poison or for rodenticides. Who exactly alerted the police is not known but the first two officers from Scotland Yard visited Litvinenko on the evening of 18 October. Those were Detective Inspector Brent Hyatt accompanied by Detective Sergeant Christopher Hoar from one of the MITs or Major Investigation Teams, specialised homicide squads within the Met. They reported to Detective Superintendent Clive Timmons, head of Serious and Organised Crime Command.

'When the medical assessment became more complex,' Hayman writes, 'implying that Litvinenko might have been poisoned by a radioactive chemical, and it became clear that he was going to die, we were called in.'[2] Sasha's poisoning became 'radioactive' five days later. That means that the police were informed in the late afternoon of Thursday, 23 November, just a couple of hours before Litvinenko passed away.

Initially, the Metropolitan Police was called when it became clear that 'a former KGB spy', as Litvinenko was unanimously described by the world media including in Hayman's book, was most likely poisoned. Because UCLH doctors were not forensic experts and thought their patient had somehow ingested thallium, Sasha was treated with Prussian blue, a compound not soluble in water which is used as a sequestering agent for certain toxic heavy metals including thallium or radioactive caesium.

As mentioned, DI Hyatt and DS Hoar visited Litvinenko assigned to investigate an allegation that somebody had poisoned a British subject in an attempt to kill him. They knew absolutely nothing about the person they were going to interview, had a rather vague idea about the country he was coming from and the secret service of which he once used to be a senior investigations officer. Even their knowledge of the City of London left much to be desired. Both of them spoke no Russian and at first it did not occur to them to invite an interpreter. They just came to talk to an unknown individual who claimed he had been poisoned.

'I born in Soviet Union in (INAUDIBLE) city thirty kilometres from Moscow, thirty, three, three hundred kilometres from Moscow, south area,' Litvinenko started.

> 'I grew, I grew up, up (INAUDIBLE) months. I sent to my, my family in (INAUDIBLE) I grew up in North Caucauses [*sic*]. It's (INAUDIBLE) Republic. It's near Chechnya. It's North Caucauses. After, after education in school I been recruited to Soviet Union Army. For one years I been Private. After this I have, I had education in High Military School, and Russian Interrogate [*sic*] Ministry.'

DI Hyatt: 'The Russian?'

Litvinenko: 'Russ, no Soviet Union Interrogate Ministry and Police Ministry, Home Office were Ministry, High Military School. 1985 I had first Officer rank, Lieutenant, second Lieutenant. After this I sent to Moscow special for two years. I duty in special mechanised rifle division. It's in, near Moscow. Our division worked Politburo and central office of (INAUDIBLE) communist party of Soviet Union, together with KGB. In 1987 I sent to KGB for one years. I had education in Siberia in (INAUDIBLE) city and Operation Officer for Military Counter Intelligence Service. After 1988 I been sent to Central Office of KGB, after of FSB. Until 1999 for eleven years I been Officer of, Central Office of KGB. I now have, I enough,

I have meeting face of face every head of FSB; Mr KOVEROFF (phonetic),[3] Mr PUTIN, Mr. Head of FSB, Mr. General, General Colonel Mr TRAFIMA (phonetic)[4] of yeah sorry.'

DI Hyatt: 'Take your time...'

Litvinenko: '1997 I sent to top secret department of KGB my, my department has duty killing, without, killing political and high business men person without verdict, Judge verdict.'

DI Hyatt: 'Sorry just explain that to me again Edwin?' [They used the name under which the patient was registered.]

Litvinenko: 'Sorry.'

DI Hyatt: 'That, that last part.'

Litvinenko: 'Yeah, yeah.'[5]

Police officers had to change the tape every thirty minutes, each time starting with a full introduction. Litvinenko quickly got tired and once said he was born in 1992 (instead of 1962). He was also told that he was being interviewed 'as a significant witness', not a victim, which was rather strange.[6] This nerve-racking conversation continued for quite long until finally, at 20.00, an interpreter arrived. This dramatically improved the situation and the interview went on until about midnight.

When the two policemen reported the results of their preliminary investigation, it was decided that the stakes were potentially high because it was obvious that (thanks to Goldfarb's efforts backed by Berezovsky's money and Lord Bell's connections) the media had started to get interested in the case. Finally, a meeting was called at Scotland Yard to decide whether the investigation should go to the Homicide and Serious Crime Command (SCD1) of the Specialist Crime Directorate or to the Counter Terrorism Command (CTC) of Specialist Operations – Andy Hayman's turf, where CTC was overseen by Peter Clarke, Deputy Assistant Commissioner. He was in charge of several specialist units including Protection Command, Security Command, and Counter Terrorism Command (SO15). A bit confusing, but never mind.

Until quite recently, it was all different. An investigation like that would be carried out by MI5 assisted by the Special Branch (SB), but on 2 October 2006 the Special Branch of the Metropolitan Police ceased to exist. In an attempt to modernise the Service and improve its efficiency, the SB, renamed 'Special Operations 12' (SO12) in 1986, was merged with the Anti-Terrorist Branch (SO13) to become SO15. 'The move was greeted with dismay by past and present members of the redundant department,' the SB historians write, 'who were proud of its fine traditions and felt that the knowledge and expertise that had been accumulated and honed for well over a century were to be diluted and allowed to disappear into thin air.'[7]

Notwithstanding, the scale of the Metropolitan Police Service's response was considerable. It involved at times about 100 detectives and about 100 uniformed police officers.[8] Clive Timmons's Serious and Organised Crime Command was fully involved and it was one of its officers, DS Mike Jolly, who later suggested it would be useful to try to establish if radioactivity was damaging Litvinenko's internal organs causing acute health effects.

On 16 November toxicology tests at Guy's hospital confirmed the presence of thallium. On the next day, David Leppard of *The Sunday Times* was invited to interview Sasha in the cancer ward of Barnet hospital, where he had now been moved from an accident and emergency (A&E) department. Alex Goldfarb and Marina were present with Alex translating. They were not yet aware of the toxicology test results but the doctors had already informed the Met. In his article, published on Sunday, 19 November, David mentioned that a police spokesman confirmed an inquiry had been launched: 'The Specialist Crime Directorate are investigating a suspicious poisoning.'[9] In formal language it meant that as soon as it was medically determined, the Metropolitan Police decided to conduct a criminal investigation into attempted murder by poisoning to ascertain whether a person should be charged with an offence.

An important breakthrough in the interviews, although without any influence on the investigation, came on 20 November late in the afternoon when Litvinenko was asked whether he met somebody on 31 October with whom he had a meal or a drink.

'On the 31st October at about four p.m. I had a meeting arranged with a person about whom I wouldn't really like to talk here because I have some commitments,' Sasha explained. 'You can contact that person on that long telephone number which I gave to you.'[10] At that moment, the interview stopped. The time was 17.16. DI Hyatt dialled the long telephone number and the phone was picked up at 85 Albert Embankment in Vauxhall.

Interlude: The spy games

Charles Farr headed the Russian desk at Vauxhall Cross until 2004 when he was succeeded by Christopher Steele, having been promoted to MI6's director of security and public affairs. Steele was educated at Girton College, Cambridge, where he studied Human, Social and Political Sciences (HSPS) and was elected president of the Cambridge Union. Recruited to MI6, after training and an intensive Russian course Steele was sent to Moscow in April 1990 posing as a young diplomat, Second Secretary (Political). In April 1993 he was back at the head office. A year later the British government officially acknowledged the existence of SIS for the first time.

In 1998 Steele was sent to Paris, now as First Secretary (Financial), together with Nigel Backhouse. France has long been an intelligence ally and Steele was almost certainly a declared officer, so it was not a big problem when his name appeared in the list which was published on the internet in May 1999. The list of more than a hundred MI6 officers gave his full name, year of birth, and mentioned his Moscow posting. Anyway, Steele successfully completed his tour of duty in France, coming back to London in 2002.[11] The only side effect of the publication was that he could not go to Russia anymore. Instead, two years later he was promoted to command the Russian desk at head office, on the balance sheet of which in London were Soviet defectors Vladimir Rezun, Vladimir Kuzichkin, Oleg Gordievsky, Mikhail Butkov, Viktor Oshchenko, Viktor Makarov, Sergey Skripal, and probably a few less-known others. Shortly before his appointment, in January 2004, Vasili Mitrokhin died. The old defectors, however, did not interest him much because in his work Steele primarily focused on politicians and oligarchs in (as well as from) Russia, CIS, and the former Warsaw Pact countries and their associations with organised crime groups in Europe and the USA. In this work, Steele was following in the footsteps of his predecessor who would eventually be appointed Director of the Office for Security and Counter-Terrorism (OSCT) in July 2007. This role made him one of the most senior civil servants responsible for security and organised crime strategy.

What became known in the trade as Criminal Intelligence was a rather new development caused by the collapse of the Soviet Union. Although MI6 have always provided intelligence about possible terrorist threats, organised crime was not their turf. But with Mikhail Gorbachev's perestroika (restructuring) and glasnost (openness), the situation radically changed. According to the experts,

> Though the [traditional forms of] organized crime existed throughout Soviet history, it was the syndicated form that began to emerge in the late 1950's, expanding during the corrupt Brezhnev years (1964–82), exploding during perestroika, and reaching pandemic levels after the demise of the Soviet Union in 1991. The abrupt transformation of the Russian society from a centralized command economy to one driven by the forces of market capitalism created the socio-pathological conditions for the malignant spread of mercenary and especially syndicated organized crime. New criminal syndicates were created by an alliance of criminal gangs/groups and former members of the Soviet Union's communist nomenklatura (bureaucracy) and the consequence was the criminalization of much of the Russian economy.[12]

But this was not all. After travel abroad became accessible to everyone who could afford it and the former KGB (now SVR, FSB, FSO, and so on) had completely restored their all-powerful status by 1996–98, high-level official corruption, money laundering, and various criminal activities ranging from prostitution and drug trafficking to international bank and stock exchange fraud started to move out of Soviet shores and massively spread beyond its borders. With Putin's coming to power in 2000, the merger of Russian secret services and state officials with organised crime groups was completed, leading to the Kremlin's use of crime as an instrument of state policy.

In Britain, MI6 opened a counter-narcotics section as early as 1988, and after Charles Farr left the Russian desk in 2004, the intelligence work against Russian organised crime, which had quickly developed to represent a global threat, had become a daily routine.[13] In this work Litvinenko turned out to be a very valuable asset indeed. And not only for the British secret services.

There are at least ten different kinds of agents who are usually employed by intelligence agencies for different operations, but unsurprisingly Litvinenko didn't fit into any of those categories. Although Marina Litvinenko did not know the details of her husband's work for MI6, she instinctively guessed that he was not a 'spy' or 'secret agent' whose job would be to produce secret information for his handler. She admitted that Sasha had shared with her some of the information he was supplying to British intelligence but correctly reasoned that what he shared with his controllers related to Russian organised crime, including its presence in the UK.

'The reality of Russian organised crime in the UK is that they prey on the most vulnerable members of their own community,' one of the London newspapers wrote shortly after the Litvinenkos arrived in Britain. The reason why Sasha asked a contact to recommend him to one of the British secret services in early 2003 was because he wanted to continue doing what he did in Russia. That is, to contribute to fighting Russian organised crime. Now in Britain and the rest of the Western world.

In this work Litvinenko was also collaborating with several private British corporate investigations firms. For obvious reasons, those were not in the primary league like, for example, Hakluyt, K2 Intelligence, or FTI Consulting. The London-based international NGO Global Witness was also not in his list of contacts. Known to the media as an anti-corruption group, they had a special projects team specialising, among other things, in exposing bribes paid to politicians in developing regions by companies eager to exploit a country's resources in the oil, gas, and mining sectors. Beginning from 1997, Alexander Yearsley was Head of Special Projects for Global Witness. In the mid-2000s, he and his team began to investigate a company in Ukraine allegedly involved in the operation of a major natural gas pipeline that supplied energy to Western Europe. Global Witness had reason to suspect that Semion Mogilevich, a Ukrainian-born Russian organised crime figure, secretly controlled the Ukrainian company.[14] The organisation described Mogilevich as 'the most dangerous mobster in the world'.

Litvinenko was one of a few persons in the West who could claim insider knowledge of Mogilevich's vast criminal organisation and his ties to the Russian Intelligence Services (RIS) and corrupt state officials. In addition to what he had learned about Mogilevich as a senior FSB officer in the Anti-Organised Crime Directorate (URPO) in Moscow, he got some additional information from the so-called Melnichenko tapes: an eavesdropping operation in the office of the former Ukrainian president. Recorded in 1998–2000, conversations in the president's office reveal that Putin was close to Mogilevich during his early days in Leningrad.[15] Litvinenko knew the contents of the tapes, having been part of Berezovsky's team of Goldfarb, Felshtinsky and Shvets directly involved in this project.

When Yearsley investigated Mogilevich's crime networks, he knew nothing about Litvinenko but collaborated with the WSJ journalist Glenn Simpson, who in December 2006 wrote a front-page article about Mogilevich and the pipeline company.[16] 'The U.S. is worried that the Russian mafia will spread its influence in the energy industry and use its natural-gas profits to increase its economic and political clout,' he reported. Those were prophetic words. When this book was sent to press, Mogilevich (born in 1946) was on the FBI's Most Wanted List with a US government offering a reward of $5 million for his arrest.

Glenn Simpson and Christopher Steele first met in 2010, introduced by Alex Yearsley. By that time all three of them had left their employers and were working as private investigators. Steele co-founded Orbis Business Intelligence, Simpson – Fusion GPS, and Yearsley was Managing Director of Martello Risk.

When the 2016 presidential campaign of Donald Trump was formally launched, Fusion GPS was hired to look into the candidate's finances. After almost a year of work, it became necessary to employ a Russia specialist because it became clear that the focus of Fusion's research would be on Trump's entanglements with Russia, so Simpson engaged the services of Steele. In June 2016 Orbis was subcontracted to compile a series of reports that subsequently became known as the Steele Dossier or Trump–Russia Dossier.

The story did not end here because the best-kept secret of the dossier was the identity of Steele's 'primary source with access to multiple Kremlin insiders', as it became known. For quite some time, a group of four amateur detectives interested to uncover this secret source suspected that it was Yuri Shvets.[17] Although Shvets trashed Steele's reports after the dossier was published, they still thought that his disparaging comments about Steele's claims might have been a 'false flag' operation to steer attention away from him.

People obviously had reason to think so. It will be remembered that Shvets and Litvinenko had worked together on similar projects prior to Litvinenko's poisoning. Shvets was asked to testify at the Litvinenko Inquiry and, according to Luke Harding, MI6 appointed Steele to internally investigate Litvinenko's murder, so they had reasonable grounds to believe that Steele and Shvets crossed paths one day.[18] As should have been expected, the results of this internal investigation have never been made public.

***

After Brent Hyatt introduced himself to the person on the other end of the line, it was quickly explained to him who was answering his call and he was asked to get Litvinenko to the phone. With his interlocutor Sasha spoke Russian, which the man who would become known as 'Martin' when some details leaked to the media in December 2012, learned in a crash course before being sent to Moscow years before. Martin promised to come to the hospital immediately. He did arrive and quite certainly presented his credentials to the full satisfaction of the police officers. What he explained to them in indirect terms was later clearly and unambiguously formulated by Ben Emmerson QC representing Marina Litvinenko: Mr Litvinenko, aka Edwin Carter, had been for a number of years a registered agent in the employ of Her Majesty's Secret Service.[19] After you've heard it, forget about it.

As soon as he left, the microphone was switched on again with Nina Tupper translating. The time was 19.29, so two hours had passed since the last recording.

> DI Hyatt: 'Okay, I don't want you to tell me the name of that person [in the Waterstones bar on 31 October] but can you tell me if that person is the person that I've been speaking to in your presence in this hospital around about fifteen minutes ago?'
>
> Litvinenko: 'Yes, that is absolutely correct.'

It seems the detective inspector decided to show vigilance and also demonstrate his knowledge of some basic techniques of working under cover. Specifically of what is known in the trade as 'going grey'. This refers to the skill of moving amongst other people blending in the crowd so that you do not attract attention. In Hyatt's professional opinion, Martin was a bit too tall and slightly stooped to be able to go grey when necessary. Besides, he possessed a big head, protruding ears, and was wearing glasses, so the detective thought it would be better to double check.

> DI Hyatt: 'And I don't want to ask you what you talked about with that person. But can you confirm whether or not you had anything to eat or anything to drink at that time [during that meeting]?'
>
> Litvinenko: 'During that meeting we were drinking. He was drinking coffee, and I was drinking hot chocolate, and I also took three French pastries, such puff ones, and nothing else. Yes, small croissants.'
>
> DI Hyatt: 'And aside from your wife and your son, did you meet with anybody else on that day?'
>
> Litvinenko. 'No.'[20]

He actually did see Zakayev and his family that evening, but that was not so important. Just in case their house was later checked for alpha radiation.

In his interview with David Leppard at Barnet hospital and his long conversations with Brent Hyatt and Christopher Hoar at UCLH, Litvinenko spent a disproportionate amount of time describing his meeting with Scaramella on Piccadilly Circus and their lunch at Itsu on November 1, the day he was poisoned. In his final report on the Litvinenko Inquiry, its chairman Sir Robert Owen devoted a few paragraphs to this fact, stressing that in his talks to the people who visited him at hospital Litvinenko 'either delayed in telling them, or did not tell them at all about his meeting with Mr Lugovoy and Mr Kovtun on the same day'. The chairman disagreed with the opinion expressed by some of Sasha's friends that he deliberately did it having in mind luring those two back to London. According to Sir Robert,

The reluctance on the part of Mr Litvinenko to tell his friends about his meeting with Mr Lugovoy and Mr Kovtun on the day that he became ill cannot be explained by his strategy to try to lure the two men back into the jurisdiction, since these were private conversations with trusted friends. The answer seems to lie in what Mr Shvets described as Mr Litvinenko's 'wounded professional pride'. He said: 'He was agonised by the understanding that as a professional he failed. I mean Sasha as a professional failed in this case. He was always saying that I can identify my enemy a mile away ... But this particular case when it comes to his own life, he badly failed.'[21]

This seems like a wrong conclusion. The day after Leppard's visit, discussing the details with Hyatt and Hoar (Police exhibit no. CH/3A, 18 October), Litvinenko told the police about his meeting with Lugovoy and Kovtun asking them not to tell anybody, including his wife. 'If I show, if we make it public,' he said, 'we would not be able to arrest them. Mario [Scaramella] is no problem, he is in Italy.'[22] His hastily spoken words may have sounded like a gabble to the ears of both police officers and the interpreter, but that's exactly what he meant.

***

The Counter Terrorism Command and their SO15 team was called in when it was clear that Litvinenko was going to die soon. After Leppard's article in *The Sunday Times*, many international media outlets picked up the news. The RFE/RL's Russian Service interviewed Gordievsky in London, who was in telephone contact with Sasha and Marina, read the *Sunday Times* article, and figured out all the rest to brew a plot. Andrey Shary from the Radio Liberty Prague studio produced a special programme based on that interview, also accompanied by a text version. Simultaneously it appeared in English in a slightly abridged form. The next day, Tuesday, 21 November, Roy Greenslade wrote in *The Guardian* that the Litvinenko poisoning was dominating the British news like never before. 'Unless it's a catastrophe – tsunami, 9/11 – it's rare for both the red-top papers and the serious press to lead on a story involving a foreigner,' he admitted. The journalist noted, not without surprise, that the mainstream British media like 'the *Daily Telegraph*, *The Times*, *The Guardian*, *The Sun* and the *Daily Mirror* all devote their front pages to pictures of Alexander Litvinenko, the former Russian agent who has been poisoned by a deadly toxin called thallium.' 'The *Financial Times*,' he added, 'also carries a picture with its front page cross-ref.' Finally, my article 'Russian Venom' was published by *The Wall Street Journal* on 22 November, suggesting it must have been a radioactive poison.

On 23 November 2006, Andy Hayman was woken at 6.00 am by a call from the Operations Centre. An officer on duty informed him that Litvinenko was dying and that a COBRA meeting was scheduled at eight. He asked his deputy Suzanna Beck to take care of the planned meetings and appointed Peter Clarke to head the investigation. Andy himself put together a team of five officers who were happy to be available 24/7 through the duration of the investigation, giving them an initial brief instruction before he left for the meeting. 'Though we wouldn't go public with it yet,' he later recalled, 'as far as we were concerned this was no longer a poisoning inquiry: it was an international murder investigation – doctors were telling us the poisoned man had only hours to live.'[23] There was still no mention of polonium.

According to Andy Hayman, the closed-door COBRA meeting was on the same day, but it actually was on Friday, 24 November. The meeting was chaired by a senior civil servant who wanted information for the home secretary, John Reid, that no one was able to deliver at that stage. Almost certainly John Prescott (Baron Prescott), Deputy Prime Minister, whose office controlled the day-to-day emergency planning in the Cabinet Office, was present. Also present were Andy Hayman, his deputy Peter Clarke, who was in charge of the investigation, Dr Pat Troop, the Health Protection Agency's chief executive, Eliza Manningham-Buller of MI5, and several most senior government figures.[24] Peter Clarke did the police briefing: so far, the police had searched several locations that Litvinenko visited on 1 November – the Itsu sushi bar on Piccadilly, the Mayfair Millennium Hotel near the American Embassy in Grosvenor Square, and his home in Muswell Hill in North London. Traces of residual radioactive material polonium-210 were found in each of them. They were also found in the vehicle that had taken Litvinenko to hospital.

In reality and contrary to conventional wisdom, there is no COBRA crisis management group nor any fortified bunker 'in the bowels of Whitehall'. The Cabinet Office at 70 Whitehall has a suite of rooms for the use of government ministers and officials. The name for the strategy group is the Civil Contingencies Committee which is supported by a small secretariat. COBRA is an acronym of 'Cabinet Office Briefing Room A', where this strategy group supposedly meets, but given the popularity of the term, it is a synonym for all the government's immediate strategic response meetings.[25] Given the date of the COBRA convention several hours after Litvinenko's death when the traces of polonium were just discovered, there was nothing more to report except that polonium-210 was a by-product of the nuclear industry also found in devices that eliminate static. To be somehow used in the poisoning, it would have required high-grade technical skills and a sophisticated scientific process to produce, probably within a nuclear lab. At least this was reported immediately after the COBRA meeting on Friday.[26] When John Reid was questioned by the MPs in the House of Commons three days later, the Litvinenko case was still considered not even as a suspicious, but as an unexplained death.

'The following day, as the list of contaminated addresses grew, the prime minister [Tony Blair] stepped into the fray in a bid to reassure,' Andy Hayman writes. 'He pledged that there would be no "diplomatic or political barrier" standing in the way of this police investigation.'[27] Could the London police investigate a complex, state-sponsored intelligence operation planned and carried out by the secret service of another country?

In the meantime, the Russian ambassador Yury Fedotov was called to the Foreign Office. According to the home secretary, 'he was asked to convey to the

Russian authorities our expectation that they should be ready to offer all necessary co-operation to the investigation as it proceeds'.

About five weeks after Litvinenko had been poisoned, nine CTC officers were briefed by the Security Service (MI5) as well as by MI6 and finally allowed to fly to Moscow after much diplomatic wrangling. One may only guess what they expected to find there.

By the end of the year, Andy Hayman and Peter Clarke were confident that their officers had collected enough evidence to bring their prime suspect to court. On 31 January 2007 the Metropolitan Police handed their investigation file to the Crown Prosecution Service (CPS) to review the evidence and consider whether they could bring a prosecution. 'I was cock-a-hoop,' the Assistant Commissioner was obviously pleased about his department's achievement. 'I was proud that we had managed to produce strong evidence, despite the health, media and diplomatic complexities. And we'd put our case together in a very short time.'[28] Well, there's an English idiom 'haste makes waste'. Like a similar Russian proverb, it is used to say that doing something too quickly causes mistakes that result in time, effort, and human as well as material resources being wasted.

Until the end of May, CPS lawyers and prosecutors from CPS Counter-Terrorism Division studied the case. On 22 May 2007 Sir Ken McDonald, the director of public prosecutions (DPP) of England and Wales, announced publicly that 'among the people of interest to police in this inquiry was a Russian citizen named Andrei Lugovoi [sic].' After four months of deliberations and discussions about whether criminal charges should be brought against anyone who might have been involved in this case, the DPP concluded that the evidence sent to his Service by the Metropolitan Police was sufficient to charge Lugovoy with the murder of Litvinenko by deliberate poisoning. The CPS lawyers were instructed to take immediate steps to seek his extradition to the UK.

Hayman was absolutely happy. He remembered talking to someone from MI6: 'The moment this man steps on UK soil we'll nab him.'

Almost certainly it was Charles Farr who had served on the Russian desk and several weeks later would be appointed Director of the OSCT. He looked over his glasses and said: 'I admire your enthusiasm Andy, but you've got no chance of ever speaking with Lugovoy again.' He was right, of course.

Kovtun's name was not even mentioned. In July, Britain expelled four Russian diplomats and three days later, in a tit-for-tat move, Russia expelled four British diplomats from Moscow. Assistant Commissioner Hayman resigned from the Service in December 2007. The government decided to end the role of the British police in the Litvinenko case there.

* * *

As if nothing whatsoever had happened, on Thursday, 2 August 2012, Putin was in London again. This time, he was visiting the former hospital in the Custom House area of Newham, now an exhibition centre turned into a sports arena for the

London Summer Olympics. Accompanied by the new British prime minister David Cameron, Putin attended the judo finals at ExCeL, an abbreviation for Exhibition Centre London. 'The pair had met earlier at Downing Street,' *The Guardian* reported, 'though Cameron had prefaced the judo outing by explicitly insisting he'd use it to press the recalcitrant Putin on Syria. But of course – what else does one do at the judo?'

As should have been expected, it could not work with Putin – an avid judoka and a judo black belt who co-authored a book titled *Judo: History, Theory, Practice* (2004). He was also elected honorary president of the International Judo Federation (IJF). 'It's rather difficult to tell from the back of someone's head,' the *Guardian* reporter continued to tease, watching Putin, Cameron and William Hague, First Secretary of State and Secretary of State for Foreign and Commonwealth Affairs, himself a judo fan, in the VIP guest lodge, 'if they're mouthing the words "military-backed humanitarian corridors" as the venue sound system blasts *I'm A Survivor*, but reading the body language at the ExCeL, it didn't look like it.'[29] Remarkably, DSU Clive Timmons acted as the Operational Commander of Olympic Intelligence Centre at the time of Putin's visit.

Until the Russian president departed from London, nothing happened, but several days later, on 7 August, the Assistant Coroner Sir Robert Owen was appointed to conduct the inquest proceedings,[30] six years after the death of Litvinenko.

In mid-May 2013, the coroner reluctantly agreed to William Hague's request to hide material which suggested the Russian Intelligence Services (RIS) were behind Litvinenko's killing. In his ruling, Owen said the inquest might now result in an 'incomplete, misleading and unfair' verdict. By that time, the inquest, a judicial inquiry into the cause and circumstances of a person's death, had been adjourned, put on hold. Sir Robert said he was considering inviting the government to hold a public inquiry instead, which would be allowed to hear the sensitive evidence which the foreign secretary wanted to bury. 'Ben Emmerson QC had previously accused Hague of attempting to stage a cover-up and of placing Britain's trade interests with Moscow ahead of justice,' Luke Harding reported. 'Both Hague and Cameron were shamelessly "dancing to the Russian tarantella", he told a pre-inquest hearing.'[31] In early June, Sir Robert wrote to the Lord Chancellor and Secretary of State for Justice, calling for a public inquiry stressing that 'any investigation of the death which excludes a proper analysis of the HMG material will be inadequate'. After much deliberation, the government refused.

On 17 July, Theresa May, the home secretary, responded on behalf of the government. In her letter, she first of all stated that the coroner 'had access to whatever sensitive governmental material' he had thought it proper to call for. The government noted, she wrote, that the coroner indicated that essentially two issues would be of central importance to this case: the Russian state responsibility for Litvinenko's death and whether it could reasonably have been prevented by the British government.

Among five factors pointing, in the government's view, against accepting the coroner's proposal for public inquiry, two clearly stood out. First, the government believed that it would be perfectly possible to conduct an inquest aimed at answering the statutory questions, that is, the cause and circumstances of a person's death, 'without considering the sensitive material at all'. Finally, the letter stated, it is true that international relations have been a factor in the government's decision making. 'An inquest managed and run by an independent coroner is more readily explainable to some of our foreign partners, and the integrity of the process more readily grasped, than in inquiry,' May wrote. In short, the factors militating against establishing an inquiry 'substantially overweight those in favour'.

The last sentence of the letter, rarely quoted, gave Marina's lawyers some hope. 'The Government undertakes, however, to keep this matter under close review and, if the balance of the competing considerations were to change, to revisit this decision.' In February and March 2014, Russia invaded and shortly after annexed the Crimean Peninsula from Ukraine. On 22 July Theresa May announced, in a written statement laid before the House of Commons, that an inquiry into the death of Alexander Litvinenko was to be held and Sir Robert Owen was appointed its chairman. It happened when Putin and his clique began to steer away from the civilised world. When the Russian army attacked Ukraine and started a war there, Putin's honorary presidency of the IJF was suspended with all his titles removed.

**

The Litvinenko Inquiry chairman notes in the Preface to the Inquiry Report, 'My conclusions on the central issues in this Report are to be found at Parts 8, 9 and 10. Those Parts of the Report, and the conclusions they contain, are based on the totality of the evidence that I have heard – that is, both the "open" and the "closed" evidence.' Therefore, those seem like the most relevant parts to revisit, review, and reassess. Especially in the light of Professor Robert Service's statement during the Inquiry hearings. 'In 10 or 20 years,' Professor Service said, 'we will know more about what we're talking about today, and we will be able to go further, and it will probably be very dispiriting, the verdict that we will come to.'[32] Alas, a chair of the public inquiry has no power to determine any person's civil or criminal liability. Public inquiries do not come to verdicts, only conclusions and recommendations, but those can also be dispiriting. That said, it was an obvious achievement of Sir Robert that he insisted on a public inquiry to replace the inquest (the initial refusal was challenged in the High Court by Marina Litvinenko's lawyers). The advantage of a public inquiry over the inquest is that the rules governing an inquiry allow for sensitive evidence to be heard, albeit in closed session.

Sir Robert Owen held closed hearings of the inquiry over several days in May 2015 in a government building in London. During those hearings, he heard oral evidence from witnesses and was able to study some documents submitted by the government. In Part 7 of his Report ('The closed evidence'), Sir Robert described this work and its results as much as he was allowed to do by the rule of law known as public interest immunity. Without having access to those witness statements and sensitive documents, it is, however, possible to speculate what could have been the principal issues that were of interest to the inquiry.

As is clear from all available documents, the sensitive information that the HMG did not want to disclose was (1) to confirm that Litvinenko was a paid agent of British intelligence; (2) that MI6 had sent him on several undercover assignments abroad; (3) the intelligence requirements for those missions; and finally (4) whether everything was done to prevent placing the life of the agent in grave danger.

As expected, the government preferred the NCND approach. During the hearings, it was established that Litvinenko was recruited in early 2003. In his witness testimony Goldfarb stated: 'Sasha first told me that he was working for MI6 sometime in early 2003.'[33] He also introduced Goldfarb to his MI6 contact 'Charlie', who was none other than Charles Farr, head of the Russian desk.

As follows from the inquiry material, Litvinenko told his wife and some of his friends: Berezovsky, Goldfarb, and Felshtinsky, plus those whom he considered his friends (Zharko, Lugovoy, Limarev and Chekulin) that he was working for British intelligence. Because Sasha did not trust Mario Scaramella much, he told him he was not associated with any secret service. There could have also been other reasons for not telling Mario.

The meeting with 'Charlie' was arranged at Caffè Nero in Piccadilly. Goldfarb immediately understood that he was dealing with the MI6 head of the Russian desk because 'Charlie' said that Simon Butt 'was his counterpart at the FCO'. Mr Butt, a career member of the British diplomatic service, served as Deputy Head of Mission at the British embassy in Kiev until 2000, and then worked for four years at the FCO in London as Head of the Eastern Department.

'Charlie asked for my reaction to the theory that Badri [Patarkatsishvili] had secret ties with the Kremlin, and was instrumental in advancing Russia's goals in Georgia,' Goldfarb testified, adding that he said to Charlie he did not believe that. When Alex visited Tbilisi later that year, Badri told him that he had met with a British representative there and hoped that he was able to prove that he was not working for the Kremlin. Charlie also asked Goldfarb, a professional microbiologist, whether he knew anything about Russian assistance to Iraq in microbiology, certainly having in mind the biological weapons programme. Goldfarb said he didn't know anything on the subject. The US-led invasion of Iraq began on 19 March.

'In the course of these interactions,' Goldfarb further testified, 'Sasha told me that he was consulting MI6 on Russia's organised crime in Europe, and was travelling on their behalf to various countries in the EU assisting local law enforcement. He showed me his cover document, a British passport with his photograph. He was not a British citizen at the time.'[34] That leaves no doubt about Litvinenko's affiliation with British intelligence.

Another issue is what Theresa May called 'preventability' in her July 2013 letter to Sir Robert Owen.

An agent, especially operating undercover in a foreign state, is always at risk, independent of what he does. This is especially so when he or she is operating against criminal or terrorist organisations. Nothing happened to Litvinenko when he was on assignments in foreign countries. An important element of risk reduction was that he had never been sent on an espionage mission abroad but was rather seconded by MI6 to allied services to consult and help. It is well known that Rezun, Gordievsky, Mitrokhin, Skripal, and others used to travel a lot providing consultations for friendly services, and so did Litvinenko. At home, the professional risk for all members of secret services also exists (like that for policeman, firefighters, lifeguards, even ambulance workers) but it is generally considered to be much less to compare with the above categories. Anyway, the intelligence services, especially in Britain and the USA, do their utmost to prevent risk in every possible way. The 'preventability' is at the highest level.

***

It was established without any reasonable doubt that Litvinenko ingested the fatal dose of radioactive poison when he drank tea in the Pine Bar of the Millennium Hotel on 1 November 2006. There is an obvious question that arises: if Sasha did not put it into the teapot himself, then who did? Sir Robert devoted considerable time trying to answer this important question – perhaps the most important question of the whole inquiry. Who administered the poison? Richard Horwell QC in his closing submissions made on behalf of the Metropolitan Police Service asserted that 'the evidence points resolutely to Lugovoy and Kovtun and no one else as having administered the poison which killed Litvinenko'.[35] The chairman, however, pointed out that 'the evidence gathered by the Metropolitan Police, their views as to where that evidence points have been accorded no special weight'. He stressed that he had approached the evidence with an open mind and even 'considered it objectively'. Whether any person, a judge, a coroner, or whoever else can consider anything 'objectively' is highly debatable, but here is no place for philosophical discussions.

The problem of this particular public inquiry lies in the fact that although public inquiries are major investigations, the British government considers 'preventing recurrence' to be the primary purpose of public inquiries. According to Jason Beer QC, the UK's leading authority on public inquiries, the main function of inquiries is to address three key questions: What happened? Why did it happen and who is to blame? What can be done to prevent this happening again?[36]

Litvinenko was poisoned and died in November 2006. It took ten years to complete the inquiry – the Report was delivered in January 2016. Now, more than sixteen years after the death of Alexander and seven years after the publication of the inquest results, only the first question can be answered. And while the second question remains open, the answer to the third question will inevitably be very short. Due to the initial false approach to the first point: why it happened and who was to blame, despite (or maybe because of) the inquest chairman's single recommendation, nothing had been done to prevent this happening again. As a result, we had three dead bodies in London right after Litvinenko. And those are only people from the Berezovsky circle: Patarkatsishvili, Berezovsky himself, and Glushkov. With Litvinenko, it makes four.

Because nothing had been done to prevent this happening again, the Skripal poisoning in March 2018 was a surprise attack and a shock. It was investigated by the same Counter Terrorist Command. Remarkably, in all above cases the inquiry was not initiated, there were only inquests to determine the cause of a person's death, and in the Berezovsky case the inquest returned an open verdict on death. In simple words, the Berkshire coroner was unable to reach a conclusion on how the former deputy secretary of the Security Council of Russia died. In my book *The KGB's Poison Factory* (2017) and its sequel *Assassins* (2019), I am seeking to prove that in most of the cases the use of poisons as an element of Russian special operations (not to mention highly sophisticated modern technologies that could only be imagined in the past) cannot be detected during a forensic test with very few exceptions. In the Litvinenko case, even the identified radioactive poison had been named wrongly in all investigation and inquiry documents, which led to multiple errors.

As a result, there were also errors in conclusions because many people – journalists, writers, policemen, lawyers, and amateur detectives – rushed to study nuclear physics and the decay chain of uranium-238 and radium-226 as well as the life and work of Marie and Pierre Curie. In his already mentioned article, Edward Jay Epstein wrote:

> Lab tests showed that he [Litvinenko] had in his body one of the world's rarest and most tightly controlled radioactive isotopes, Polonium-210 ... Polonium-210 is of great interest to the UN's nuclear proliferation watchdogs because it is a critical component in early-stage nuclear bombs. Both America and Russia used it as part of the trigger in their early bombs. ... As a declassified Los Alamos document notes, the detection of Polonium-210 remains 'a key indication of a nuclear weapons program in its early stages.' ... When Polonium-210 was discovered in London in late November 2006 in Litvinenko's body, however, no such proliferation alarm bells went off. Instead, the police assumed that this component of early-stage nuclear bombs had been smuggled into London solely to commit a murder.[37]

And so on. Trying to detect an unstable toxic isotope of a rare highly radioactive metal with the symbol Po, Alex Goldfarb and others spent a lot of time, effort, and money trying to obtain documents to prove that a certain cargo was transported from the Balakovo Nuclear Power Station, about 900 km (560 miles) south-east of Moscow, to the Forensic Research Centre of the FSB in August 2006.[38] Moreover, in August 2010 Alex travelled to Austria to meet an alleged FSB agent who contacted him by email about a month before. The man, whose name was Alexey Potemkin, claimed he was an FSB major sent to Austria undercover together with his wife Polina, also an intelligence officer.

The man was quite certainly a plant and that was a typical sting operation, clumsily organised by the FSB who do not have experience in foreign operations.

Potemkin tried to interest Goldfarb by providing details of what he called secret transportation of polonium from Russia via Austria to Britain in 2006. He even handed over copies of some FSB documents and promised to deliver much more if Goldfarb would arrange his political asylum in the UK. 'He told me,' Goldfarb reported, 'he was prepared to give evidence to British police, and ask for permission to enter the UK and claim asylum. Outside the UK he feels he is exposed to criminal charges as a spy, a smuggler of radioactive materials, and as a false claimer of asylum [in Austria].'[39] Potemkin even managed to squeeze ten thousand dollars from Goldfarb for the documents pertaining to polonium transportation, but those documents never arrived. Instead, Goldfarb received six other documents described in detail in his witness statement. All this material was later adduced into evidence.

In the meantime, the Austrian security police found the internet site of the so-called Russian Nobility Assembly in United Europe (La Réunion Russe Noble de l'Europe Unie). Among other things, the site declared that as of 4 December 2009 Potemkin had been the chairman of the Austrian section of the Assembly at the same time serving as the plenipotentiary of the All-Russian Monarchist Union and Peter and Paul Imperial Society in Europe. In October 2022 it was not possible to find Potemkin's traces in Austria anymore but the site was still active.

So much ado for nothing!

To the so-called earlier poisoning attempts. 'Tests conducted on Mr Litvinenko's hair demonstrated that he had ingested polonium 210 on not one but two occasions … The first dose was much smaller, and had been ingested by Mr Litvinenko several days earlier.'[40] The chairman was sure that Litvinenko did receive that small dose of poison (on 16 October, fifteen days before the meeting at the Pine Bar) and that the scientific evidence in this regard is compelling.

First, the scientists using autoradiography methods were unable to provide a precise answer to the 'when' question. 'The best they could do,' the Report states, 'was to offer probable time brackets.' Not to mention that an error can be in every scientific analysis, it will be remembered that very serious errors in this investigation happened at least three times. Or maybe more?

The police documents, part of Operation AVOCET (INQ017900-905), show that the table where Litvinenko and Scaramella were sitting at Itsu at about three o'clock on 1 November (more than one hour *before* Litvinenko was poisoned in the Pine Bar) was contaminated in many places. The contamination was quite irrelevant, maximum about 70 cps, but it led to Scaramella being placed at hospital. Here starts the most interesting part.

> Mr Mario Scaramella was found by the Nuclear Weapons Establishment (Atomic Weapons Command of the British Army) to have significant radioactive poisoning from Polonium 210 following the analysis of urine collected using scientific police procedures by Scotland Yard's Antiterrorism Unit at the protected locality of Ashdown Park in England on 27 November 2007. Following orders of the Health Protection Agency and further checks that showed

level of contamination equal to 2.0 Gy in the marrow, 9.5 Gy in the kidneys, 4.9 Gy in the liver and 1.2 Gy in the colon, he was admitted to University College London Hospital on 01/12/06, where he was guarded. The significant and fatal dose of alpha radiation identified, even in light of the absence of immediate effects of the contamination (e.g. marrow collapse) was recalculated with other modelling techniques which suggested a lower effective contamination and new analyses, carried out this time by a civil laboratory on a sample from 3 December 2006, showed very low levels of contamination and from a new sample from 6 December the same laboratory found 'no worrying' levels. In any case, the British government convened an emergency committee (COBRA) classified analysis and medicines relating to the health of Mr Mario Scaramella.[41]

The UCLH did more tests. The tests showed levels of polonium that may be found in many people. The hospital noted that Scaramella had been well during his admission and all his results – blood test and chest X-ray – had been within normal limits. On 6 December he was discharged from the ward. 'We do not believe that he will suffer any immediate or long-term effects of polonium exposure. There is no risk to his contacts,' the doctors concluded.[42]

While at hospital, poor Mario was calling his father and his girlfriend to say a farewell, only hoping that he might still have a bit of time to write his will. 'Initial tests indicated that Mr Scaramella was himself heavily contaminated with polonium 210. As Dr Harrison [the same expert who made the autoradiography test of Litvinenko's hair] explained in evidence, however, the results of these tests were unreliable. Mr Scaramella was not in fact contaminated at all.'[43] Why should one test be considered unreliable and another reliable?

With all this, the table at Itsu remained a problem. The Report explained it rather simply: the police were wrong and Litvinenko and Scaramella were sitting at another table (!?). There was no direct evidence as to where they sat, it said, but 'given the primary contamination at the Erinys boardroom, it is a reasonable inference that the contamination found at Itsu was left by Mr Lugovoy, Mr Kovtun and/or Mr Litvinenko at the time of their visit on 16 October'.[44] However, as was previously established, the plan of the Erinys boardroom made by the police was wrong, the place where Litvinenko was sitting was not contaminated, and even if one, purely theoretically, admits that Sasha was poisoned there, he would not leave any radioactive traces after that short period of time. Besides, the traces at Itsu clearly point to only two persons, not three. Finally, after 16 October and until 1 November, Litvinenko never left any radioactive traces at all and was feeling so well that, as mentioned, three days before he was really poisoned, he was able to run his perfect 10K in record time. The conclusion? The thesis that Litvinenko was first poisoned on 16 October is false.

A very careful study of Part 8 of the Report, especially Chapter 6 titled 'Who administered the poison?' will inevitably lead an attentive reader to the conclusion formulated by Sir Robert himself. And namely – 'Given the findings ... regarding the time and place at which, and the means by which, Mr Litvinenko ingested the fatal dose of polonium 210, these matters are clearly sufficient to raise a question as to the possible involvement of Lugovoy and Kovtun in the poisoning. On their own, however, these facts do not establish anything more than that.'[45] One could probably add that a hundred suspicions don't make a proof.[46] With all evidence and witness statements available to the inquiry, there exists no direct proof that either both of them or Lugovoy alone administered the poison. In his closing submissions that lasted for three hours made on behalf of the Metropolitan Police Service, Richard Horwell QC was only able to provide circumstantial proofs of their involvement that a good British lawyer could successfully contest in a court. The accused did not confess and no one saw any of them putting poison into the teapot used by Litvinenko. The police and the inquiry were seriously misled because they investigated a separate murder supposedly committed by two alleged culprits instead of investigating a complex intelligence operation. In that case, officers and prosecutors qualified to investigate such operations would almost certainly come to different conclusions.

There is no doubt that in London both Russians handled the radioactive poison, and that at least twice Kovtun was exposed directly to polonium radiation and Lugovoy at least once, but this established fact could in no way prove that Lugovoy and Kovtun were 'common murderers', as Mr Horwell stated.[47] It seems that in all three cases they rather tried to abandon the mission to which they had been sent but at the end themselves got contaminated. After a long disease, Kovtun died in June 2022.

Regarding the theory of the possible second attempt (after an alleged 'first unsuccessful attempt' on 16 October) to poison Litvinenko, no proof exists except that Lugovoy quite obviously had direct contact with radioactive poison in his hotel room. However, it could have also been an attempt to poison Badri, with whom a meeting had been prearranged with all the signs of a possible operation planned against him while a meeting with Litvinenko happened by chance. Not to mention that any special operation to which the murder by poisoning refers, is performed according to certain rules that cumulatively differ it from, say, an amateur poisoning. In any case, whatever had been planned in Moscow, the operation was without doubt abandoned on that day.

A few words about witnesses to the inquiry. Because the investigation and the inquiry were only interested in homicide as a crime committed on British soil, they ignored other important issues. For example, they took all witness statements at face value.

In this complex, multi-stage intelligence operation involving members of all Russian intelligence services, many people who provided witness statements or testified during the hearings (or those, like Tatiana Lugovaya or Maxim Begak, who were not even interviewed) took direct part in the operation playing different roles. Many of them have already figured in previous chapters. At least two registered British companies, CPL and Eco3 Capital, were completely ignored by the investigation and their staff were questioned as if they were really who they pretended to be. Again, because they investigated the murder, no one took the trouble to order at least a simple due diligence report on Continental Petroleum Limited, dissolved in May 2012, or Eco3 Capital Limited, dissolved in April 2016, or take a deeper look at their so-called 'directors', 'secretaries', and business documents. At different times, Alexander Shadrin[48] served as director and secretary of both companies alongside twelve other directors or secretaries, whose biographies are of great interest. However, at the time of the Litvinenko operation, Vladimir Voronov (aka Voronoff) was registered as one of CPL's directors (from May 2006). What they called their oil business in Russia could as well become a separate investigation if a good private spy was hired to compile a report.

Among many interesting figures there is the Hon Charles George Yule Balfour, the younger brother of Lord Balfour,[49] who was director of CPL from June 2005 to August 2009, and of Eco3 from December 2004 to May 2007. Balfour registers himself as a banker. Not to mention the dates of his involvement with two Russian shell companies, the documents show that he had been director of eleven other similar companies in London. Like with other 'directors', it was as usual only nominal directorship. In 2006 and even much later (when the inquiry was opened in July 2014 and until it was completed), it was still possible to employ a good private intelligence firm like, for example, Hakluyt to dig up all information on both CPL and Eco3, as well as others, and their declared activities in Russia and elsewhere. Alas, it had never been done. Remarkably, in May 2010 the CPL office was moved to Esher, Surrey, the county where Berezovsky, Patarkatsishvili, Perepilichny, Glushkov (New Maiden is only about seven miles from Esher), and even this writer lived.

Another shell company in St John's Grove, Archway, London, with a share capital of £3 (three pounds) was incorporated in March 2007 with two directors: one Duncan Jeremy Naylor (graphic designer) and Vladimir Voronkov (consultant). Mr Naylor traditionally resigned in September 2015 while Mr Voronkov is still there. It is not the same Vladimir Voronkov who was ambassador and permanent representative of Russia to the International Organisations in Vienna, and who at the time of writing served as the Under-Secretary-General of the United Nations Office of Counter-Terrorism (UNOCT). No, this is a diplomat whose career is well known.

His namesake, Vladimir Anatolyevich Voronkov, a journalist, born in November 1955, is only known to a few people. He did not think long of how to name his new company and it was named simply as its postal address – St John's Grove No. 22 Limited.[50] Even an experienced manager of a private business intelligence company will find it difficult finding anything on Mr Voronkov because all information about him was carefully deleted from internet sites. The police and the inquiry counsel in their turn did not want to ask him questions for very long. Andrew O'Connor QC informed the witness from the very beginning: 'You know that we are investigating the circumstances of Mr Litvinenko's death. I will ask you mainly some questions about 1 November.'[51] Naturally, Mr Voronkov was very helpful but could not contribute anything of value.

His biography was of no interest to the investigation because what could it have to do with 'the circumstances of Mr Litvinenko's death'? If Yuri Shvets or Christopher Steele were looking into the case, they would immediately notice that several years after university Mr Voronkov was sent as a TASS correspondent to Copenhagen, Denmark, and in September 1991 arrived in London, also as a TASS correspondent. Both of them would know that this is a traditional cover for KGB officers. The former KGB Major Shvets, who worked in Washington under the cover of a TASS correspondent in 1985–87, would also know that the 3rd department of the KGB's First Chief Directorate was responsible for sending spies to Denmark and Britain. One of the officers there in Moscow, Copenhagen, and London was Oleg Gordievsky.

When Berezovsky was only visiting London before he settled there forever, he met Voronkov, whose reports about the family of Nicholas II and other news from the British Isles he read in Moscow newspapers. He immediately hired him to take care of his family and business and – in January 2001 – his private business. After a while, Boris asked Voronkov to find a good office for the company and Voronkov soon found appropriate premises at 7 Down Street, where Berezovsky and Co. moved following substantial repairs and refurbishment in January 2003. Thus, Mr Voronkov had worked as Berezovsky's personal assistant from early 1996, running his office and looking after his other properties both in the UK and abroad until early 2007. He was then fired and opened his own company in London. In the meantime, he became a British citizen.

As in the case of Vladimir Voronov, another friend of the tycoon, no one can say that Mr Voronkov is or was a KGB agent whose acquaintance with Berezovsky was carefully arranged and whose work with him all those ten years was controlled by Moscow. Of course not. This might be considered a defamatory statement, libel, that cannot be published in the UK. Libel is a tort (civil wrong) under common law, for which a defamed party can sue for damages so no journalist or writer can ever dare to put it on paper. When Catherine Belton tried, the British lawyers of Putin's friends quickly found her and her publisher HarperCollins.

It is important to say that the Counsel to the Inquiry: Robert Tam QC, Hugh Davies OBE QC, and Andrew O'Connor did a marvellous job during the inquiry hearings. Their preparedness and extremely high qualifications were demonstrated in full and greatly appreciated by those who were present at sessions. It is not their fault that the government sent them down the wrong road from the very beginning. It is clearly also not the fault of the chairman, Sir Robert Owen. When the inquiry was formally set up in July 2014, he was a serving High Court judge who usually deal with most complex and difficult cases. Sir Robert retired from that post in September to serve full time as the chairman of the inquiry.

The Litvinenko murder was an intelligence operation that had become history by now. All intelligence cases, like intelligence history in general, must be revisited and reassessed every twenty or so years. This account must also be reviewed after several decades and maybe a new historian will find what was not possible to find or see when this book was written, and will be able to go further. As one modern Japanese artist said, there is nothing eternal in this world.

Epilogue

No analysis works if you have been deceived.

Adage attributed to Boris Berezovsky

One famous Ukrainian journalist reminded me of his interview with Berezovsky in London in February 2012. 'Putin will be executed by hanging from the yardarm,' Boris said, 'but I shall probably be hanged before him...'[1] In addition to all other qualities, Boris Berezovsky also possessed the gift of foresight. 'He was on the right side of history,' Goldfarb said in an interview. 'Berezovsky was quick to recognise his mistake and start criticising Putin. He was most consistent in his opposition to Putin's regime.' After a second, Alex added: 'When this aberration that is plaguing Russia is finally over, Berezovsky will be vindicated.'[2] Spoken ten years ago, today these words are more relevant than ever. There is much to be said about Litvinenko's patron (protector, sponsor, friend), whose life Sasha Litvinenko saved maybe more than once, but this book is not about Boris, it is about Sasha. As soon as they got rid of him, Berezovsky's own life expectancy had been drastically reduced. 'I shall probably be hanged before him...' – these words uttered by the tycoon must have been duly brought to Putin's attention. A year later, Berezovsky was gone.

Back to the Litvinenko Inquiry Report, I found several conclusions recorded by the chairman unconvincing. For example, Sir Robert writes: 'I have already made a finding that Mr Lugovoy and Mr Kovtun poisoned Mr Litvinenko with polonium 210 at their meeting in the Erinys boardroom on 16 October 2006 ... an operation in which Mr Kovtun was intended to play, and did play, a key role.'[3] As already stated, having studied all relevant documents I must say that this is at best a supposition regarding both – the allegedly established fact of poisoning and the 'key' role of Kovtun.

In Part 9, I disagree with Chapter 11, 'Conclusions regarding Russian State responsibility', except for one principal point.[4] There must be no doubt at all that the Russian State including its Security Council, Presidential Administration, Foreign Ministry, secret services, scientific research centres, and its propaganda machine are fully responsible for this murder. But due to the fact that the inquiry was misled about the character of this clandestine operation (which subsequently became covert, that is, if not completely secret than at least deniable), all arguments about where the polonium had been manufactured, whether it came from the Avangard facility or from another place, or the role of the FSB in this affair, are simply not correct. The explanation is very simple: as has already been established a long time ago, there is what I call the 'KGB's poison factory', a research laboratory specialising in complex poisons and other substances for secret services (SVR, FSB, GRU and GUO/SBP). Various components for this laboratory come from different places. The Litvinenko operation was masterminded, coordinated, and directed by the SBP and carried out by former GUO officers – Lugovoy, Sokolenko and Valuyev – supported by officers, agents, and co-optees from other Russian intelligence services.

Likewise, the next chapter discussing the involvement of Nikolai Patrushev, as the then director of the FSB, and Vladimir Putin, still the President of Russia at the time of writing and back in 2006, is irresolute because it is based on false assumption. The famous conclusion made by Sir Robert Owen and reproduced by the media all around the world is this. 'Taking full account of all the evidence and analysis available to me,' the chairman announced, 'I find that the FSB [!?] operation to kill Mr Litvinenko was *probably* approved by Mr Patrushev and also by President Putin.'[5] Alas, Sir Robert came to this conclusion at least partially because of his choice of the Russia expert for this inquiry. It was Robert Service, a well-known British historian and a former professor of Russian history at Oxford University who compiled the report for the Litvinenko Inquiry.

There is no place here to analyse the multiple errors of his report. Suffice it to say that Professor Service is not a specialist in Soviet and/or Russian secret services and intelligence operations and knows little or nothing about them. His only book remotely dealing with the subject and entitled *Spies and Commissars* (2011) is equally full of factual errors and misrepresented evidence. It was an unfortunate choice for the inquiry while quite obviously the very best candidate would be Professor Christopher Andrew of Cambridge University, the doyen of espionage historians.

In brief, the responsibilities for intelligence operations abroad are divided between the SVR (foreign intelligence service), GU (former GRU, military intelligence) and FSB (federal security service). We shall not discuss Russian military intelligence, which was probably not directly involved in the Litvinenko operation. The responsibilities between two other secret services have been divided, with the FSB in charge of all intelligence operations inside Russia and on the territory of the former Soviet Union, and the SVR in the rest of the world. The SVR has several specialised units like Zaslon, or departments within the Illegals Directorate capable of conducting all kinds of 'special tasks', including poisoning. But my firm conviction is, based on personal experience and years of research, that this operation was masterminded by the most secret, powerful, and rogue Presidential Security Service (SBP) headed by Viktor Zolotov.

Like all other similar crimes – the shooting of Anna Politkovskaya on Putin's birthday, the poisoning of Litvinenko on the anniversary of his arrival in Britain, the assassination of Boris Nemtsov on the Russian Day of Special Forces, and Berezovsky's 'suicide by hanging' – the 'unlucky' thirteen (Judas betrayed Jesus) years after Putin was elected president for the first time in March 2000 – Litvinenko's murder was carefully tailored to suit the perverse taste of Zolotov and his master. In this relation, it would be interesting to know why a number of Zolotov's photos were adduced in evidence while his name had not been mentioned in any available inquiry document.

There had been a lot of discussions about why anyone would wish to kill Alexander Litvinenko. A possible murder motive or motives had been analysed in detail. Probably many of them played their role to a greater or lesser extent. My personal opinion is that the so-called Ivanov Dossier, actively promoted by Yuri Shvets as the main motive, was in reality less important than Sasha's work for MI6 or his collaboration with the Mitrokhin Commission of the Italian parliament.

Litvinenko's activities in Spain could have become known first of all because there was a mole working for Russia deep inside the Spanish official intelligence agency Centro Nacional de Inteligencia (CNI), a partner of SIS. Robert Flórez García had been betraying all CNI's secrets that he knew to his SVR controllers, among other things reporting on Sergey Skripal's involvement with MI6 sometime in 2004.[6] I have left Spain to future researchers because it is an interesting, complex, and little studied subject. José Grinda in Madrid was not able to tell me anything of value but a more or less coherent picture of the Spanish authorities' fight against the Russian organised crime could be made based on multiple publications in English and Spanish. Here, Litvinenko's role was not so crucial, having in mind that the Spanish prosecutors began active operations against the Russian mafia in 1997 and never stopped ever since. In December 2020, the newspapers reported on Spain's 'biggest Russian mafia swoop in a decade' with twenty-three people arrested for money laundering. This joint operation with Europol became known as Operation TESTUDO. The investigation started in 2013 and culminated in eighteen raids across the country. Naturally, after Flórez García was arrested, Moscow received information about Litvinenko's contacts in Spain from Lugovoy, who was scheduled to fly to Madrid with Sasha on 10 November 2006.

About the prime suspect, a former bodyguard recommended to Berezovsky personally by the then Russian prime minister Yegor Gaidar, Boris acknowledged, 'I trusted Lugovoy completely.' And then said: 'The emotions tell me against Lugovoy being a murderer, because I have known him for many years.'[7] Maybe his being a bodyguard and not a trained assassin was the reason why Lugovoy was able to beat the polygraph in 2012. Asked whether he had ever been dealing with polonium and whether he had poisoned Litvinenko, Lugovoy firmly said, 'No,' and at the end of the test the polygraph examiner had to announce: 'I can tell you the result was conclusive, you were telling the truth, no deception indicated.'[8] The chairman expressed his doubts with the results and, as he said, placed no weight at all on the outcome of the examination, but that was it.

The most important question of the whole Litvinenko Inquiry is whether Putin was personally involved. In spring 2007, one of the Russian investigators was sent to London to interview Berezovsky in connection with the Litvinenko case. The interview was carried out at one of the London police stations in the presence of the Metropolitan Police officers.

Epilogue

> Q. In your opinion, who could have wished the death of Mr Litvinenko?'
>
> A. This is Putin himself. There are two facts confirming this. The first is the way how Sasha was murdered. And second, what were the actions of the Russian government after his death.[9]

I was very surprised that the legal team of the Litvinenko Inquiry, not to mention the MPS, did not even think about studying the appropriate Russian legislation, although like SIS in Britain, Russian secret services are governed by Russian law. In the meantime, to establish the extent of Putin's involvement it is enough to read the Federal Law No. 5-FZ of 10 January 1996 'On Foreign Intelligence' which, somewhat similar to Intelligence Services Act, makes provisions about RIS.

> Chapter 12: Russian Intelligence Services (RIS) operate under the authority of the President of the Russian Federation.
>
> The President of the Russian Federation.
> (1) determines the tasks of RIS;
> (2) controls and coordinates the activities of RIS;
> (3) makes decisions, within the limits of authority determined by federal laws, on issues related to foreign intelligence operations of RIS.

Words like 'probably' or 'likely' are simply not applicable here. Whoever came up with an idea to murder Boris Berezovsky and his close friends, including Sasha Litvinenko, there must be no doubt that like Stalin before him, in such operations President Vladimir Putin would be having responsibility and power in the final instance. His personal decision regarding who should live or die became final once it had been delivered. And although there can be no 'definitive story' where secret services are involved, this conclusion should probably be accepted as the final analysis. Especially under the nightly threats of nuclear war on Russian television that Putin not only silently encouraged but openly supported.

'The war with Ukraine will eventually end and Putin will go,' a former British ambassador in Moscow wrote in December 2022 when Ukraine plunged into darkness after the wave of Russian attacks. But whether Putin passes from the scene sooner or later, the bitter memories of this war will outlast him. He might have succeeded in silencing several brave men and women, in killing many people and children in Georgia, Ukraine, and elsewhere, but Litvinenko's last words came true and the howl of protests from around the world would reverberate in Putin's ears for the rest of his life. Sasha concluded his message with the words, 'May God forgive you [Mr Putin] for what you have done, not only to me but to beloved Russia and its people.' I do not think this is going to happen.

APPENDIX

The KGB Successors: December 1991– December 2022

March 1954 – KGB (Komitet Gosudarstvennoi Bezopasnosti)

The Committee of State Security of the USSR directly accountable to the Council of Ministers was established on 13 March 1954. It consisted of several chief directorates, directorates, and services, but the most important were the First Chief Directorate (FCD), one of the Soviet foreign intelligence services, like the British SIS tasked mainly with the covert overseas collection and analysis of secret political, economic, scientific, and military intelligence; and the Second Chief Directorate (SCD), the principal security agency of the Soviet Union. The KGB was dissolved on 3 December 1991 after a failed coup d'état and collapse of the USSR. In the course of its long history, only one of its former chiefs, Yuri V. Andropov, became the actual head of the state as General Secretary of the Communist Party (November 1982–February 1984) and Chairman of the Presidium of the Supreme Soviet (June 1983–February 1984). The KGB head office was located in Moscow at 2 Lubyanskaya Square.

February 1990 – Protection Service of the KGB

Sluzhba Okrany was the successor of the 9th Directorate of the KGB, responsible for personal protection of the leaders of the Communist Party and the Soviet government.

August 1991 – Protection Department, Presidential Staff

Upravlenie Okrany pri Apparate Prezidenta SSSR was the successor of the 9th Directorate of the KGB, responsible for personal protection of the leaders of the Communist Party and the Soviet government.

September 1991 – Presidential Security Service, RF

Sluzhba Okrany Prezidenta RSFSR was a new service responsible for the personal protection of Boris Yeltsin, then President of the Russian Federation. The Service was established by Alexander Korzhakov, Yeltsin's bodyguard, on 3 September 1991.

October 1991 – Security Service

Mezhrespublikanskaya Sluzhba Bezopasnosti SSSR (MSB) was a successor of the Soviet KGB. It was headed by Vadim Bakatin and existed until 19 December 1991 when it was transformed into the Ministry of Security and Internal Affairs of the RSFSR. In January 1992, the Constitutional Court declared the previous decision invalid and the Security Service was dissolved again, now becoming part of the Security Ministry of Russia (MBR). This ministry existed until December 1993 and was headed by General Viktor P. Barannikov.

December 1991 – GUO

Glavnoe Upravlenie Okhrany (GUO) of the Russian Federation was a successor of the Presidential Security Service, which was dissolved.

December 1991 – FAPSI

Federalnoe Agenstvo Pravitelstvennoi Svyazi i Informatsyi (Federal Agency for Government Communication and Information) under the President of the Russian Federation. Among other specialised agencies, former 16th KGB directorate (electronic intelligence/ELINT, radio interception and decryption) then headed by Lieutenant General Igor V. Maslov became part of the FAPSI. At the end of 1992, the FAPSI department responsible for presidential communications was attached to the GUO. As a separate government agency, FAPSI existed until March 2003, when its functions were divided between the FSO, FSB and SVR.

December 1991 – SVR

Sluzhba Vneshnei Razvedki (SVR) of the Russian Federation is a direct successor of the KGB's FCD. Like its predecessor, it is tasked mainly with the covert overseas collection and analysis of secret political, economic, scientific, business, and military intelligence. Almost all of its operational stuff are commissioned officers of the Russian army, navy, or air force. The legal basis for the SVR operations is the Law on Foreign Intelligence signed by the President on 10 January 1996. Since 2012, Russian President Vladimir Putin had been authorised to personally issue any secret order to the SVR without consulting parliament. In June 1972, Soviet and then Russian foreign intelligence, internally known as 'the Centre', moved and since then had been located in Yasenevo near Moscow. Its foreign outposts are known as the *rezidentura* (residency or station), always hidden under the roof of a Russian embassy. Officers of the residency may operate undercover as diplomats, trade representatives, journalists, bankers, and so on. Specific areas of the residency's activities are known as lines: for example, officers of the PR line are responsible of political intelligence operations; S&T line is in charge of collecting scientific and technical intelligence; VKR line officers are its counterintelligence staff; while officers of the N line support so-called 'illegals' who operate in this particular country without any legal cover. Depending on the country and the residency's size, there may be other lines like line EM, which deals with the Russian community in the country where this residency is located.

December 1993 – FSK

Federalnaya Sluzhba Kontrazvedki (FSK) of the Russian Federation was a successor of the MBR, formed on 21 December 1993. The FSK inherited the structure of the Security Ministry with the exception of the border troops transformed into the separate Federal Border Service of Russia – the main command of the border troops of the RF. Between December 1993 and February 1994, the FSK was headed by Nikolai Golushko, a former chairman of the Ukrainian KGB. His former deputy Sergey Stepashin headed the Service in March 1994 and remained the FSK director until June 1995, dismissed from this post at his own request. He was subsequently appointed head of the administrative department of the Cabinet staff.

April 1995 – FSB

Federalnaya Sluzhba Bezopasnosti (FSB), the Federal Security Service of the Russian Federation. The FSB is Russia's domestic counterintelligence and security agency and is part of its intelligence machinery alongside the FSO, SVR and the GU (former GRU), Russian military intelligence. Its main tasks are formulated as ensuring the security of the Russian Federation, protection of its borders, internal waters, territorial sea and exclusive economic zone (EEZ), Russian continental shelf and natural resources. The FSB is also directed to protect Russian economic interests, ensure information security, counter terrorism and espionage within the territory of the Russian Federation. Its Fifth Service is also responsible for collecting intelligence on the territory of the former Soviet Union (FSU). FSB is directed by the President of Russia. In the period from July 1995 to December 2022, the Security Service had been headed by five directors: General of the Army

Mikhail Barsukov (July 1995–June 1996), General of the Army Nikolai Kovalev (June 1996–July 1998), Colonel Vladimir Putin (July 1998–August 1999), General of the Army Nikolai Patrushev (August 1999–May 2008), and General of the Army Alexander Bortnikov (May 2008–present). The headquarters of the FSB are at the same address as the former KGB – No. 2 Lubyanskaya Square, Moscow.

May 1996 – FSO

Federalnaya Sluzhba Okrany (FSO), the Federal Protective Service or Federal Guard Service of Russia, is a federal government agency, successor of the GUO, tasked to provide personal security to the political, administrative, and spiritual leaders of Russia and to ensure security of federal properties defined by the law 'On State Protection' (27 May 1996). For sixteen years from May 2000, the FSO had been headed by General Yevgeny Murov, succeeded by General Dmitry Kochnev in May 2016. Before this appointment, General Kochnev headed (June 2015–May 2016) the most secret Russian secret service – Putin's Presidential Security Service, which is formally part of the FSO. The staff of the FSO is estimated to number 50,000 servicemen and women.

May 2000 – SPB

Sluzhba Bezopasnosti Prezidenta (SPB), the Presidential Security Service of Russia, was formally established in November 1993. However, in its current form, it has existed since May 2000, when Vladimir Putin became the president and appointed Viktor Zolotov, his former personal bodyguard and member of Yeltsin's protection team, to head his security service. Zolotov had headed the SBP with an undeclared number (estimated 2,500–3,000) of personnel for thirteen years. The agency was created to protect the president and his family but is now said to protect also the prime minister. According to some unconfirmed leaks, in the 1990s several departments of the service were in charge of fighting corruption and other white-collar crimes within the government and the Kremlin staff. Several sources mention the so-called Psychological Security Department of the SBP as responsible for collecting and analysing intelligence about possible threats to the life of Vladimir Putin. It is said to rely on a panel of unnamed experts from all Russian secret services. In June 2016 Putin appointed Alexey Rubezhnoy to head his SBP. All information about the man is classified.

July 2013 – AII

Agentstvo Internet Issledovanii, the Internet Research Agency or Glavset, better known in the West as a troll factory, is a Russian private company based in

St Petersburg and engaged in online propaganda, influence operations, and political warfare. This troll factory is a modern version of Service A (active measures) of the KGB's FCD. At that time, Soviet overt and covert propaganda and disinformation operations were conducted by the KGB with the help of corrupt Western journalists and so-called agents of influence. After Putin's coming to power and before the Russian invasion of Ukraine, the regime was actively using the services of Ketchum, FleishmannHillard, Publicis Groupe, WPP, and other global PR, marketing, and corporate communications firms 'to improve its reputation' in the West. According to the media, Ketchum alone had received more than $60 million from the Kremlin for their work (2006–2014). In March 2022, *PRWeek* reported that major companies are pulling out of Russia due to the Kremlin's military operation in Ukraine. A report issued by the US Office of the Director of National Intelligence, 'Assessing Russian Activities and Intentions', described the IRA as a troll farm: 'The likely financier of the so-called Internet Research Agency of professional trolls located in Saint Petersburg is a close ally of [Vladimir] Putin with ties to Russian intelligence.' In the absence of professional Western PR firms, the role of IRA and such outlets as Russia Today (launched in December 2005) has considerably increased.

April 2016 – Rosgvardia

Federalnaya Sluzhba Voisk Natsionalnoy Gvardii RF, the National Guard of Russia, is an independent agency and military force reporting directly to the president. It was formed on 5 April 2016 and has since been headed by Putin's former bodyguard, now General of the Army Viktor Zolotov. It is usually referred to as a private army or Praetorian Guard of Vladimir Putin. By the time Putin's armed forces attacked Ukraine, the National Guard numbered over 340,000 personnel in eighty-four units across Russia, having consolidated the Internal Troops of the Interior Ministry (MVD), the Special Rapid Response Squad (SOBR) of the state police, and the Special Purpose Mobile Unit (OMON), formerly a special forces unit of the militia of the MVD, plus the Federal State Unitary Enterprise 'Okhrana' (The Guard). Before the war in Ukraine, the Rosgvardia was the internal special forces intended for use in domestic security roles against the opposition, protest demonstrations, and all other forms of anti-government unrest including individual picketers to ensure the continuity of Putin's regime. Since the beginning of the war, Rosgvardia have played an important role in both combat and rear-area security in the Ukrainian territory occupied by the Russian troops. One British Defence Intelligence update in late September 2022 stressed that 'with a requirement to quell growing domestic dissent in Russia, as well as operational taskings in Ukraine, Rosgvardia is highly likely under particular strain'. It was also noted that Rosgvardia units were especially ill-prepared for combat.

Notes

The Murder of Alexander Litvinenko: A Short Bibliographical Essay Instead of Acknowledgements

1. James Robinson, 'Smile when you do that, Mr President', *The Observer*, Sunday, 16 July 2006. See also, Boris Volodarsky, *The KGB's Poison Factory: From Lenin to Litvinenko* (Barnsley, S. Yorkshire: Frontline Books, 2009), 205. Angus Roxburgh is a journalist. He was the *Sunday Times* Moscow Correspondent in the 1980s until he was expelled from the Soviet Union in a tit-for-tat spy scandal. Roxburgh returned in the 1990s and was the BBC's Moscow correspondent during the Yeltsin years. Subsequently, he worked as an advisor and speechwriter for Putin's communications team.
2. Eli Lake, 'Confessions of a Putin Spin Doctor', *Daily Beast*, 11 March 2014.
3. Dimitri Konstantinovich Simes was born in Moscow and before his emigration worked at the Institute of World Economy and International Relations. Immediately upon arrival in America in 1973, he made contact with Richard Pearl, assistant to Senator Henry Jackson, Brent Scowcroft, future National Security Advisor to Presidents Gerald Ford and George H. W. Bush, and James Schlesinger, former CIA Director and US Secretary of Defense. Soon, Simes got a job at the Carnegie Endowment's Center for Soviet and European Studies and became a naturalized American citizen despite FBI suspicions of his collaboration with the KGB. Since the mid-1980s, he has been an adviser to President Richard Nixon. In 1994, shortly before Nixon's death, Simes founded the thinktank Nixon Center for Peace and Freedom (later Center for the National Interest) of which he is now the President and CEO. See Putin's List, www.spisok-putina.org/en/personas/simes.
4. Christopher Booth, 'The true story about Russian lying', *The Spectator*, 22 March 2022.
5. In an Australian international documentary series *Dateline*, reporter Nick Lazaredes asked many people including Lekarev, 'Who killed Litvinenko?' Lekarev, born in 1935, according to his own words had been a non-staff employee of a research institute working for the technical-operational directorate (OTU) of the KGB in 1959–62. The institute did not work with polonium. In the interview, Lekarev did say that Nikolai Khokhlov was poisoned with polonium 'but was later saved by the British physicians' – both of these assertions are not correct. See Boris Volodarsky, *Nikolai Khokhlov:*

Self-Esteem with a Halo (2005); *The KGB's Poison Factory* (2009), 164–81; *Assassins* (2019), 81–104.
6. Cowell, *The Terminal Spy*, 347–8.
7. Litvinenko Investigation, INQ003016.
8. Litvinenko Investigation, INQ003101.
9. Litvinenko Investigation, Operation AVOCET, Itsu Restaurant, INQ017900-905.
10. Call Site Analysis Report, Operation WHIMBREL, INQ019348-72; Telephone Calls Data, INQ020044-50; Maps showing movements of Alexander Litvinenko, 1 November 2006, INQ018243-51; and Maps showing movements of Andrey Lugovoy (and Dmitry Kovtun) on 1 November 2006, INQ018252-66.
11. Having begun her police career with the Met long time ago, Lisa has served at every rank from Detective Sergeant to Detective Superintendent, becoming the most senior female detective within the CT Command. After Litvinenko, among other important operations, DSU Harman also led the Met's forensic response in the two Wiltshire investigations involving Sergey and Julia Skripal and two British subjects poisoned with the Novichok class of nerve agents. Like the Litvinenko poisoning, this posed unique and unprecedented forensic challenges. In December 2019 she was awarded the Queen's Police Medal for Distinguished Service.

Definitions of Key Terms

1. In *The Fist of God* (1994), Forsyth writes that by the end of the 1990s there were 2,000 sayanim (singular *sayan*) in London alone, 5,000 in the rest of Britain and ten times that number in the USA. He also explains how the system operates. For example, a Mossad team arrives in London to mount an operation. They need a car. A motor-trade sayan is asked to leave a legitimate second-hand car at a certain place. It is returned later, after the operation. The sayan never knows what it was used for. The same team needs a 'front'. A property-owning sayan lends an empty shop, and a confectionary sayan stocks it with sweets and chocolates. They need a mailing 'drop' – a real estate sayan lends the keys to a vacant office on his books, and so on.
2. On 15 March 2022, Professor Peter Mathieson, Principal and Vice-Chancellor, made the following statement on behalf of Edinburgh University: 'Since the invasion of Ukraine by the Russian Government, colleagues across the University have been working tirelessly to support members of our community and I wanted to update you on some key developments. First, I want to reiterate that we join our colleagues in the sector in condemning this invasion. Our thoughts are with Ukrainian people and their family members in Edinburgh and beyond, and we fully endorse the Universities UK statement on this issue … In line with others in the sector, we have been reviewing our relationships with Russia. We have instructed our investment managers to divest of all our Russian investment holdings at the earliest opportunity. We have agreed to review, as a matter of priority, the honorary degree awarded to the Head of

the Ruskiy Mir Foundation, Vyacheslav Nikonov, and are now progressing the formal process to do this.'
3. Alan S. Cowell, *The Terminal Spy: A True Story of Espionage, Betrayal and Murder* (New York, NY: Doubleday, 2008), 32.
4. In 1987, as part of the KGB operation PHANTHOM, Zhomov approached Jack G. Downing, the CIA station head in Moscow (1986–9), and offered to sell very sensitive top-secret information in exchange for a handsome sum of money and resettlement in the USA. The offer seemed too good to be true, but the CIA bought Zhomov's story, which in reality intended to protect a very important KGB source inside the CIA. After a while, Zhomov, codenamed GT/PROLOGUE by the CIA, disappeared. Downing later served as the Agency's Deputy Director for Operations (DDO), succeeded by his deputy James Pavitt in July 1999.
5. Although it looks similar, this FSB Centre differs from the British Centre for the Protection of National Infrastructure (CPNI), formed in February 2007. The CPNI works with the Security Service (MI5) and the Government Communications Headquarters (GCHQ) and its role is formulated as 'to reduce the vulnerability of the UK to a variety of threats such as Terrorism, Espionage and Sabotage' by providing protective security advice to businesses and organisations across the country. The Centre is accountable to the DG of MI5.
6. *Wimpel* in German, which means 'pennant' or 'pennon' in English.
7. See *National Intelligence Machinery*, London, September 2001, 15.
8. *Task Force Report: Organized Crime – Annotations and Consultants' Papers*. The President's Commission on Law Enforcement and Administration of Justice (Washington, DC: US Government Printing office, 1967), 41.
9. Richard Norton-Taylor, 'Alexander Litvinenko accusation puts MI6 in an unflattering light', *The Guardian*, Friday, 14 December 2012.

About This Book
1. OMSDON, now Separate Operational Purpose Division or ODON, a rapid deployment internal security forces of the Internal Troops of the Ministry of Internal Affairs (MVD).
2. At the time it was the Third Chief Directorate of the KGB, now FSB's 3rd Department, military unit no. 70850. Litvinenko's recruiter was Nikolai A. Andryushin, who left the Service in 1995 aged 41 to start a career in security business working for the big Russian companies. In December 2014 he became a member of the Supervisory Board of the ProCommerce Bank in charge of economic and information security.
3. Alex Goldfarb with Marina Litvinenko, *Death of a Dissident: The Poisoning of Alexander Litvinenko and the Return of the KGB* (London: Simon & Schuster, 2008), 46.
4. Yuri Felshtinsky, 4 February 2007. Foreword to *Blowing Up Russia* (2022), x–xi.

5. Cf. Stephen M. Walt, 'How to start a war in 5 easy steps', *Foreign Policy*, 2 April 2018.
6. Cf. the relevant passage in Gail W. Lapidus, 'Russia's second Chechen war: Ten assumptions in search of a policy', in Lena Jonson and Murad Esenov (eds.), *Chechnya: The International Community and Strategies for Peace and Stability* (Stockholm: The Swedish Institute of International Affairs, 2000).
7. Pavel K. Baev, 'Chechnya and the Russian military: A war too far?' in Richard Sakwa (ed.), *Chechnya: From Past to Future* (London: Anthem Press, 2005), 117.
8. Forsyth, *The Fist of God*, 623.
9. Philip A. Karber, 'New generation warfare'. The article published by National Geospatial-Intelligence Agency (NGA), Springfield, Virginia, 4 June 2015. See also, James Derleth, 'Russian new generation warfare: Deterring and winning the tactical fight', *Military Review*, September–October 2020, 82–94.
10. A radiological attack is the spreading of radioactive material with the intent to do harm, according to the US Department of Homeland Security. The experts define radiological terrorism as the deliberate use of radiological weapons. These weapons would not cause massive numbers of deaths. In most scenarios, only a few people may die immediately or shortly after the exposure to radiation, although many people could develop cancer within several years after the attack. Such an attack, they write, might spur panic and result in high economic costs because of the need for decontamination and possible tearing down and reconstruction of contaminated structures. Thus, radiological weapons must be considered weapons of mass disruption, posing the greatest immediate threat to human health and wellbeing. For details, see Pavel Kuna, Zdenik Hon, and Jiří Patodka, 'How serious is threat to radiological terrorism?' *Acta Medica*, 52/3 (2009), 85–9.

Prologue
1. Luis Gómez, 'Litvinenko dio pistas de mafiosos rusos en España', *El País*, 6 July 2008.

Chapter 1
1. For whatever reason, Catherine Belton calls IIASA 'A KGB-linked institute of economics in Austria' in her book *Putin's People: How the KGB Took Back Russia and then Took on the West* (London: William Collins, 2020), 189.
2. Mike Cummings, 'Aven offers inside account of the making of modern Russia', *Yale News*, 13 November 2017.
3. In October 1994, Aven met Mikhail Friedman, one of the co-founders of Alfa Group, and soon became an Alfa-Bank shareholder (by 2022, one of its co-owners) and was also involved in other Alfa Group ventures. In 2012, the Alfa Group together with Viktor Wechselberg (President, Renova Group, Russia) and Leonard Blavatnik (Chairman, Access Industries, USA) sold their aggregate 50 per cent stake in TNK-BP to state-owned Rosneft for $28

billion. A year later, Aven joined the board of LetterOne Group, an investment business founded by Friedman and focused on the telecoms, technology, and energy sectors. The Group owns companies and has investment in companies with operations in thirty-two countries around the world.

At the end of February 2022, the EU sanctioned Aven as 'one of Vladimir Putin's closest oligarchs'. In April, the French Ministry of Culture seized one of the valuable paintings owned by Aven, *Autoportrait* (1910) by Pyotr Konchalovsky, as part of the personal sanctions imposed on him in relation to the Russia's war in Ukraine. In May, Bloomberg reported that around thirty officials raided Aven's English home, seizing cash and scrutinising his money transfers to the UK. Previously, he resigned from the board of directors of Alfa-Bank and LetterOne Group to help them avoid sanctions, together with Friedman filing a lawsuit in the European Court of Justice against the EU. The court's spokesperson, Jacques Zammit, said that it would be a long time before judgements would be handed down (Leonie Kijewski, 'Abramovich is suing the EU. He is not alone', *Politico*, 3 June 2022). Earlier that year, Russia was expelled from the Council of Europe and in September ceased to be a Party to the European Convention on Human Rights.

4. Sergey E. Prikhodko was a career Russian diplomat who had been deputy chief of the AP (1998–2004) under Yeltsin and Putin, and also headed its Foreign Policy Directorate, his last job being deputy prime minister and head, later first deputy, of the Cabinet Office (Prikhodko died in January 2021). Although very close to President Putin, Prikhodko remained largely in the shadows until 2016. He came to fame in early 2018 when *The Telegraph* reported about a rendezvous on a yacht between Prikhodko and Oleg Deripaska, a Russian oligarch. 'It reportedly took place in August 2016,' Alec Luhn writes, 'a month after Mr [Paul] Manafort, then Mr Trump's campaign manager, offered "private briefings" to Mr Deripaska ... Mr Deripaska hired Mr Manafort on a $10 million annual contract in 2006 after the Washington insider proposed a campaign to "greatly benefit the Putin government" by influencing US politics and media' (*The Telegraph*, 8 February 2018).

Alexey A. Gromov, another career Russian diplomat who had worked in Prague, Karlovy Vary, and Bratislava between 1982 and 1996, a period when Russian intelligence services were especially active recruiting and controlling agents in the Czech and Slovak republics and Austria. In November 1996, President Yeltsin appointed Gromov chief of the Press Office. He became Putin's press secretary in January 2000, remaining in this post until May 2012, succeeded by Dmitry Peskov. Gromov was promoted to first deputy head of the AP. According to a report by investigative journalists from *The Project*, an independent media outlet, Gromov, whom Putin trusts, managers the Kremlin's grip on the media and is also its chief censor, controlling all major Russian propaganda resources. See 'Master of Puppets: The Man Behind the Kremlin's Control of the Russian Media', *The Project*, 5 June 2019.

5. Petr Aven, *Vremya Berezovskogo* (Moscow: Corpus, 2018), 206.

6. Goldfarb with Marina Litvinenko, *Death of a Dissident*, 66; Boris Yeltsin, *Midnight Diaries* (London: Weidenfeld & Nicolson, 2000), 20–21. Yeltsin's book was ghostwritten by Valentin Yumashev.
7. When Mikhail Gorbachev launched perestroika ('restructuring'), the Soviet version of Okhrana was still known as the 9th Directorate of the KGB, headed by General Yuri Plekhanov. By August 1991, it was transformed into the Protection Directorate under the President's Office briefly headed by Generals Gennady Bashkin and then Vladimir Redkoborody, who was the first GUO chief. Between June 1992 and July 1995, the GUO was subordinated to the Commandant of the Moscow Kremlin Mikhail Barsukov. He was succeeded by Yuri Krapivin (July 1995–June 1996). Under his leadership, in May 1996, it became the Federal Protective Service (FSO), which Goldfarb cleverly translated as Federal Service of Okhrana.
8. As a member of the GUO protection team, Lugovoy was reported to have at different times acted as a bodyguard to Yegor Gaidar (PM between June and December 1992, later first deputy PM), Sergey Filatov (Kremlin Chief of Staff, January 1993–January 1996) and Andrey Kozyrev (Russian foreign minister, October 1990–January 1996). By 1996, Valuyev, Sokolenko, and Lugovoy had resigned from the service.
9. Goldfarb with Marina Litvinenko, *Death of a Dissident*, 72–3.
10. Ibid., 37.
11. Ibid., 92–3.
12. Yeltsin, *Midnight Diaries*, 97.
13. Gevorkyan et al., *First Person*, 125–9. Alexey A. Bolshakov had served in St Petersburg between July and October 1991 as head of the Committee for Economic Development of the Mayor's Office. He was then transferred to Moscow, was appointed deputy PM (November 1994), and in August 1996, first deputy PM, serving until 7 March 1997, after which he returned to St Petersburg as Chairman of the Board of Trustees of the St Petersburg and NW Regional Development Fund.
14. 'It was me who invited Putin to the Kremlin', interview with P. Borodin by Andrey Mozzhukhin for Lenta.ru, 8 December 2015.
15. For details, see Sami Nevala and Kauko Aromaa (eds.), *Organised Crime, Trafficking, Drugs: Selected Papers Presented at the Annual Conference of the European Society of Criminology, Helsinki 2003* (Helsinki: European Institute for Crime Prevention and Control, 2004), 6–8.
16. See *Russian Money Laundering*, Hearing Before the Committee on Banking and Financial Services, US House of Representatives, 106th Congress, First Session, September 21, 22, 1999, Serial No. 106-38 (Washington, DC: GPO, 1999), 317.
17. In his letter to the Communist chairman of the State Duma, Gennady Seleznyov (also spelled Seleznev), Skuratov asked about the fate of $50 billion of the country's hard currency reserves allegedly funnelled to the West through Fimaco. In her book *Putin's People* (2020), Catherine Belton claims that she

has a copy of this six-page letter to Seleznyov dated 1 Feb 1999 (see pages 117 and 525).
18. Litvinenko Inquiry Hearings, Day 15, 25 February 2015, 10.
19. See Rodrigo Fernández, 'Felipe Turover, un aventurero en el Kremlin', *El País*, 29 Aug 1999; and Yegor Khobotov, 'To the biography of Philipp Turover', Compromat.ru, 14 March 2000.
20. Benton, *Putin's People*, 91–2.
21. Fernando Peinado, 'Vacation rental nightmares: Living with "a former KGB spy" in the room next door', *El País* (English), 13 January 2022. The next article by the same author was published on 17 March 2022. By that date, Turover had still not vacated the room for which he had not been paying.
22. Goldfarb with Marina Litvinenko, *Death of a Dissident*, 134–5.
23. Alexander Volkov, *Viktor Ilyukhin: President Hunter*, in Russian (Moscow: Algoritm, 2012), 74–82. Dyachenko was Tatyana's second husband. They divorced in 2002 and she married Yumashev, who divorced his first wife and was then living with Svetlana Vavra, the wife of Andrey Vavra, whom Yumashev invited to work in the AP and who was one of Yeltsin's speechwriters.
24. See Boris Volodarsky, *The KGB's Poison Factory: From Lenin to Litvinenko* (Barnsley: Frontline Books, 2017), 11, 12, and 255. In this first volume, the date is erroneously given as February 1997. In the second volume, it was corrected to March 1996, see *Assassins: The KGB's Poison Factory Ten Years On* (Barnsley: Frontline Books, 2019), a photo insert after p. 146, where Olga was photographed in Salzburg by the author. See also Goldfarb with Marina Litvinenko, *Death of a Dissident*, 37–8.
25. Catherine Bolton writes that in an interview with her in October 2017, Yumashev said that it was Voloshin who initially voiced the idea of nominating Putin as PM, which may or may not be true.
26. Several different versions exist. Goldfarb, who should be informed best of all, writes that after visiting Lena's birthday party in February 1999, which was an unusually modest celebration for Berezovsky because the inevitable purge of his empire by Prosecutor General Skuratov had been the talk of the town in the past weeks, Putin became a fully-fledged member of the Family. Belton refers to an episode from Masha Gessen's book *The Man Without a Face: The Unlikely Rise of Vladimir Putin* (New York: Riverhead Books, 2012), 18–19, telling the story of an alleged meeting between Putin and Berezovsky in the lift anteroom in the old KGB head office. There, the two men were allegedly discussing Putin's possible running for the presidency. Remarkably, describing the scene that Masha borrowed from Goldfarb's book (163–5) because she simply couldn't know it herself, Masha writes that 'Berezovsky met with Putin almost every day' (19). In her turn, quoting from Masha's book, Belton suggests that 'the two men had met only fleetingly prior to that, when Berezovsky visited St Petersburg in the early nineties' (142–3). Regarding Berezovsky vising Putin in Biarritz in July 1999, Gessen writes that they actually spent the whole day in conversation. In the end, Putin said, 'All right,

let's give it a shot. But you do understand that [President Yeltsin] has to be the one to say it to me.'
27. See 'Bernard Bertossa declares Pavel Borodin guilty', *The Jamestown Foundation Monitor*, 8/47 (7 March 2002).
28. Andrew Higgins, 'Swiss money-laundering probe finds a Kremlin link and a wall of silence', *Wall Street Journal*, 23 July 2001.
29. Kruglov occupied this post between 1992 and 1998. See 'London Court upheld sale of Tchigirinski villa to Sibir subsidiary', RAPSI News, 5 December 2012.
30. Mikhail Khodorkovsky was arrested at Novosibirsk airport on 23 October 2003. He was charged with fraud, tax evasion, and other crimes and put into prison but later transferred to the labour camp. He was released on 20 December 2013.
31. Edward Jay Epstein later published an article 'The spectre that haunts the death of Litvinenko', *The New York Sun*, 19 March 2008, followed by a chapter, 'The Case of the Radioactive Corpse', in his book *The Annals of Unsolved Crimes* (New York: Melville House, 2012). There Epstein writes, 'Despite a surfeit of speculation, there is no satisfactory explanation how the polonium-210, which can be used as a trigger in an early-stage nuclear weapon, got to London.' For an explanation, see Chapter 8.
32. Interview with Vitaly M. Greenberg, June 2014, Moscow.
33. Andy Hayman with Margaret Gilmore, *The Terrorist Hunters* (London: Bantam Press, 2009), 241–5.

Chapter 2

1. In 2020, in an article for *The Times*, Tom Ball called Dubov 'the last surviving member of a group of businessmen opposed to President Putin'. Others were Boris Berezovsky, Badri Patarkatsishvili, and Nikolai Glushkov. According to the article, Dubov said that he and other Russians in Britain had called on MI5 to devote more resources to the Kremlin. 'British intelligence services,' the newspaper writes, 'repeatedly ignored warnings from Russian dissidents about the threat from Moscow' (*The Times*, Tuesday, 4 August 2020).
2. Petr Aven, *The Time of Berezovsky* (Moskva: AST/Corpus, 2018), interview with Yuri Shefler (in Russian).
3. Goldfarb with Marina Litvinenko, *Death of a Dissident*, 236. The channel was finally sold for $175 million. According to Goldfarb, Abramovich allowed the Kremlin to nominate five new board members. Contrary to the promise, Glushkov remained in prison.
4. Ibid., 238–239.
5. UK Parliament, Publications and Records, Hansard written answers for 13 January 2004: Column 654W.
6. Goldfarb with Marina Litvinenko, *Death of a Dissident*, 321–2.
7. The judge overseeing the case was Dame Elisabeth Gloster. 'It turned out,' Catherine Belton writes, 'that Mrs Justice Gloster's stepson had been paid nearly £500,000 to represent Abramovich in the early stages of the case'

Notes

(Catherine Belton, *Putin's People: How the KGB Took Back Russia and Then Took on the West*, London: William Collins, 2020, 4). Mrs Justice Gloster declined to comment, Belton adds in a footnote, while the Judicial Office, which represents judges, said she had declared the matter.
8. This is the King James Version, 2 Samuel 17:23. It ends with 'So he died and was buried in his father's tomb'. The Revised Standard Version is different: 17:23 'hanged himself'. No doubt the premonition that Absalom had embarked on a disastrous course prompted the rejected counsellor to take his own life lest he die the death of a traitor at the hands of David.

Chapter 3

1. Felshtinsky to the author, 5 July and 16 October 2022. See also Yuri Felshtinsky and Alexander Litvinenko, *Blowing Up Russia* (London: Gibson Square, 2022), foreword by Felshtinsky, 4 February 2007.
2. Dr Medish grew up in the USSR, where he experienced the brutality of the Soviet regime first-hand. His father, Mark's grandfather, was arrested by the NKVD, Soviet secret police, in 1942 and his family never heard of him again. The younger Medish was conscripted into the Red Army and took part in the Battle of Stalingrad, after which he was taken prisoner of war by the German troops and released three years later by Allied forces. Having then moved to the United States, Vadim Medish received a doctorate in Russian history from the American University in Washington before joining the faculty in the languages and foreign studies department in 1963.
3. See Goldfarb and Marina Litvinenko, *Death of a Dissident*, 4–5.
4. See Alexander Litvinenko, *The Lubyanskaya Criminal Gang* (New York: Grani, 2002), Instead of a Foreword: 'Unforeseen Circumstances' by Alexander Goldfarb, 14–15; and Goldfarb with Marina Litvinenko, *Death of a Dissident*, 4–5.
5. Litvinenko Investigation, 'Interview of Litvinenko by Scaramella', INQ019495.
6. Christopher Andrew and Vasili Mitrokhin, *The Mitrokhin Archive: The KGB in Europe and the West* (London: Penguin Books, 2000), xxiii and 17–19.
7. See Goldfarb with Marina Litvinenko, *Death of a Dissident*, 8–10.
8. Gina C. Haspel, Central Intelligence Agency Career Timeline, 1 May 2018, declassified.
9. See Goldfarb with Marina Litvinenko, *Death of a Dissident*, 13–15. From Alex Goldfarb's witness statement to Scotland Yard dated 20 May 2013: 'I was not paid for my role in bringing the Litvinenko family to the UK. However, travel, accommodation, legal and other associated costs in the amount of US$131,813.86 were fully paid by Berezovsky. I attach my financial statement to him dated 24 November 2000 (exhibit 2)', LITV 2-DNX-Z, p. 3, declassified on author's request, FOIA.
10. T. Rees Shapiro, 'Vadim Medish', obituary, *The Washington Post*, 25 May 2011.
11. This circulation figure is mentioned in *Case of Novaya Gazeta and Borodyanskiy vs Russia* (Application no. 14087/08), European Court of Human Rights, Strasbourg, Judgement of 5 March 2013 (Final of 28/06/2013).

12. Published in *Novaya Gazeta* no. 6, 27 January 2003.
13. Sergey Guriev, 'Putin's dictatorship is now based on fear rather than spin', *Financial Times*, 17 April 2022. The writer is a professor of economics at the Paris Institute of Political Studies (Sciences Po).

Chapter 4

1. The letter was posted in May shortly after Melnichenko's meeting with Petro Shatkovsky, deputy chief of the SBU. For more details, see Boris Volodarsky, 'The Ukrainian Tapegate Dilemma', *The Salisbury Review*, 24/2 (Winter 2005), 15–17.
2. See Melnichenko's letter to Oleksandr Turchynov, Director of the Security Service of Ukraine (February–September 2005), *Obozrevatel*, 1 April 2005.
3. Litvinenko Investigation, INQ020257.
4. The Mitrokhin Commission Archive, Personal File LIMAREV. According to his 'Autobiography', after 1993 Limarev was invited to NORDEX, whose president was Grigory Luchansky, and 'became one of the first 6 directors-partners of NORDEX in Moscow, Zurich and Vienna'. In 1996, then-director of the CIA John Deutch called Luchansky's company Nordex 'an example of an organization associated with Russian criminal activity moving out of Russia'. A year later, the chairman of the House Committee on International Relations asked FBI Director Louis J. Freeh: 'Is there any evidence that former KGB officials are involved in the Russian organized crime syndicates?' to which Freeh answered: 'Yes, sir, there is; both in investigations in Russia, as well as in other parts of Europe, in companies such as Nordex, which is a Vienna-based company, a multinational company.' See Roman Anin, Olesya Shmagun, and Jelena Vasic, 'Ex-Spy Turned Humanitarian Helps Himself', OCCRP, 4 November 2015.
5. Anton Romashin, 'Oleg Sultanov: I am not going to pull the oligarchs' chestnuts out of the fire any more', *Nezavisimaya Gazeta*, 3 April 2003 (in Russian).
6. [11] David Satter, 'The Shadow of Ryazan: Who Was Behind the Strange Russian Apartment Bombing in September 1999?' *Project on Systemic Change and International Security in Russia and the New States in Eurasia*, The John Hopkins School of Advanced International Studies, 19 April 2002, 14.
7. A letter of Yuri Shchekochikhin to President Putin, 25 March 2002, published on his political party's website: www.yabloko.ru/Press/Docs/2002/0325Schek-Putin-letter.html, retrieved on 21 June 2022.
8. For details, see Mark Franchetti, 'Moscow says it has MI6 spy recruited by Litvinenko', *The Sunday Times*, 8 July 2007; Adam Rawnsley, 'Pablo Miller: The mystery man who "recruited" Putin's poisoned spy', *Daily Beast*, 16 March 2018; Pavel Borisov, 'A hundred grand and hundreds of betrayed agents', *Meduza*, 6 March 2018; and Alexander Hinstein, 'A spy who took French leave', *Moskovsky Komsomolets*, 2 July 2007 (in Russian).

Chapter 5

1. Barry Maier, *Spooked: The Secret Rise of Private Spies* (London: Sceptre/Hodder & Stoughton, 2021), 5, 11, 34.
2. He was allegedly convicted by the Savelovsky Regional Court of Moscow on 12 March 2002 under Article 313, Part 1 of the Russian Criminal Code which is 'escape from a place of confinement, arrest or custody'. This, however, is not applicable because Lugovoy had never been placed in confinement, arrested or in custody, and therefore could not escape.
3. Litvinenko Inquiry Hearings, Day 7, 9 February 2015, 31–3.
4. Litvinenko Inquest, INQ002838-49.
5. Litvinenko Inquest Hearings, Day 7, 9 February 2015, 48.
6. Litvinenko Inquiry, INQ 005973-79 (INQ005974).
7. Litvinenko Inquiry, INQ002972-79 (INQ002974).
8. An excellent report with pictures and details of the investigations was published by *The Insider* on 16 June 2022.
9. To the best of my knowledge, no one ever investigated what he was doing in Canada. By sheer coincidence, a Russian spy who called himself Paul William Hampel was detained on 14 November at the Pierre Elliott Trudeau International Airport in Montreal just prior to boarding a flight to Europe. When searched, the counterintelligence officers found in his possession a fraudulent Ontario birth certificate, a large sum of US dollars in five currencies, a short-wave radio, two digital cameras, three mobile phones, and five SIM cards. After three weeks of detention, the man finally admitted that he was not Hampel but a Russian citizen born on 21 October 1961, and that he had no legal status in Canada. 'He is ready to leave Canada,' his lawyer said, 'but he does not admit being a spy.' Hampel, whose Russian name was not disclosed, was deported from Canada in December 2006 and the scandal was hushed up. Whether Lugovoy was acting as his contact or courier remains unknown.
10. Litvinenko Investigation, INQ005973-79.
11. Litvinenko Inquiry Hearings, Day 13, 25 Feb 2015, 67–8.
12. Litvinenko Investigation, INQ006481-88. See, for example, Luke Harding, 'Litvinenko report on Putin ally was motive enough for murder, inquiry told', *The Guardian*, 23 February 2015. See also, TV Dozhd, report of 30 April 2015.
13. A fifty-page BND report on drug trafficking and money laundering in Liechtenstein involving SPAG, dated 8 April 1999, was published by the Transborder Corruption Archive in June 2020 alongside other relevant documents, see https://tbcarchives.org/bnds-report-on-drug-trafficking-and-money-laundering-in-liechtenstein-1999-spag-company. See also, Roman Shleynov, 'Have some questions to ask the witness: The President of Russia', *Novaya Gazeta*, 18 (14 March 2005), in Russian.
14. Litvinenko Inquiry Hearings, Day 23, 11 March 2015, 162–8.

Chapter 6

1. Litvinenko Investigation, INQ003088.
2. Before joining the university, Mr Gannon served as the CIA's Director of European Analysis (1992–95), Deputy Director for Intelligence (1995–97), Assistant Director of Central Intelligence for Analysis and Production (1998–2001), and as Chairman of the National Intelligence Council (1997–2001).
3. Litvinenko Investigation, INQ003088.
4. One written by Litvinenko with Goldfarb and Akram Murtazaev, in Russian (2002), another with Felshtinsky, translated into English (2002 and 2007), and the last book, *Allegations* (London: Aquilion, 2007), which is a collection of Litvinenko's articles and interviews translated from Russian and edited by Pavel Stroilov.
5. Litvinenko Inquiry Hearings, Day 27, 18 March 2015, 66.
6. Including the protocols of the Parliamentary Investigation into Terrorism in Italy (established by law no. 499 of 23 December 1992), where one section is entitled 'The KGB's Influence on Italian Politics' ('l'Ombra del KGB sulla Politica Italiana'), 27 July 2000, 66–126, in addition to the set of documents shared by the British government with SISMI.
7. Litvinenko Investigation, INQ019505. Here and throughout the whole text, translators from Italian used the word 'exploration' instead of 'intelligence'. It is difficult to say how this misleading error could occur because in Italian it is 'servizi segreti e di intelligence', practically a calque of the English term.
8. Andrew and Mitrokhin, *The Mitrokhin Archive* (London: Allen Lane, 1999), 389 and 631. However, based on the analysis by the Office for the Documentation and Investigation of the Crimes of Communism (ÚDV) of the Czech police, researchers conclude that in the absence of a complete archival record, given that important documents were shredded, the full truth about the fact and nature of any Czechoslovak assistance to the Red Brigades remains unclear.
9. Litvinenko Investigation, INQ019505-07.
10. Litvinenko Investigation, INQ015758. It was established that a TASS correspondent with this name was accredited in Conakry, Guinea, in October 1968.
11. Litvinenko Investigation, INQ017459-60.
12. Velichko was a former mayor general of the KGB who had served in the 9th Directorate, where Lugovoy, Valuyev, and Sokolenko also served, from 1986 to 1991, during which time Velichko was also temporary seconded to Muammar Gaddafi's personal security detail and, as a security adviser, to the Soviet UN delegation in New York. In August 1991, Velichko supported the so-called State Committee on Emergency Situations, a coup d'état attempted by a group of the KGB officers and Communist Party officials against Mikhail Gorbachev and his reforms. Velichko was dismissed from the KGB and after a long investigation forced into retirement. In the 1990s, he was one of the founders of first private security companies, among others, the Russian

National Service of Economic Security together with Lt. General Vitaly M. Prilukov, Lt. General Leonid V. Shebarshin, and Lt. General Nikolai S. Leonov, all former KGB top brass investigated and fired for their support of the coup. In 2006, Velichko was President of the State Security Veterans Club. He is the author of the book *From the Lubyanka to the Kremlin* (Moscow: Aqua-Therm, 2013).
13. Litvinenko Investigation, INQ013784 (email of Monday, 30 October 2006, 12.58 pm).
14. Litvinenko Investigation, INQ017458.
15. Litvinenko Investigation, INQ019858.
16. Catherine Belton, *Putin's People* (London: William Collins, 2020), 335 and 343. One of the highest points was probably a secret meeting at a party in Italy (April 2018) between Boris Johnson, then Foreign Secretary, and Alexander Lebedev, a former KGB spy in London. In December 2020, Lebedev junior assumed office as a Member of the House of Lords, nominated for a life peerage by Boris Johnson, British prime minister and leader of the Conservative Party.
17. Roman Kupchinsky, 'Berlusconi, Centrex, Hexagon 1 and 2 and Gazprom', *Eurasia Daily Monitor*, 5/228 (1 December 2008).
18. Kristie Macrakis, *Seduced by Secrets: Inside the Stasi's Spy-Tech World* (Cambridge/NY: Cambridge University Press, 2008), 131; and Helmut Müller-Enbergs, *MfS-Handbuch, Hauptverwaltung A (HV A): Aufgaben – Strukturen – Quellen* (Berlin: BStU, 2011), 199.
19. Deutscher Bundestag, Beschlußempfehlung und Bericht des 2. Untersuchungsausschusses nach Artikel 44 des Grundgesetzes, Bonn, 28 May 1998, 176–182. The company was Forel Handels GmbH, through which 170 million DDR Marks were laundered.
20. Guy Chazan and David Crawford, 'A friendship forged in spying pays dividends in Russia today', *Wall Street Journal*, 23 February 2005. See also, Macrakis, *Seduced by Secrets*, 49.
21. Gidi Weitz, 'The Schlaff saga probe finds Austrian billionaire helped Lieberman fund his party', *Haaretz*, 8 September 2010; Barak Ravid and Ekiva Eldar, 'Liberman's support for Putin stuns many in foreign ministry', *Haaretz*, 9 December 2011; Anonymous, 'Russia-Ukraine conflict: Israel's Lieberman condemns war crimes but says there are "mutual accusations"', *Haaretz*, 4 April 2022.

Chapter 7
1. In the Litvinenko Inquiry Report, it is erroneously stated that 'in early 2003, Mr Ponkin came to London and tried to involve Mr Litvinenko in a plot to kill President Putin' (para 4.46, p. 60).
2. His book on the case is entitled *A Very Expensive Poison: The Definitive Story of the Murder of Litvinenko and Russia's War with the West* (2016).
3. The Litvinenko Inquiry Report (January 2016), para 4.46, p. 60.
4. Felshtinsky to the author, 3 July 2022.

5. Anonymous, 'Poisoned spy accused Putin of being a paedophile', *Mail Online*, 20 November 2006. See also, Litvinenko Inquiry Report, 5.27 page 92, and Litvinenko Investigation, BLK000134.
6. For details, see Alexander Litoy, 'From grenades to state awards', *The Insider*, 30 December 2021. See also, Transborder Corruption Archive, 'Lalakin junior (Podolskaya gang)'s property in Luxemburg' and 'Alexander Litvinenko's videotape transcript: protection of organized crime by FSB, parts 2 and 3', 1 August 2022.
7. Natalia Morar, 'Delo o Diskonte', *The New Times*, 15 (11 May); 16 (28 May); and 28 (20 August 2007).
8. Nataliya Gevorkyan, Natalya Timakova, and Andrei Kolesnikov, *First Person: An Astonishingly Frank Self-Portrait by Russia's President Vladimir Putin* (New York, NY: Public Affairs, 2000), 206.

Chapter 8

1. Litvinenko Inquiry Hearings, Day 11, 16 February 2015, 68.
2. Litvinenko Inquiry Hearings, Day 25, 16 March 2015, 38–43.
3. Litvinenko Inquiry Hearings, Day 9, 11 February 2015, 38–48; and INQ002850-51.
4. Litvinenko Inquiry Hearings, Day 10, 12 February 2015, 83.
5. Litvinenko Investigation, INQ002885-8.
6. 'In fact, their clothing was so oddly matched and coloured it was almost comical so it stuck in my mind. Kovtun was wearing a shiny silvery metallic polyester type suit with a shirt and tie … Lugovoy was wearing a dark grey checked suit, shirt and tie and similar shoes, both men were wearing a lot of gold jewellery, bracelets and rings, I believe.' Litvinenko Investigation, INQ002885-88. It seems Mr Krgo watched a Russian mafia film shortly before he gave this evidence.
7. As part of his legend, Lugovoy claimed to have been affiliated with three private security companies in Moscow: Gardé X, Capital-Shield, and Ninth Wave, but was never able to produce any proof confirming his involvement with or ownership of a stake in these companies. At the time of writing, Vladimir Valuyev was registered as the owner and founder of Ninth Wave. A small private company, EVP-Holding, possibly a dummy, was incorporated in April 2005 as a consultancy, registered by a bogus founder/director and dissolved shortly after the Litvinenko Inquiry was completed. It is possible that during that 1.34 pm telephone call from Moscow, Lugovoy told his controllers about his and Kovtun's exercises with poison in the room.
8. Litvinenko Inquiry Report, 6.109–6.111, 132–3.
9. For details, see E. Carvalho, S. Fernandes, S. Fesenko, E. Holm, B. Howard, P. Martin, M. Phaneuf, D. Porcelli, G. Pröhl, and J. Twining, *The Environmental Behaviour of Polonium* (Vienna: IAEA, 2017), 175. The becquerel (Bq) is defined as the activity of a quantity of radioactive material in which one nucleus decays per second.

Notes

10. Professor Dr Bogdan Skwarzec to author, 10 June 2022.
11. John Harrison, Tim Fell, Rich Leggett, David Lloyd, Matthew Puncher and Mike Youngman, 'The polonium-210 poisoning of Mr. Alexander Litvinenko', *Journal of Radiological Protection*, 37 (2017), 266–278.
12. VOLNA was a KGB name of one of the secret channels of delivery of hazardous materials to and from the USSR. Usually, the Aeroflot flights were used for the purpose and the container was placed in the pilots' cabin where one of the pilots was an intelligence officer, agent, or a co-optee. According to published evidence of at least one former KGB officer who used to deal with VOLNA before and after the collapse of the Soviet Union, after 1991 the use of this method of transportation increased. See Volodarsky, *The KGB's Poison Factory*, 265n24.
13. Litvinenko Inquiry Report, 6.111, 132.
14. Litvinenko Inquiry, INQ014291 (p. 8) and INQ016745 (p. 10).
15. Litvinenko Inquiry Hearings, Day 19, 11 Feb 2015, 124.
16. That evening after they parted, a telephone exchange is registered between Litvinenko and Lugovoy. At half past ten (22:35:12), Litvinenko called and left a voice message. Half an hour later (22.08.41), he repeated the call, again without success. Lugovoy called back twice (at 22:50:10 and 23:09:27), telling Sasha that they were having good time riding rickshaw in Soho. The last two times, Litvinenko dialled Lugovoy's number (23:35:14 and 23:35:25) but no one picked up the phone, so he left voice messages and switched off.
17. Litvinenko Inquiry Hearings, Day 14, 24 Feb 2015, 181–2.
18. Litvinenko Inquiry, INQ002838-49; Litvinenko Inquiry Report, Day 11, 16 Feb 2015, 1–99.
19. Litvinenko Investigation, INQ002820.
20. Litvinenko Inquiry Hearings, Day 10, 12 Feb 2015, 192.
21. Litvinenko Inquiry Hearings, Day 11, 16 Feb 2015, 128–30.
22. Evidence obtained as part of Operation WHIMBREL and not included in the Inquiry documents.
23. Litvinenko Investigation, INQ016604, Litvinenko interviews at UCLH, Critical Care Unit, 19 Nov 2006, 1900–1930 hours, p. 7 of 11.
24. For a comprehensive story about Badri and Boris, their longtime friendship and 'divorce', see Suzanne Andrews, 'The Widow and the Oligarchs', *Vanity Fair*, October 2009. Martin Pompadur and Vladimir Voronoff were also interviewed for this article.
25. Litvinenko Investigation, INQ016341.
26. Litvinenko Inquiry Hearings, Day 14, 24 February 2015, 48.
27. Lugovoy was lying as usual when he said that Berezovsky or his secretary called him when he was at Badri's mansion. In reality, he himself called Berezovsky's office twice, at two (14:09:06) and five o'clock (17:16:58) and Berezovsky's secretary called him back a few minutes later (17:19:51) to arrange a meeting for Friday, October 27, in the afternoon.

Chapter 9

1. Litvinenko Inquiry Report, 145 and 277.
2. Litvinenko Inquiry Hearings, Day 14, 24 Feb 2015, 118 and 122.
3. Litvinenko Investigation, INQ003141.
4. Litvinenko Investigation, INQ012693. Darya left Eco3 Capital in late 2007.
5. Litvinenko Inquiry Hearings, Day 14, 24 Feb 2015, 188–9.
6. Litvinenko Inquiry Report, 6.173, 145.
7. There are four telephone calls from Lugovoy to Berezovsky at 10:44:26, 11:21:07, 11:36:20, and 12:06:05.
8. Lugovoy first called Litvinenko at 16:38:10, then Litvinenko called back (16:47:37) leaving a message, and then Lugovoy called Litvinenko again twice (16:47:51 and 16:48:04).
9. Litvinenko Investigation, INQ002907-08, INQ016371-72. See also, Litvinenko Inquiry Hearings, Day 17, 27 Feb 2015, 21: 'Q. It is possible that you might have got the date of this wrong, that it might actually have been 27 October? Glushkov. No.'
10. A call from Litvinenko to the Pescatori was registered at 18:23:11. On the way to his tube station, he called Shamil Zakayev (18:32:10), the son of Akhmed Zakayev, probably asking him whether his father was planning to travel back home and could perhaps pick him up. It seems Akhmed was busy and Sasha travelled by tube.
11. Litvinenko Inquiry Report, 6.183–4, 146.
12. Litvinenko Inquiry Hearings, Day 20, 4 March 2015, 49–57; Litvinenko Inquiry, INQ017917.
13. See Anan Sadovnikova, Hans Hoyng, Thomas Hüetlin, and Uwe Klußmann, '"Walking dirty bomb" tells of London meetings', *Spiegel International*, 11 December 2006. Before this article was published, Anna Sadovnikova visited London with a team from Spiegel TV discussing details of the Litvinenko case with Oleg Gordievsky and this writer. I am grateful to Anna for sending me the footage of her interview with Kovtun.
14. Litvinenko Investigation, Operation WHIMBREL, INQ015298-5305.
15. Litvinenko Investigation, Operation WHIMBREL, INQ013877-885. At the time, Frau Wall cohabitated with her partner Hartmut Kohnke in Haselau. Herr Kohnke was managing director of Garant Private Vermögensverwaltung, a private property management company which owned the house where Marina and Kovtun lived alongside other rental properties. In one of them, at Max-Brauer-Allee in Hamburg-Altona, Kovtun was still registered as the principal tenant, a businessman from St Petersburg, at least until April 2009.
16. Litvinenko Investigation, Operation WHIMBREL, INQ015282.
17. Litvinenko Investigation, Operation WHIMBREL, INQ013886-92 of 9 December 2006.
18. Litvinenko Investigation, INQ013557.
19. Litvinenko Investigation, Operation WHIMBREL, 20 November 2006, INQ016643-44. When Mr Hyatt made a telephone call to the number provided

Notes

by Sasha, it turned out the person on the other end was an SIS officer from the Russian Desk at the Vauxhall Cross head office who figures in the Inquiry documents as 'Martin'.
20. Litvinenko Investigation, INQ013811-12.
21. Litvinenko Investigation, Operation WHIMBREL, INQ002747.
22. Ibid., INQ002748.
23. In the Declaration that he made at the British embassy in Moscow on 23 November 2006, Kovtun gave a different explanation for this trip: 'The second time that I came to London was on 1 November 2006. I came from Hamburg having agreed my visit with Continental Petroleum Ltd, with the aim of passing several documents to one of the members of the Board, Dr Shadrin. Mr Lugovoy was present at the talks with Dr Shadrin as my main partner in the oil field development projects.' Litvinenko Inquiry Report, 6.242–6.250, 157–159.
24. Litvinenko Inquiry, INQ019296, Part 2.
25. See Boris Volodarsky, *Assassins* (Frontline Books, 2019), 248–64.
26. Litvinenko Investigation, INQ012674-5.
27. Litvinenko Inquiry Hearings, Day 16, 26 Feb 2015, 23–4.
28. Litvinenko Investigation, Operation WHIMBREL, INQ015216-17. To be fair – no one asked Sokolenko about SMS messages.
29. Litvinenko Investigation, Operation WHIMBREL, INQ002748.
30. In digital forensics, Cell Site Analysis is the process through which the raw Call Data Records (CDRs) for a cell phone are used to identify the potential location of the phone (James Matthews, cyfor.co.uk).
31. Litvinenko Inquiry Hearings, Day 25, 16 March 2015, 23.
32. Litvinenko Investigation, INQ015656-7.
33. Litvinenko Investigation, Operation WHIMBREL, INQ002748.
34. Litvinenko Inquiry Report, 6.253, 160.
35. Litvinenko Investigation, INQ012693.
36. 'Andrew O'Connor QC, Counsel to the Inquiry: Is it right that for this period that we're now looking at – so between about 11.00 and 12.00 and the early afternoon of 1 November – you have not undertaken the more sophisticated cell siting on Mr Lugovoy's phone? Mascall: No. Due to, you know, the cost of doing cell siting, the more extensive cell siting, and at the time that was not done for that particular period.' Litvinenko Inquiry Hearings, Day 16, 26 February 2015, 45–9 (47).
37. Litvinenko Inquiry Hearings, Day 14, 24 Feb 2015, 191–3.
38. Litvinenko Investigation, INQ003101.
39. Litvinenko Investigation, Operation AVOCET, INQ017900-905; Radiation schedule INQ017973-82.

Chapter 10
1. Litvinenko Investigation, INQ003118-9 and INQ016310.
2. Litvinenko Investigation, INQ016310.

3. Veterans of the US secret service's Office of Technical Service, after retirement – widely popular writers and masters of disguise, who specialised in support of clandestine and covert CIA operations in various places including Moscow.
4. Litvinenko Investigation, Operation AVOCET, INQ017916.
5. An article in *The Washington Post* (by Erica Frantz and Joseph Wright, 2 March 2022) mentioning Putin's brazen decision to invade Ukraine compares him with other dictators whose decisions appeared unpredictable and misguided – men like Libya's Moammar Gaddafi, Uganda's Idi Amin, and Turkmenistan's Saparmurad Niyazov. 'In these and other instances,' the paper writes, 'paranoid and erratic authoritarian behaviour was a product of years of "personalist rule" – when leaders successfully concentrate powers in their own hands.'
6. For details, see Tatsuji Namba, 'Cholinesterase inhibition by organophosphorus compounds and its clinical effects', *Bull World Health Organ*, 44/1-2-3 (1971), 289–307. The Wikipedia (English) article describing Navalny's poisoning is wrong in many aspects.
7. Although the foreign intelligence service of Russia underwent many changes, Directorate S (S for special operations) still exists and its officers continue to work at the Yasenevo headquarters, in the SVR stations (residences) under the roof of Russian embassies abroad (Line N), and as Russian 'illegals' in the West. Several of this directorate's departments had been responsible for planning and carrying out 'special tasks', known in the West as executive actions and in Directorate S as 'direct actions'. This is a euphemism for subversion, sabotage, terrorist acts, and targeted killings. One of the units, Department 8, specialised in using complex poisons and bio-agents in addition to other deadly substances in their covert operations.
8. Litvinenko Investigation, COM00181003-4.
9. It is a translator's mistake. Should be spelt Vadim. Due to his condition, Sasha had mixed up two similar sounding names – Vadim and Dima. Lugovoy was calling Kovtun by his first name: Dima, which is a Russian diminutive for Dimitry or Dmitry – Dmitry Kovtun. Instead of 'Dima', Litvinenko said 'Vadim' and the translator transcribed it as 'Vajim'.
10. Litvinenko Investigation, INQ002479-81 (compilation).
11. In his critical condition, Sasha mixed up the names again. Volodya is a short form for Vladimir. During an earlier meeting with Lugovoy, Vladimir Valuyev was introduced to him as Lugovoy's 'business partner', and on 16 October it was Dima, a Russian diminutive of Dmitry, Kovtun's given name.
12. Litvinenko Investigation, INQ016595-6.
13. Litvinenko Investigation, INQ017502.
14. Litvinenko Investigation, INQ016596. This interview was conducted at hospital by DI Brent Hyatt between 18.00 and 18.57 on 19 November 2006, four days before Litvinenko died. Taking his condition, Sasha could not think clearly and he confused Dmitry Kovtun, who was present at that meeting, with Vladimir ('Volodya') Valuyev, whom he had met earlier in the company of Lugovoy.
15. Litvinenko Investigation, INQ002903-4.

Chapter 11

1. Hayman with Margaret Gilmore, *The Terrorist Hunters*, 226–68.
2. Hayman with Margaret Gilmore, *The Terrorist Hunters*, 231. In reality, on Clive Timmons's instructions, samples of Litvinenko's blood and urine were sent to AWE for testing, arriving there in the early evening of 21 October. On the next day, during a meeting between police officers, the forensic science service, AWE, and Porton Down, the results, which revealed the presence of polonium, were discussed but dismissed. Then DSU Timmons requested that a 'living post-mortem' be carried out on Litvinenko in order to establish the cause of his condition. The results, which confirmed the polonium contamination, were communicated to the police between 3.00 pm and 5.00 pm on 23 November. See Litvinenko Inquiry Report, 39.
3. Nikolai D. Kovalyov, FSB director (June 1996–July 1998).
4. Anatoly V. Trofimov, colonel general, Deputy Director of the FSK and Chief of the FSK (from April 1995 – FSB) Directorate for Moscow and Moscow Oblast (January 1995–February 1997).
5. Litvinenko Investigation, INQ002076-79.
6. Litvinenko Investigation, INQ002450.
7. Ray Wilson and Ian Adams, *Special Branch: A History, 1883–2006* (London: Biteback, 2015), Introduction.
8. Litvinenko Inquiry Hearings, 33/8.
9. For a transcript of a conversation, see INQ016789-96; for David Leppard's article in *The Sunday Times* of 19 November 2006, see INQ018413-6.
10. Litvinenko Investigation, INQ016641.
11. See Luke Harding, 'How Trump walked into Putin's web', *The Guardian*, 15 November 2017.
12. See Joseph L. Albini, R. E. Rogers, Viktor Shabalin, Valery Kutushev, Vladimir Moiseev, and Julie Anderson, 'Russian organized crime: Its history, structure and function'. See also, Michael J. Waller and Victor J. Yasmann, 'Russia's great criminal revolution: The role of the security services', both in *Journal of Contemporary Criminal Justice*, 11/4 (December 1995).
13. On 9 February 2004, the creation of what would become known as the Serious Organised Crime Agency (SOCA) was announced. The SOCA was formed in April 2006. Its first founding non-executive chairman was Sir Stephen Lander, former DG of the security service (MI5). It operated within the UK, also collaborating with British and foreign intelligence services and law enforcement agencies.
14. The Wikipedia (English) article on Mogilevich states that 'according to the U.S. diplomatic cables, he controls RosUkrEnergo, a company actively involved in Russia-Ukraine gas disputes', and that RosUkrEnergo is a partner of Raiffeisen Bank (Austria).
15. As follows from the audio files, Putin personally knew Mogilevich. On 8 February 2000, Kuchma's recorded conversation with General Derkach, the head of the SBU at that time, revealed they were discussing some issues that

Mogilevich promised Kuchma he would solve. In the course of the conversation, it transpired that Derkach recently met with Mogilevich. By that time, the latter had already settled down in Russia, bought a summer house near Moscow and had a good personal relationship with Putin in St Petersburg. The next conversation about Mogilevich took place two days later, on 10 February 2000. The head of the GUR (military intelligence of Ukraine) General Smeshko reported to Kuchma that Mogilevich had been the KGB (and later SVR) agent since Soviet times. See the database of the Free Russia Forum PUTIN'S LIST 'Mogilevich Semyon'.

16. Glenn R. Simpson, 'U.S. probes possible crime links to Russian natural gas deals', *Wall Street Journal*, 22 December 2006.
17. For details, see Meier, *Spooked*, 259–61. See also, Glenn Simpson and Peter Fitsch, *Crime in Progress: Inside the Steele Dossier and the Fusion GPS Investigation of Donald Trump* (New York: Random House, 2019). 'Shvets' overall analysis of the Steele dossier was uncannily accurate – far more accurate and far more prescient that any contemporary US observer,' Barry Meier writes.
18. See Harding, 'How Trump walked into Putin's web'. 'One reason for this [Steele's involvement in the Litvinenko investigation on behalf of MI6,]' he writes, 'was that he wasn't emotionally involved with the case, unlike some of his colleagues who had known the victim. He quickly concluded the Russian state had staged the execution.' It is interesting where the journalist obtained this information. In his opening statement on the first day of the Litvinenko Inquiry hearings, Neil Garnham QC, who appeared on behalf of the then home secretary Theresa May, explained the position of the British government 'to neither confirm nor deny assertions, allegations, or speculation in relation to security and intelligence agencies' and this specifically concerned the Litvinenko investigation.
19. See Terri Judd, 'Strange truth of a life caught up with MI6's "Martin" and the KGB', *Independent*, 14 December 2012.
20. Litvinenko Investigation, INQ016643-4.
21. Litvinenko Inquiry Report, 3.135–3.137, 40–41. See also Litvinenko Inquiry Hearings, Day 24, 12 March 2015, 92.
22. Litvinenko Investigation, INQ002465.
23. Hayman with Margaret Gilmore, *The Terrorist Hunters*, 231–2.
24. Given the importance of the matter, Sir Peter Ricketts (later Lord Ricketts), PUS for Foreign Affairs, Sir Richard Mottram, Security and Intelligence Coordinator (later retitled Permanent Secretary, Intelligence, Security and Resilience in the Cabinet Office) and chairman of the Joint Intelligence Committee, and Sir John Scarlett, the Chief of SIS, were probably also present.
25. COBRA is usually chaired by the home secretary or prime minister and brings together 'all of the various elements from the various departments and intelligence agencies' to 'supply support, [and] make sure that in real time everybody is working on the same information picture'. COBRA is reactive,

temporary, and ad hoc and formed in the immediate aftermath of an attack for a 'specific purpose [and] for a specific period'. COBRA is chiefly responsible for the production of the Commonly Recognised Information Pattern, or CRIP. The CRIP helps ensure that after an attack everybody involved in counter-terrorist activity is sharing information and working from the same information. See House of Commons, HC 117-I (London: The Stationary Office Limited, 2 February 2010), 5.
26. See, for example, a long and detailed report by Alan Cowell, 'London riddle: A Russian spy, a lethal dose', *The New York Times*, 25 November 2006.
27. Hayman with Margaret Gilmore, *The Terrorist Hunters*, 237.
28. Hayman with Margaret Gilmore, *The Terrorist Hunters*, 239–40.
29. Marina Hyde, 'London 2012's judo highlight: David Cameron v Vladimir Putin', *The Guardian*, 2 August 2012.
30. An inquest into Litvinenko's death was opened on 30 November 2006 but was adjourned pending the police investigation and any criminal proceedings. On 13 October 2011, the inquest was resumed by the Coroner Dr Andrew Reid, it having become clear that there was no realistic prospect of the suspects facing a criminal trial. On 7 August 2012, Sir Robert Owen was appointed to conduct the inquest. See 'In the High Court of Justice, Queen Bench Division, Divisional Court', Case No: CO/12683/2013, 11 February 2014.
31. Like Harding, 'Litvinenko inquest coroner agrees to keep crucial evidence secret', *The Guardian*, 17 May 2013.
32. Litvinenko Inquiry Hearings, Day 33, 30 July 2015, 73. Robert John Service is a British historian who until 2013 was a professor of Russian history at Oxford University. He was invited as an expert witness on certain topics of recent Russian affairs.
33. Litvinenko Investigation, INQ017563. As sometimes happens, Litvinenko was recruited on his own initiative. That is, he asked a contact to recommend him, and a meeting was arranged with an officer in a quiet café in Central London.
34. Litvinenko Investigation, INQ017563-4.
35. Litvinenko Inquiry Hearings, Day 33, 30 July 2015, 61.
36. See Institute for Government: Public Inquiries, 21 May 2018. The Institute for Government in London is the leading thinktank working to make government more effective.
37. Epstein, 'The spectre that haunts the death of Litvinenko', *The New York Sun*, 19 March 2008. In her supportive article, Mary Dejevsky argues that 'we're still not being told the whole, chilling story'. 'There is another, and perhaps bigger, problem,' she writes. 'Scientists who know anything about polonium-210 find it hard to believe that anyone would choose it as a murder weapon against one individual, even if the purpose was to evade detection. For a start, it is extremely expensive. But it also fits much more comfortably into another scenario: that of nuclear smuggling. It seems far more likely that the polonium tracked in London was part of some sort of deal – a deal that, for whatever reason, went disastrously wrong. … Demand for polonium-210

on the illegal international market is as a key element in detonating a nuclear explosion. This is why it commands such a fantastically high price – hundreds of thousands, if not the many millions, of dollars mentioned by some.' See 'The Litvinenko files: Was he really murdered?' *Independent*, 1 May 2008.
38. Litvinenko Investigation, INQ014611-2. See also INQ014613.
39. Litvinenko Investigation, INQ018946-61.
40. Litvinenko Inquiry Report, Chapter 4, 8.28–8.33, p. 187.
41. Litvinenko Inquiry Evidence, LUG000062, Confidential report.
42. Litvinenko Inquiry Evidence, LUG000045, UCLH discharge summary.
43. Litvinenko Inquiry Report, Chapter 5, 9.28, p. 213. See also, Litvinenko Inquiry Hearings, Day 19, 3 March 2015, 67–73.
44. Litvinenko Inquiry Report, Chapter 6, 6.101 and 6.292.
45. Litvinenko Inquiry Report, Chapter 6, 8.70, p. 193.
46. Porfiry Petrovich, F. M. Dostoevsky, *Crime and Punishment* (1866).
47. Litvinenko Inquiry Hearings, Horwell 33/13.
48. In addition to several already mentioned companies, and there are many, many more where Shadrin (DOB: 11 October 1965) figures as director or secretary, one should pay attention to Eco3 Corporate Administration Ltd, Company No. 5989663, incorporated five days after the Litvinenko operation on 6 November 2006. By the time of this book's publication, it had been renamed Innovation Admin Ltd with Dr Alexander Shadrin (dir.), Nikolai Gorokhov (dir.), Valery Dyskin (dir.), and Dariya Pridmore (secr.) – bah, familiar faces! The company was initially registered at the same address at 58 Grosvenor Street, W1K, but was then reregistered to number 60, together with Hamilton Bradshaw, a management consultancy.
49. In December 2017, the British newspapers ran a story how Roderick Francis Arthur Balfour (Lord Balfour) was terribly upset and outraged that his children would inherit neither the title nor the family home because all four were female. Instead, the earldom would pass to his younger brother Charles.
50. He previously worked for Tower Management Ltd, 4–6 Savile Row, then as director of Xtra, a private company of Boris Berezovsky, and then as 'managing consultant' at SFR Solutions at 7 Down Street.
51. Litvinenko Inquiry Hearings, Day 16, 26 February 2015, 188. Previously, he was also interviewed by DC B. Eager on 24 November 2006 (INQ003176) and DC Philip Booth on 18 January 2007 (INQ016356).

Epilogue
1. Dmitry Gordon, 'We don't choose the times we live in' – interview with Boris Berezovsky, part 2, *Bulvar Gordona*, 9 (28 February 2012).
2. Luke Harding, 'Boris Berezovsky: A tale of revenge, betrayal and feuds with Putin', *The Observer*, 23 March 2013.
3. Litvinenko Inquiry Report, 8.97, 196.
4. Litvinenko Inquiry Report, 9.187–9.200, 239–40.
5. Litvinenko Inquiry Report, 9.215, 244.

Notes

6. See Volodarsky, *Assassins*, 14 and 229.
7. Litvinenko Investigation, INQ017600 and INQ017655.
8. See Litvinenko Inquiry Report, 8.132–8.147, 203–5. The inquiry chairman was not satisfied with these results. He concluded: 'In summary, I have no doubt that I should place no weight at all on the outcome of this test – in part because of shortcomings in the way that the test was conducted, in part because of Mr Lugovoy's unsuitability as a subject of the test, and in part because of the risk that Mr Lugovoy took deliberate steps to defeat the test.'
9. Litvinenko Investigation, INQ017655. Boris Berezovsky interviewed by Alexander Otvodov, investigator for major cases of the Russian Prosecutor General's Office, 30 March 2007.

Index

A1 (scientist, unidentified Inquiry expert) 120, 125, 134, 141
Abdullayev, Yaragi 'Yasha' 107, 173
Abramovich, Roman 7, 14, 16, 26, 30, 63, 134
Agartanov, Vladimir (KGB Dresden, later emigrated to Czechia, pen name 'Usoltsev') 19
Akimov, Andrey 97
Aksenov, Yuri (GRU) 95
al-Zawahiri, Ayman 88
Albert II, King of the Belgians 174
Albright, Madeleine 38, 40
Alexander I, Emperor of Russia, King of Congress Poland and Grand Duke of Finland 22
Aliokhin, Aleksey 103–4, 105
Amendola, Giorgio 89
Amundsen Minneside, Ivar 114, 115
Ananyev, Yevgeny 15, 16
Andrade, Noberto 161–4, 168
Andrew, Professor Christopher M. 40, 42, 197
Androsov, Stanislav (head of KGB station in Washington, 1982–6; then head of the FCD's 1st department: USA, Canada, 1986–89) 19
Antonov, Anatoly Ivanovich, Russian ambassador in Washington from August 2017, the only ambassador in the world under international sanctions 100
Atlangeriev, Movladi, nicknamed 'Lord' and 'Lenin' 31, 32
Attew, Dean Martin 70, 71–2, 77–80, 81, 84, 135, 146, 147, 154, 157, 158, 160
Austria (see also Vienna) 2, 8, 15, 19, 47, 51, 95, 96, 97–8, 99, 110, 190, 191
Aven, Petr 1, 2, 3, 8, 9, 11, 12, 14, 16, 17–18, 21, 22, 111
AVOCET, Operation 159, 191

Babinov, Oleg 152–3
Balfour, Hon Charles George Yule 137, 194
Barnett, Neil 157
Barsukov, Mikhail 4, 203
Batten, Gerard 114, 159, 160
Beck, Suzanna 183
Beckett, Margaret 18
Bedford, Peter 32
Beer, Jason 189
Begak, Maxim 146, 149, 162–3, 165, 170–1, 172, 193
Bell Pottinger 29, 30
Bell, Lord Timothy 'Tim' 29, 30, 33, 177
Belton, Catherine 11, 97, 195
Beltsova, Olga 15, 16
Berezovsky, Boris Abramovich
    in Britain – Platon Elenin 1–19, 20–33
    and Litvinenko's escape from Russia 34–45, 46
    political asylum in the UK 102
    and IFCL 21, 27, 54, 106, 115

Index

and Litvinenko's funeral 114
and Litvinenko's retainer 115, 116
'I shall probably be hanged...' 196
Berezovsky's Time (2018) 1
Berlusconi, Silvio 91, 95, 96–7, 108
Bertossa, Bernard 14
Black, Dr Stuart (expert) 125
Blair, Tony 18, 175, 184
Blake, Heidi 17
Blears, Hazel Anne 28
Bloomberg 8, 97, 209
Bolshakov, Alexey 7
Bonetti, Mario 133
Bonini, Carlo 11, 83
Bonner, Elena 27
Booth, Philip 154
Bordyuzha, Nikolai 13, 14
Borodin, Pavel 7, 8–9, 12, 14–15, 16, 25
Bortnikov, Alexander 103, 110–11, 203
Brightwell, Tony 75
Brinkmann, Professor Bernd 32
Brown, Nigel 74
Bukovsky, Vladimir 50, 113, 114–15
Bulgakov, Mikhail Afanasyevich 85
Bush, George W. 14, 38, 44–5, 205
Bushlanov, Konstantin 13
Butkov, Mikhail (KGB Oslo under journalistic cover, defected) 179
Butterworth, Matthew 131

Cadman, David 101
Cameron, David 186
Carter, James 'Jimmy' 34
Chekulin, Nikita 59, 60–61, 65, 66–9, 70, 188
Chemezov, Sergey (KGB Dresden, later – CEO of Rostec Corporation) 19
Chibber, Akshay 77
Chubais, Anatoly 17, 87
Churchill, Sir Winston Leonard Spencer 17
Churchill Archives Centre 87
Clark, Paul 105

Clarke, Peter 177, 183, 184–5
Clinton, William Jefferson 'Bill' 38
Connor, Gregory John 16
Cormac, Graham Neil 158
Cossiga, Francesco 90
Cotlick, Michael (aka Misha Kotlik) 72, 78, 115, 116
Cowell, Alan S. 104
Curie, Pierre and Marie (Maria Skłodowska) 121, 190
Curtis, Stephen 74, 136, 138

D'Avanzo, Giuseppe 11, 63
Davies, Barry 168
Davies, Hugh 116, 124, 126, 128–9, 137, 155, 160, 195
Davison, Dariya (aka Dariya Pridmore) 126, 128, 136, 155
de Klerk, Frederik Willem 172
del Ponte, Carla 8, 10, 12–13
Deniau, Jean-Charles 63
Denisenko, Maria 55
Deripaska, Oleg 73, 209
Derkach, Leonid 81
Dewhirst, Martin 30, 48, 135
Diana, Princess of Wales 69
Dodin, Lev 83
Dorenko, Sergei 26
Douglas, David 69
Draper, Frances 41
Dresden 19, 24, 47, 97, 98, 109
Dubov, Yuli 21, 27, 33, 65, 83, 102, 172
Dudayev, Dzhokhar 5, 24, 94–5
Dyachenko, Leonid 12
Dyachenko, Tatiana (née Tatiana Yeltsina aka Tatiana Yumasheva) 9, 12, 211n23

Ecclestone, Bernard Charles 'Bernie' 70
Elizabeth II, Queen of the United Kingdom and other Commonwealth realms (from February 1952 to September 2022) 160

Elyashkevich, Alexander (Oleksandr Yeliashkevych) 52
Emmerson, Ben QC 81, 182, 186
Epishin, Dmitry 51
Epstein, Edward Jay 17, 190
Ernst, Konstantin 26
Eurasia Daily Monitor 97, 217
Evans, Garym 73, 74–5
Evans, Mary Anne, known by her pen name George Eliot 115

Faraday, Michael 115
Farr, Sir Charles 'Charlie' 18–19, 178, 180, 185, 188
Federyakov, Sergey (codename Comrade ALLEN) 51
Fell, Nicholas 137
Felshtinsky, Yuri 2, 14, 17, 20–21, 34–7, 45, 46, 48–9, 50, 52–3, 54, 60, 63, 82–3, 107, 109, 113, 180, 188
Flint, Martin 61, 63, 68–70, 135
Fomichev, Ruslan 138
Forsyth, Frederick 28, 206
Friedman, Mikhail 3, 19, 208–9
Frolov, Mikhail 109
Fuglevaag Warsinski (later Warsinska-Varsi), Maria 114

Gaidar, Yegor 119, 198, 210
Galeotti, Mark 110
Ganchev, Andrey 88
Gannon, John 87, 216
García, Robert Flórez 198
Gazelle, Charles 63
Gent, Dr Robert Nicolas (expert) 125
Gerashchenko, Victor 10
Gessen, Masha 211
Glushkov, Nikolai 13, 22–3, 54–5, 58, 62–3, 72, 106–8, 139, 151, 154, 189, 194, 212
Goldfarb, Alexander 'Alex' 3, 4–5, 11, 12, 14, 16, 21, 25, 27, 29, 31, 33, 37, 38–39, 40, 42–5, 48, 50, 52–5, 58–61, 62, 73, 83, 94, 101, 106–7, 112, 114–15, 175, 177, 178, 180, 188, 190–91, 196, 210–11, 213, 216
Golushko, Nikolai 202
Gongadze, Georgy 49, 51, 52–3
Gorbachev, Mikhail Sergeyevich 10, 179, 210, 216
Gorbunova, Elena aka Helena (aka Lena Berezovskaya) 13, 16, 18, 25, 114
Gordeyev, Alexey V. 76–7, 128
Gordievsky, Oleg (MI6 codename FELIX, after defection codenamed GNAT by the KGB) 31, 53, 77, 116, 159, 168, 179, 183, 189, 195, 220
Gore, Albert 'Al' 38
Gorokhov, Nikolai 130, 136–7, 155, 226
Greenberg, Vitaly 17
Greenslade, Roy 183
Grinda, Gonzalez José 78, 109, 198
Gromov, Alexey 'Liosha' 2, 209
Gusak, Alexander 103
Gusenbauer, Alfred 97
Gusinsky, Vladimir 3, 74
Guzzanti, Paolo 87, 88, 91, 92, 95, 99, 159

Haaretz 97, 99, 217
Hague, William 186
Hain, Peter 69
Harding, Luke 33, 104, 181, 186
Harman, Lisa 137, 206
Harrison, John 122, 125, 192
Hason, Michael 98
Haspel, Gina Cheri Walker 43, 44
Havel, Václav 172
Hayman, Andy 18–19, 174–7, 183, 184–5
Heifetz, Grigory (also spelled 'Kheifetz' and 'Kheifits') 54
Hinstein, Alexander 59, 214
Hitler 46, 110

Index

Hoar, Christopher 'Chris' 170, 175, 176, 182–3
Hoban, Michael 76
Höhne, Inna (née Davletova, after her first marriage Yamatina) 143
Höhne, Frank 143
Hollingsworth, Mark 138
Holmes, John Taylor 70–71, 77, 79, 81
Horwell, Richard 189, 193
Hunter, Keith 73, 74–76, 111
Hussein, Saddam 48
Hyatt, Brent 147, 170, 175, 176–8, 181, 182–3, 220, 222

Idrisova, Angelina 119, 120, 127, 146, 154, 158, 163
Idun, Zac 82
Ilyukhin, Viktor 12, 211
Ivankov, Vyacheslav, mob nickname 'Yaponchik' 110
Ivanov, Viktor Petrovich (former KGB, later chairman of Aeroflot, currently President of the Association 'Russian House of International Scientific and Technical Cooperation') 80–81, 110, 198

Jackson, Andrew 7
Johnson, Boris 29, 217
Jolly, Mike 178
Jost, Patrick 76

Kabayeva, Alina 26
Kadyrov, Akhmad 31
Kadyrov, Ramzan 31
Kalugin, Oleg D. 53, 80–81
Kalugin, Yuri V. 104
Kalvītis, Aigars 52
Kennedy, Edward M. 38
Khodorkovsky, Mikhail 3, 16, 74, 212
Khokhlov, Nikolai (codename WHISTLER) 53
Khokholkov, Yevgeny 24, 94
Kirillov, Sergey 108

Kiriyenko, Sergey 12
Klebnikov, Paul 21, 31
Klima, Viktor 98
Knuckey, Clifford 'Cliff' 74–5, 128–9
Kodanev, Mikhail 22
Köhler, Herbert 98
Kolesnikov, Andrei 218
Konopikhin, Felix 91
Korpan, Dr Nikolai 54
Korzhakov, Alexander 3, 4, 55, 201
Koshkariova, Tatyana 26
Kovalev, Nikolai 203
Kovtun, Dmitri 83, 84, 108, 117, 118–20, 122–31, 137, 140–45, 146, 149, 150–57, 161, 162–3, 167, 168, 170–72, 182–3, 185, 189, 192–3, 196, 206, 218, 220–21, 222
Kozlov, Andrei 110
Kozlov, Vladimir 58, 60
Kravchenko, Yuri 51
Krgo, Goran 119, 218
Krikun, Serafim 47
Kruglov, Anatoly 16, 212
Kryuchkov, Vladimir 57
Kuchma, Leonid 48–51, 53, 65, 81, 106, 223
Kudrin, Alexey 7, 25
Kudykov, David 115
Kupchinsky, Roman 97
Kuzichkin, Vladimir 179

Lady, Robert Seldon 87
Lalakin, Sergey, nicknamed 'Luchok' 110, 218
Lansley, Stewart 138
Lavrov, Sergey 100
Lebedev, Alexander 133, 217
Lebedev, Sergey (KGB Karlshorst, head of Washington station, later executive secretary CIS) 47
Lekarev, Stanislav 205
Lenin 103, 165
Leppard, David 28–9, 101, 103, 178, 182–3

Leshchev, Yury (KGB Karlshorst, controller of KGB station in Dresden BV) 47
LeVine, Steve 65
Lewis, Julian 28
Lichfield, Patrick 35
Lieberman, Avigdor 99, 217
Limarev, Lev 55, 56–7
Limarev, Yevgeny or Eugeny 'Zhenya' 10, 55, 56–60, 63, 73, 91, 92, 153, 158–9, 160, 188, 214
Litvinenko, Alexander (Sasha), alias 'Alexander Volkov', in Britain – Edwin Redwald Carter:
  attempted defection to the USA 36, 38–9, 42–3, 44
  author's meeting with 48, 52–3, 54
  Berezovsky assassination attempt and 4, 23
  books written by 1, 46, 60, 105
  Chechnya and 5, 6, 94
  collaboration with the Mitrokhin Commission 15, 16, 85, 86–99, 108
  death of 22, 100, 173
  early career 93, 94
  escape from Russia 34–45, 46
  final statement of xli, 199
  funeral of 22, 114–15
  Kovtun and 150, 161, 162–73
  Limarev and 59, 90, 92, 159
  Lugovoy and 73, 74, 76, 79, 109, 119, 124, 125–6, 127–30, 135, 139–40, 149, 154, 161, 162–73, 185
  Nevzlin and 78
  Politkovskaya and 82, 83, 112
  Putin and 109
  Scaramella and 86–99, 158–9, 160, 173
  Shvets and 80, 81, 84, 146, 173, 181
  trip to Switzerland with Berezovsky 13
  URPO, work in 23, 24
  Zakayev and 5, 6, 74, 172, 182
Litvinenko, Marina, in Britain – Marie Anne Carter 5, 21, 34–7, 39, 40, 42–5, 61, 67, 81, 105, 107, 109, 112, 114–16, 156–7, 173, 175, 178, 180, 182–3, 187, 207, 210–13
Litvinenko, Maxim 85, 114
Litvinenko, Walter 36, 114
Lugovoy, Andrey:
  alleged business activities 71–72
  as Duma deputy xl
  at the Best Western Premier Shaftesbury Hotel 118–19
  at the Millennium Hotel 148–72
  at the Parkes Hotel 127, 129–30
  at the Pine Bar 164, 165–70
  at the Sheraton Park Lane Hotel 131–2, 136, 141
  Badri and 72, 132, 133–4, 143
  Berezovsky and 72, 106, 139, 143
  early career 4
  probable contacts with polonium-based poison 119, 120, 123, 134, 141
  meetings with Litvinenko in London 71, 73, 74–75, 76, 79, 106, 117, 118, 124, 131, 132, 135, 139, 140, 157
  preparation for the London operation 108
Lugovaya, Galina 151
Lugovaya, Svetlana 148, 151, 152, 170–71
Lugovaya, Tatiana 127, 146, 148, 193
Lugovoy, Yegor 148, 151, 152, 170–71

Makarov, Viktor 179
Manningham-Buller, Eliza (later Dame) 174–5, 184
Marchuk, Yevhen 48–9
Marckwald, Willy 121
Margelov, Mikhail 'Misha' 55, 56, 58
Margelov, Vitaly 55, 56–8

Index

Marino, Filippo 87
Marx, Karl 115
Mascall, Craig 128, 136, 139, 150, 152, 155, 156, 221
Maskhadov, Aslan 5
Matassa, Lorenzo 86–7
MATRIOSHKA, operation 15
Matveyev, Lazar (KGB Dresden, later retired) 19
May, Theresa 186–7, 188, 224
McLaren, Charles 25
McNally, Malcolm 157
Medish, Mark C. 38, 46
Medish, Vadim 38, 46, 213
Medvedev, Alexander 96–7
Medvedev, Vadim 104
Meier, Barry 68, 224
Melnichenko, Mykola 48–51, 52, 59, 65, 81, 106, 180, 214
Mendez, Tony and Jonna 162
Mentasti-Granelli, Bruno 96
Menzies, George 61, 68, 69
Miller, Alexey 78, 79
Miller, Pablo 'Paul' 64, 214
Milligan, James Kerr 55
Mitrokhin, Vasili 15, 40–43, 44, 57, 86, 87–8, 89, 91, 92, 95, 96, 99, 108, 159, 179, 189, 198, 213, 214, 216
Mityukhov, Mikhail 6
Mogilevich, Semion, mob nickname 'Seva', alias 'Sergey Yuryevich Schneider' 180–81, 223, 224
Montesinos Torres, Vladimiro 15
Morar, Natalia 110, 218
Moro, Aldo 89, 90–91
Mucibello, Fulvio 88
Muratov, Dmitry 53
Murdoch, Rupert 134
Murov, Yevgeny 166, 167, 203

Nagiyev, Ramin 58
Navalny, Alexey 29, 77, 79, 112, 167, 222
Naylor, Duncan Jeremy 194

Nekrasov, Andrei 114
Nemtsov, Boris 6, 12, 33, 111, 112, 167, 197
Nerodenkov, Andrey 16
Nerodenkova, Margarita 16
Nevzlin, Leonid 78
Nicholas II, Emperor of Russia 195
Nikonov, Vyacheslav 207
Norman, Sir Henry 25
Noukhaev, Khozh-Ahmed 31
Nowikovsky, Robert 98

O'Callaghan, John 64
O'Connor, Andrew 150, 152, 194, 195, 221
Okulov, Valery 54
Okulova, Yelena 9
Oshchenko, Victor 179
OSOAVIAKHIM, operation 94
Owen, Sir Robert 30, 109, 120, 125, 138, 154, 182, 186–7, 188, 195, 197, 225

Pacolli, Beghjet 8
Palumbo, Louis F. 87
Papini, Andrea 92
Patarkatsishvili, Arkady 'Badri' 13, 22, 26, 29, 55, 62, 63, 69, 107, 108, 132, 133, 137, 143, 151, 188, 189, 194, 212
Patrushev, Nikolai 24, 31, 103, 197, 203
Paul I, Emperor of Russia 22
Pearson, W. Robert 38
Penkovsky, Oleg 44
Perepilichny, Alexander 194
Pershin, Eugene 71, 72
Pershina, Irina 71
Peskov, Dmitry 209
Phillips, Quentin James Kitson 'Ken' 64
Picasso, Pablo 25
Piccinelli, Gian Maria 86
Pichugin, Alexey 78

Pickering, Thomas R. 'Tom' 38–40, 45
Pietras, Radoslaw Michal 142, 145
Piguzov, Vladimir 57
Politkovskaya, Anna 53, 62, 82–3, 92, 108, 111, 112–3, 139, 159, 167, 197
Polli, Gert-René 98
Pompadur, Martin 'Marty' 132, 133, 134, 219
Ponkin, Andrey 37, 103, 104–5, 124, 217
Popov, Vladimir 2
Potanin, Vladimir 3
Potemkin, Alexey 190, 191
Prescott, John 184
Pribylovsky, Vladimir 14
Pridmore, Darya, *see* Dariya Davison
Priest, Nicholas 'Nick' 122
Prikhodko, Serge 2, 209
Primakov, Yevgeny 11, 14, 57
Princes William and Harry 160
Prodi, Romano 88, 89, 90–91, 97, 99, 108, 159
Prokhanov, Alexander 61
Putin, Vladimir, KGB school alias 'Comrade Platov' (KGB Dresden, later – president of the RF): and Litvinenko 1, 104, 109, 112, 199

Quirke, Daniel 'Dan' 75, 76–7, 115, 127, 128–9, 134–5, 157

Rea, Nicolas, 3rd Baron Rea 115
Reddaway, Peter B. 110, 111
Reid, John 18, 184
Reilly, Timothy 'Tim' 77, 78, 79–82, 118, 124, 125, 134
Rezun, Vladimir, pen name 'Victor Suvorov' 35, 87, 179, 189
Riley, Alan 99
Rizzo, Giulio 115
Roberts, Colin 178
Robinson, James 205
Rose, Simon 101, 105

Rossetti, Christina 115
Roxburgh, Angus 205
Rumyantsev, Dmitry 10
Rushailo, Vladimir 23
Rutherford, Ernest 121
Rybkin, Ivan 6
Ryzhov, Nikita 89

Safonova, Olga 13
Sakharov, Andrei 27
Samuel, Richard 41
Sandoval, Joseph 39
Satter, David 60, 214
Scaramella, Mario 58, 63, 85, 86, 87, 88–95, 99, 108, 158, 159, 160, 163, 172, 182, 183, 188, 191, 192, 213
Scarlett, John (later Sir) 41, 103, 224
Scaroni, Paolo 99
Scheffler@Shefler, Yuri 23, 212
Schlaff, Martin (Stasi codename LANDGRAF) 97, 98–99, 217
Schroeder, Gerhard 97
Scott, Spencer 117–8
Sechin, Igor 110, 111
Seijó, Rosa 9
Seleznyov, Gennady 10, 57, 210, 211
Service, Robert 187, 197
Shadrin, Alexander 117, 118, 126, 127, 128, 130, 132, 136, 137, 138–40, 149, 153, 154, 155–6, 171, 194, 221, 226
Shakespeare, William 22
Shary, Andrey 183
Shaw, Peter 63, 69, 135
Sheinwald, Sir Nigel 18
Shubsky, Kirill 146, 147, 157
Schuppe, Georgy 'Egor' 149
Shuvalov, Igor 80
Shvets, Yuri 50, 52, 53, 77, 78, 80, 81, 82, 84, 146, 157, 159, 160, 173, 180, 181, 183, 195, 198, 224
Siletskaya, Yekaterina 15
Siletsky, Andrey 8, 15
Simpson, Glenn 181, 224

Index

Skripal, Sergey 29, 100, 179, 189, 190, 198, 206
Skuratov, Yuri 10, 12, 55, 210, 211
Skwarzec, Professor Bogdan 121, 122–3, 219
Slater, Alan 132, 133, 148
Smirnov, Alexander 102
Sobchak, Anatoly 7, 24, 25
Sokolenko, Vyacheslav 4, 84, 108, 135, 140, 141, 143, 148–51, 152–3, 167, 170–71, 172, 197, 210, 216, 221
Soskovets, Oleg 62
Spain 1, 9, 19, 78, 96, 135, 147, 198
Stalin 110, 165, 166, 199
Steele, Christopher 178, 179, 181, 195, 224
Steier, Dr Peter 122
Steindling, Rudolfine, known as 'Red Fini' 98
Stepashin, Sergey 14, 202
Stern, German magazine 97–8
Stolpovskih, Viktor 8, 9, 16
Stroilov, Pavel 114, 216
Sudoplatov, Pavel 23, 24
Sultanov, Oleg 59, 214
Szucsich, Marco 96

Tabunov, Alexander 157
Tam, Robin QC 82, 88, 113, 139
Tarasov, Evgeny 152, 153
Tatum, Paul 88
Taylor, Nathan 133
Terlyuk, Vladimir 28, 30, 31, 65, 66–67, 100–101, 102, 105, 110
TESTUDO, Operation 198
Thatcher, Margaret (Baroness Thatcher) 29
Timmons, Clive 175, 178, 186, 223
Tokarev, Nikolai (KGB Dresden, later – president of Transneft) 19
Tregubova, Yelena 139
Trofimov, Anatoly 90, 223
Troop, Pat 184
Trotsky 21, 24, 27, 166

Trump, Donald 181
Tugolukov, Yevgeny 78
Tupper, Nina 182
Turchynov, Oleksandr 52, 214
Turover, Genrikh Yakovlevich (in Spain – Enrique) 9
Turover, Philipp aka Felipe (in Russia – Philipp Turover-Chudinov) 8, 9, 10–11, 211

Vaino, Anton 166
Valuyev, Alexey 75, 83, 129, 130, 149, 150, 154, 171
Valuyev, Vladimir 4, 75, 76–77, 83, 84, 108, 119, 127, 129, 130, 135, 139, 141, 142–5, 146, 150, 151, 167, 170, 197, 210, 216, 218, 222
Velichko, Valery 92, 216, 217
Vienna 13, 48, 51, 54, 64, 95, 96–99, 121–2, 194
VLADIMIR, operation 108
Vlasov, Igor 92
Voinovich, Vladimir 37
VOLNA, operation 122, 219
Volokh, Vyacheslav 4
Voloshin, Alexander 6, 13, 211
Voloshin, Pavel 60
Voronin, Vladimir 139
Voronkov, Vladimir 139, 194, 195
Voronov, Igor 10
Voronov@Voronoff, Vladimir 127, 128, 132–3, 134, 137, 138, 139, 140, 154, 163, 194, 195, 219
Vranitzky, Franz 98

Wall, Dr Eleonora 142, 146
Wall, Marina 142, 143, 220
Wallace, Ben xviii
Waring, Mathias 98–9
Weitz, Gidi 97, 217
West, Dave 131
Wolf, Franz Thomas Alexander 19
Wolf, Markus 'Misha' 19
Workman, Timothy 27, 28

Yakovlev, Vladimir 95
Yandarbiyev, Zelimkhan 5
Yanukovich, Victor 51, 106
Yau, Alan 104
Yearsley, Alexander 180, 181
Yegorov, Nikolai 7
Yeltsin, Boris 2, 3, 6, 7, 9, 10–13, 14, 20, 33, 38, 54, 55, 94, 201, 203, 205, 209, 210, 212
Yeltsina, Elena 54
Yeltsina, Tatiana, aka Tatiana Dyachenko and Tatiana Yumasheva 9, 12, 211
Young, Scott 138
Yumashev, Valentin 2, 3, 6, 8, 9, 11, 12–13, 14, 24–25, 210–11

Yushchenko, Viktor 52, 54, 106
Yushenkov, Sergey 21, 22, 27

Zakayev, Akhmed 5, 6, 17, 31, 74, 104, 107, 108, 114, 115, 154, 171, 172, 182, 220
Zakayev, Shamil 154, 157, 220
Zakharova, Maria 100
Zharko, Vyacheslav, alias 'Slava Petrov' 61, 62–63, 64, 73, 159, 188
Zhomov, Alexander (CIA codename GT/PROLOGUE) 207
Zolotov, Victor 103, 166, 167, 175, 197, 198, 203, 204
Zolotukhin, Boris 21, 22
Zubkov, Alexey 78
Zyuganov, Gennady 3, 57